D1499866

THE BEST PLAYS OF 1956–1957

THE BURNS MANTLE YEARBOOK

Illustrated

with drawings by HIRSCHFELD

from "Long Day's Journey into Night"

THE BEST PLAYS
OF 1956–1957

EDITED BY LOUIS KRONENBERGER

DODD, MEAD & COMPANY

NEW YORK · 1969 · TORONTO

"Separate Tables": By Terence Rattigan. Copyright 1955 as an unpublished work by Terence Rattigan. Copyright © 1955 by Terence Rattigan. Reprinted by permission of Random House, Inc., New York. All inquiries should be addressed to author's agent: Harold Freedman, c/o Brandt & Brandt, 101 Park Avenue, New York 17, N. Y.

"Long Day's Journey into Night": By Eugene O'Neill. © 1955 as an unpublished work by Carlotta Monterey O'Neill. © 1955 by Carlotta Monterey O'Neill. All rights reserved under International and Pan-American Copyright Conventions. Reprinted by permission of Carlotta Monterey O'Neill and Yale University Press. All inquiries should be addressed to Richard J. Madden Play Co., Inc., 522 Fifth Avenue, New York, N. Y.

"A Very Special Baby": Copyright © 1957 by Robert Alan Aurthur. Copyright © 1955 by Robert Alan Aurthur. Reprinted by permission of the author and of Dramatists Play Service, Inc., 14 East 38th Street, New York 16, N. Y.

"Candide": Book by Lillian Hellman, lyrics by Richard Wilbur, John Latouche and Dorothy Parker. Copyright © 1957 by Lillian Hellman. Copyright © 1955, 1957 by Leonard Bernstein. Copyright © 1957 by Richard Wilbur, John Latouche and Dorothy Parker. Reprinted by permission of Random House, Inc., New York, N. Y.

"A Clearing in the Woods": By Arthur Laurents. Copyright © 1957 by Arthur Laurents. Reprinted by permission of Random House, Inc., New York. All inquires should be addressed to author's agent: Harold Freedman, c/o Brandt & Brandt, New York, N. Y.

"The Waltz of the Toreadors": By Jean Anouilh, translated by Lucienne Hill. Copyright © 1953 by Jean Anouilh and Lucienne Hill. First American edition published by Coward McCann, Inc., New York, 1957. Reprinted by permission of the publishers.

"The Potting Shed": Copyright © 1956, 1957, by Graham Greene. Reprinted by permission of The Viking Press, Inc., New York, N. Y. All rights strictly reserved. All inquiries should be addressed to author's representative: Monica McCall, Inc., 667 Madison Avenue, New York 21, N. Y.

"Visit to a Small Planet": Copyright © 1956, 1957, by Gore Vidal. Reprinted by permission of the publishers, Little, Brown & Company, Boston, Mass.

"Orpheus Descending": Copyright © 1957 by Tennessee Williams. Selections reprinted by permission of the author and New Directions, 333 Sixth Ave., New York 14, N. Y. All inquiries should be addressed to author's agent: Audrey Wood, MCA Management, Inc., New York, N. Y.

"A Moon for the Misbegotten": By Eugene O'Neill. Copyright © 1952 by Eugene O'Neill. Reprinted by permission of Random House, Inc., New York, N. Y.

© 1957 BY DODD, MEAD & COMPANY, INC.

Library of Congress Catalog Card Number: 20-21432

CAUTION: Professionals and amateurs are hereby warned that the above-mentioned plays, being fully protected under the copyright laws of the United States of America, the British Empire, including the Dominion of Canada, and all other countries of the Copyright Union and the Universal Copyright Convention, are subject to a royalty. All rights, including professional, amateur, motion picture, recitation, public reading, radio broadcasting, television, and the rights of translation into foreign languages, are strictly reserved. In their present form these plays are dedicated to the reading public only. All inquiries regarding them should be addressed to their publishers or authors.

PRINTED IN THE UNITED STATES OF AMERICA

PN 6112
.B45

EDITOR'S NOTE

IN editing this fortieth volume in the *Best Plays* series, I continue to find myself under very pleasant obligations. Once more my wife, Emmy Plaut, has provided help that is more fairly called collaboration. For editorial assistance, I am immensely indebted to Barbara Kamb and Phyllis Terry. For the use of photographs, I must thank the Editors of *Life* Magazine and Doris O'Neill, and for the use of its tabulation of Hits and Flops, *Variety* and Mr. Abel Green. Particular thanks are due, for their reports and articles, to Miss Cassidy, Mr. Hope-Wallace, M. Josset, Mr. Kook, Mr. Mielziner and Mr. Sherwood, and for very kindly granting the use of their sketches, to Donald Oenslager, Oliver Smith, David Hays, Ben Edwards, George Jenkins, Frederick Crooke, William and Jean Eckart, Alvin Colt, Motley and Irene Sharaff.

And, as always, it is a great pleasure to be associated in this project with Mr. Hirschfeld.

LOUIS KRONENBERGER

CONTENTS

THE BEST PLAYS OF 1956–1957

SUMMARIES AND COMMENTARIES

THE SEASON ON BROADWAY

DOUBTLESS for a long time to come, 1956-57 will be able to hold its head high as the season that brought forth Eugene O'Neill's *Long Day's Journey into Night.* At the same time, it might equally well hide its face as the season that offered inexcusably little else. To be sure—if accuracy insists on squelching antithesis—there were a few other very rewarding things: among the new plays, a *Waltz of the Toreadors;* or, among the old ones, a serenely classical *Misanthrope* and a glitteringly heterodox *Troilus and Cressida.* There was an outstanding evening of slick theatre; possibly half a dozen evenings that boasted some measure of brilliance or buoyancy or intensity; still other evenings that might preen themselves on their acting though apologize for their words. All in all, however, it was a depressingly bad season—and not least for coming on the heels of an uncommonly good one.

Just why it was so bad is a little hard to explain. What lends, however, a peculiar shabbiness to the story is not that some of Broadway's better established playwrights proved such keen disappointments but that a whole slew of unestablished playwrights raised such pitifully weak hopes. One could accept the fact that, among all the plays by Broadway's relative newcomers, none should show genuine achievement; what, again and again, one sighed for in vain was evidence of real talent. On Broadway, to be sure, talent is a wonderfully misused word; it is bestowed on people with a knack for being breezy, or crudely melodramatic, or even just topical; and it is excitedly hailed in people who write photographic scenes full of the phonographic talk of platitude-clogged minds; or in people with a fair command of purely journalistic eloquence or platform rhetoric. And if some of this involves, at times, something more than mere tricks, it is still—in any creative, any artistic, any even deeply personal sense—not talent. Whatever its stage virtues, nothing could be more genuinely *untalented* than, let us say, *Inherit the Wind;* but it is the measure of how sadly 1956-57 fell short that such stage journalism as *Inherit the Wind* would have been welcome.

Actually, there was something worse about 1956-57 than a dearth of the right sort of talent; there was a kind of spread, or growth, of the wrong sort of sail-trimming. A consistent lack of inspiration can only be lamented, but a pervasive lack of aspiration needs to

3

be decried. Somehow, there are fewer and fewer of the kind of "bad" plays that—as with the corresponding category of bad novels —can not only be respected for what they attempt but can even be admired in places for what they achieve. In a fair number of quite unsuccessful novels, there will jut up a genuinely creative scene, there will break through an intensely personal vision. But few authors of plays at the same level can even boast—what with all the rewrites and compromises and cuts—of "an ill-favored thing but mine own." For it is clearly not their own, and one reason why it is not is that often it isn't even the theatre's own. Less and less of what appears in the Broadway theatre originates there; the theatre has fewer and fewer accredited architects, and more and more— often quite bungling—remodelers. This involves not only the new, and still very knotty, problem of plays made from TV scripts, or after the fashion of TV scripters; it also involves the old, and always very questionable, business of plays derived from books. From books, last season, were made *The Tunnel of Love, The Happiest Millionaire, Auntie Mame, The Hidden River, Too Late the Phalarope, Eugenia, Child of Fortune, The Loud Red Patrick;* and beyond the fact that none of them made a really satisfactory play, the very few among them that derived from books of any stature somehow took the story and let the stature go. The real trouble, however, is that while a certain amount of adaptation is inevitable, often understandable, even irresistible, Broadway now—what with book and magazine sources to tap on the one hand, and TV on the other—is fostering a whole race of adapters, many of them hacks, so that in a season like the present one, beyond one's asking disconsolately "Where are the good plays?" one asks scarcely less, "Where are the legitimate playwrights?"

All the same, the poor showing last season among unestablished playwrights was much accentuated by the failure—or inactivity— of the established ones. O'Neill's other play, *A Moon for the Misbegotten;* Tennessee Williams' *Orpheus Descending;* Arthur Laurents' *A Clearing in the Woods;* Robert Sherwood's posthumous *Small War on Murray Hill;* Richard Nash's *Girls of Summer;* and (from among the superior adapters) Ruth and Augustus Goetz's *The Hidden River*—all these ranged from the disappointing to the close-to-disastrous. It was equally a season in which nothing appeared on Broadway by Thornton Wilder or Arthur Miller or William Inge or George Kelly or John van Druten or T. S. Eliot or Christopher Fry or S. N. Behrman or Maxwell Anderson or Sidney Kingsley or Paul Osborn or Elmer Rice or Clifford Odets or Mary Chase or Noel Coward.

*Rosalind Russell as
"Auntie Mame"*

In the circumstances, it would be no less foolish than fraudulent to claim real merit for all the Best Plays. The problem of selection is always thorny, involving as it must the play without benefit of the production, the words without reference to gesture or tempo or inflection. With my least dazzling choices, where the problem is such a minimum of merit, the deciding factor has been a minimum of meretriciousness. A-for-Effort can never fairly take precedence over actual achievement; but other things being equal—or worse yet, absent—aims do signify. Hell may be paved with good intentions, but not so Broadway: most of Broadway's paving stones represent compromise and the quick buck. In any case, though I think it wildly misguided, *A Clearing in the Woods* was not shabbily begotten. Whatever its miscalculations, again, *Candide*—even shorn of its music—stares Broadway down. *Visit to a Small Planet* is a hand-me-down (or rather a fatten-me-up) from TV; but it does boast a fresh idea and fitful exhilaration. On the other hand, if an *Auntie Mame*, with Rosalind Russell, is agreeable strictly-popular entertainment, without Miss Russell it is very little indeed. And on the stage *A Tunnel of Love* has so vulgarized the talent of Peter DeVries as to invalidate it.

The special approach to O'Neill's *Long Day's Journey into Night* demands a word of comment. The feeling of Mrs. O'Neill that so intensely personal a work should nowhere be synopsized has resulted, it seems to me happily, in our including instead the full text of Act I.

The season's first drama to deserve any mention, *Too Late the Phalarope,* was a striking example of the dangers of turning novels —particularly serious novels—into plays. It is much as though the best way to construct a chair were to cut down a sofa; and Robert Yale Libott's adaptation of Alan Paton's well-known novel quite forfeited the amplitude and swell of fiction without acquiring any of the force and drive of drama. Parts of the play were much too obvious, other parts too obscure; and scenes were choppily joined to one another like so many train coaches, with the engine at the wrong end.

The play, involving the division between the English and the Afrikanders as well as between whites and blacks, centers in a young policeman whose sinning with a native girl both breaks the law and violates a rigid social code; both offends a bigoted father and alienates a narrow, unresponsive wife. Indeed, *Too Late the Phalarope* possesses so many sources of voltage and causes for crossed wires, constitutes such a complex of race and religion, family and sex, that the novel cannot be cut down without having, also, the heart cut out of it. Mr. Libott nowhere vulgarized the story, but neither did he vitalize it; and its various important strands, which should have formed a tight, tragic nooselike knot, never even properly intertwined. Only at the end when the father cast out his son and sealed up his house, did the play vibrate; but the last scene was a standing broad jump of a scene, without the running start and rising momentum of the play itself behind it.

In late October Terence Rattigan's *Separate Tables* gave Broadway its first big hit and brought quicksilver to a season already plainly lacking in blood. *Separate Tables* is exceedingly good theatre, but in no sense anything more. It is not even a play, but rather two playlets; it is as much stunt as drama; and its appeal necessarily owed much to production. Two very skillful performers, Margaret Leighton and Eric Portman, were successively cast in roles quite garishly unlike and hence brilliantly contrasted. The scene and minor characters were, for both playlets, the same: a small, drab English seaside hotel crammed with character-part guests. In *Table by the Window* a once-married couple meet again after having messed up each other's lives. The now desperately chic woman, who might have married millions, is reduced to modeling and drugs; the once talented tough proletarian, who might have become a Labor cabinet minister, is reduced to penny-a-lining and drink. In the other playlet, *Table Number Seven,* the man is a natty fraud who has fabricated for himself a dashing military past, while proving to be a sexually timid duffer who gets pinched for molesting women in cinemas. The woman is an angular, sniffy spinster who is in love with the fraud, and whose dragon of a mother is determined to expose and, if possible, expel him.

In both plays Rattigan sounds a theme (expressed in the symbolism of separate tables) of how lost and alone and in need of others are the down-at-heel and the down-at-heart. In all other respects, two lives badly lived are sharply contrasted with two never lived at all. Except for a touch of wordiness, Mr. Rattigan very expertly contributed everything that could have been asked of him to make such stunt-writing prosper. The characterizations were sharp, the details adroit, the atmosphere was vividly dreary, the big scenes were vigorously emotional. It was all a little too much a triumph of theatre; or a defeat, at any rate, of truth. The first play, after honest moments in a rather too worn stage situation, wobbled into a regulation happy ending. The second play, which might have seemed a protest against something amiss in English life, wound up an instance of what is amiss with English playwriting: the engines were reversed, the sentimental faucets turned full on. *Separate Tables* could also be regarded as a parable for playwrights: writers also have need of others, writers too crave the comforting arms of the public; but the artist's independence of stance, his solitary, separate-table insight is his one source of lasting strength. Mr. Rattigan lacks the courage of his conceptions; all's right with the world when the curtain comes down, and accordingly very brisk at the box-office; but something is just a little too obliging about the play.

All slick theatre, *Separate Tables* was soon followed by something removed from it *toto caelo*—O'Neill's unsparing levy on his own darkened past, *Long Day's Journey into Night*. Not reaching Broadway till sixteen years after it was finished, this relentless chronicle of O'Neill's riven and tormented family, mingling the fierce thrust of unblushing theatre with harsh, unsoftened truth, may very possibly come to seem O'Neill's most substantial legacy to the American stage. It offers the kind of illumination born of a compulsive prodding and clawing in dark places. In this turbulent autobiographical drama, O'Neill—as Addison said of Marlborough—rides in the whirlwind, yet directs the storm.

A nearly four-hour-long play about the "Tyrone" family—actually the young O'Neill, his father, mother and older brother—it occupies a single harrowing day in 1912. The touchy, hard-drinking father—a gifted actor who has dwindled into a perennial matinee idol—is a miser. His closefisted reliance on cheap quacks has helped make a hopeless dope fiend of the mother. The older brother is a cynical, shiftless lush; the 23-year-old O'Neill an unconfident and tuberculous fledgling writer. Nothing "happens": four people simply resent and taunt and bludgeon one another as they slowly, stammeringly, but at length explosively, reveal themselves. The play's movement, rather than forward, is downward and inward. In an accursed, bedevilling propinquity, the drugged and the drunken exhibit spectral moments of love, or convulsive moments of guilt; make accusations that are at bottom confessions; practice cruelties that constitute spewings of self-hate. Over and over they go on saying the same thing, while somehow blurting out things not meant to be said at all. Over and over they assume the same perverse or clearly posturing roles, while yet betraying some vivid corner of their actual selves.

As almost everywhere with O'Neill, the play is overlong and often cumbrous and clumsy; but these weaknesses, as very seldom with O'Neill, are not without value. The repetitious speeches are at least in character, as coming from broken-willed neurotics needing the

Eugene O'Neill and José Quintero: Author and Director of "Long Day's Journey into Night"

solace or the savagery of words. The plotlessness of the tale very considerably derives from the impotence of the characters. The language—merely blunt and straightforward, except where the posturing actor and fledgling writer empurple it—has, in the theatre, much more trenchancy than the flabby poetical prose so frequent in O'Neill. And even the excessive length does weight and certify a story that, if told neatly and concisely, might merely seem lurid. *Long Day's Journey* does not seem lurid. If only by writing about the family nightmare could O'Neill expunge it from his mind, then by waiting half a lifetime before he wrote, O'Neill achieved a strange and self-governing, but an assured perspective. In this most personal of all his plays O'Neill seems, as a writer, the least self-conscious: the play suggests a kind of emotional total-recall rather than any subjective or self-pitying involvement. O'Neill has succeeded, not—as is usual in fictionized autobiography—through assuming some kind of mask, but by stripping himself bare; and memory has had for him an incandescence that imagination almost always lacked. On his own doorstep he was to find characters more vibrant than any he could easily invent. The mother may pass too directly from the sheltered girl we are told about to the shattered wreck we see; but the O'Neill men, with their still-far-from-extinct volcanic fires, their bitter humor and biting anger, are fiercely damned. Whatever its rating as art, the play is a notable experience; the characters are nowhere softened into victims or flattened into villains: always, with however wayward or mocking or spastic an autonomy, they stay people.

On the heels of *Long Day's Journey* came another rather agitated family play, Robert Alan Aurthur's *A Very Special Baby*. The title referred to a 34-year-old man, the youngest child (whose mother died when he was born) in a large Italian-American family. Simultaneously babied and belittled by his rich, tyrannical, self-made father—who resents him because of his mother's death—he has never found his feet. When, at length, there seems a chance he can, the father blocks the way; and there are troubled scenes before, presumably, the son escapes.

Beyond some effective scenes and dialogue, the play's chief merits are its real honesty of purpose and a title character who is still a far from worn-out stage type. If *A Very Special Baby* never becomes more than respectable playwriting, it is from never achieving any real urgency or rising to any real distinction. It suffers, to a degree, from a certain thinness of material, but the more decisive limitation is the drabness of its method. The people involved have been conscientiously studied; their difficulties have been resolutely stressed.

But—what so often characterizes an age of oppressive naturalism—one looks in vain for a truly personal pigmentation, for a unique or enlarging vision of life. What one finds instead is something photographic (which is more of a close-up than a view) and something theatrical (which too often mistakes the loud pedal for the resonant chord).

Whatever its limitations, Arthur Laurents' *A Clearing in the Woods* has no traffic with naturalism or interest in photography. Mr. Laurents' concern was not the sitting room's furniture but the psyche's: what he sought to do was to take an overwrought romantic egoist of a young woman and have her delve back into her past—into her troubling memories of herself, her father and the men in her life—as a way toward self-understanding and self-acceptance. Mr. Laurents' method of rendering visual and concrete what his heroine remembered was provocative and yet readily grasped. The mental "clearing in the woods" was assigned a physical counterpart, Oliver Smith's fine woodland set providing a sort of field-and-stream of consciousness. The heroine's three earlier selves were played by three other actresses who resembled her; and people and incidents wove in and out of the story inside the self-determining and telescoping time-scheme of memory.

If the attempt to physically landscape a woman's troubled mind and to flesh her rasping memories failed of dramatic impact, and often even of valid stage effect, the failure seemed basic, indeed all but foredoomed. In certain individual scenes, in particular moments of stress or touches of fantasy, Mr. Laurents' method proved both striking and successful; and in other places, the interest in what he was attempting might in some degree offset his failure to bring it off. On the whole, however, he was attempting something glaringly unsuited to the stage—which is at the same time the merest commonplace of the novel. In using in the theatre an ultra-subjective method, in seeking the equivalent of interior monologue and stream-of-consciousness, in trying to externalize a floating mass of introspection and retrospection and reverie, it was as though a sculptor should sweat and struggle after an effect that any painter can do far better with no effort at all. Drama works centripetally from the outside in, so that in the theatre even the soliloquy seems at most a serviceable makeshift, and the aside a clumsy contrivance. And in *A Clearing in the Woods* not only did everything proceed from the inside out, but it sought to make concrete a whole mass of conflicting and competing impressions in the heroine's mind, of all that is sly, ambivalent, aberrant in such deep-sea mental voyaging. In practice, not too much could be made to seem plausible, let alone

real; or cumulative, let alone dramatic. The heroine's general predicament never produced any truly dramatic situation; while the
various past situations that helped bring on the present predicament
were, psychologically, much too familiar to be individualizing. But,
however misguided, *A Clearing in the Woods* is at least a courageous
and a reasonably ingenious try.

Like his earlier *The Living Room*, Graham Greene's *The Potting
Shed* is more trenchant than it is artistically rounded or right, and
leaves a final impression that the playwright is more important than
the play. This is partly because the playwright is in places still a
novelist, and partly because the play itself is, however vividly, a
tract. Mr. Greene's Roman Catholicism has as crucially conditioned the substance of *The Potting Shed* as earlier it did that of
The Living Room, though the crux, this time, is not sin but faith.

The Potting Shed is that most truly dramatic of detective stories,
a what-done-it, a shadowy trek backward from an effect to a cause.
James Callifer is divorced from a wife who loves him and is not
welcomed among his implacably rationalist family. Incapable of
love or of feeling really alive, he is just as incapable of understanding why: everything preceding a moment in the family potting shed
when he was fourteen is blotted out of his mind and has been so
carefully blacked out of his family's that his psychoanalyst can nowhere hit on a chink of light. The journey back, with Greene using
a cocky teen-ager to get him round some tough corners, has all the
pull of a good detective yarn; while the disclosure of what happened
in the potting shed—of how a miracle brought the dead boy back
to life, and how it was born of a vow made by the priest who was
the boy's uncle—constitutes the very heart of the play.

In moving from effect to cause, Greene has also moved from a
character's question to a playwright's answer. Once that answer
is given, once the tremendously theatrical revelation scene is past,
once a psychological mystery has passed into a theological solution,
the play has no further voltage. For two acts, however, the story-
telling and much of the writing have the power to grip; during those
two acts, indeed, *The Potting Shed* has something more than narrative tension or suspense; it has an emotional force born of its characters' harassed bafflements and needs. The road leading to the
light is steeply twisting and darkly landscaped. And if Greene, in
treating the rationalist Callifers, sharply satirizes the bigotry of disbelief, he himself never brings bigotry to faith. But it is faith, it
is indeed theology, that in his own way he celebrates at last.

If *The Potting Shed* is much less dour than *The Living Room* was,
this is not just because the hero finds a measure of faith, but because

the whole play is concerned with faith and not with sin, and because it pivots on a priestly uncle who fortified rather than fails the protagonist. All this, along with better dramatic technique and an immeasurably better theatre production, won for *The Potting Shed* a far higher rating—both popular and critical—than was granted *The Living Room*. All the same, once *The Potting Shed's* very genuine theatrical excitement becomes less vivid, the play seems much less valid; and, for me, it is still the granitic, bleakly intense first half of *The Living Room* (the second half I admit is a failure) that stands out as Greene's best writing for the stage.

O'Neill's *A Moon for the Misbegotten* is laid in time some ten years after *Long Day's Journey into Night*. Set on a Connecticut farm, it reintroduces the hard-drinking older Tyrone brother, Jim, who by now is a wholly dissipated, used-up drunk whose last reserves vanished with the death of his mother. A huge, sweet-natured, healthy, hulking daughter of an Irish tenant farmer—a virgin who pretends to be a wanton—has long been wildly (and unrequitedly) in love with Jim. The two of them come together alone one night; but beyond a quickly aborted and drunken impulse of lust in Jim, nothing happens. Partly from knowing he must spoil the girl's life by sharing it, and even more from having nothing left inside himself to share, Jim goes away for good.

To this story, which has about it very little of the first-hand urgency of *Long Day's Journey,* O'Neill has brought scarcely a fraction of the power. It has everywhere—which in so synthetic a theatre as ours, and so impoverished a season as this, gives it a cachet—O'Neill's honest and pervasive compassion. It has some very nice raffish first-act comedy, and moments thereafter that give resonance to certain scenes, and a face to O'Neill's feeling of lostness. But it only stirs very fitfully to life: O'Neill's great—and greatly damaging—fault, his using too many and too flaccid words, flattens out a story that at best is never intense enough. And beyond a limitation of talent, there seems to me a kind of failure of toughness—of that toughness that tempers O'Neill's compassion, and imparts a certain tragic sense to life. Everyone in *A Moon for the Misbegotten* comes round to behaving a little too decently, so that there is no tussle of sick, bitter, angry, thwarted, even petrified emotions; and the play leaves an impression of being too soft. It was the last play that O'Neill wrote, and in view of his own physical handicaps it is easier to understand why it should offer so little of his power.

Tennessee Williams being one of the few big-name playwrights of the season, the hopes inspired by his *Orpheus Descending* made the play itself all the greater a disappointment. A rewrite of his *Battle of Angels,* which in 1940 halted at Boston on its way to Broadway, *Orpheus* conveyed a sense of having been remodeled; of altered corridors and stairs, of trapdoors that had been inserted and windows that had been bricked up. But at no matter what the stage or the style of construction, the builder's identity was never in doubt. Mr. Williams wrote of life in a backward, bigoted Southern town, and of a young guitar-playing itinerant who happened by. He became involved with the unhappy women of the town, and as a result with its unreasoning men, to be chewed to death at last by its chain-gang bloodhounds. Against a background of the town's eccentrics and outcasts, its bullies and racists, Mr. Williams wrote more intensively of the young man's affair with a woman whose Italian father died of mob violence, her own husband being part of the mob. Symbols of lostness and loneliness, the young man and the young wife become victims of corruption and brutality.

At some point in the play, one encounters everything that Mr. Williams does well and even does uniquely: the harshly funny humor, the whiplash of recrimination, the corrosive bite of evil, the shaking fingers of fright. But the play, for all that, clearly fails as a whole, and fails for visible reasons—faultiness of structure, obsessiveness of attitude, an unbridled, empurpling theatricalism. In Williams' attempt at a kind of outer and inner story—in his ferocious portrayal of a whole community's lynch-law intolerances encircling his tense, sordid, sometimes maudlin idyl—there is more awry than a certain sprawl and a shifting tone. There is too little causation, there is no vital connection: the destructive social forces fail to bear down honestly, or even credibly, on the personal tale. But it is just here that the obsessive attitude enters in, that the overwrought social critic in Williams helps lead the craftsman astray. Preoccupied with violence, corruption and sex, Williams sees life through a cracked glass darkly, and at the end—exactly as the Marines used to dash to the rescue—he brings on hoodlums for the kill.

It is hard, finally, to separate material from method, to distinguish the world's violence from Williams' own, because of the garish way he orchestrates his protest and the sheer fireworks of his pessimism. Talent as vivid as Williams' is quite often as lopsided: few strikingly individual visions of life are notably balanced or panoramic. But what tells against *Orpheus Descending* is less something personally limited about it than something gratuitously lurid; what vitiates the play, even as it momentarily animates it, is its all too canny theatre sense. There is an immense amount of evil in life; but it is the stage's melodrama, and not the world's malevolence, that so exultantly wears its heartlessness on its sleeve.

The Hidden River, which Ruth and Augustus Goetz adapted from Storm Jameson's novel, was a split-level kind of play, being partly a mystery yarn over who informed on a Resistance fighter during World War II, and partly a moral inquest into varieties of French behavior under the Nazis. At neither level did the play really manage to score: a split-level whodunit should have more concealed and built-in features—here the guilty person was very quickly obvious; and the moral drama quite lacked flesh and innards. To begin with, it was the problem that created the people, rather than the other way round; and the people, besides, were portrayed too much under mere scrutiny and too little under actual stress. In its latter half *The Hidden River* did have, however, some good old-fashioned emotionalism—a mother faced her son's murderer; brother stared wildly at brother—and though the effect might be familiar, the moment was theatrical.

N. Richard Nash's *Girls of Summer* was concerned with a mixed-up young woman and her mixed-up kid sister; a mixed-up young hipster, a mixed-up male teacher of ballet, and a cocky, Jaguar-driving stranger who—converting two pair into a full house—turned out to be terribly mixed-up also. Not for a long time had any play so much featured unquiet desperation. Showing only glints of the humor that brightened his *The Rainmaker,* Mr. Nash wailed and moaned, in rondo form, the woes of upset psyches and sexual distempers. Though plainly overwrought itself, the play was yet the victim of even more overwrought staging; and seemed as lacking in power as it was laden with pain.

Twice, in the course of the season, a Henry James novel was dramatized and done in. In the case of the "serious" one, *Child of Fortune,* Guy Bolton had chosen to adapt perhaps the most spacious and intricate of all James' fictions, *The Wings of the Dove;* and on that score alone needed great luck to succeed. But, faced with the book's amplitude and complexity, Mr. Bolton chose to simplify it for the stage by clinging to the story and reducing the characters to the merest plot carriers. And in doing so, he burned away the gold of James' great moral drama to leave the dross of James' somewhat too fictional period tale. The central situation—two worldly, hard-up people in love and secretly engaged; a doomed young heiress who is a friend of the girl's and in love with the man; the girl's idea that the man make the heiress happy by marrying her, and simultaneously insure their own future by becoming her heir—obviously makes for stage drama. But just as obviously such a central situation comes only in very small or very large sizes; will

only succeed as something quite trashy or as something truly tremendous. To achieve the tremendous, all the ethical dilemmas and
moral betrayals involved must be given full play; James' populous,
resplendent canvas of London and Venice must be done at full
length; while his characters, with all their perceptions and perturba-
tions and sensibilities, must be studied in depth. Unhappily, Bolton
not only could never flesh his story, but the very bones he reduced
it to cracked and broke. *Child of Fortune* was as lacking in nour-
ishment as in distinction.

The weak showing of the season's drama derived honorably
enough, in many cases, from sheer lack of art. But the weak showing of the season's comedy seemed less forgivable—there was frequently, too, an obvious lowness of aim. Except for *The Waltz of
the Toreadors,* a serious—indeed, a fundamentally quite sad—play
for all that it is an often hilarious farce, no comedy all season had
any real distinction; while only *Visit to a Small Planet* had even
the grace of novelty. For the rest, everything was either respectably
pallid, as with Robert Sherwood's posthumously produced *Small War
on Murray Hill,* or trivially pallid, as with Terence Rattigan's *The
Sleeping Prince,* or blatantly vulgarized, like *Tunnel of Love,* or
shamelessly vehicular, like *Auntie Mame,* or soggy-sprightly, like
The Happiest Millionaire, or more snobby than sprightly, like *The
Reluctant Debutante,* or ducking-the-issue, like *A Hole in the Head,*
or to-be-seen-and-not-read, like *Hotel Paradiso.*

The season's first mentionable comedy, Mr. Douglas Home's *The
Reluctant Debutante,* told—in a series of glossy costume changes—
of a determined London society matron's efforts to find her unco-
operative debutante daughter a suitably rich and right husband,
while the girl herself fell for a cad. In one of those splendid, if
hardly novel, reversals, Mother's shakoed palace guardsman turned
out to be morally unworthy, while the seeming cad was not just a
parfit gentil knight, but an honest-to-God duke. All this dishing
up of leftovers from belowstairs-fiction was served swimming in
snob appeal; but the play did have some fun with snobs. The
characters were mostly as illbred as they were wellborn; the hen-
brained, hard-driving Mama and her great friend Lady Crosswaithe,
who also had a marriageable daughter, cooed at each other like
doves while scratching like wildcats; and so much of the dialogue
was delivered into a telephone that the instrument was listed among
the cast of characters. The dialogue, if pleasantly droll in places,
was seldom witty, and even the small talk went, all too often, from

badinage to worsinage. For something so frightfully trivial, the play was never sufficiently smart.

The season's second mentionable comedy, like the first, came from London; but if just as trivial, Mr. Rattigan's *The Sleeping Prince* was infinitely more tedious. An "occasional fairy tale" laid in Carpathia's London Legation at the time of George V's coronation, it told of a fetching young American chorus girl whom a Grand Duke invites for supper—and the night. But after a night rendered blameless by too much vodka, the girl stays on to meet and beguile the family, to go with the young King of Carpathia to a ball, with the Grand Duke's wife to the Abbey, and at length into the next room with the Grand Duke. Though Carpathia plainly should border on Ruritania, it had none of its dashing absurdity or charm. In terms of costumes, orders, ribands, monocles and curtsies, the play was almost cinematically royal; but it came off about as frivolous and frothy as an Iron Cross. It seemed no accident that amid all the Coronation whirl and glitter Their Carpathian Highnesses were being left severely to themselves, for they were indeed crashing bores; and the author of *Separate Tables* was here blindly scattering poppy while contriving poppycock.

Two American comedy hits next emerged, each a very obvious book dramatization. In *Auntie Mame,* the authors of *Inherit the Wind* turned Patrick Dennis' novel into a romp for Rosalind Russell. Thanks to the inherent appeal in any lovable stage lunatic, coupled with the tremendous skill and vivacity of the lady enacting the part, *Auntie Mame* had no trouble becoming the season's favorite popular comedy. Adapted from a sophisticated comic strip of a novel, the play—if rather less vulgar—was even more of a comic strip; and the adapters, doubtless wisely, went in for a kind of scene-a-minute technique. Their slapdash method, if wholly uncreative, did manage to make speed a kind of substitute for wit: all these quick-changes went well with Auntie Mame's own scatterbrained nature, and in the theatre allowed for a splendid succession of new costumes, hair-dos, wall-treatments, gaffes, predicaments and men. Outside the theatre and devoid of Miss Russell, however, *Auntie Mame* can scarcely be regarded as playwriting.

When Cordelia Biddle wrote a biography of her father, Anthony J. Drexel Biddle, Kyle Crichton served as a sort of daughter's helper; and it was he, again, who adapted the book for the stage. Certainly *The Happiest Millionaire* told of a man who cried out to be a stage character: Biddle was the most redblooded of bluebloods, the most warmhearted of hotheads, the most brotherly-loving of Philadelphia eccentrics—a man who turned teetotaler and collected alligators, who boxed with professionals and gave a song recital without possessing a voice. The problem in bringing Biddle to the stage was how to connect up his disconnected crazes and sudden whims; how to make a negotiable narrative out of a heap of anecdotal small change. In the attempt, the book got pommeled and knocked about like one of Father's sparring partners, and Father himself, at times, got kept out of sight in his corner. The play was restricted to 1916-17, when Cordelia became engaged and married to Angier Duke; and Angier and his sharp-tongued mother took much of the limelight. There were many moments when Father or fisticuffs, or Mrs. Duke and her son, made life at 2104 Walnut Street enjoyable. But there were even more when Philadelphia might as well have been Kansas City, when the Biddle clan might have been cut from cardboard, when there was neither elegance nor stuffiness to particularize Father's antics. Even a Biddle is no match for a Broadway, and all too often a truly unconventional man dwindled into utterly conventional farce.

Robert Sherwood's last play, *Small War on Murray Hill*, was also his mildest. Telling how Britain's General Howe, not happy about the issues of the American Revolution, dawdled, while occupying New York, to enjoy the charms of a patriotic American lady, Sherwood introduced Minerva into the classic conflict of Venus vs. Mars. Smacking less of the bedroom than the drawing room, and most of all perhaps of the library, the play turned speculative as to just how, while a war is actually going on, people feel and behave about it. Clearly, the impact of a far greater war had colored Sherwood's thinking; and it gave his play, at moments, a certain pensive grace. But *Small War* was small beer: it had neither dramatic fiber nor intellectual focus, the writing suggested neat prose rather than lively dialogue, and the effect was much too heavy for light comedy and much too unstimulating for a comedy of ideas. Venus all too often covered her flesh, Mars muffled his drums, Minerva mumbled her words; and the Muse of Comedy simply turned her back.

At last, well on in January, arrived Anouilh's *Waltz of the Toreadors*. A French sex farce, it proved (as just that) perhaps the best envelope Anouilh has yet found for conveying his philosophic approach to life, with its bitter personal tang, its over-protesting cynicism, its disillusionment so dark as to imply illusions once far too rosy. In *The Waltz of the Toreadors,* by reducing to caricature the romantic attitudes that get men betrayed, Anouilh rises nearer to truth than when he wallows in man's betrayal or whiplashes the betrayers. As *Ring Round the Moon* revealed earlier, Anouilh is capable, in a world of fantasy, of a kind of detachment quite denied him in a world of "fact." Laid in 1910, the play is concerned with a retired French general, chained—for all his infidelities—to the sickbed of his not-really-sick jealous shrew of a wife; and chained equally to his high-romantic memories of a girl he waltzed with years ago and who now very suddenly reappears. A Don Quixote when not a Don Juan, Anouilh's General St. Pé needs, as he grows older, stronger and stronger rose-colored glasses; he is only the more romantic, indeed, because of the day-to-day realities of a vixen wife and two ugly daughters. In the end his foundling secretary—who turns out to be his son—has carried off his dream woman, and the General is left disconsolate and alone in the dusk. But at length he finds a pretty new housemaid to steal out with into the darkness.

Often uproarious farce from the blunt savagery of its incidents— aborted female "'suicides"; aborted man-of-honor duels; the wife shifting hilariously from an invalid's helplessness to an athlete's violence—the play bears, all the same, an almost tragic burden. From out of the mouth of farce—like cold water from the mouth of a fountain gargoyle—flows a stream of comfortless cold wisdom. Anouilh needs the coarse exaggerations of caricature to offset the genteel evasions of life painted in water-colors. The general's foundling son may be no more than a Gilbertian hand-me-down; but the lostling father, the middle-aged satyr with his subaltern dreams, is part of a darker comic vision. General St. Pé inspires the thought that there would be less war between men and women were there not so often war, in the same breast, between man and boy. And yet it is through pitilessly mocking and exposing the General's dreams that Anouilh wins sympathy for the dreamer: in the very degree that he is brutal, Anouilh is humane. So long as man's heart has its own convenient method of dating things, and a waltz its own hypnotic power of transforming them, a chronicle like Anouilh's must have its wistful and touching side. And so long as the French have their special ambivalent insights—remain the wittiest of fools, and the most rational of madmen, and look most like dandies when wearing their hearts on their sleeves—a chronicle like Anouilh's will have genuine verve and flavor.

The second Henry James debacle, *Eugenia*, tells—under its maiden name of *The Europeans*—of two elegantly hard-up nineteenth-century Continental worldlings, a baroness and her brother who descend in a fortune-seeking mood on their rich, staid, starchy Boston kinfolk. Light, bright, early, "easy" James, the novel is not so much a comedy of intrigue as a comedy of attitudes; of dull innocents who are shocked by Europe, and gay intriguers who are stupefied by Boston. Much of all this must doubtless, at best, evaporate in a stage adaptation: it seemed all but annihilated in the *Eugenia* that served as a vehicle for Tallulah Bankhead. To give Tallulah no competition, it was staged as though all the other characters were waxworks; to give her sufficient stimulation, she performed as though surrounded by leopards. Turning a pastel into a circus poster, Tallulah snorted and snarled, and in her own unmistakable, misguided way was at times amusing. But at other times only Mae West as Snow White could have seemed more unsuited to a part.

Gore Vidal's *Visit to a Small Planet* brings up the problem—which will surely more and more recur—of how a good saucerful of TV fun can be made to fit a regulation soupbowl of a play. Good TV fun was Mr. Vidal's yarn of a man from a far-off, highly civilized planet who arrived, via flying saucer, to visit his "hobby," the Earth. And in terms of the stage, the problem was met, after a fashion, by not turning *Small Planet* into a play at all, but by simply converting it after a while into a vaudeville show for two expert comics, Cyril Ritchard and Eddie Mayehoff. But without Mr. Ritchard and Mr. Mayehoff to handle the routines, the problem snaps back into place, the soupbowl seems only half-full, the satire only fitfully present.

Visit to a Small Planet gets off to a good start, with a genuine and entertaining first act. The visitor arrives from afar, his timing a bit askew—he had hoped (and dressed) for the Civil War. He glances about, inquires, reacts, compares; decides, if waging war is really Earth's sovereign talent, he will wage a very big one himself. But with two acts still to go, war—on however titanic a scale—is satirically not quite sufficient; so there are imitations of jungle noises, and animal acts, and mind-reading acts, and songfests and monologuists; with Mr. Vidal, every time satiric inspiration burns low, hastily throwing another monologue on the fire. In a dreary season, *Small Planet* does have definite merits—its very palpable bright idea, its very pleasant first act, some amusing thrusts and perky sallies. But if a small bright spot in a bad season, it casts (by dint of its TV origin) a disproportionately dark shadow: TV-and-water is presumably going to become a very popular theatrical drink.

Joseph Fields' and Peter DeVries' *The Tunnel of Love* shows how saleable a drink, already, is fiction-and-cheap-fizz. This adaptation of Mr. DeVries' novel also started off as a satire—as a sort of cannonade on that citadel of the Exurbanites, that bohemia with a seacoast, Westport, Connecticut. But it quickly jettisoned anything so highbrow and became a mere illustrated joke book on styles in childbearing. When married women weren't having children in *Tunnel of Love*, unmarried ones were; or couples were adopting; or the sins of the fathers became the adoptees of their wives. The play

Elizabeth Fraser, Darren McGavin, Nancy Olson and Tom Ewell in
"The Tunnel of Love"

had funny lines and an occasional amusing scene; but it as much bogged down as a tale as it went out of bounds in the telling. Whether or not motherhood is sacred, it cannot very happily be, for three long acts, profane: the theme turns something more than dubious, it turns dull. And the telling was no help: a yarn about errant husbands, expectant wives and unwed mothers needs a very light touch that leaves no smudge, a swift skating tempo that outrides thin ice. But *The Tunnel of Love* gives even its brightest remarks the flashy neon lighting of the wisecrack; and tends to spell out every last word, where it shouldn't even finish the sentences.

Arnold Schulman's *A Hole in the Head* very possibly began as a fairly straightforward problem play, as a study of a roughneck Jewish rolling stone left to bring up a 12-year-old motherless son. The way Mr. Schulman ultimately treated it, however—introducing much Miami-hotel atmosphere and Jewish-family antics—it was rather as a problem play that *A Hole in the Head* wound up. For nothing had been straightened out, and very little had even been explored. The central situation had simply been used as a come-on and a catch-all: there is the matter of the roughneck's on-the-skids hotel; of a blonde he goes with and a widow he ditches her for; of his rich lout of a brother and the brother's warmhearted wife—all of whom leave the story exactly as they found it, with the father much what he was and the boy still gallantly at his side. That Mr. Schulman waywardly exploited his material rather than purposefully organized it would have mattered less had the details been fresher and the detours more rewarding. But *A Hole in the Head* studied human reactions far too little and audience responses far too much, and in the very act of milking the comic side of Jewish family life, sadly watered it down. Mr. Schulman belongs, indeed, to the two-faucet school of playwriting—anything not comedy must be sentiment; and at the end anything knotty or troublesome simply gets chucked out of sight. The play has its amusing moments; indeed it functions as a sort of new theatre form, the problem farce—a form not to be encouraged, since by its very nature one side of it tends to betray the other side.

Late in the season came *Hotel Paradiso,* an exceedingly French French farce, co-written in the '80s by the once-famous and prolific Georges Feydeau. Such French farce means sex first but not, in the long run, foremost: eventually slapstick and speed become more important than spice; the bed, in such goings-on, is only a prop, the actual objective is bedlam. In the play Bert Lahr, who is married to a battle-ax, somehow gets out from under her thumb to sin with a beautiful blonde; and in due course, he and the lady and a great many other people known to one another are all cheek-by-jowl or better in a Paris fleabag. Upstairs and down they scamper, in and out of rooms they dash; and as entertainment, *Hotel Paradiso* was rather in-and-out itself. It had lively spurts and was nicely dotted with mad scenes, but even in the theatre—where alone it could come alive—*Hotel Paradiso* seemed more like a brightly instructive exhibit of how French farce operates than an occasion of genuine merriment.

Just one costume piece remains to be mentioned; and just one whodunit. *The First Gentleman* chiefly exhibited England's rakish, selfish, stylish Prince Regent as a father: he insists that the Princess Charlotte marry the Prince of Orange, though ultimately he allows her the Prince Leopold she loves. The play abounded in gaudy family scenes culminating in Charlotte's death in childbed at 21. Gorgeously costumed, *The First Gentleman* had a nice storybook air, but no vibration as story. Why Mr. Norman Ginsbury chose to display so hopeless a family man almost exclusively among his family is hard to grasp; quite pointlessly slighted is the Regent who was not always fatuous, or even fat, and who had adorned as well as tarnished a picturesque society. Moreover, the writing had neither a period gloss nor a better-than-period glitter; and if fun enough to look at, the play proved a heavy burden to listen to.

The whodunit, *Speaking of Murder,* had an incidental virtue or two, but quite failed to raise goose pimples. The plot concerned an English blonde who, during a lengthy visit in Connecticut, does in a wife from a desire to marry her husband; only to have the husband marry a movie star, so that now she must do in the second wife as well. The play never paid off as a scare piece, both from making no attempt at mystery and from arousing no real shudders or suspense. Thanks to Estelle Winwood, as the murderess' hard-drinking, hard-bargaining blackmailer, there were some stylish cat-and-mouse scenes: but only where the two ladies were speaking of murder did *Speaking of Murder* come alive.

Broadway, which in late years had simply ceased to do anything about quality revivals, last year leaned as far backward as 1906 and 1929 and went so dangerously far afield as Shaw. But a passable *Apple Cart* and a generally very rewarding *Major Barbara*—what with reinforcements from London's Old Vic and Paris's Renaud-Barrault troupe—at least demonstrated that Broadway had heard tell of the classics and definitely approved of cultural foreign aid.

The Apple Cart marks the point in Shaw's career where he plainly began to collect dust as well as kick it up, and to seem rather a past master than a present one. He could still, however, chessboard his old ideas into seeming momentarily like new gambits; which is why, in 1929, *The Apple Cart,* with its Socialist playwright seeming to put in a good word for monarchy, caused a mild furore.   Shaw's retort, that royalty and democracy were not in conflict, but rather that both were menaced by plutocracy, gave him the chance to juggle variations on an old theme and—if never to upset any apple carts—to toss out numerous apples of discord.   The play, for all its dead spots and familiar noises, has perhaps just enough scattered brilliance and second bounce for a superlative production to bring it off.   On the other hand, a merely competent production (starring Maurice Evans), if it did not exactly let Shaw's play down, failed to give it all the holding up that it requires.

Major Barbara—unlike *The Apple Cart*—is, of course, major Shaw; though, quite like *The Apple Cart,* it too suggests a Shavian about-face.   Here, indeed, in his exalting a great munitions maker, the Socialist Shaw fired (as never again) into his own ranks.   The Salvationist Barbara learns from her munitions-making father that it is the destroyers of bodies who keep the savers of souls in funds, and that it is men like himself who abolish that greatest of all crimes, poverty.   If *Major Barbara* wisely demonstrates the folly of all absolute positions, it nevertheless glaringly ousts the Life Force in favor of the Death Force, and seems to suggest that the best way to keep half the world well-fed is to blow up the other half.   Whatever Shaw's logic, however, *Major Barbara* makes a decidedly good show. Beyond its chattering upperclawss idiots and bellowing lower-class bullies, it abounds in glittering intellectual pinwheels and ideological *trompe-l'oeils.*   Furthermore Charles Laughton, as the play's director, contrived as many bright tricks of staging as Shaw had contrived of thought.   For a while the two expert showmen got in each other's way, but in time they managed very well to set one another off.   This was partly owing to a generally accomplished cast, top honors going to Mr. Laughton himself as Andrew Undershaft.

Shaw also reached Broadway via Second Avenue and the Phoenix Theatre, with Siobhan McKenna enacting the title role in *Saint Joan.* No one who had previously acted it on Broadway—Winifred Linehan, Katharine Cornell, Uta Hagen—had proved so memorable. Miss McKenna's blatantly peasantlike Joan was all drive and no dreaminess; displayed a fanatic's certitude rather than a heretic's defiance.   Such one-track-mindlessness has its acting limitations and Miss McKenna played with a sort of fierce monotony; but by subordinating effect to essence, what Joan does to what Joan is, she brought her audience into a real relationship with Shaw's heroine. An otherwise torpid production diminished the occasion; and in its fourth season the Phoenix generally proved unexciting. The trouble may lie less in choice of material than in the want, at the Phoenix, of anything close to a sound repertory company, of any real signature in the way of style, and in sufficient display of what can only be called showmanship. Some of the trouble may even lie in the great size of its theatre, which hurts and distorts the modest, or the offbeat, or the informal nature of many of its projects.

Shakespeare reached Broadway, thanks to the Old Vic. The Old Vic had less lustre, and much fewer triumphs, than when last over in 1946; indeed, what for me was its one exciting production, the *Troilus and Cressida,* was generally its most controversial. An opening *Richard II,* if smooth enough, was much weakened by John Neville's over-elaborate performance in the title role. His reach, quite possibly, butterfingered his grasp, for nothing vivid or even very definite emerged from his interpretation; and in this violin concerto of a play, where Richard's sad-fiddled woes alternate with England's full-choired fortunes, a poor Richard is calamitous. A *Romeo and Juliet,* despite Claire Bloom's beguiling looks and moments of poetry, was no better: Miss Bloom dipped talent in tediousness and seemed too mannered and too slow-paced; while in that tender trap of a part—Romeo—Mr. Neville was seldom more than graceful. The *Macbeth* that came next did not strikingly differ, as a production, from the *Richard* and the *Romeo;* but the rewards were greater, from its reverberating so much more powerfully as a play. And here, as was not true earlier, the chief roles were forcefully handled: Paul Rogers' Macbeth and Coral Browne's Lady Macbeth lacked depth, but were commandingly theatrical; and there was between them, also, a fierce connubial bond that helped humanize a woman who all but lacks humanity, and a man who all but loses it. As for the production generally, if it could not counter such real difficulties as the terrific fourth-act drop in pressure, it succeeded with things more compassable—caught the poetry almost throughout; the rushing theatre and rising drama of the first three acts; and the feudal, night-lighted atmosphere, with its sense of a haunted world no less than a haunted man.

But only the Old Vic's final production proved really noteworthy: even those who disliked the *Troilus and Cressida* would concede, I think, that it ventured challengingly; while those who, like myself, were won over by it were almost everywhere engrossed. An understandably neglected play—being quite as "difficult" as it is imperfect —*Troilus* is unwarrantably neglected for all that. There is not only much that is special, fascinating and even fine about it, but there is much in its mood that a modern audience can particularly respond to. In *Troilus,* with its bitter and debunking cynicism, Shakespeare slashed at the vast fabric of the Trojan War to rend its romance and heroism to tatters; to reduce its Ajaxes and Nestors to caricature; to make love harlot-like and friendship homosexual; to show honor traduced and war grotesquely fumbled. What with the violence of its mood and the slackness of its method, with its fierce fanged bite yet its biting off more than it can chew, *Troilus and Cressida* resembles a little those Huxleyan "sophisticated novels" of the 1920s.

In staging the play, Tyrone Guthrie boldly evoked an Edwardian world full of prance and panoply, all his Trojans deliberately very British and his Greeks very German. A siren Helen lolled against a cream-and-gold piano; Pandarus was frockcoated and effeminate; Thersites a disheveled Cockney war photographer. Guthrie's picture of two aristocratic military castes who sup together when not slaughtering one another involves a Hector and Ajax who were quite as much first cousins as were the Kaiser and George V. But more important, if Guthrie's treatment discolored Shakespeare's play, it yet unified it better than Shakespeare did. At times Guthrie's inventions might be pretty toys rather than useful tools; at other times, by deleting or smothering words, he might keep Shakespeare from speaking for himself; and most dubiously of all, the tone of his *Troilus* was too gaily farcical for Shakespeare's guilty merriment. But he only brightened, he never softened or bowdlerized: Nestor still driveled, Thersites still sniveled, Achilles could be a sufficient gangster, Cressida a sufficient bawd. Guthrie's *Troilus* was like a very free but very robust translation—a fair exchange, if not a full equivalent.

Four years after their first visit to Broadway, Madeleine Renaud and Jean-Louis Barrault returned with their Paris troupe to offer *chef d'oeuvres variés*—Molière, Lope de Vega, Ben Jonson—along with such moderns as Salacrou and Giraudoux. For people a little at a loss with spoken French, the fine points of their production may be all too often lost. But with a great and familiar classic like *The Misanthrope,* it was clear how beautifully interwoven all things were —and how delicately stressed while nowhere coarsely emphasized. Madeleine Renaud's final leavetaking, a kind of simple exit that released in the audience the most complex sensibilities, supplies an instance of how the whole production was managed. M. Barrault, whether as Alceste (where he seems too old) or as Claudel's Columbus (where, on the other hand, he seems too *gamin*) is a less distinguished actor than a director and showman. The *Christophe Colomb* itself is not a play but rather a pageant, a piece of "total theatre" that makes use of language, music, choruses, crowds, ballet, a movie

Ethel Merman in "Happy Hunting"

screen and a narrator. It is encrusted, moreover, with philosophic thought and suffused with Claudel's intense Catholic feeling. Along with Claudel's picturesque and wittily etched episodes and Milhaud's lovely music, it had—after the fashion of pageants—its doldrums and longueurs. But in it Barrault's brilliant sense of stage management and remarkable gifts of showmanship found time and again their opportunities, which were time and again fulfilled.

For musicals, it was a busy season: though most of the ranking musical-comedy composers (Richard Rodgers, Cole Porter, Harold Arlen, Frank Loesser) were no part of the scene, there was an impressive clutch of librettists (Betty Comden and Adolph Green, Howard Lindsay and Russel Crouse, Lillian Hellman, George Abbott) and a true galaxy of female stars (Judy Holliday, Ethel Merman, Beatrice Lillie, Eartha Kitt, Gwen Verdon). But despite such names, and an attempt to set to music such unusual works as Voltaire's *Candide*, Al Capp's *Li'l Abner*, Don Marquis' *archie and mehitabel* and O'Neill's *Anna Christie*, more went awry than went right. But among musicals, more than anywhere else in '56-'57, there was a certain amount of adventurousness; and in view of how much fitting together a large-scale musical demands, there was more than anywhere else an excuse for falling short.

Li'l Abner had its high points; but the distance from one to another was often uncomfortably long. Suddenly, with something fine and deafening from the orchestra, or fine and floor-shaking from the chorus, Al Capp's comic-strip community bounced to life. At still other times, behind musical-comedy goggles, there was Capp's satirical eyeing of conformity and stupidity and skullduggery. But all too often the Capp menagerie, let out of their neat newspaper cages, lost their way stumbling in too many directions. It is a question whether successful pen-and-ink characters can ever do as well in flesh and blood; but on Broadway it is less the characters than the characteristics of comic-strip life that cause snags. The essential repetitions, the churning status quo that go down fine a spoonful a day in a newspaper can sadly pall as an evening-long drink on the stage. Hence, on the stage, *Li'l Abner* has been swamped with plot —which not only palls but plods; and which, by never letting anyone relax, robs Dogpatch of its homey, ferocious day-by-day charm. Happily, there were genuine compensations: if the Dogpatchers were dull when they walked, they could be dazzling when they hoofed it— Michael Kidd provided some epical choreography, once in a matrimonial-chase ballet, and again in a Visigothic descent on a formal ball that wound up a glorious shambles. There was such rousing music as *Jubilation T. Cornpone,* along with some very lively satirical ditties: if much of *Li'l Abner* damply spluttered, its best things exploded with a bang.

Bells Are Ringing showed no such violent ups-and-downs: it was a pleasantly undistinguished, an everywhere Broadway show that, with Judy Holliday to sweeten and individualize it, could not but be a hit. Miss Holliday played a warmhearted New York answering-service operator who brought hope, cheer, confusion and the vice squad into the lives of various clients who aroused her interest, while with one of them, naturally enough, she fell in love at first hearing. The love story proved almost defiantly orthodox, and Judy's forest of switchboard wires promised wacky snarls and entangling alliances that seldom appeared. From the Comden and Green who wrote *On the Town,* and even *Wonderful Town,* there was a certain falling off in sass and wit, and in the usual fresh, crisp Comden-Greenness. But there was sprightliness to their lyrics, and briskness in Jerome Robbins' staging, and often schmaltz to Jule Styne's tunes; and this, with Judy Holliday looking engagingly blank or beguilingly large-eyed, being inimitably daft or sly or small-girl or strong-minded or pathetic, made for a diverting enough—if also a disappointing—show.

Candide eschewed Broadway in the degree that *Bells Are Ringing* embraced it, and courted problems quite as much as the usual musical shuns them. The result, perhaps not too surprisingly, was a medley of the brilliant, the uneven, the exciting, the earthbound, the adventurous and the imperfectly harmonized. Voltaire's famous satire against facile optimism and idealism—wherein the young Candide goes forth chanting his tutor's insistence that this is the best of all possible worlds, only to be drenched in misfortune and witness more crime and suffering than exist in all Greek tragedy—is equally one of the bitterest books ever written and one of the gayest. Moreover, it gallops at such speed as to make its fantastic pile-up of catastrophes almost as hilarious as it is horrifying. To convert *Candide* into a "comic operetta" is plainly a major operation: Voltaire's volley of incident needs a corresponding musical, visual, verbal and choreographic vivacity. Perhaps more than any single element, this crucial problem of fusing and harmonizing plagued the production—the more so as Voltaire's book is innately better suited to the movies (which could duplicate the breakneck pace and wallow in the calamities) or to pure opera (which almost wholly in musical terms could match the book's speed, wit and mocking elan).

Beyond the question of the operetta medium itself, difficulties arose over the crucial blending and balancing of the libretto and the music. Leonard Bernstein's score had, notably, a sort of mocking verve: for show tunes it substituted musical jokes—spoofs of such operatic standbys as coloratura jewel songs, duets, quartet finales, and period dances; and without being a strictly eighteenth-century score, had a mischievously gay and glittering period quality. As opposed to Bernstein's deliberate pastiche, Lillian Hellman's libretto bore much of her own strong impress, which is quite foreign to Voltaire's. Where, as Lytton Strachey once said, Voltaire's style is, like a rapier, all point—and indeed ironic and glancing and bland—Miss Hellman's is hard-hitting and sharp in proportion as it is blunt and explicit, with an effect of body blows. Equally, where Voltaire was diabolical, Miss Hellman was humanitarian. The results seemed too weighty for the lyrics and music, and perhaps too overt in itself. But at the very least this libretto—by comparison with almost all others—is really *written* and bears a signature. Furthermore, it can now be seen, certain actual ornaments of the production—the sumptuous sets and expertly elaborate staging—tended to slow down and overweight the script, and were equally un-Voltairean. Voltaire's *Candide* being episodic and indeed virtually anecdotal, its best stage equivalent might almost be a series of blackouts. On the stage, too, the fireworks and *fioratura* of the music tended to muffle Richard Wilbur's (and some additional) lyrics. But when read, they generally stand forth as more than just clever or high-spirited, they have an elegance and breeding altogether uncommon in our musical theatre. And for all its miscalculations and its lack of sustained effect, *Candide* at its best is as much above Broadway in achievement as it seems everywhere unlike it in aim.

Unorthodox, too, was *Cranks,* a pint-sized English revue displaying a full jeroboam's worth of frills. Three men and a girl squealed or knelt or sat with their backs to the audience; climbed things while they rhymed things; and contorted and configurated while singing ballads and blues. Now and then, the essential idea was fresh and amusingly satiric; here and there the production embroidery was ingenious and witty. But beyond offering little in the way of tunes and eschewing everything in the way of skits, *Cranks* achieved an awful sameness of effect from so many frantic efforts to be different; and at times, with its self-conscious posturings, less suggested a revue than the religious rites of the Stanislavsky methodists.

With *Happy Hunting,* things reverted unmistakably to Broadway. The show could boast Ethel Merman, if almost nothing else; but for box-office purposes that was quite enough. As a musical, *Happy Hunting* is more than not out of the top drawer; it is plainly from a discontinued line of furniture. Even what was most up-to-date about it—its background of the Grace Kelly wedding—was, satirically, already down to peanuts. The Lindsay and Crouse book, at its very best, had nothing beyond a routine sprightliness; a tune could somehow seem reminiscent while at the same time having no lilt; and the dancing largely suggested the hotcha of a generation ago. But however often Ethel might have resembled a forsaken Merman, she always comported herself like the Queen of the Deep; outflanked her material wherever possible, outstared it wherever not; and in a show business that so often turns the funny into the vulgar, once more at times converted vulgarity into fun.

In the Ziegfeld *Follies* another great star was forced to go it almost alone. The *Follies* brought Beatrice Lillie back to Broadway after four years away from it but brought back nothing of its own old fabled self. There were, to be sure, the required number of stately showgirls with whole gardens in their hair, and the remembered number of semi-nudes descending the staircase. But if, as of yore, the flesh was willing, the spirit was dismally weak. The spirit, in fact, had all but vanished: the songs had no tunefulness, the lyrics no bounce, the sketches no crackle; and though the dances had moments of color, they quite lacked distinction. In the circumstances, it was not surprising that Miss Lillie was at her best when she spoke not a word—in a restaurant pantomime where she dined quite grandly and madly alone. Elsewhere she had briefer, sometimes merely momentary, triumphs, where a *grande dame* lurched or a veiled maiden looped or culture splintered into anarchy: in this *Follies* indeed the famous chill Lillie stare, as from an insulted mermaid, or the disdainful Lillie glide, as of a sneering sleepwalker, might very easily have been addressed to her material.

If neither of the season's final two musicals was successful, both were in some degree unhackneyed. *Shinbone Alley* was concerned with Don Marquis' archy (the literary cockroach who typewrote free-verse memos by hurling himself head-downwards on the keys) and with Marquis' mehitabel (the gallantly bedraggled, *"toujours gai"* cat whom archy reported on). The two friends are an easy pair to feel affectionate toward, but far less easy to endow with stage life. For one thing, they still need to seem like insect and animal; their story, again, is a problem because there actually is no story. And beyond that, they reflect a very personal and crinkly humorist and they represent a whole dimming era of vers libre and the Volstead Act. *Shinbone Alley* made a brave trial and at least for a time had a faint chance; but after a time things went almost unbrokenly downhill; and only now and then all evening was the Don-Marquis strain triumphant. Now and then, also, *Shinbone Alley* proved enjoyable show business; and Eartha Kitt, with her feline grace and mannered charm, was frequently mehitabelish, or at the worst gave Kitt for cat. But the show's plotless proceedings had almost no lift, while its music was unexciting and its dancing dated.

New Girl in Town, which ended the season, also introduced the season's most resurgent playwright into a new medium. A musical version of O'Neill's *Anna Christie,* it was an amusing reflection as well on American show business. No one in the American theatre has trudged so far or so heroically or so alone, or been so indifferent to pace or careless of pitfalls, as Eugene O'Neill; yet it was George Abbott—than whom no one in the American theatre has been more of a steam calliope down the Main Stem, or shown more knack for whizzing pace and social razzle-dazzle—who both wrote the libretto and staged the show. The result was no more a miraculous meeting (and mating) of extremes than a head-on catastrophe; it was instead an often pleasant but an always misguided show. The trouble was that extremes didn't meet, that oil and water made no attempt to mix: when traffic moved north and south for O'Neill, it stopped dead east and west for razzle-dazzle. O'Neill's simple primitivist black-and-white was framed inside a gaudy, frilly, foolish turn-of-

Cameron Prud'homme, Gwen Verdon, Thelma Ritter and

George Wallace in "New Girl in Town"

the-century lace valentine. Far from being ruthless with *Anna Christie,* Abbott was only too faithful to her in his fashion, hewing closely to the plot line and merely jettisoning all mood, unity and cumulative effect. *Anna Christie* might make a good serious musical drama that would actually sustain O'Neill's story better than O'Neill did; but for a capers-and-confetti musical comedy it could only prove a death's head at a feast. Perhaps its worst crime was to ration Gwen Verdon's dancing—her wonderful comic dancing in particular. When the capers-and-confetti had right of way there was some nice waterfront folderol; Bob Merrill provided some agreeably undistinguished music, and Bob Fosse some attractively lively dances. But leading such a left-hand, right-hand existence, *Anna Christie* was not its old familiar self, nor really a New Girl either.

THE SEASON IN CHICAGO

By Claudia Cassidy

Drama Critic, Chicago *Tribune*

THEATRES made more news than theatre in the Chicago season of 1956-57. The Studebaker was reopened by local backers whose internal tug of war reduced a hopeful repertory idea to amateurish stock. The once cherished Selwyn gave up the ghost to Michael Todd, who remodeled it discreetly and rechristened it hideously. As Todd's Cinestage it bolstered the booming advance sale by disposing of $100,000 worth of tickets to a merchant who used them to cajole customers. Rumor persisted that Mr. Todd also had acquired the Selwyn's next door twin, the Harris. Gossip alleged that when he drove his bride past the sandblasted Cinestage and its mellowed neighbor, Miss Elizabeth Taylor remarked, "I suppose the dirty one's mine."

On another theatre front Orchestra Hall, long the home of the Chicago Symphony Orchestra, cracked and creaked when a new building to its north caused some resettling. There was talk of "a new temple of music," as when is there not? The talk faded as the plaster was patched, and attention again focused on the chances of restoring the Auditorium, that long neglected and altogether remarkable monument to the genius of Adler and Sullivan. The Ravinia Festival, meanwhile, has restored a forgotten theatre on the grounds of its North Shore park, and will extend its summer season of concerts to include some preliminary skirmishes in playgoing.

Inside the theatres, the winter season was the familiar story of too little too late. There were exceptions, of course. The freshness and offbeat brilliance of Ruth Gordon and *The Matchmaker* had a producer of little faith doubling the booking. *No Time for Sergeants* was the season's champion for thirty-three weeks, and not as an inferior duplicate of a major success. With William Holden's astringent innocence making the most of Pvt. Will Stockdale, inadvertently of the Air Force, this was uproarious comedy, deceptively relaxed.

The Lunts flourished in the preposterous hocus-pocus of *The Great Sebastians,* giving the lonely Great Northern its sole glow of the

35

long, dark season. Mr. Lunt said the spacious old house conformed to Jean Anouilh's definition of what a theatre should be—"a large room."

The Old Vic came rather timorously for two weeks at the Shubert and piled up a gross of $104,000 for its four plays—*Richard II, Macbeth, Romeo and Juliet* and the Tyrone Guthrie flourish of *Troilus and Cressida*. Maurice Evans looked in late with *The Apple Cart*. *Witness for the Prosecution* had four brilliant weeks with the original cast before new management and less distinguished actors took over.

Orpheus Descending was booked here on the tryout tour, at Tennessee Williams' request, and suddenly detoured. The persistent story was that the producers of *Cat on a Hot Tin Roof* did not want the newer Williams play to precede it. True or false, it made little difference about *Cat on a Hot Tin Roof*. By the time that play arrived at the tag end of the season, it was a bitter disappointment. Thomas Gomez as Big Daddy was its powerhouse. In general, the idea seemed to be that if the peripheral violence made enough noise you would not notice the pernicious anemia of the acting. The caricatured direction underestimated Tennessee Williams and overestimated Elia Kazan.

Shirley Booth improved *The Desk Set*, but hardly enough. *Damn Yankees* was a dim copy, though it had a hopefully sulphuric Mephisto on the old Bobby Clark prowl. *A Hatful of Rain* with Vivian Blaine in the Shelley Winters role was at least different.

The Studebaker Theatre Company, which began so bravely and struck so serious a snag, turned out to have a disastrous case of split managerial personality. Some of its backers were interested in a resident professional company with a growing backlog of classic and contemporary plays. Others, either silent or outnumbered at the start, hankered for the vanished days of a local amateur group known as the Playwrights Theatre Club. Until this was public knowledge Studebaker subscribers were a baffled lot, as the season played Jekyll and Hyde.

There were two series of five plays each, and so interesting was the outlook that the first series had 13,000 subscribers. It struck its crest in a distinguished performance of *The Immoralist*, with Geraldine Page and Hurd Hatfield, which could profitably have moved to another theatre to continue its run. The second series began with another box-office favorite, the London or extended version of Arthur Miller's *A View from the Bridge*, starring Luther Adler. This one was moved to the Harris when displaced by the next subscription play.

Maurice Evans and Signe Hasso in "The Apple Cart"

Peter Palmer as "Li'l Abner," pursued by Charlotte Rae, Joe E. Marks, Stubby Kaye and Edith Adams

Unfortunately, that next subscription play struck rock bottom. It was to have been *The Cherry Orchard* with Elisabeth Bergner, but Miss Bergner canceled because of illness. *Lysistrata* with Vicki Cummings was substituted, and the director took one look and fled. What finally reached the stage was possibly the worst performance of *Lysistrata* since the Athenian première. Next in line was a version of *The Guardsman* so inept that those who remembered the Lunts in that same theatre were reduced to mild hysteria by the playbill note, "The fragrance in the theatre is Nostalgia."

Where was *My Fair Lady?* Booked to open at the Shubert in November, 1957, after a summer on the West Coast. Managers prefer to do their touring, then settle down here for the run. In that case it has to be special, to be worth the wait.

For the 1956-57 record twenty-nine shows played 159 weeks in seven theatres. This is how they were subdivided:

Erlanger Theatre: 38 weeks—*No Time for Sergeants,* 33; *Cat on a Hot Tin Roof,* 5, so far.

Studebaker Theatre: 35 weeks—First Series, 4 weeks each, *Androcles and the Lion, Desire Under the Elms, A Month in the Country, The Immoralist, Much Ado About Nothing;* Second Series, 3 weeks each, *A View from the Bridge, Lysistrata, The Guardsman, The Flowering Peach, Waiting for Godot.*

Harris Theatre: 31 weeks—*Bad Seed,* 4 held over, 9 in all; *Witness for the Prosecution,* 15; *Janus,* 3; *A View from the Bridge,* 3; *The Desk Set,* 6.

Shubert Theatre: 26 weeks—*The Joy Ride,* 3; *Silk Stockings,* 2; Danny Kaye and All Star International Revue, 7; *Damn Yankees,* 12; Old Vic repertory of *Romeo and Juliet, Troilus and Cressida, Macbeth* and *Richard II,* 2.

Blackstone Theatre: 22 weeks—*The Boy Friend,* 11; *Anniversary Waltz,* 1; *The Matchmaker,* 8; *The Apple Cart,* 2.

Great Northern Theatre: 4 weeks—*The Great Sebastians.*

Selwyn Theatre: 3 weeks—*A Hatful of Rain.*

THE SEASON IN LONDON

By Philip Hope-Wallace

Drama Critic, The Manchester *Guardian*

A NOT uncommon sight at theatre time in Piccadilly is a couple of country cousins standing forlorn on the curb and scanning a list of amusements. What theatre to go to? In most cities—other than London, New York and Paris—it's a case of take it or leave it, usually a revival of *Hedda Gabler* at the one-and-only Stadtheater. But with some forty stages to pick from, choice is hard. And the name of the theatre, still less of the play, is no help nowadays. The ones you can get into you don't want to, and the ones you want, you can't. Then plays which have been running four years (*The Boy Friend*) are likely to be run down. It's difficult; as a critic functioning in London, who hasn't seen Broadway for ten years and only makes two big yearly fugues to Paris, I find it hard to know where to begin.

After all, you in the States have usually had the best of the things that trickle over here, or get them from us—*The Waltz of the Toreadors,* say. *The Chalk Garden* seemed more wonderful to us here because at the Haymarket as it originally was cast (with Edith Evans and Peggy Ashcroft, as chatelaine and governess, fighting for the laughs, not to mention the way John Gielgud produced the luncheon scene, with Felix Aylmer as the judge and George Rose as the manservant), the playing was just something almost holy—like that eve-of-war *Importance of Being Earnest*—sheer heaven-sent acting which blinded us from noticing (what we noticed well enough when Gladys Cooper stood in for Edith) that the play, though original and stilted and quite a good study in loneliness, wasn't really the old rose of English comedy I thought I'd smelled on the opening night. Equally you won't now want to be told about *The Waltz of the Toreadors* (not well cast here but more a success than in Paris). And what about our wonderful parade of foreign visitors?—Mme. Feuillère regally swanning through Racine; J. L. Barrault as a cock-sparrow Columbus; and even the widow Weigel, Brecht's relict, pulling Ma Courage's go-cart.

We've had two shockers from Paris as well—both premières: *Fin de Partie* by "Godot" Beckett in French, which pulled the wool even farther over some eyes. This was all about the Godforsaken despair of a blind bore and his shuffling servant (like that other pair in Godot) with a couple of oldsters (the bore's parents) stuffed into two garbage cans on the off-prompt side, occasionally popping up their heads and whining. Not a bad symbol of family life and tensing one's nerve in its obsessive, Kafka-like pessimism and nightmare. But such works seem to me to lack objectivity. You read into them what you will, like the mark on the hospital wall which you study on the way round from surgery.

The Arts Theatre, which can defy the fatuous Royal Censor (who forbade *Tea and Tedium,* of all mild plays!) put on *The Balcony* by Jean Genet—which caused a rumpus and upset the prairie Hazlitt of the London Evening *Standard,* Mr. Milton Schulman, who was nauseated. With some reason, too. The scene is a perverts' brothel and the concernment is that of dressing-up or illusion, so well treated in Pirandello's *Enrico Quatro* (where a mad, rich egotist lives a fantasy life as the emperor day and night). Genet has a sort of special genius for giving pornography an intellectual status. Like Sade, he is valuable; but as a playwright he seems in only a primitive stage of development, well short of puberty.

Speaking of which, *Tea and Sympathy* was quite well done, and so too was *A View from the Bridge* which Arthur Miller had expanded—and made more portentous than the one-acter you saw in the States. I find his attitude to the proletarian, inarticulate hero insufferably patronizing and god-look-down-ish, and the whole rather hysterical piece is nowhere to go for a laugh. But like *A Hatful of Rain,* these American "tough" plays pull on a strong swell of feeling, and Antony Quayle in particular got a good deal out of Miller's perplexed docker. But when Miller has the dock-side doctor say, as a chorus, "This man let himself be wholly known," did we really agree? I doubt it. A side-thrill, of course, was that this again was a "banned play" (allegations of homosexuality are allowed in music-hall jokes but not in serious plays). To defeat the ban, a "club" was formed at the Comedy Theatre, so the New Watergate Theatre Club, entrance fee five shillings, is now the world's biggest private theatre club for showing plays which may be about homosexuality: a situation which has given even us hypocrites at home a good laugh!

Graham Greene's *The Power and the Glory* drew a fine priest-portrait from Paul Scofield, but was distinguished otherwise only by Peter Brook's production and the fact of being in competition with the usual duds, some American (like *Janus,* mildly amusing only), and some native (like the implausible, snobbish and fatuous *Iron*

Duchess by Douglas Home, author of *The Reluctant Debutante,*
which seeks to prove that the uppercrust is usually right after all
and foreigners, cooks and Labour M.P.'s are wise to truckle under).
Would this "go" in America? So preposterous a view of England
well might—it *is* that view which does best abroad.

For instance the Angry Young Man, John Osborne, is wafting to
international glory on the strength of his play *Look Back in Anger*
(in my opinion, the most overrated play of the last ten years), which
is being exported to Moscow where it will no doubt be seen as a
true picture of life of Britain. One wonders how Peter Ustinov's
sapient, clever-clever jape about Russian, British and American diplomacy, *Romanoff and Juliet,* would fare in Moscow. True, his

*The Old Vic's "Troilus and
Cressida": Jeremy Brett,
Rosemary Harris, Ronald
Allen, Coral Browne, Paul
Rogers and John Neville*

The Love of Four Colonels has run two years in Paris, but *Romanoff* (just closed after a long London run) seemed to me only a satirical revue sketch stretched to play length. *Under Milk Wood,* an inspired, bawdy, poetic and touching radio play for sing-song Welsh voices by Dylan Thomas, has such richness of imagery and raciness of dialogue that it even survived the wax works illustrations which put it clumsily on the stage. It delighted its audiences, but cannot quite rank as more than a memorably funny entertainment, hardly as a play at all.

These international fluctuations are strange: for instance, I'm told *Camino Real* is much better *here* than it was on Broadway. Some

people complain they can't make it out; it seemed dead simple to me, just the limbo of middle age. Such lines as "What you call corruption, I call simplification" still mark out Tennessee Williams as a man with a natural ear for theatre. Young Peter Hall, a producer on the way up, did wonders with it: just as Peter Brook made the Parisian cast of *Cat on a Hot Tin Roof* (as yet unplayed in London) very nearly plausible.

But of the exotics, the one which hit us with a smack was the first Australian drama with an all-Australian cast ever to reach London. This is Ray Lawler's *The Summer of the Seventeenth Doll*, and though technically it is no advance on Galsworthy, it is really about something: about real, raw, childish, sawn-off Australian optimists who can't seem to grow up. It is a half-comic study of a barmaid's revulsion from the idea of giving up a traditional good time, which is poignant just because this ideal of a sweltering annual "beano" of bottled beer and carnal congress with her he-man —shattered (like the souvenir dolly) when he is seen to be slipping —is the *one* sacred thing in the baked suburban boredom of this vast, empty country full of muscled-up cockneys with their childish, bar-room optimism which can't stand the truth about maturity. It was strangely moving for us cool, supercilious Britons (who find our Australian cousins at once loud and prickly), but perhaps it would show to Americans too many seams and prentice shifts. All the same the blind, shouting misery of this pair—June Jago, all chin and elbows, and Kenneth Warren as a sort of Aussie Lee J. Cobb—stick in the mind like a cactus thorn.

The real talking point of the year, however, has been—not the Old Vic nor the Arts nor the Watergate, nor yet the endless succession of slick Broadway musicals (a waning vogue), nor amateurish and "different" British musicals (à la *Boy Friend*)—but the earnest, uncomfortable doings of our London Brechtians at the Royal Court Theatre, Sloane Square (a bit off the theatre map though, in postal fact, "West End" as you could wish). The "writers' theatre" which George Devine and the English Stage Company hoped to see flourish in this cosy little red-plush playhouse (where once Shaw and Barker trounced the actor-manager's romantic theatre of Tree and Irving) brought in some lean harvests. Angus Wilson is a shrewd novelist, but his play *The Mulberry Bush* (about the failure of high-minded liberal parents to avoid making a mess of the next generation) was better as an idea than as a play.

Their effort at Brecht, in spite of Peggy Ashcroft, put the fame of *The Good Woman of Setzuan* back some way. But with Mr. James Osborne and *Look Back in Anger* they certainly got a playwright of kinds, as I had the wit to perceive, thank goodness, in my first notice of him—though, hating the whole play and the whole outlook, I was a long way from estimating how eagerly the younger generation were going to respond to his iconoclasm.   Apparently something in Mr. Osborne's father-hating, sneering, anti-filial attitude rings a loud bell for the rising children of the Welfare State who feel, of all things, that they have been baulked even of the right to die for a lost cause!   It was this and certainly not the novelettish story of the sufferings of Jimmy Porter, social misfit, who hurt his better-educated wife's feelings, bedded her girl friend (when she smacked his face) and yet had the wife crawling back to him at the end.   True there was a feeling for atmosphere, and some heat and indignation; quite a lot of ribald, wounding youthful humor too.   But as a play it was just too bad.

Now *The Entertainer,* which is currently a sell-out and given the boost of an Olivier star performance, along with Brenda de Banzie *and* Dorothy Tutin (quite wasted), is much less of a novelette and much more of a well-motivated, symbolic case history.   It's rather like a try at an English *Death of a Salesman.*

"England is a garden," said Kipling—or someone.   But in these days of a shrinking empire, England, as Mr. Osborne sees her, is a ramshackle music hall, staging those semi-nude burlesque shows which are about all the living theatre that our industrial jungle now gets.   His hero, The Entertainer, is a squalid little hoofer named Archie Rice.   "Have-a-go" Archie is in debt, drunken, played out but still "game," still, in a sordid way, loyal to the tradition of "The Show must go on"—in fact, a Mr. Britannia.   The play takes the form of a series of music hall turns—something which Sir Laurence Olivier anyway does with an inside-out genius and zest at charity shows and the like, his preferred "turn."   We see Archie back-stage too, nagging a second wife, riling a boring old father (one of the old breed of pre-1914, pre-American-invasion vaudevillians), cheating himself and his family and proclaiming himself dead to feeling.   All this is revealed to a daughter, visiting home and disapprovingly looking on—the little prig has jilted her upper-class lover who disapproved of her anti-Eden Suez views (it's just as native as that).   Yet when, melodramatically, a war-office telegram announces that a soldier son, expected hourly home from fighting in Egypt, has been murdered by treacherous "Wogs," Archie Rice is smitten with real anguish: which of course Olivier puts over in a big way, for a moment a Lear plus Willy Loman.   This incident, clearly based on the recent fate of poor Lieut. Moorhead, struck me as cheap—passable in Coward's *Cavalcade,* but hardly a climax for a pretentious parable of this sort. After it (it is the second-act curtain) the piece goes into disintegration, with Archie showing a trace of the old "grit" and not, for instance, selling out to the New World (by emigrating to Canada, as his more prosperous brother suggests). In other words, this says, "With all her faults, Britain can still take it. But it's up to us enlightened younger generation . . ." etc., etc.

Olivier's performance needs no extolling. He is a marvelously endowed actor. Everything comes to him from outside, as it were. Here is antithesis of "Method" acting, such as Sam Wanamaker gives us in *A Hatful of Rain*. Olivier "gives" a cheap, down-at-heel, adulterous hoofer, as naturally as a bird flies or a fish swims and it is finally acting which defies description . . . though for a lifetime one won't forget him leering out over the footlights of the half-empty burlesque theatre and saying, "Don't clap too loud, ladies: it's a very old building."

THE SEASON IN PARIS

By André Josset

Playwright; and Secretary-General of the International Theatre
Institute, UNESCO

TO begin with, the 1956-1957 theatrical season was better as a whole, and, if I may say so, better ventilated, than the seasons which preceded it, in the sense that its presentations were more varied and more flavorsome.

It all began with a new play by Julien Green, who, as you know, is of American origin but writes in French. I remember having spoken of his talent as a novelist and his career as a dramatist as far as I could plot its development three or four years ago. Since then, my prognosis has been proved correct and Green's new play, *L'Ombre* (The Shade) does nothing to modify my opinion. I admire Green as a novelist of extraordinary intensity, but I don't believe that he can adapt himself to the demands of the theatre. His text is beautiful, but it lacks the special point of view, the particular orientation, of the dramatist. And this, it seems to me, is Green's inherent defeat in the theatre.

Two days later, Albert Camus presented, at the Mathurins Theatre, the adaptation of a Faulkner play that has become famous in Europe: *Requiem for a Nun.* You are no doubt acquainted with its great and terrible subject. I had seen the play's world première in German, at the Grand Theatre of Zurich, directed by the Austrian Leopold Lindtberg, and I recall being deeply moved by the simultaneously realistic and fantastic atmosphere, the Biblical background created by Negro spirituals sung in muted voices during pauses between the scenes. Albert Camus' presentation, although extremely searching, did not give me the same impression of strange intense poetry, no doubt because of the tiny framework of the Mathurins Theatre.

Then, on September 24th, Armand Salacrou, who last year had a great hit with a play dating from 1945, gave us a new work called *Le Miroir* (The Mirror). Its success was unfortunately not as great, but Salacrou could later console himself for this with the success of a second new play. On September 26, Bernard Shaw came out of limbo with *Mrs. Warren's Profession* under his arm, a play in which Valentine Tessier wound up capturing public attention, although the old-fashioned adaptation constituted rather a difficulty than an advantage.

More and more, during the past few years, Italy and France have been exchanging their new works. As a whole, Italian plays in Paris have not yet fetched the general public, though the quality of many of the plays has been good. This was true of a play called *Au Delà du Mur* (Beyond the Wall) which has a novel theme. It is concerned with the telepathic influence, exercised at a distance, of an individual upon a young girl; but though intelligently constructed, the play is a bit cold. Nevertheless I believe we must welcome themes that constitute a change from those that forever crop up in so-called "light" plays. The public has been led to appreciate, above all, those comedies which we call "boulevard plays," while applying to more ambitious plays what I would call the policy of the snigger.

At the beginning of October, Marcel Pagnol gave us a play written years ago but never performed—*Fabien*. Its press was not very good and the public did not listen long to the words of this work by the author of *Fanny*.

The celebrated inventor of science-fiction, Jules Verne, inspired the adaptation of his unforgettable *Twenty Thousand Leagues Under the Sea*, under the new title of *Nemo*. The Grenier Hussenot company showed us very amusingly the inside of a submarine, with visions of watery depths, fish, octopi and other weird animals. But though the play received a hearty welcome, its success was not all that could have been desired.

The Comédie Française showed us an "antique" by Alexandre Dumas *fils: Le Demi-Monde*. I used the word "antique" because the characters in this play really seem out of a far-distant world. The incredible, stupid and odious way that women of the demimonde were treated a century ago ended by making the audience laugh, and we followed with interest a very well-constructed plot on a prehistoric subject by a master architect.

Now we come to a sensational theatre event, in a sense that Jean Anouilh's new play *Pauvre Bitos* (Poor Bitos) started a battle, unprecedented for many years, on the evening of its première. The hero of the play is Robespierre, who during the French revolution caused the greatest bloodshed while he himself was an intolerable sentimentalist. The author's great talent allowed him to discover a special way of presenting his character: thanks to a very interesting scenic subterfuge, what we call in France "les dîners de têtes" (head masks), he moved Robespierre up into modern times. That is, the

guests at these little worldly ceremonies are asked to mask themselves from the neck up as historical characters, while otherwise
wearing modern dress.   In this way, the past is made to talk through
the mouth of the present and to say things of current interest.
Anouilh regards Robespierre as the perfect symbol of all those
mediocrities who have governed, and still govern, the world, and
who occupy unmerited places in society.   On the evening of the
première, politics got mixed up in this; and, above all, some critics
and spectators seemed to take the satire personally.   Let me say
frankly that the political satire strongly displeased me, the satire
on the mediocrities very much amused me, and the construction of
the play seemed to me extraordinary.   I will add, however, that the
business of a Frenchman insulting his country seemed to me a bit
indecent; and that the author would have shown more courage to
have launched his insults when it was dangerous to do so—that is,
in 1945.   This said, and dissociating oneself from any consideration
of internal politics, the play is full of talent which the public appreciated, for *Bitos* has become a great success and is still playing.   On
this subject I must pay homage to the intellectual sang-froid of the
Paris public, which could pass beyond what it did not like in the
text to make the play itself a success.   Furthermore, it seems that
Anouilh, feeling that the subject of his play concerns only the French,
has refused up to now to let it be put on abroad.

On October 20th, we were given an adaptation of *The Sleeping
Prince,* which did not have any success.   A new comedy by Monther-
lant, presented at the Comédie Française under the title *Broceli-
ande,* also quickly disappeared from the stage.   It shared billing
with a comedy by Jules Romains, *Amédée, ou Les Messieurs en
Rang* (Amedee, or Gentlemen in a Row), which had been produced
in the past by Louis Jouvet.

The Théâtre National Populaire of Jean Vilar again had a very
successful season with two important works, *Ce Fou de Platonov*
(That Madman Platonov) by Chekhov, and *Le Faiseur* (The Brag-
gart) by Balzac.   One might say that these two great works had
almost never been performed until now.   *Le Faiseur,* shown later in
the season, but which I insert here for greater convenience, had been
put on well before the last war by Charles Dullin.   Its success then
was only so-so, but the grace, the lightness, the rapidity of Vilar's
direction, joined to the flavor of Balzac's characters, gave us an evening that was amusing, charming, even thrilling.   Perhaps the critics
of the past, who consistently decreed that *Le Faiseur* was a bad
play, were led astray by Balzac's reputation as a great novelist and
did not see in him an authentic dramatic author.

Almost at the same time, the Comédie Française put on Shakespeare's *Coriolanus,* a play which in 1934 aroused violent reactions in the audience (and even in the streets) since it presented rival political philosophies, which later led to World War II. Today, the public seems completely vaccinated against such things. The flaming tirades of Coriolanus against democracy, and the flaming tirades of the plebs against Coriolanus, were received by the audience without excitement.

A charming and imaginative play at the Théâtre Grammont, *Irma la Douce* (Gentle Irma), continues its pleasant and amusing career. Also, after the half-failure of *Nemo* at the Marigny Theatre, there appeared *L'Hotel du Libre Echange* (Free Exchange Hotel), a vaudeville of high buffoonery by Feydeau.

I now come to another of the great successes of the season, *L'Oeuf* (The Egg), a bitterly satiric play on society, the way to live in it and the way to snuggle up in it in order to succeed. Lies, conventions, traditions, betrayals, and even murders ably disguised are, it appears, the best means to achieve success. A young man, at first naive, manages to make his way in this society, which is as closed as an egg-shell, once he has understood that the expression "to follow the right channels" means to follow the worst ones. For me, the conclusion went too far in a rather systematic pessimism, but as I know the need for rigid concentration in the development of a dramatic work, I feel indulgent toward the author.

In December, Marcel Pagnol's famous play, *Topaze,* was once more revived with great success. Then, *Cat on a Hot Tin Roof,* by Tennessee Williams, appeared at the Théâtre Antoine. I find it pointless to explain to Americans everything this American play can be: I will only note that it was very well received—I mean, with much curiosity—and that it is still playing today. The critics, however, were not very kind to it. But the Théâtre Antoine has what we call solid flanks and was able to resist converging attacks.

At the Théâtre National Populaire, Beaumarchais' famous *Marriage of Figaro* again allowed Jean Vilar to have a lively success, at least as an animator. Although I enjoyed the whole thing, it seemed to me that this presentation was not up to the standard of, for example, Balzac's *Le Faiseur.* But remarkable moments made up for certain weaknesses; and it is always a delight to go to the Théâtre National Populaire and to note the existence of an enthusiastic audience, madly in love with worth-while plays.

I pass on to a play written by Marcel Achard, entitled *Patate* (Spud). It has been the greatest success of the Paris season in French. Powerfully acted by Pierre Dux, it is the story of two friends who hate each other. The humbler of the two friends finally

Tallulah Bankhead
in "Eugenia"

gets the upper hand, thinking he will find great pleasure in vengeance. But he learns at the same time that the voluptuousness of vengeance counts for nothing, and that true happiness rests in the love of his wife, whom he has been neglecting.

The latest of André Roussin's plays, entitled *La Mamma* (The Mamma), received a rather bad reception. For some time past, Roussin seems to have become a punching-bag for a certain number of critics. But he has the merit not only of seeking original subjects, but also of developing them in a clear and comic manner. Obviously, the theme of *La Mamma* does not make one smile; or rather, it makes one smile wanly. It concerns male impotence treated as comedy. The action takes place at Naples under the exhilarating sun of Southern Italy and has as its victim a handsome young seducer who suddenly trembles with fear from having met with a disaster in love. The mother of the young man, a formidable woman, decrees that her beloved son, the seemingly washed-up great seducer, shall be reinvigorated the very same night whether he wishes or not. Everything takes place as she demands, because the word impossible does not exist where a love-affair is concerned. The extraordinary "Mamma" is played with irresistible comic power and incredible authority by Elvire Popesco. Despite the critics, the play continues and I salute an able and courageous author.

Next appeared, at the Marigny Theatre, *La Visite de la Vieille Dame* (The Old Lady's Visit), by a Swiss author, a play whose cruelty is almost sadistic. It concerns an aged millionairess who returns to her native village to revenge herself on those who made a hell of her youth. The ferocity of the subject and the cruel comedy it breathes do not prevent this play from being a terrifying fantasy. Fortunately Sacha Guitry's delicious, adorable comedy, *Faisons un Rêve* (Let's Build a Dream), came along to tear us very quickly out of this accursed if extremely vigorous garden. Guitry's incomparable imagination twinkled anew in this little masterpiece. As far as I am concerned, I admit that I can't resist Sacha's plays. I resist his films better, but I fall under his spell when I see this sick old man, pushed about in a wheelchair, still living so intensely and directing his works with such great lucidity.

I must now speak at some length about the great success of the new Theatre of the Nations in Paris. You perhaps know that the three international festivals of the past three years presaged a permanent theatre devoted to foreign plays, put on in Paris in their original languages and their original productions. The International Theatre Institute, of which I am Secretary General, encouraged the realization of this dream when its Dubrovnik Congress unanimously requested the French Government to do what was necessary toward establishing such a theatre in Paris. The request was honored, and at present the Théâtre Sarah Bernhardt each evening houses Theatre of the Nations productions.

The first production, in April, was *Don Quixote,* a magnificent little-known opera of Massenet's, which had a triumph thanks to the very talented conductor, the voices of the Opera of Belgrade and the marvelous sets. I cannot tell in detail about all the works which followed *Don Quixote.* I will simply make a selection from a program whose ensemble is extraordinary. To start off, I will cite *Galileo Galilei,* by Bertolt Brecht, a play presented by East Germany. Slow, heavy, abundant, powerful, occasionally interminable, this is a play which yet holds you under its spell. Galileo, who believed he had discovered that the earth was not the center of the universe, had to pay dearly for his daring affirmation. His conscience as a scientist gave in to the pressure of the religious authorities of his time, and he ended his life in a rather miserable state of dejection. Naturally, this work is full of cruel anti-religious attacks, but aside from a few passages which the satire exaggerates, the play holds the stage remarkably. The end of the play, where we see Galileo all alone, under surveillance, carrying within himself the heavy weight of his denial, eating his soup in a porringer like an old man in an asylum, attains a kind of grandeur.

Then came Vittorio Gassmann with Alfieri's romantic tragedy, *Orestes.* It seems that Alfieri used to say that, of all the Orestes that existed, his was by far the best. However that may be, it moved us greatly. It is constructed in the purest, sparest fashion, and the presentation was as successful as the text.

And suddenly a thunderclap shook the stage: Laurence Olivier, Vivien Leigh, Anthony Quayle and the entire company of the Shakespeare Memorial Theatre came before us with *Titus Andronicus.* I believe that I myself suggested to Olivier, two years ago at Stratford, that he bring to Paris this unknown play by Shakespeare (or, if it is not by Shakespeare, it is by his twin brother). And on the evening of the opening, I shivered a bit in my seat, thinking of all the butchery this play exhibits. Hardly had the curtain gone up than the miracle took place. We now feel in Paris that there has never been such a divine cripple as Vivien Leigh, violated, her tongue torn out, her two hands cut off; and we also feel that Olivier is an actor of genius. In the midst of an extravagant mixture of epochs, of Goths, of Moors, we saw rise up a prodigious old Roman of the republican era, an aged Roman peasant, somewhat narrow, stubborn, savage, tender, immensely merciless and immensely human. Surrounding the Oliviers was a production daring but always realistic, with a background of ferocious poetry, of strange sounds halfway between cries and music. Moments which have been judged absurd achieved a savage power. I am thinking now of the reappearance of Lavinia, the victim; of the presentation in iron cages of the severed heads of Titus' sons; of Olivier's bursts of laughter followed by a fainting-fit; of the tale of the horrors committed by the monstrous Moor, of the indignant clamors of the soldiers. The triumph was such that it obliged putting the very steps of staircases on sale.

It was perilous to follow up such an exploit, but without equaling *Titus Andronicus*, the Comic Opera of East Berlin presented, with considerable success, *The Intelligent Little Fox*. The music, composed forty or fifty years ago, is strangely modern, and the spectacle of this drama, taking place among the animals of the forest, was delightful.

A few days ago, Jean-Louis Barrault presented the French contribution to the Theatre of the Nations, *Le Partage de Midi* (Division at Noon) by Paul Claudel. Aboard a ship, with the reflections of the water playing over the sails, began the drama between the carnal Isé, the sorrowful Mésa, halfway between earth and heaven, and the bubbling Amalric. I find it unnecessary to depict for you the action of this play, which is a famous one; besides there is very little action; its beauty lies in its dialogue and in the verve of the subject. It was a revival, but the success achieved by Jean-Louis Barrault equaled that of the original production. The evening marked the return of Jean-Louis Barrault, who, as you may know, no longer has a theatre in Paris. One is being sought for him on all sides; naturally, everybody hopes it will be found. In any case, once the international season is over, Barrault will be installed in the Theatre of the Nations for five months, presenting French plays.

Most recently the Theatre of the Nations offered the Soviet Beriezka Ballets, which were an enchantment from beginning to end. These were folklore ballets danced exclusively by women, full of poetry, variety, emotion, humor, linked to one another with extraordinary rapidity; presenting, successively, flower bouquets shining with garlands that tied and untied themselves to the gay or melancholy music of an accordian. It seemed that we had entered an enchanted kingdom which bore at its portals the happy inscription: "Here, all the world's misfortunes are forbidden."

We are now looking forward to a week in the French language, to Nō plays from Japan, to days with the Dublin Gate Theatre (which will offer Dennis Johnston's *The Old Lady Says No*), to several Italian operas and to your American contributions—a symphony concert by the Cleveland Orchestra and O'Neill's *Long Day's Journey into Night*, with Fredric March and Florence Eldridge.

OFF BROADWAY

By Garrison P. Sherwood

WHERE to draw the line between Off Broadway and Broadway is becoming more difficult each year. It is now often a matter of geography rather than of professionalism. Off Broadway is an established feature in New York life. This is becoming evident in the publicity given the better productions; even the "ads" are mixed right in with the Broadway offerings, and the reviewers subject the plays to far less easy-going and far more Broadway-like standards. Off-Broadway's status has been given a real boost by the fact that the Circle-in-the-Square group—Leigh Connell, Theodore Mann and José Quintero—are now represented on Broadway with O'Neill's *Long Day's Journey into Night,* which won both the Critics' Circle Award and the Pulitzer Prize for the year. Add to this the fact that Carmen Capalbo and Stanley Chase, whose production of *Three-penny Opera* has had a fabulous run at the Theater de Lys, also set up on Broadway by taking the Bijou Theatre and presenting, first, Graham Greene's *The Potting Shed* and later Eugene O'Neill's *A Moon for the Misbegotten.*

Theatregoers still must look Off Broadway for most of the classics and much that is "difficult" or "highbrow." There was, for example, Sean O'Casey's *Purple Dust* at the Cherry Lane, James Joyce's *Exiles* at the Renato, Sophocles and Euripides at the Theatre Marquee, *The Misanthrope* very well done at Theatre East, *Hamlet* and *Twelfth Night* beautifully performed by the Shakespearwrights at their new home on West End Avenue. Add to these Gorki's *The Lower Depths* at Alhambra Hall, Ben Jonson's *Volpone* at the Rooftop, Ibsen's *Lady from the Sea* at the Tempo, Molière's *The Doctor in Spite of Himself* also at the Tempo, Chekhov's *The Sea Gull* and Strindberg's *Easter* at the Fourth Street and three one-act plays by J. M. Synge—*Riders to the Sea, The Tinker's Wedding* and *In the Shadow of the Glen*—at Theatre East.

Revivals of old and not-so-old plays also continued to play an important role. There was a fine revival of Louis Peterson's *Take a Giant Step* at Jan Hus Auditorium which ran all season, and such others as *Arms and the Man* at the Downtown, *Camille* at the Cherry

Erudite Intermission Dialogue Among

Off-Broadway Theatregoers

Lane, van Druten's *I Am a Camera* at the Actors' Playhouse, Leslie and Sewell Stokes' *Oscar Wilde,* Pirandello's *Right You Are* with Erik Rhodes, *The Lady's Not for Burning* with Henry Brandon and Margaret Phillips at the Carnegie Hall Playhouse and *No Exit* at Theatre East. The American Saroyards presented a Gilbert and Sullivan repertory. There were also the twenty-year-old *Johnny Johnson, The Eagle Has Two Heads* and *Idiot's Delight.* Mention should be made of the Heights Players of Brooklyn, a new group who did some fine acting in John Patrick's *The Hasty Heart* and whose second production, Arthur Miller's *The Crucible,* was not only well acted but exceptionally well directed.

Of the new plays—beyond the long-delayed premières of Shaw's eighteen-year-old *In Good King Charles's Golden Days* and the aforementioned eleven-year-old *Purple Dust*—there was Walt Anderson's *Me, Candido* which was vigorous and fresh; *The River Line* by Charles Morgan with such featured Broadway players as Beatrice Straight, Peter Cookson and Gene Lyons in the cast; *A Land Beyond the River,* a desegregation play by Loften Mitchell; Kenneth Sylvia's *The Shadow Years,* a drama about Mary Todd Lincoln; *Career* by James Lee and *A Box of Watercolors* by G. Wood. On the lighter side, there was an entertaining Off-Broadway revue, *Shoestring '57,* and Langston Hughes' Harlem-set musical play, *Simply Heavenly.*

It would take far too much space to mention all the Off-Broadway productions: the week of February 18th brought in seven alone. The chief Off-Broadway weakness continues to be with new plays by unestablished writers, few of which display much merit.

Along with all the Off-Broadway successes, the headaches have also increased. Off-Broadway producers have learned, as Broadway learned long ago, that quality is expensive. And so, apparently, is success. Budgets are rapidly rising—what with such matters as increased wages and theatre rentals and union contracts. Four years ago a production might cost $500; today anything from $7000 to $15,000 is not unusual. Shows used to break even with a 35% capacity; nowadays it takes a minimum of 50%. Rents used to be around $125 a week: these days landlords are asking—and getting—$575. With the growing approach to really professional standards, Off-Broadway producers must everywhere have professional talent. It will be interesting to watch how it will come out. It is safe to say Off Broadway is here to stay and a real challenge to Broadway itself.

Judy Garland in the "All-Star Variety Show"

SCENE DESIGNING AND THE FUTURE

By Jo Mielziner

WHAT about the scenic art of the 1956-1957 season? Technical and artistic standards continued to be comparatively high. There is certainly no dearth of talent in this field in the American theatre. But is this element of our stagecraft really keeping apace with the contemporary playwrights' needs? I think the answer must be no. As an active designer of stage scenery and lighting for the past thirty-three years, I feel we should do more but we are seriously handicapped. I don't mean the handicaps of budget limitation or time pressure. These may be more trying today than they were in past decades, but they will always be there and the artist must face them as part of his job. But in the name of my fellow designers and directors, I do cry out in anguish and protest at the strangling restrictions imposed on us all by the theatre buildings' antiquated walls, within which we strive to produce dramatic magic. This is not just a plea for the scenic artist to achieve a better setting; in the broader sense, it's a plea for him to be able to do more for the play.

Stage directing, as well as set designing, is conditioned by the architectural limitations of the auditorium and backstage. Our Broadway theatres are relics of a bygone day. The movies have perfected 3-D, Cinemascope, Todd-A-O and many other improvements in the short fifty-odd years of their existence. The motion-picture industry constantly tries to keep up with the evolution of new approaches. In little more than ten years of large-scale activity, the television industry has taken great strides in improving its techniques of production. But the living theatre in New York has not improved itself physically in over thirty years. It has not even provided *adequate* facilities for the employment of techniques proven worth-while in the professional theatre in Europe or in college theatres throughout the United States.

At last, after many years of fruitless talk about the urgent need for building new theatres for New York, the Lincoln Square Project was launched in the fall of 1956. This major redevelopment program for the Sixties west of Broadway included—besides new housing, a university campus, a new home for the Philharmonic and a new Metropolitan Opera House—a complex of six dramatic theatres.

Although the theatre project was later dropped from the general plan, the designs for it—with all that they envisage—remain. The thinking behind these designs was far deeper than a simple urge to have new, comfortable buildings to house Broadway's plays. It would have been comparatively easy to recreate in a new area some larger, more comfortable theatre buildings, which reflected contemporary needs of transportation and parking and thereby reglamorized theatregoing with every aid that luxury could supply. But something more significant went into these plans. The designer and the architects involved made a study of production methods and trends, which brought out some very interesting ideas. This survey showed how poorly designed were the playhouses of even thirty years ago in relationship to contemporary playwriting and "the new stagecraft."

In general, playwriting through the first decade of the twentieth century was pretty much conditioned by the dramatic conventions of the three-act play. The pauses required for scene changes within these acts were completely acceptable to the audiences of this period. Theatre architects from 1850 to 1925 reflected this technique in their basic designs. Excessively high real-estate values in the New York theatre districts led to theatres with stages far more cramped than European stages of the same period. But the comparatively leisurely approach to scene-changes, plus the simple, old-fashioned floodlit lighting equipment, prevented these handicaps from being serious, right through the nineteenth century and up into the first decade or two of the twentieth. In the late 'twenties, however, the influence of Continental stagecraft and modern playwriting combined to make our ill-designed stage houses a most serious handicap, under which we've been struggling for a quarter of a century.

Influences were equally strong on audiences as well as on creative teams behind the curtain. Audiences were no longer content to sit in a half-lit auditorium during protracted scene changes. All of us have been too deeply conditioned by heightened communication— by motion pictures, newsreels, wirephotos, radio and television. The age of restlessness, of condensation and of rapid transportation, has its influence on both the storyteller's technique and the audience's habits of receptivity. Today a scene change of more than a minute or two creates a restlessness in the audience that the theatre no longer can tolerate. The playwright is no longer content—nor should he be—to submit to conventions of forty or fifty years ago. The rigid forms of the nineteenth century are too limiting for today's author. He feels the need for fast-moving action. He demands an unlimited stage picture, where multiple scenes are employed simultaneously or in flashback.

The new stagecraft inherited from Europe and developed in this country during the teens and early 'twenties has to a great degree kept pace with the needs of the new playwright. To meet these needs, simpler forms, more imaginative concepts, the development and use of flexible and fast-moving stage lighting have been developed. But the poor design and physical limitations of our theatre buildings seriously hamper the director, the designer and their technical specialists. All the new techniques must still be crowded into backstage areas which were not designed for any such stagecraft. The result is not only enormously limiting, but enormously expensive; and it is one of the back-breaking forces in the economic stranglehold on living theatre.

Even the larger stages designed for musical comedies have proved to be woefully inadequate. Not that the spectacle shows and musicals of the early 1900s didn't have a great many settings; they often had two or three times as many as we now employ. But there was a difference. Stage lighting in those days was a matter of floodlighting—pure illumination: little narrow borderlights and floodlights in the wings, with no control whatsoever. Another limiting factor was the convention (completely acceptable up to about 1925) that a musical-comedy story could be written with the assurance that though five or ten minutes were needed for major scene shifts, the audience would be entertained by something known as a "Number in One"—by something done in front of a curtain or drop. But the revolution that occurred in the 'twenties and 'thirties—when musicals became more and more legitimate, and straight dramatic plays used more and more of the freedom and imagination previously associated with musicals—posed a new problem: the scene "In One" had to make sense. It had to be part of the continuity; it was no longer a moment of light entertainment unrelated to the plot. Today the nightmare of everyone connected with the preparation of a musical is, "How do we handle the scenes 'In One'?" Unlike European theatres, which for seventy-five years have used huge turntables, mechanical stages and other techniques in order to change large sets, we have no room in our old, poorly designed buildings to include important stagecraft innovations.

This business of so-called "padding" with a scene "In One" is not even limited to the musical theatre of today. Many a legitimate playwright and his director are faced with this question. Our contemporary playwright should not have to be so hampered by problems of scene-changing in the basic writing of his script. There are times when it takes the maximum ingenuity of author-director-designer to stage a multi-scene play without the padded writing often needed to overcome these serious limitations of our stages. A scene pause, like punctuation marks, is often most necessary, but surely these pauses should be determined by the playwright in terms of their dramatic effectiveness, and not on a mere mechanical basis of getting to the next setting.

The Lincoln Square theatres were designed to free the playwright and his director from these limitations. This can be accomplished with stages larger in area and depth and with the use of techniques that are almost impossible today—wagon stages, turntables, jackknife platforms, etc. In these theatres, if a scene is "padded," it will be the playwright's choice and not because of mere marking time to make a scene change.

Of the hundreds of manuscripts that are turned down every season by producers, a number are totally unproducible; there are, however, many scripts about which there are serious questions. They are good manuscripts full of potential values. These are weighed in the producers' minds not in terms of "Is it a good—or bad—script?" but, "Is the potential interest and audience for this script large enough to warrant the enormous financial risk involved the moment that script is bought for production?" Not that all scripts haven't got the risk element—just as the producer's judgment is itself a risk, even when he is convinced that he has a potential hit. If in his judgment a script has great worth, but is considered financially too risky for normal production means, there is no recourse but to return the script with regrets.

The plans for five of the Lincoln Square theatres constituted an attempt to design auditoriums and stages that would embrace the newest ideas for tomorrow's director and playwright and yet be altogether serviceable for plays and musical productions conceived in terms of Broadway or the Road as they exist. The gap from the turn of the century to 1950 is a tremendous one, but we believed that five of these theatres would be able to bridge it. The sixth theatre, on the other hand, was conceived in a different light. Here we decided to experiment with an entirely new concept of a theatre building. This building, which we designated as "Q" Theatre for want of a formal title, would be dedicated to the performing of plays of known value but unknown potential audience—the kind of plays which producers feel they should do, but in the last analysis can't, because of enormous production costs and guarantees. So a study was made as to where the greatest expenses lie in producing an un-

*Siobhan McKenna as
Shaw's "Saint Joan"*

known play, and on the basis of this study a very unconventional theatre was designed.

It is a startling fact that existing theatre buildings, which have to pay high overhead 365 days in the year, actually earn income only eight times a week for three-hour performances. This helps account for the extremely high guarantees that theatre owners must demand of producers. In existing theatre buildings there is only storage space for one production at a time—and even that is limited. Even if additional storage space existed, there would not be the means to shift from one production to another in an hour or two, which would be absolutely necessary if more than one tenant regularly used the same theatre during a given week.

In "Q" Theatre a new technique would provide very simply for having two or more productions share both facilities and overhead. Instead of a conventional backstage house for hanging scenery in the customary manner, this theatre would stress the simplest and most flexible elements in stagecraft—the actors' costumes, properties and stage lighting. This theatre would be equipped with very modern and expressive lighting equipment for projected scenery and for lighting such small-scale units as screens, which enable either a single set or a multi-scene production to be easily handled and stored. To facilitate rapid scene changes, there would be built-in sliding platform stages. This technique encourages the performing of plays demanding multiple playing areas seen simultaneously.

Flexibility in the stage picture, though much desired, is often limited because of basic sight-lines in the seating arrangement. In other words, in a given conventional seating plan, the larger the playing area, the more space can be at the mercy of the sight-lines. On the other hand, because of its unique design, "Q" Theatre would have much greater flexibility in the size of its productions, as regards both width of the proscenium opening and depth of the usable stage: from the intimate forestage for a dramatic reading all the way to a large opening and great depth for a musical production.

The theory behind "Q" Theatre's design was to minimize the cost of production as well as the risks involved in heavy overhead. Besides avoiding heavy physical production costs, it aimed at freeing the production from the enormous costs of out-of-town tryouts. With the technique involved, one production could have dress rehearsals during the day on the same stage that, within an hour, would be cleared for the evening performance of a currently running play.

As an example of the potential value of such a theatre, examine eight productions that were done in the 1955-1956 season in New

York—all unusual projects of definite artistic worth, but terribly risky economically. Had these been done in "Q" Theatre, their economic fates might have been far more satisfactory and their dramatic value not harmed in the least, and perhaps even augmented. The revival of *The Skin of Our Teeth*, with Helen Hayes and Mary Martin, played only twenty-two performances; the revival of *Othello* played for eighteen. Marcel Marceau gave sixteen performances at the Phoenix and sixteen uptown, but had to move out because other productions were scheduled in the theatres. Maurice Chevalier's "Songs and Impressions" had only forty-six performances but could easily have gone on for much longer by sharing the overhead. *Island of Goats* could have been tried out in "Q" at perhaps less than half the original production cost. *The Lark* would have been a natural for this theatre, and after proving its enormous power, might have moved elsewhere or kept on in "Q" and reduced the overhead through other performances on weekday afternoons, Saturday mornings and Sunday; *Tamburlaine the Great* was a worth-while production but had a very limited audience; *Waiting for Godot* was an unusual and worthy venture, and a natural for this kind of theatre. The Shakespeare Festival Company in Connecticut, or any other repertory group of classical presentations, would find "Q" not only an interesting stage to perform from, but one that prevents enormous losses and promotes possible profits.

If "Q" Theatre ever opens its doors, many a so-called "unproducible" new manuscript will get a professional production under sympathetic conditions. If, after this type of showing, any of these plays proves of major commercial value, there will always be the opportunity to engage a standard theatre for a solo run. Revivals for which there may be a limited but enthusiastic audience will get a production opportunity without the present risk of overwhelming losses.

New bricks and fresh mortar will not basically affect the American theatre, but they will make theatre-going more enjoyable and creative playwrighting more workable.

THE IDEA OF LIVING LIGHT

By Edward F. Kook

Lecturer in Stage Lighting, Columbia University

ROBERT EDMOND JONES in his inspired book, *The Dramatic Imagination,* quoted Professor Max Reinhardt: "The art of lighting a stage consists of putting light where you want it and taking it away from where you don't want it."

This definition suggests a wide spectrum of possibilities—the creation of light and shade, the balance of light intensities, the elimination or the inclusion of a shadow at a precise area, exaggeration in size, a silhouette or a close-up, a sense of infinite sky, an object advancing or receding, a ghost appearing or a form disappearing. Color and harmony with light—all made possible. Sometimes it is complicated and means a great number of lighting instruments. One theatrical producer, on seeing vast quantities of lighting equipment strewn all over the stage, quipped: "Kook, so much lighting equipment to make it dark!" Other times so little is used to make it bright. . . .

The artist responsible for designing the set is usually the man who creates the light. This individual is a thinking, creative artist who knows his *material* pigment. He should have a similar knowledge of light. It would be inconceivable for him not to know how to handle his *tool,* the brush. Therefore, why should he know less about the tool of lighting? The theatre demands that he know his way in both crafts. Too many artists in the theatre of today are unaware of the great possibilities of modern lighting. The theatre is all-demanding. The artist's work, while individual, cannot make a separate bid for attention, for the theatre today is a collaborative effort and the dramatic art is a composite of all the arts. Through understanding this, the artist learns to work with other men.

As designer he should conceive in terms of light. The question is: Should he call upon someone else to create the lighting plans? This makes the designer less than a well-rounded theatre artist, and the producer has to hire a separate lighting specialist. The lighting specialist is supposed to follow the conception of the so-called designer in creating the basic forms and colors in his lighting plans, but sometimes he fails to integrate lighting with design.

Lighting is an integral part of the stage design, but it should seldom dominate the final form. A division of the work between several designers often leads to a lack of unity. This may not always follow, of course, because the lighting specialists can contribute to the production without necessarily taking away from the designer's fundamental concept. It will be interesting to see whether this division of responsibility in design will fare well or ill in the future.

The concept of the lighting grows from the very first reading of the script. The type of play is stated by the playwright and the style of the production depends on the interpretations given it by the director. The director relates the living human form, the actor, to the concept of Time and Space. He creates the movements and gestures of the players which are integrated into the dramatic action of the play. (One wonders why directors in the American theatre, so unlike those in Great Britain and Germany, fail to assume the responsibility for "lighting the play.") From these numerous meetings and from attendance at rehearsals there spring ideas which the designer translates into line, form, pattern and color. All of it must harmonize with the emotional and spiritual sequences of the play. Spatial relationships are coupled with the actors' activities, which are in turn linked to the audience through the living element of light.

It is the audience that completes the magic circle of the theatre. As a vital segment, the audience's support and enthusiasm are essential to a great production. Since the most active of human senses is vision, it is to the eye that greatest appeal should be directed. The eyes are more keenly receptive than the ears, and in the words of Gordon Craig—"The audience would be more eager to see than hear." And if the observers do not see well, the indications are that they will not hear well. The audience will believe what it sees more readily than what it hears. Even in dreams it is a succession of visual images which we experience. As unreal as a ghost may be, the one in *Hamlet* is the more easily accepted when seen. Therefore, first and foremost, the actor and the environment through which he moves must be clearly visible. The spectators will not enjoy the performance if they cannot see the players' faces.

Thus the attitude of lighting designers regarding the eye must be elevated to a more scientific level. It is essential to understand the way light affects the eye, to know the characteristics of light sources and its spectral qualities and also the means of controlling light. No less attention must be given to materials and how they receive and reflect light. Just as too much light creates glare and discomfort, so too little will accelerate fatigue. Seeing should be clear and certain, immediate and easy. Above all else, the director will insist upon high visibility. I recall the time a prominent director remarked: "The only time the actors' faces were clearly visible was when they took their curtain calls." A little late in the evening, all will agree.

Whereas the playwright seems to be concerned with our seeing the actors' faces, there is no doubt that he is primarily interested in the time of day, season and place. He does not want it left to the audience's imagination. In another era, the imagination of the people was perforce permitted to be exercised. In the time of Shakespeare, when *Macbeth* was first played, there were not the means to darken the stage. "Light thickens, and the crow makes wing to the rooky wood," he says, and the audience took it from here—and in the proper light, if one may be permitted a pun.

In today's theatre of illusion it requires truckloads of scenery to simulate rocks, trees and backdrop and countless lights to create a sense of darkness, perhaps with a beclouded moon for good measure. There can be cerebration in the mind's eye; none in the eye itself.

Having attained visibility and specified the time of day, the designer also strives to make the plastic elements of light illuminate not only the painted scenery but the acting areas. Movement of light can make any part of the stage its center. Highlights will focus attention on the central meaning of the play and the living human forms; spotlights can place the player's living shadow where it is wanted or pierce the darkness with penetrating precision. This is not unlike the cruel blast of light that revealed the darkened, pitiful figure of Blanche du Bois in *A Streetcar Named Desire.*

Through the application of colored lights the heavens can be made to appear vast and infinite, remote and receding, or rolling and soft and separate in their ties to living man. Or in direct contrast: the sky is made black and foreboding, angry and menacing, as the Deluge floods the earth and drowns its human beings. The artist-visionary Robert Edmond Jones creates these effects magically in *Green Pastures;* yet simply and beautifully, too.

Painting with light is the supreme means employed by Jo Mielziner to express the inner life of the actor. He uses integrated lighting in direct association with the architecture. In his mounting of *Cat on a Hot Tin Roof,* the stage becomes brilliantly welded with the audiencee.

In *Long Day's Journey into Night* the lighting ideas, slow-moving and imperceptible, accent and dramatize the varying emotions of the

"The Taming of the Shrew" at the American Shakespeare Festival Theatre, with Morris Carnovsky, Pernell Roberts, Nina Foch and Mike Kellin

players. Without intrusion and very much a part of the players, the lighting advances the atmospheric qualities of the drab, dreary, realistic living room. The audience remains spellbound as it travels through the tragic, agonizing and long journey. The lighting idea is truly a tone poem. In *A Clearing in the Woods* fluid and flexible light helped to capture the many moods of the play. Movements of the human form were sharply delineated as they were silhouetted against the mass of sky.

Subtle fluctuations of light or sometimes the absence of light can bring greater allure to a scene which introduces what appears to be the naked form. Little light intended for little seeing is appropriate to a good old-fashioned murder or a tender love scene (who makes love in broad daylight?). Show girls in shimmering light answer the eye's cravings for beauty and will hold the audience better than the most absorbing story. Flo Ziegfeld knew all this. The opulent Ascot scene in *My Fair Lady* is a delightful eye-opener. Nevertheless, the final lighting idea will be part of, rather than separate from, the total endeavor: for if it is to remain a beauty unto itself, then, in the words of Francis Beacon, it is a "petty wonderment."

Dramatic art is a union of all the arts; lighting is an integral part of the whole. Light must be recognized as an emotional language, with power to create dramatic visibility. It is capable of bringing heightened composition values in combination with the proper mood to express the "inner nature of all appearance."

Finally, the playwright must unleash his tamed mind from the confines that he believes the physical limitations of our present-day stage have imposed. He must come to know what Adolph Appia described as the "livingness of light." Through the livingness of light the actors will be seen in the full roundness of their being, and will stand much nearer to their audiences. Through the livingness of light the meaning, no less than the movement, of a whole play can be augmented and enriched.

THE TEN BEST PLAYS

SEPARATE TABLES

Two Plays

By Terence Rattigan

[TERENCE RATTIGAN *was born in London in 1912. He attended Harrow and Oxford, and was headed for the diplomatic service when he wrote a play called "First Episode," later renamed "College Sinners." He is known in England as a screen writer as well as a dramatist. His plays include "French Without Tears," "While the Sun Shines," "O Mistress Mine," "The Winslow Boy" and "The Deep Blue Sea."*]

I. TABLE BY THE WINDOW

A Play in Three Scenes

IN the dining room of a small, slightly seedy Bournemouth private hotel, all the guests, except one couple, are seated at their separate tables. The only unoccupied tables are a single by the window and another toward the center of the room.

The none too attractive dinner is served by none too attractive waitresses—one very old and rugged, the other very young and flip. The menu offers few choices, and these are further limited by what is "off" in the kitchen by the time the guest orders.

The guests, with the exception of a young couple who are each reading a book, are all somewhere between sixty-five and seventy. Oddly dressed Miss Meacham, deep in her racing forms, pays attention to food only when it causes her to have nightmares. Her contemporary, Mrs. Railton-Bell, whose jewelry and silver foxes are as conspicuous as her grande-dame manner, carries on conversations at various tables—with Lady Matheson, a mousy widow, and Mr. Fowler, a quiet, elderly, ex-public-school master.

"Separate Tables": By Terence Rattigan. Copyright 1955 as an unpublished work by Terence Rattigan. Copyright © 1955 by Terence Rattigan. Reprinted by permission of Random House, Inc., New York. All inquiries should be addressed to author's agent: Harold Freedman, c/o Brandt & Brandt, 101 Park Avenue, New York 17, N. Y.

Mr. Fowler, looked after by the young waitress, takes her word that there is no more goulash, accepts her advice not to order the stuffed pork, and meekly agrees to what she recommends. As the girl disappears into the kitchen, it is Mrs. Railton-Bell's opinion that "she won't last." Lady Matheson feels the same way.

MRS. RAILTON-BELL—Still, it's disgraceful that the goulash's off, and two people not even in yet.

LADY MATHESON—I know.

MRS. RAILTON-BELL—Of course Mr. Malcolm's never on time— (*she indicates the table by the window*)—and he deserves what he gets. (*In another confidential whisper.*) Anyway, after those long sessions at the Feathers I often wonder if he ever really knows what he's eating. But the new lady—(*she indicates the other unoccupied table*)—I mean, my dear, what will she think?

Lady Matheson causes her friend some irritation by having already seen the new arrival. And Miss Meacham, totally lacking in curiosity about human beings, nevertheless absorbed every detail of and about the new guest when she met her on the stairs. "She's called Mrs. Shankland," Miss Meacham volunteers. "She comes from London, she arrived by train, she has four suitcases and a hatbox and she's staying two weeks." Mrs. Railton-Bell is impressed. Lady Matheson offers the finishing touches: "She was awfully smartly dressed. Nothing flashy—very good taste—but—well —Mayfair, if you know what I mean." Having had enough, Mrs. Railton-Bell shifts back to the weather as Mrs. Shankland appears.

Anne Shankland, about forty, stylish but not too stylish, dressed as for a smart London restaurant, seems very much out of place here, as she waits almost timidly to be shown to her table. Mabel, the maid, merely points to it. Not a guest glances at Anne as she takes her place.

There is a possibly explosive moment when Mabel offers Anne goulash. Mr. Fowler, stuck with spam, glares furiously at Mabel but decides against making a scene.

Mrs. Railton-Bell's voice, more self-consciously well-bred than ever, descants on the weather, with caustic asides about the sloppy dress and manners of the young couple who have now left the room. She also upbraids Oxford for failing to teach them better manners. Lady Matheson, whose husband was Oxford, echoes this. Mrs. Railton-Bell does not care to be reminded that Lady Matheson's husband went to Oxford, when her own did not.

The youngish manageress, Miss Cooper, comes in to make sure

that Anne is comfortable. She is momentarily put out because Anne has refused the soup, till Anne explains that she has to watch her figure: "I work at modeling, you know." Assuming that Anne has come for a little rest, Miss Cooper urges her to ask for anything she wishes. She offers a cordial smile, turns away with it extinguished. Noticing the still unoccupied table at the window, Miss Cooper calls Mabel. Will she go to Mr. Malcolm's room? Mabel already has. Has the kitchen kept something hot for him? They have, but will continue to do so for only another five minutes.

It has not been so much the food that upset Mr. Fowler as his not receiving a telephone call from an expected guest. "Please don't worry about the room, Miss Cooper," he frets. "If anything's gone wrong—which I don't believe, mind you—I'll pay for it, I promise you."

Miss Cooper—That won't be necessary, Mr. Fowler. But I *would* rather like to know—if you don't mind—as soon as possible. (Mr. Fowler *goes.* Miss Cooper *takes up the vase from his table.*)

Mrs. Railton-Bell (*sympathetically*)—It's too bad, Miss Cooper. This is the third time, isn't it?

Miss Cooper—I expect he'll turn up. Just forgotten to phone, that's all. You know what these Bohemian young people are like. (*She goes out.*)

Mrs. Railton-Bell—I don't, as it happens. I don't care for Bohemians. (*In her confidential whisper.*) We have one too many here, I should have thought. (*With her head she indicates the table by the window.*) And I'm beginning to doubt the very existence of Mr. Fowler's famous young painter friend.

Lady Matheson—I know he exists. Mr. Fowler showed me an article on him in *Picture Post.* He was the head boy of Mr. Fowler's house at Tonbridge, I gather. So proud of him, Mr. Fowler is—it's really quite touching to hear him go on—

Mrs. Railton-Bell—Well, I think it's a disgrace that he keeps on letting him down like this—(Miss Meacham *suddenly closes her book.*)

Miss Meacham—It's not a disgrace at all. Why should we old has-beens expect the young to show us consideration? We've had our life. They've still got theirs to live. Seeing us can only remind them of death and old people's diseases. I've got two of the prettiest nieces you ever saw. You've seen their photographs in my room. But they never come near me, and I wouldn't like it if they did. God knows I don't want to remind them of what they've got to become.

Miss Meacham, book in hand, now leaves. A moment later, Mrs. Railton-Bell sweeps regally into the lounge. Lady Matheson has yet to finish her sweet. Anne toys with her food as Mabel brings in the final course.

Suddenly John Malcolm gives a violent push to the door and enters. In his early forties, rugged, with unruly hair and untidy dress, he looks quickly at his watch, next at the kitchen door, then hurries toward his window table. Anne watches him remotely, expressionless. As he passes her table, conscious of her stare, he looks in her direction and stops dead—his back to the audience. After a moment he walks on.

His eyes on the tablecloth, Malcolm answers Doreen, the waitress, in monosyllables. After a final reference to his drinking, she withdraws to the kitchen. The silence is broken by Lady Matheson's "Good evening," as she, too, leaves the room.

Looking now at Anne, Malcolm asks whether it is mere coincidence that she is here. If, as she answers, she came for a rest, why did she choose this of all places? Anne says that a man at a party recommended the hotel. "He didn't tell you I was here?" Malcolm asks. She admits: "He did say something about a journalist—called John Malcolm. Is that you?" Then Anne recalls that these are his Christian names. But before she can answer his savage demand why she hadn't gone to one of the grand hotels, the waitress returns to remove his untouched soup. Then Malcolm resumes his attack.

John—He pays you alimony, doesn't he?

Anne—Seven fifty a year. I don't find it very easy. You see, I'm not getting work these days—

John—I thought he was a rich man.

Anne—Michael? Oh, no. His antique shop lost a lot of money.

John—He gets his name in the papers a lot.

Anne—Oh, yes. Quite a social figure—first nights and all that.

John—How long exactly were you married to him?

Anne—Three years and six months.

John—Beating me by three months? I saw the headlines of the divorce. They were quite juicy—but not as juicy as ours—you'll admit. It was cruelty again, wasn't it?

Anne—Yes.

John—Did *he* try to kill you too?

Anne (*quietly*)—No.

She says that her divorced husband showed his cruelty in a lot of small ways. . . . "They can all be summed up by saying that he doesn't really like women." When she admits that she went into.

this marriage with her eyes wide open, Malcolm laughs a bitter laugh. "A nice poser for a woman's magazine," he taunts her. "Girls, which husband would you choose? One who loves you too little—or one who loves you too much?"

John Malcolm proposes to leave for London during Anne's two-week stay, but agrees only too readily when she says that she will leave instead, though she doesn't understand why.

JOHN—Do you think these old women don't notice anything? They spend their whole days gossiping. It would take them less than a day to nose out the whole story and wouldn't they have a time with it! They're suspicious enough of me as it is. They know I write in the *New Outlook* under the name of Cato—and how they found that out I'll never know, because none of them would sully their dainty fingers by even touching such a bolshie rag.

ANNE—I read it every week.

JOHN—Turning left-wing in your old age?

ANNE (*quietly*)—My old age?

She is grateful when he says that she doesn't look eight years older since he saw her last. He accepts her excuse for not visiting him in prison, and when she reassures him that she will leave in the morning, he gets up abruptly, crosses over and says awkwardly: "Well, what do we do—shake hands?" Anne rises quickly and kisses his cheek, saying how glad she is to see him again. "It may seem boorish of me not to be able to say the same," John replies, "but then I am a boor, as you know. In fact, you must still have a scar on the side of your head to prove it to you." The eight years have healed Anne's scar, but it is apparent that John's kind of scar remains. He brushes by Miss Cooper at the door, determined to go out into the stormy night. Perturbed, Miss Cooper follows him to unlock the main door for him.

Alone, Anne stares for a long time at herself in her hand-mirror. Wishing to introduce Anne to her fellow-guests, Miss Cooper returns for her. She hates any of her guests to feel lonely. "Loneliness is a terrible thing," Miss Cooper says conversationally, "don't you agree?" Anne answers, "Yes, I do agree. A terrible thing," and follows Miss Cooper to the lounge.

SCENE II

In the lounge two hours later, the young couple are seated together on the sofa. They still read, but now, between long silences, make occasional remarks. Jean has all the guests ticked off. She even knows where they are: "The new one's gone up to her room. So has old Dream Girl. The Bournemouth Belle and Minnie Mouse are in the television room. Karl Marx is out boozing. Mr. Chips is still ringing up his painter friend."

And Jean, having finished her Chaucer, starts pestering Charles, who is still at his Anatomy. Over his objections, she closes his book; she wants to hear what Charles told his father about them. "Oh, for God's sake," Charles cries, "that we were in love with each other and were going to get married." He pulls his book back. Jean's reaction is that *that* was a dirty lie. Charles admits there was no other way to make his father understand, and tries to open his book. Jean tells him that if he goes on much longer, he'll be old before his time. This registers with Charles, who wonders "if all old people are as miserable as these." Jean, eliminating boarder after boarder, proves that out of the whole crowd, there is only one who is really miserable. Mrs. Shankland, she is sure, has been through some form of hell, and wears no wedding ring. Charles retorts: "According to your ideas on marriage, it ought to make her the happy one." "My ideas on marriage are only for us, Charles," Jean replies, "because I'm going to have a career and you're going to be a famous surgeon and don't want hordes of children cluttering up your consulting room. But most people aren't as sensible as we are. They get married and are miserable when it goes wrong. Thank heavens that can't happen to us. We're too integrated. At least I am, I know, and I hope you are too—" Wanting to kiss her, Charles wouldn't mind seeing Jean ever so slightly disintegrated. As they embrace, the ladies can be heard in the hall. Jean orders him to wipe his mouth. "Damn it all," Charles protests, "even the old girls know the facts of life." "They may know them," says Jean, "but they don't like them." They say their good-nights to the ladies.

Nothing gets by Mrs. Railton-Bell. Since the young couple came here ostensibly to study, she takes it as a personal offense that they may be in love, too. She hates anything "furtive." But a television speech by a member of the Conservative party is of more importance to her and Lady Matheson. Taking their accustomed seats by the fire, they are about to discuss the worth-while things the speaker had said, when John, drunk and sopping wet, brings the storm with him through the French windows. Mrs. Railton-Bell orders him to shut the windows and, along with Lady Matheson, decides to ignore him. They resume their discussion of the Conservative speech. John, drying in front of the fire, appears not to listen. Mrs. Railton-Bell concludes: "And then he said that every wage increase meant a smaller cake for cutting—" Abruptly John asks: "Who said this?"

MRS. RAILTON-BELL—Sir Roger Williamson, on television.

JOHN—I might have guessed it.

MRS. RAILTON-BELL—I gather you don't agree with what he said, Mr. Malcolm?

JOHN—Of course I don't agree. You know damn well I don't agree. That's not the point. They've got some clever people in that party. Why do they have to put an old ass like that on television—with a falsetto voice, a face like an angry walrus, and the mind of a backward child of eight?

MRS. RAILTON-BELL—That was *not our* impression of Sir Roger. (JOHN *doesn't answer. He seems, for the moment, to be lost in reverie.*)

JOHN—Poor old Roger. I suppose he needs the dough to make a little back on what he spends on all those girl friends of his.

Mrs. Railton-Bell is appalled and asks whether John is personally acquainted with this man he libels. John, remembering where he is, says he isn't, and asks what further things Sir Roger said. Had he mentioned the go-slow in the docks? Mrs. Railton-Bell's comment that the dock workers seemed to have no sense of national responsibility draws John's reply: "There's no body of men in England with more," and that is something he *knows*, having been a docker himself. This does not surprise Mrs. Railton-Bell.

Still in his dripping mackintosh, John seats himself—despite their cold looks—near the ladies. Between alcoholic burps, he finds out that it was Lady Matheson who uncovered John's being "Cato." She remembers, to her horror, his article on *Dividends and Wages,* the typescript of which he had left on the table nearby. Showing unusual spirit, Lady Matheson lets him know how monstrous she thought it: "Do you realize that I have to live on a little less than half of what the average dock worker makes a year? My husband was in the Civil Service and died before the pension scheme came into force. Still, the sum he left me seemed perfectly adequate at the time. And now—"

JOHN—I know. You can't afford to have your wireless repaired —and you live by it. You had to move into a small back room when they raised the hotel prices last year. You can only afford one cinema a week, in the front rows. I bet you don't even buy the *New Outlook*—you borrow it. In short, by any reasonable standards you're well below the poverty line, and, as the poor have always had my passionate sympathy, Lady Matheson, you have mine.

LADY MATHESON—Thank you, but I can do very well without it.

JOHN—I wonder if you can. You're the unlucky victims of our revolution—you and Miss Meacham and Mr. Fowler and the others. You should appeal to our humane instincts, Lady Matheson.

LADY MATHESON—By voting for your side, I suppose.

JOHN—That would be the most practical way, I agree.

LADY MATHESON (*staunchly*)—Never. Never till I die.

MRS. RAILTON-BELL—Tell me, why didn't you mention *me* just now, when you were talking of victims?

JOHN—Because you're not one, and won't be, either, until our capital levy gets at that tidy little nest egg of yours.

Outraged, Mrs. Railton-Bell wishes to sweep out of the lounge, but is delayed by Lady Matheson's having mislaid her spectacles. Miss Cooper, entering with Mrs. Railton-Bell's coffee, takes in the chilly scene. Upbraiding John for coming through the French windows and messing up the lounge, Miss Cooper orders him to take off his mackintosh in the hall. John very humbly excuses himself and goes out. Mrs. Railton-Bell refuses to discuss the matter now with Miss Cooper, but conveys her intention of registering a formidable complaint in the morning. Lady Matheson's spectacles found, both ladies leave. All patience, Miss Cooper next listens to fretful, ever hopeful Mr. Fowler, who has come back for more supplies of writing paper.

When at last she is alone, Miss Cooper kneels to tackle the mud on the carpet and tidy up the room. On John's moody return, she first offers him Mrs. Railton-Bell's coffee, then sympathy. Perching on the arm of his chair, her head affectionately on his shoulder, Miss Cooper tries to find out why he was so troubled that he got drunk. When he won't tell her, she asks in a cheerful way about his contretemps with the old women. John thinks he may have to leave. "You won't have to," she assures him, "I'll see to that. But was it so bad?" "Not very bad," John says . . . "Just an ordinary show-off, a rather sordid little piece of alcoholic self-assertion. Taking it out on two old women, telling them what a brilliant political thinker I am, hinting at what a great man I once was. I even gave away that I used to work in the docks." He hopes that he covered up knowing Roger Williamson. He can't remember what else he did and, with an affectionate arm around Miss Cooper, apologizes miserably. He doesn't know why he does these things; he used to know how to behave. "I'd do them too," says Miss Cooper, kissing him gently, "in your place." She refuses to let him think the less of himself, reminding him: "But before you were even thirty you'd been made a Junior Minister." "Yes, yes, yes," exclaims

John, rising brusquely. "It doesn't matter. The world is full of promising young men who haven't in middle age fulfilled their promise. There's nothing to that. Nothing at all." Though she quietly tries, Miss Cooper can't find out what made John get drunk. "Couldn't you *ever* get back?" she ventures. John laughs sharply: "God, what a field day for the Tory press that would be! John Malcolm Ramsden has decided to stand as a Labour Independent for his old constituency. It will be recalled that Mr. Ramsden, who was a Junior Minister in the 1945 Administration, went to prison for six months in 1946 on the triple charge of assaulting a police officer in the course of his duty, of being drunk and disorderly, and of causing grievous bodily harm to his wife. . . ." He can see the headlines, that's enough. Knowing Miss Cooper's desire to help, John tells her that he loves her "sincerely," causing her to smile and say that smacks of brotherly feelings. When he retorts that she should know better, Miss Cooper does, and is grateful for "all that." They draw together, then hearing someone at the door, draw apart as if from long practice.

Anne wishes a word with John. Miss Cooper is disturbed that she knows who he is, but leaves them. Anne hopes John doesn't mind this coming back to say good-bye; she was afraid that he hated the very sight of her. Really looking at her for the first time, John says: "The very sight of you, Anne, is perhaps the one thing about you that I don't hate."

There is some nervous hedging. Anne is sure John always got her wrong; John is sure she is as predictable as always. He just wants her to leave him now, and to disappear quietly in the morning. She begs to stay, to sit down. He feels that this is a reminder of his bad manners. She wants to know why—if he always finds her predictable—he ever married her in the first place? Indulging her vanity, he says: "Because my love for you at that time was so desperate, my craving for you was so violent, that I could refuse you nothing that you asked—not even a marriage that every prompting of reason told me must be disastrous." As a former Hull docker, John has viewed a wife's obligation very differently from Anne, who, as a model, refused to have children. Angrily protesting John's refusal to believe that she married him for love, Anne asks what other reason could have prompted her to choose him over her more glamorous admirers? They rehash all their old arguments: John maintains that she only wanted to enslave him; the other suitors with their millions and their titles were too tame for her. Anne needed wilder game: ". . . a genuine, live, roaring savage from the slums of Hull, to make him grovel at the vague and distant promise of delights that were his anyway by right, or goad him to such a frenzy of drink and rage by a locked door that he'd kick it in and hit you with his fist so hard that you'd knock yourself unconscious against a wall—that must really have been fun."

Pleased to discover that his drinking tonight was because of her, Anne becomes much more self-confident. She tells John that he is the only person in the world that she had ever been really fond of. "You notice," she says, "how tactfully I leave out the word love. Give me a cigarette." Refusing his distasteful brand, Anne asks for her handbag and her gold cigarette case.

They continue to talk of their love, of their past dissensions; John continues to stare at Anne. Contentedly, she tells him not to, it makes her embarrassed. He finds, to her delight, that she has not changed a bit. "If you wanted an obedient little *hausfrau*," she purrs, "why didn't you marry one—like that manageress I caught you canoodling with a moment ago? That *was* a canoodle, wasn't it?" "A canoodle is what you would call it—yes," answers John. He couldn't marry Miss Cooper because he doesn't love her. "Couldn't you—" Anne suggests—"as they say—*learn* to love her? After all, she's your type." "I have still only one type in the whole world, Anne," John tells her. "God knows it does little for my pride to have to admit that to you, but I never was very good at lying about myself." Looking at her, he repeats: "Only one type. The prototype." "I'm glad," says Anne.

They talk quietly of her second husband, who wasn't enough of a man for her. Taking his hand, Anne confesses that some of the things John had predicted would happen to her are happening. She is without friends. She hasn't the gift to make them. John sweetly says: "There's no gift. To make people love you is a gift, and you have it—" "Had it," says Anne bitterly. "Have it," John repeats. Anne feels time is slipping by. "God, it goes fast, doesn't it?" she cries.

JOHN—I haven't found it to, these last eight years.

ANNE—Poor John. I'm so sorry. (*She squeezes his hand.*) But it's such a wonderful fluke, our meeting again like this, that we really shouldn't waste it. We must see some more of each other now. After all, when fate plays as astounding a trick as this on us, it must mean something, mustn't it? Don't send me away to-morrow. Let me stay on a little while. (JOHN *makes no reply. He is staring at her.* ANNE *continues, gently.*) I won't be a nuisance. (JOHN *still does not answer; he is still staring at her.*) I won't, John. Really I won't.

JOHN (*at length, murmuring thickly*)—You won't be a nuisance. (*He embraces her suddenly and violently, and she responds. After a moment she begins to say something.* JOHN, *savagely*—) Don't speak. For God's sake, don't speak. You'll kill this moment.

Anne, at the risk of killing his moment, reminds him that they are in the public lounge. Telling him the number of her room, taking a cigarette from his shaky hand, smoothing out her dress and hair, she blows John a kiss, asks, "Half an hour?" and starts for the door. At the door is Miss Cooper, calling her to the telephone for a London message.

Miss Cooper knows, and lets John know, that Anne is the one he told her about. "Carved in ice, you said once," she remembers. She won't let John reply; she understands. She also knows that if Anne took all this trouble to track John down, she won't let him go very easily. John answers: "She hasn't run me to earth. It was a coincidence, her coming down here." Miss Cooper lets slip that she doesn't believe this. John starts shaking information out of her. "Don't knock *me* about, John," Miss Cooper says quietly. "I'm not her, you know." But she reveals that Anne is now talking to the one man who knew John was here—the editor of the *New Outlook*.

When Anne, happy and unruffled, returns, she leaves her order for the morning with Miss Cooper and says good-night. John, dismissing Miss Cooper, stops her dead. He insists on having it out right now. "When fate plays as astounding a trick as this, it must mean something, Anne, mustn't it?" John mimics.

Mocking her the while, he advances menacingly. Anne, though scared, stands her ground. Accusing her of lying to contrive this reunion, John pulls her around to peer at her. He sees now the lines that weren't there before and tells Anne: "It won't be long now before this face will begin to decay and then there'll be nothing left to drive a man to—" He slips his hands around her throat. Anne's quiet "Why don't you?" has him stare for a moment, then push her violently away. She falls from her chair, as once more John dashes out into the rain.

Miss Cooper finds Anne sobbing uncontrollably and takes her to her own room, to quiet her.

SCENE III

Having faced Mrs. Railton-Bell's morning complaint, Miss Cooper enters the dining room. She greets the young couple and Miss Meacham. She reassures Mabel that John's bed was not slept in because he was called away unexpectedly last night. The new lady, Miss Cooper tells Mabel, will not be having breakfast; she has to watch her figure. Miss Meacham is aware that Anne is leaving, and not at all surprised. Miss Meacham knew she couldn't stick it out. She tells Miss Cooper that Anne simply is not an "alone" type. According to Miss Meacham, Miss Cooper is. Having had no sleep, Miss Cooper finds this compliment hard to take. Rising, Miss Meacham elaborates: "No. What I've always said is—being alone, that's the real blessed state—if you've the character for it. Not Mrs. What's-her-name from Mayfair, though. I could tell that at a glance. A couple of weeks here and she'd have her head in the gas oven. It's pork for lunch, isn't it?" "Yes, Miss Meacham," Miss Cooper answers. "I loathe pork," says Miss Meacham. "Ah, well," she adds, "I'd have a bit on Walled Garden, dear, if I were you. He's past the post if the going's on top."

Alone in the emptied room, Miss Cooper slumps into a chair. John, needing money to get away, finds her there. Told that's not necessary, that Anne's not hurt and is leaving herself, John is greatly relieved. Miss Cooper, for propriety's sake, straightens his collar and tie and seats him at his table. Doreen, the waitress, takes his order and leaves.

Miss Cooper tells John that Anne has been taking drugs for nearly a year. "The damn little fool," John says, "why does she do it?" With a shrug, Miss Cooper asks: "Why do you go to the Feathers? —Yes—there's not all that much to choose between you, I'd say. When you're together you slash each other to pieces, and when you're apart you slash yourselves to pieces. All told, it's quite a problem." Against her own interests, she now urges him to see Anne. He is ready to slip out again, but Miss Cooper reasons that he should speak to Anne because he loves her and she needs his help. Once again the manageress, Miss Cooper goes to the lounge. John just sits.

Anne arrives and is greeted by the waitress, who goes off to get her some coffee. Anne says "John" in a pleading voice and continues to stand by his side. He advises her to go to her own table. Once seated, she apologizes, in a desperate tone, for lying to him. She knows she's always been an awful liar: "It was nearly always about my lying that we used to quarrel in the old days, do you remember?" "Yes," answers John, "I remember." Anne is near to tears as the waitress returns, but controls herself. When they are by themselves again, Anne confesses she doesn't know what's going to happen to her. It's the living alone. John tells her to give up those drugs. Anne promises to try.

JOHN—Tell me, Anne. When you say you need me, is it me you really mean, or just my love? Because if it's my love you must know now that you have that. You have that for life.

ANNE—It's you, John.

JOHN—But why? Why, for heaven's sake?

ANNE—I suppose because you're all the things I'm not. You're honest and true and sincere and dependable and—(*She breaks off and tries to smile.*) Oh dear, this is just becoming a boring catalogue of your virtues. Too embarrassing. I'm sorry and that damn waitress will come in and catch me crying again.

JOHN (*slowly*)—I may have had some of those virtues once, Anne. I'm not at all sure that I have them now, so I don't know if I'd be able to satisfy your need. I do know, though, that you can never satisfy mine.

What's more, John is sure that even if they both tried, they'd both fail. "Because," John says, "our two needs for each other are like two chemicals that are harmless by themselves, but when brought together in a test tube can make an explosion as deadly as dynamite." Knowing she's always been a coward, Anne can't face getting old. The tears start again, and when finally she lowers her handkerchief, she finds John sitting at her table. Aware that they haven't much to hope for together, though more than when apart, John answers Doreen's "Do you two want to sit at the same table for lunch?" with "Yes, I think we do." "Oh," says Doreen, "I'll make up a double for you from now on, then. It's just so long as we know—"

II. TABLE NUMBER SEVEN

A Play in Two Scenes

EIGHTEEN months later. New slipcovers in the lounge and summer weather outside are not the only changes: the young couple is a married couple with baby. Jean no longer speaks English; she now talks baby talk. But Charles, in spite of Jean's prattle, is still at his studying. He gets rid of his wife, only for Major Pollock to provide a fresh interruption.

The Major is in his middle fifties. With his clipped military mustache and very neat clothes, he seems almost too much the retired major. Even before his entrance from the garden, he could be heard telling Miss Meacham that it wasn't like the old days, "When one would ring up the hall porter at White's and get him to put on a couple of ponies." His unsought-after conversation with Charles is sprinkled with references to Sandhurst, Clausewitz, and the Black Watch. Needing quiet, Charles chooses his baby's brand, and leaves the Major as fast as he can.

Eric Portman and Margaret Leighton changi

makeup for their dual roles in "Separate Tables"

Next, the Major teases Mr. Fowler about a letter he has had from yet another ex-student. Miss Cooper, entering with the Major's copy of the *West Hampshire Weekly News,* which was almost impossible to find, can't imagine his wanting to read it. "Oh," says the Major, "I just wanted to have a look at it, you know. I've never read it—strange to say—although I've been here . . . what is it, almost four years?" "I'm not surprised," Miss Cooper answers; "there's never anything in it except parking offenses and cattle shows."

Straightening the room, Miss Cooper hears Mr. Fowler out on his new letter. Major Pollock, unobserved, quickly seeks and finds what he was looking for. His eyes glaze. He closes the paper sharply. Mr. Fowler remembers that the Major, as well as his student Macleod, was in the Highland Division. The Major, coming to, says fiercely that he had never said so, but in the next breath says he doesn't think he knew Macleod. Mr. Fowler, chuckling, leaves the room. "Curly Macleod," he reminisces. "He once elided a whole word in his Greek Iambics . . ."

The Major tries to find out whether anyone else has this paper. Mrs. Railton-Bell, he learns, subscribes, though the Major can't imagine why. Miss Cooper doesn't know, but makes a stab at it: "There's not a lot that goes on in the world, even in West Hampshire, that she likes to miss. And she can afford fourpence for the information, I suppose." In a jolly vein, the Major wishes he had borrowed hers and saved his money. He laughs heartily; Miss Cooper smiles politely and leaves the room.

Alone, the Major, having ripped out the offending page and stuffed it into his pocket, conducts a feverish search through the magazines on the table for the other copy. He has it in his hand when Mrs. Railton-Bell walks in. Her timid-looking, wizened, dowdy, thirty-odd-year-old daughter, Sybil, follows. The Major is caught; he asks to borrow the paper. Permission is granted until Mrs. Railton-Bell discovers the other copy on the floor, and orders him to return hers and take this one. Newspaper in hand, the Major says jauntily: "Think I'll just go out for a stroll." When Sybil asks shyly to accompany him, the embarrassed Major answers: "Well, Miss R. B. —jolly nice suggestion and all that—the only thing is, I'm going to call on a friend, you see, and—" With a "Cheerie-bye," the Major leaves the embarrassed Sybil to listen to her mother. "I didn't think it was terribly wise of you to lay yourself open to that snub just now," says Mrs. Railton-Bell.

SYBIL—It wasn't a snub, Mummy. I'm sure he really *was* going to see a friend—I often *do* go for walks with the Major.

MRS. RAILTON-BELL—I know you do, dear. What is more, quite a lot of people have noticed it. (*Pause.* SYBIL *stares at her mother.*)

SYBIL (*at length*)—You don't mean—you can't mean— (*She jumps up and holds her cheeks with a sudden gesture.*) Oh, no. How can people be so awful!

MRS. RAILTON-BELL—It's not being particularly awful when an unattached girl is noticed constantly seeking the company of an attractive older man.

SYBIL (*still holding her cheeks*)—They think I chase him? Is that it? They think I run after him, they think I want—they think—no, it *is* awful. It *is*. It *is*. It *is*.

MRS. RAILTON-BELL (*sharply*)—Quieten yourself, my dear. Don't get into one of your *states* now.

Sybil likes to walk with the Major because he talks so well about London, and the war, and his regiment. "Well," she confesses, "he's seen so much of life and I haven't." Mrs. Railton-Bell can't imagine what she means. Before long, Sybil is made to proclaim her gratitude to her mother. Her mother reminds her that she can't stand any job for more than a few weeks. "Remember Jones & Jones?" she asks. "But that," cries Sybil, "was because I had to work in a basement, and I used to feel stifled and faint. But there must be something else." Not according to Mrs. Railton-Bell; not with Sybil's nervous system what it is. "There's a big difference," her mother announces, "between not having hysterical fits and being strong enough to take the job." Having settled that, Mrs. Railton-Bell asks for her newspaper. "I want to see," she says, "what the Major was so interested in."

Mrs. Railton-Bell finds she has left her glasses behind in a shelter during the afternoon's walk, and Sybil goes to fetch them. Meanwhile, Mrs. Railton-Bell, knowing where the meatier items are, turns to the right page and holds the paper close to her eyes. Lady Matheson, her glasses with her, comes just in time to read the sought-after item to her friend. What had made Mrs. Railton-Bell's hands tremble was the announcement of Major Pollock's being hauled before the local magistrate for insulting behavior in a Bournemouth cinema. Lady Matheson is upset. Mrs. Railton-Bell, ever the bloodhound, orders her to read on. A woman had complained about Pollock's persistent nudging and his attempting other liberties. The Police, called in to observe, noticed that the Major changed his seat no less than five times, always choosing a seat next to a woman. Later, the Major's lawyer made a plea, urging that his client's record be taken into account: as a second lieutenant during the war, he had held a responsible position in charge of an Army Supply Depot, and in 1946 was discharged a full lieutenant. "The Chairman of the Bench," reads Lady Matheson, "giving judgment, said: 'You have behaved disgustingly, but because this appears to be your first offense we propose to deal leniently with you.' The defendant was bound over for twelve months." Lady Matheson can only repeat: "Oh, dear." Mrs. Railton-Bell, excited but outwardly very composed, considers it a stroke of luck that the newspaper caught the story. Lady Matheson thinks it would have been better not to have known. Mrs. Railton-Bell is infuriated. "Well," says Lady Matheson, "he's been wandering around among us for four years now and there haven't been any repercussions yet." With a sigh, Lady Matheson adds: "I suppose we're too old." Mrs. Railton-Bell snaps: "I have a daughter." Lady Matheson, thus reminded of poor Sybil, begs that she won't be told details about the Major, certainly not those involving the cinema.

Mrs. Railton-Bell is ready to have the Major put out of the hotel. To do this, she is determined to tell all the guests, so that stubborn Miss Cooper will have no alternative. About to rally cohorts, Mrs. Railton-Bell considers Miss Meacham too unpredictable to bother with. With a further look on Sybil's return, Lady Matheson leaves to call the meeting. Mrs. Railton-Bell barely hesitates whether to keep the news from her daughter; in another minute she has given her the entire report to read.

Lady Matheson, coming back, is shocked at Sybil's appearance. "I did my best, my dear," says Mrs. Railton-Bell, "but she insisted, she absolutely insisted." She hovers sympathetically over her daughter: "It must be the most dreadful shock for you. It was for us, too, as you can imagine. Are you all right?" Sybil, removing her spectacles, folds the paper meticulously, murmurs: "Yes, Mummy."

When Jean and Charles come in, it develops that Sybil has crushed her spectacles in her hand. Charles immediately examines the hand professionally and ties a clean handkerchief around it. Sybil says nothing.

Mr. Fowler joins the group. Mrs. Railton-Bell announces grave news. To Charles it means that the boiler has gone wrong again; to Mr. Fowler, that prices are being raised. "Look, Mrs. Railton-Bell," says Charles, "must we play twenty questions? Can't you just tell us what it is?"

Her anger overcoming what she calls her "painful embarrassment," Mrs. Railton-Bell demotes the Major to a lieutenant in the R.A.S.C. No one is surprised: Jean and Charles had suspected it all along. Mr. Fowler doubted the Major's public-school education after his shocking mistake in quoting Horace. Implying that this is nothing,

Mrs. Railton-Bell dramatically demands her audience's attention for her "ghastly" revelation.

Charles' reaction is amazement. It is only when Mrs. Railton-Bell demands the Major's expulsion that Charles refuses point-blank. Emotionally he admits to being on her side, but logically he is not. He is very wary of passing moral judgment on things he does not understand: "It's only fair to approach it from the purely logical standpoint of practical Christian ethics, and ask myself the question: 'What harm has the man done?' Well, apart from possibly slightly bruising the arm of a certain lady, whose motives in complaining—I agree with Lady Matheson—are extremely questionable; apart from that—and apart from telling a few rather pathetic lies about his past life, which most of us do anyway from time to time, I really can't see he's done anything to justify us chucking him out into the street."

Jean, disagreeing hotly with her husband, and declaring the Major a public menace, asks Charles to think of their daughter. Charles says wearily: "I know. I know. And supposing in twenty or thirty years' time she sits next to a Major Pollock in a cinema—" "Exactly," says Jean. "It's not funny, Charles. How would you feel—" "Very ashamed of her," answers Charles, "if she didn't use her elbows back, very hard, and in the right place."

Charles is against any action whatsoever; Jean is thoroughly behind Mrs. Railton-Bell. Mr. Fowler finds it difficult when called on: "Tolerance," he says, "is not necessarily a good, you know. Tolerance of evil may itself be an evil. After all, it was Aristotle, wasn't it, who said—"

Miss Meacham, with an impatient "Oh, really," marches in from the garden, intent on getting to her room.

MRS. RAILTON-BELL—You heard, Miss Meacham?

MISS MEACHAM—I couldn't help hearing. I didn't want to. I was doing my system and you need to concentrate like billy-oh on that, but I had my chair against the wall to catch the sun, and I wasn't going to move into the cold just for you people.

MRS. RAILTON-BELL—Well, as you know the facts, I suppose we should canvass your opinion.

MISS MEACHAM—I haven't any.

MRS. RAILTON-BELL—You must have some opinion.

MISS MEACHAM—Why should I? I've been out of the world for far longer than any of you and what do I know about morals and ethics? Only what I read in novels, and as I only read thrillers, that isn't worth much. In Mickey Spillane the hero does far worse things to his girls than the Major's done, and no one seems to mind.

MRS. RAILTON-BELL—I don't think that it's quite the point what Mickey Spillane's heroes do to his girls, Miss Meacham. We want your views on Major Pollock.

MISS MEACHAM—Do you? Well, my views on Major Pollock have always been that he's a crashing old bore, and a wicked old fraud. Now I hear he's a dirty old man, too, well, I'm not at all surprised, and quite between these four walls, I don't give a damn. (*She goes out.*)

Mrs. Railton-Bell rallies and demands Mr. Fowler's vote, which after further hemming and hawing he gives in favor of action. Lady Matheson finds deciding even more difficult. Mrs. Railton-Bell impatiently snaps: "Are you on the side of Mr. Stratton with his defense of vice, or are you on the side of the Christian virtues, like Mr. Fowler, Mrs. Stratton and myself?" Charles says quietly: "I have never in my life heard a question more disgracefully begged. Senator McCarthy could use your talents, Mrs. Railton-Bell." Shutting him up, Mrs. Railton-Bell gets Lady Matheson's reluctant vote, and assuming as always that her daughter agrees with her, she reports the vote as five to one in favor of action. Charles insists on hearing from Sybil.

From a state of shock, Sybil, under her mother's questioning, emerges into hysteria. "It made me sick," she repeats over and over again. Mrs. Railton-Bell embraces her and receives her daughter's head in her arms. "I don't feel well, Mummy," cries Sybil. "Can I go and lie down?" Mrs. Railton-Bell leads her into the hall.

Irate, Charles is sure that Sybil will end up a mental case. Jean reminds him that it was he who started this. Admitting that he should have guessed her state, Charles says: "Anyway, I had an idiotic but well-meaning hope that I might get her—just this once —just this once in the whole of her life—to disagree publicly with her mother. It could save her soul if she ever did."

After Charles goes, Mrs. Railton-Bell asks briskly: "Shall we all go and see Miss Cooper in a body, or would you rather I acted as your spokesman?" The others willingly allot her the job, although Jean wouldn't mind it herself. Finding the whole thing distasteful, and Jean and Mrs. Railton-Bell of the same ruthless stamp, Lady Matheson and Mr. Fowler retreat to the television room.

Major Pollock slips back into the empty room. Sybil, entering quietly, halts his frantic search for the newspaper. "Don't pretend any more, please," she says. "She's read it, you see." What's more, everyone knows everything, and at this moment her mother is notifying Miss Cooper.

The Major collapses in a chair by the fire. Under Sybil's passionate questioning, he speaks quietly and tells her more than she bargained for about his indefensible past. She cries that it makes her ill, but listens about his furtive life and even tries to understand. On his side, he apologizes for upsetting her, of all people. He finds her so much like himself, so frightened of life: perhaps that's why they've drifted so much together.

SYBIL—How can you say we're alike. *I* don't— (*She stops, unable to continue.*)

MAJOR POLLOCK—I know you don't. You're not even tempted and never will be. You're very lucky. Or are you? Who's to say, really? All I meant was that we're both of us frightened of people, and yet we've somehow managed to forget our fright when we've been in each other's company. Speaking for myself, I'm grateful and always will be. Of course I can't expect *you* to feel the same way now.

Sybil helps him collect his possessions, including a tobacco pouch sporting Old Wellingtonian colors. She finds out that the only place the Major now can go is to a man he's afraid of. "It's rather a case of birds of a feather," he admits. Sybil says pleadingly: "Don't go to him. You mustn't go to him," and offers the Major her savings. Holding her hand gently, he thanks her but refuses. He tells her not to worry.

Miss Cooper now comes in and closes the door behind her. She makes it plain that if Major Pollock wishes to stay, he is free to. Once more grateful, the Major once more refuses, but accepts Miss Cooper's offer of a reservation in London at another of the same chain of hotels. She offers to call but the Major says: "Thank you, but I think perhaps I'd better ring them myself. In case of—further trouble, I don't want to involve you more than I need. May I use the phone in your office?" Promising Sybil that if he doesn't see her again, he'll write, the Major goes.

Sybil tries brusquely to reject Miss Cooper's sympathy. She says she can't understand Miss Cooper's offer to so wicked a man. But she breaks down suddenly. Saying, "That's better, much better," Miss Cooper takes hold of Sybil.

SYBIL—He says we're both scared of life and people and sex. There—I've said the word. He says I hate *saying* it even, and he's right. I do. What's the matter with me? There must be something the matter with me.

Miss Cooper—Nothing very much, I should say. Shall we sit down?

Sybil—I'm a freak, aren't I?

Miss Cooper (*in matter-of-fact tones*)—I never know what that word means. If you mean you're different from other people, then, I suppose, you are a freak. But all human beings are a bit different from each other, aren't they? What a dull world it would be if they weren't.

Sybil—I'd like to be ordinary.

Miss Cooper—I wouldn't know about that, dear. You see, I've never met an ordinary person. To me all people are extraordinary. I meet all sorts here, you know, in my job, and the one thing I've learnt in five years is that the word normal, applied to any human being, is utterly meaningless. In a sort of way it's an insult to our Maker, don't you think, to suppose that He could possibly work to any set pattern.

Miss Cooper finds out that Sybil, except for her one fling as sales girl, has never left her mother's side. She urges her to try again. "Mummy says no," answers Sybil. "Mummy says no. Well, then," says Miss Cooper, "you must try and get Mummy to say yes, don't you think?"

Sybil escapes on the Major's return. This time he has actually made a reservation under the simple name of *Mr*. Pollock. Miss Cooper ladles out more courage, and suggests that since he dreads a new hotel, he stay here where he won't be tempted to be "Major" again. But he feels too much of a coward for that. He realizes Miss Cooper is hoping he'll reinstate himself in Sybil's eyes. Under Miss Cooper's steady look, the Major smiles shamefacedly and says: "I expect I'll still catch the seven forty-five," and goes out.

Scene II

Except for one empty table, the dining room is filled. Mrs. Railton-Bell is going on about what a ghastly day it has been, when the Major comes quietly into the dining room. The deathly silence is broken by Doreen: "Mabel—Number Seven's in. You said he was out."

His eyes on the tablecloth, the Major orders what Doreen advises. Mrs. Railton-Bell glares at him and at the others. Her glare is immediately challenged: Charles calls a high-pitched greeting to the Major. Now Jean glares. Miss Meacham follows with a tip at Newmarket for the Major, who manages to answer both greetings. Next, Miss Cooper enters and gives particular attention to "Mr." Pollock. By now, Mrs. Railton-Bell feels the draught and turns her chair and her back on the Major. Mr. Fowler rallies, too: on his way out, he stops for a word at the Major's table. And Lady Matheson, of all people, now calls out to him: "I advise the apple charlotte, it's very good." "Thank you," says Major Pollock, "I'll have that."

Furiously, Mrs. Railton-Bell rises. She quietly tells Sybil to come with her. Sybil, equally quietly, refuses. Mrs. Railton-Bell's puzzled tones grow sharp. Sybil is adamant. "No, Mummy," she says, "I'm going to stay in the dining room and finish my dinner." Mrs. Railton-Bell's dignified exit is ruined before she reaches the door. Sybil addresses the Major: "There's a new moon tonight, you know. We must all go and look at it afterwards." "Yes. We must," the Major replies.

Doreen returns with the Major's food. "Joe got it wrong about your going, didn't he?" she asks. The Major, with Sybil's eyes meeting his, is able to answer: "Yes, he did." "That's good," Doreen says. "Breakfast usual time, then?" "Yes, Doreen," the Major decides. "Breakfast usual time . . ."

LONG DAY'S JOURNEY INTO NIGHT

By Eugene O'Neill

[EUGENE O'NEILL *was born in New York in 1888, the son of a popular American actor, most famous for "The Count of Monte Cristo." O'Neill's early plays were staged by the Provincetown Players. They were mostly one-act dramas of the sea. He has been the winner of four Pulitzer Prizes—for "Beyond the Horizon" (1920), "Anna Christie" (1922), "Strange Interlude" (1928) and last season's "Long Day's Journey into Night." Generally regarded as America's greatest playwright, O'Neill died in 1953.*]

[*Note:* As a special approach to the play, the full text of Act I only is presented here, since it was felt that so intensely personal a work should not be synopsized.]

ACT I

Characters

JAMES TYRONE
MARY CAVAN TYRONE, *his wife*
JAMES TYRONE, JR., *their elder son*
EDMUND TYRONE, *their younger son*
CATHLEEN, second girl

SCENE: Living room of James Tyrone's summer home on a morning in August, 1912.

At rear are two double doorways with portieres. The one at right leads into a front parlor with the formally arranged, set appearance of a room rarely occupied. The other opens on a dark, windowless back parlor, never used except as a passage from living room to dining room. Against the wall between the doorways is a small bookcase, with a picture of Shakespeare above it, containing novels by

"Long Day's Journey into Night": By Eugene O'Neill. © 1955 as an unpublished work by Carlotta Monterey O'Neill. © 1955 by Carlotta Monterey O'Neill. All rights reserved under International and Pan-American Copyright Conventions. Reprinted by permission of Carlotta Monterey O'Neill and Yale University Press. All inquiries should be addressed to Richard J. Madden Play Co., Inc., 522 Fifth Avenue, New York, N. Y.

Balzac, Zola, Stendhal, philosophical and sociological works by Schopenhauer, Nietzsche, Marx, Engels, Kropotkin, Max Sterner, plays by Ibsen, Shaw, Strindberg, poetry by Swinburne, Rossetti, Wilde, Ernest Dowson, Kipling, etc.

In the right wall, rear, is a screen door leading out on the porch which extends halfway around the house. Farther forward, a series of three windows looks over the front lawn to the harbor and the avenue that runs along the water front. A small wicker table and an ordinary oak desk are against the wall, flanking the windows.

In the left wall, a similar series of windows looks out on the grounds in back of the house. Beneath them is a wicker couch with cushions, its head toward rear. Farther back is a large, glassed-in bookcase with sets of Dumas, Victor Hugo, Charles Lever, three sets of Shakespeare, The World's Best Literature in fifty large volumes, Hume's History of England, Thiers' History of the Consulate and Empire, Smollett's History of England, Gibbon's Roman Empire and miscellaneous volumes of old plays, poetry, and several histories of Ireland. The astonishing thing about these sets is that all the volumes have the look of having been read and reread.

The hardwood floor is nearly covered by a rug, inoffensive in design and color. At center is a round table with a green shaded reading lamp, the cord plugged in one of the four sockets in the chandelier above. Around the table within reading-light range are four chairs, three of them wicker armchairs, the fourth (at right front of table) a varnished oak rocker with leather bottom.

It is around 8.30. Sunshine comes through the windows at right.

As the curtain rises, the family have just finished breakfast. Mary Tyrone and her husband enter together from the back parlor, coming from the dining room.

Mary is fifty-four, about medium height. She still has a young, graceful figure, a trifle plump, but showing little evidence of middle-aged waist and hips, although she is not tightly corseted. Her face is distinctly Irish in type. It must once have been extremely pretty, and is still striking. It does not match her healthy figure but is thin and pale with the bone structure prominent. Her nose is long and straight, her mouth wide with full, sensitive lips. She uses no rouge or any sort of make-up. Her high forehead is framed by thick, pure white hair. Accentuated by her pallor and white hair, her dark brown eyes appear black. They are unusually large and beautiful, with black brows and long curling lashes.

What strikes one immediately is her extreme nervousness. Her hands are never still. They were once beautiful hands, with long, tapering fingers, but rheumatism has knotted the joints and warped *the fingers, so that now they have an ugly crippled look. One avoids looking at them, the more so because one is conscious she is sensitive about their appearance and humiliated by her inability to control the nervousness which draws attention to them.*

She is dressed simply but with a sure sense of what becomes her. Her hair is arranged with fastidious care.. Her voice is soft and attractive. When she is merry, there is a touch of Irish lilt in it.

Her most appealing quality is the simple, unaffected charm of a shy convent-girl youthfulness she has never lost—an innate unworldly innocence.

James Tyrone is sixty-five but looks ten years younger. About five feet eight, broad-shouldered and deep-chested, he seems taller and slenderer because of his bearing, which has a soldierly quality of head up, chest out, stomach in, shoulders squared. His face has begun to break down but he is still remarkably good looking—a big, finely shaped head, a handsome profile, deep-set light-brown eyes. His gray hair is thin with a bald spot like a monk's tonsure.

The stamp of his profession is unmistakably on him. Not that he indulges in any of the deliberate temperamental posturings of the stage star. He is by nature and preference a simple, unpretentious man, whose inclinations are still close to his humble beginnings and his Irish farmer forebears. But the actor shows in all his unconscious habits of speech, movement and gesture. These have the quality of belonging to a studied technique. His voice is remarkably fine, resonant and flexible, and he takes great pride in it.

His clothes, assuredly, do not costume any romantic part. He wears a threadbare, ready-made, gray sack suit and shineless black shoes, a collar-less shirt with a thick white handkerchief knotted loosely around his throat. There is nothing picturesquely careless about this get-up. It is commonplace shabby. He believes in wearing his clothes to the limit of usefulness, is dressed now for gardening, and doesn't give a damn how he looks.

He has never been really sick a day in his life. He has no nerves. There is a lot of stolid, earthy peasant in him, mixed with streaks of sentimental melancholy and rare flashes of intuitive sensibility.

Tyrone's arm is around his wife's waist as they appear from the back parlor. Entering the living room he gives her a playful hug.

Tyrone—You're a fine armful now, Mary, with those twenty pounds you've gained.

Mary (*smiles affectionately*)—I've gotten too fat, you mean, dear. I really ought to reduce.

TYRONE—None of that, my lady! You're just right. We'll have no talk of reducing. Is that why you ate so little breakfast?

MARY—So little? I thought I ate a lot.

TYRONE—You didn't. Not as much as I'd like to see, anyway.

MARY (*teasingly*)—Oh you! You expect everyone to eat the enormous breakfast you do. No one else in the world could without dying of indigestion. (*She comes forward to stand by the right of table*).

TYRONE (*following her*)—I hope I'm not as big a glutton as that sounds. (*With hearty satisfaction.*) But thank God, I've kept my appetite and I've the digestion of a young man of twenty, if I am sixty-five.

MARY—You surely have, James. No one could deny that. (*She laughs and sits in the wicker armchair at right rear of table. He comes around in back of her and selects a cigar from a box on the table and cuts off the end with a little clipper. From the dining room JAMIE's and EDMUND's voices are heard. MARY turns her head that way.*) Why did the boys stay in the dining room, I wonder? Cathleen must be waiting to clear the table.

TYRONE (*jokingly but with an undercurrent of resentment*)—It's a secret confab they don't want me to hear, I suppose. I'll bet they're cooking up some new scheme to touch the Old Man. (*MARY is silent on this, keeping her head turned toward their voices. Her hands appear on the table top, moving restlessly. TYRONE lights his cigar and sits down in the rocker at right of table, which is his chair, and puffs contentedly.*) There's nothing like the first after-breakfast cigar, if it's a good one, and this new lot have the right mellow flavor. They're a great bargain, too. I got them dead cheap. It was McGuire put me on to them.

MARY (*a trifle acidly*)— I hope he didn't put you on to any new piece of property at the same time. His real estate bargains don't work out so well.

TYRONE (*defensively*)—I wouldn't say that, Mary. After all, he was the one who advised me to buy that place on Chestnut Street and I made a quick turnover on it for a fine profit.

MARY (*smiles now with teasing affection*)—I know. The famous one stroke of good luck. I'm sure McGuire never dreamed— (*Then she pats his hand.*) Never mind, James. I know it's a waste of breath trying to convince you you're not a cunning real estate speculator.

Tyrone (*huffily*)—I've no such idea. But land is land, and it's safer than the stocks and bonds of Wall Street swindlers. (*Then placatingly.*) But let's not argue about business this early in the morning. (*A pause. The boys' voices are again heard and one of them has a fit of coughing. Mary listens worriedly. Her fingers play nervously on the table top.*)

Mary—James, it's Edmund you ought to scold for not eating enough. He hardly touched anything except coffee. He needs to eat to keep up his strength. I keep telling him that but he says he simply has no appetite. Of course, there's nothing takes away your appetite like a bad summer cold.

Tyrone—Yes, it's only natural. So don't let yourself get worried—

Mary (*quickly*)—Oh, I'm not. I know he'll be all right in a few days if he takes care of himself. (*As if she wanted to dismiss the subject but can't.*) But it does seem a shame he should have to be sick right now.

Tyrone—Yes, it is bad luck. (*He gives her a quick, worried look.*) But you mustn't let it upset you, Mary. Remember, you've got to take care of yourself, too.

Mary (*quickly*)—I'm not upset. There's nothing to be upset about. What makes you think I'm upset?

Tyrone—Why, nothing, except you've seemed a bit high-strung the past few days.

Mary (*forcing a smile*)—I have? Nonsense, dear. It's your imagination. (*With sudden tenseness.*) You really must not watch me all the time, James. I mean, it makes me self-conscious.

Tyrone (*putting a hand over one of her nervously playing ones*)— Now, now, Mary. That's your imagination. If I've watched you it was to admire how fat and beautiful you looked. (*His voice is suddenly moved by deep feeling.*) I can't tell you the deep happiness it gives me, darling, to see you as you've been since you came back to us, your dear old self again. (*He leans over and kisses her check impulsively—then turning back adds with a constrained air.*) So keep up the good work, Mary.

Mary (*has turned her head away*)—I will, dear. (*She gets up restlessly and goes to the windows at right.*) Thank heavens, the fog is gone. (*She turns back.*) I do feel out of sorts this morning. I wasn't able to get much sleep with that awful foghorn going all night long.

TYRONE—Yes, it's like having a sick whale in the back yard. It kept me awake, too.

MARY (*affectionately amused*)—Did it? You had a strange way of showing your restlessness. You were snoring so hard I couldn't tell which was the foghorn! (*She comes to him, laughing, and pats his cheek playfully.*) Ten foghorns couldn't disturb you. You haven't a nerve in you. You've never had.

TYRONE (*his vanity piqued; testily*)—Nonsense. You always exaggerate about my snoring.

MARY—I couldn't. If you could only hear yourself once— (*A burst of laughter comes from the dining room. She turns her head, smiling.*) What's the joke, I wonder?

TYRONE (*grumpily*)—It's on me. I'll bet that much. It's always on the Old Man.

MARY (*teasingly*)—Yes, it's terrible the way we all pick on you, isn't it? You're so abused! (*She laughs—then with a pleased, relieved air.*) Well, no matter what the joke is about, it's a relief to hear Edmund laugh. He's been so down in the mouth lately.

TYRONE (*ignoring this—resentfully*)—Some joke of Jamie's, I'll wager. He's forever making sneering fun of somebody, that one.

MARY—Now don't start in on poor Jamie, dear. (*Without conviction.*) He'll turn out all right in the end, you wait and see.

TYRONE—He'd better start soon, then. He's nearly thirty-four.

MARY (*ignoring this*)—Good heavens, are they going to stay in the dining room all day? (*She goes to the back parlor doorway and calls.*) Jamie! Edmund! Come in the living room and give Cathleen a chance to clear the table. (*EDMUND calls back, "We're coming, Mama." She goes back to the table.*)

TYRONE (*grumbling*)—You'd find excuses for him no matter what he did.

MARY (*sitting down beside him, pats his hand*)—Shush.

Their sons James, Jr., and Edmund enter together from the back parlor. They are both grinning, still chuckling over what had caused their laughter, and as they come forward they glance at their father and their grins grow broader.

Jamie, the elder, is thirty-three. He has his father's broad-shouldered, deep-chested physique, is an inch taller and weighs less, but appears shorter and stouter because he lacks Tyrone's bearing and graceful carriage. He also lacks his father's vitality. The signs of premature disintegration are on him. His face is still good looking,

*despite marks of dissipation, but it has never been handsome like
Tyrone's, although Jamie resembles him rather than his mother.
He has fine brown eyes, their color midway between his father's
lighter and his mother's darker ones. His hair is thinning and
already there is indication of a bald spot like Tyrone's. His nose is
unlike that of any other member of the family, pronouncedly aqui-
line. Combined with his habitual expression of cynicism it gives his
countenance a Mephistophelian cast. But on the rare occasions
when he smiles without sneering, his personality possesses the rem-
nant of a humorous, romantic, irresponsible Irish charm—that of the
beguiling ne'er-do-well, with a strain of the sentimentally poetic,
attractive to women and popular with men.*

*He is dressed in an old sack suit, not as shabby as Tyrone's, and
wears a collar and tie. His fair skin is sunburned a reddish, freckled
tan.*

*Edmund is ten years younger than his brother, a couple of inches
taller, thin and wiry. Where Jamie takes after his father, with little
resemblance to his mother, Edmund looks like both his parents, but
is more like his mother. Her big, dark eyes are the dominant feature in his long, narrow Irish face. His mouth has the same quality
of hypersensitiveness hers possesses. His high forehead is hers accentuated, with dark brown hair, sunbleached to red at the ends,
brushed straight back from it. But his nose is his father's and his
face in profile recalls Tyrone's. Edmund's hands are noticeably like
his mother's, with the same exceptionally long fingers. They even
have to a minor degree the same nervousness. It is in the quality
of extreme nervous sensibility that the likeness of Edmund to his
mother is most marked.*

*He is plainly in bad health. Much thinner than he should be,
his eyes appear feverish and his cheeks are sunken. His skin, in
spite of being sunburned a deep brown, has a parched sallowness.
He wears a shirt, collar and tie, no coat, old flannel trousers, brown
sneakers.*

MARY (*turns smilingly to them, in a merry tone that is a bit
forced*)—I've been teasing your father about his snoring. (*To*
TYRONE.) I'll leave it to the boys, James. They must have heard
you. No, not you, Jamie. I could hear you down the hall almost
as bad as your father. You're like him. As soon as your head
touches the pillow you're off and ten foghorns couldn't wake you.
(*She stops abruptly, catching* JAMIE's *eyes regarding her with an
uneasy, probing look. Her smile vanishes and her manner becomes
self-conscious.*) Why are you staring, Jamie? (*Her hands flutter*

up to her hair.) Is my hair coming down? It's hard for me to do it up properly now. My eyes are getting so bad and I never can find my glasses.

JAMIE (*looks away guiltily*)—Your hair's all right, Mama. I was only thinking how well you look.

TYRONE (*heartily*)—Just what I've been telling her, Jamie. She's so fat and sassy, there'll soon be no holding her.

EDMUND—Yes, you certainly look grand, Mama. (*She is reassured and smiles at him lovingly. He winks with a kidding grin.*) I'll back you up about Papa's snoring. Gosh, what a racket!

JAMIE—I heard him, too. (*He quotes, putting on a ham-actor manner.*) "The Moor, I know his trumpet." (*His mother and brother laugh.*)

TYRONE (*scathingly*)—If it takes my snoring to make you remember Shakespeare instead of the dope sheet on the ponies, I hope I'll keep on with it.

MARY—Now, James! You mustn't be so touchy. (JAMIE *shrugs his shoulders and sits down in the chair on her right.*)

EDMUND (*irritably*)—Yes, for Pete's sake, Papa! The first thing after breakfast! Give it a rest, can't you? (*He slumps down in the chair at left of table next to his brother. His father ignores him.*)

MARY (*reprovingly*)—Your father wasn't finding fault with you. You don't have to always take Jamie's part. You'd think you were the one ten years older.

JAMIE (*boredly*)—What's all the fuss about? Let's forget it.

TYRONE (*contemptuously*)—Yes, forget! Forget everything and face nothing! It's a convenient philosophy if you've no ambition in life except to—

MARY—James, do be quiet. (*She puts an arm around his shoulder —coaxingly.*) You must have gotten out of the wrong side of the bed this morning. (*To the boys, changing the subject.*) What were you two grinning about like Cheshire cats when you came in? What was the joke?

TYRONE (*with a painful effort to be a good sport*)—Yes, let us in on it, lads. I told your mother I knew damned well it would be one on me, but never mind that, I'm used to it.

JAMIE (*dryly*)—Don't look at me. This is the Kid's story.

EDMUND (*grins*)—I meant to tell you last night, Papa, and forgot it. Yesterday when I went for a walk I dropped in at the Inn—

MARY (*worriedly*)—You shouldn't drink now, Edmund.

EDMUND (*ignoring this*)—And who do you think I met there, with a beautiful bun on, but Shaughnessy, the tenant on that farm of yours.

MARY (*smiling*)—That dreadful man! But he is funny.

TYRONE (*scowling*)—He's not so funny when you're his landlord. He's a wily Shanty Mick, that one. He could hide behind a corkscrew. What's he complaining about now, Edmund—for I'm damned sure he's complaining. I suppose he wants his rent lowered. I let him have the place for almost nothing, just to keep someone on it, and he never pays that till I threaten to evict him.

EDMUND—No, he didn't beef about anything. He was so pleased with life he even bought a drink, and that's practically unheard of. He was delighted because he'd had a fight with your friend, Harker, the Standard Oil millionaire, and won a glorious victory.

MARY (*with amused dismay*)—Oh, Lord! James, you'll really have to do something—

TYRONE—Bad luck to Shaughnessy, anyway!

JAMIE (*maliciously*)—I'll bet the next time you see Harker at the Club and give him the old respectful bow, he won't see you.

EDMUND—Yes. Harker will think you're no gentleman for harboring a tenant who isn't humble in the presence of a king of America.

TYRONE—Never mind the Socialist gabble. I don't care to listen—

MARY (*tactfully*)—Go on with your story, Edmund.

EDMUND (*grins at his father provocatively*)—Well, you remember, Papa, the ice pond on Harker's estate is right next to the farm, and you remember Shaughnessy keeps pigs. Well, it seems there's a break in the fence and the pigs have been bathing in the millionaire's ice pond, and Harker's foreman told him he was sure Shaughnessy had broken the fence on purpose to give his pigs a free wallow.

MARY (*shocked and amused*)—Good heavens!

TYRONE (*sourly, but with a trace of admiration*)—I'm sure he did, too, the dirty scallywag. It's like him.

EDMUND—So Harker came in person to rebuke Shaughnessy. (*He chuckles.*) A very bonehead play! If I needed any further proof that our ruling plutocrats, especially the ones who inherited their boodle, are not mental giants—that would clinch it.

TYRONE (*with appreciation, before he thinks*)—Yes, he'd be no match for Shaughnessy. (*Then he growls.*) Keep your damned anarchist remarks to yourself. I won't have them in my house. (*But he is full of eager anticipation.*) What happened?

EDMUND—Harker had as much chance as I would with Jack Johnson. Shaughnessy got a few drinks under his belt and was waiting at the gate to welcome him. He told me he never gave Harker a chance to open his mouth. He began by shouting that he was no slave Standard Oil could trample on. He was a King of Ireland, if he had his rights, and scum was scum to him, no matter how much money it had stolen from the poor.

MARY—Oh, Lord! (*But she can't help laughing.*)

EDMUND—Then he accused Harker of making his foreman break down the fence to entice the pigs into the ice pond in order to destroy them. The poor pigs, Shaughnessy yelled, had caught their death of cold. Many of them were dying of pneumonia, and several others had been taken down with cholera from drinking the poisoned water. He told Harker he was hiring a lawyer to sue him for damages. And he wound up by saying that he had to put up with poison ivy, ticks, potato bugs, snakes and skunks on his farm, but he was an honest man who drew the line somewhere, and he'd be damned if he'd stand for a Standard Oil thief trespassing. So would Harker kindly remove his dirty feet from the premises before he sicked the dog on him. And Harker did! (*He and* JAMIE *laugh.*)

MARY (*shocked but giggling*)—Heavens, what a terrible tongue that man has!

TYRONE (*admiringly before he thinks*)—The damned old scoundrel! By God, you can't beat him! (*He laughs—then stops abruptly and scowls.*) The dirty blackguard! He'll get me in serious trouble yet. I hope you told him I'd be mad as hell—

EDMUND—I told him you'd be tickled to death over the great Irish victory, and so you are. Stop faking, Papa.

TYRONE—Well, I'm not tickled to death.

MARY (*teasingly*)—You are, too, James. You're simply delighted!

TYRONE—No, Mary, a joke is a joke, but—

EDMUND—I told Shaughnessy he should have reminded Harker that a Standard Oil millionaire ought to welcome the flavor of hog in his ice water as an appropriate touch.

TYRONE—The devil you did! (*Frowning.*) Keep your damned Socialist anarchist sentiments out of my affairs!

EDMUND—Shaughnessy almost wept because he hadn't thought of that one, but he said he'd include it in a letter he's writing to

Harker, along with a few other insults he'd overlooked. (*He and*
JAMIE *laugh.*)

TYRONE—What are you laughing at? There's nothing funny—
A fine son you are to help that blackguard get me into a lawsuit!

MARY—Now, James, don't lose your temper.

TYRONE (*turns on* JAMIE)—And you're worse than he is, encouraging him. I suppose you're regretting you weren't there to
prompt Shaughnessy with a few nastier insults. You've a fine talent
for that, if for nothing else.

MARY—James! There's no reason to scold Jamie. (JAMIE *is
about to make some sneering remark to his father, but he shrugs his
shoulders.*)

EDMUND (*with sudden nervous exasperation*)—Oh, for God's
sake, Papa! If you're starting that stuff again, I'll beat it. (*He
jumps up.*) I left my book upstairs, anyway. (*He goes to the front
parlor, saying disgustedly*)—God, Papa, I should think you'd get
sick of hearing yourself— (*He disappears.* TYRONE *looks after
him angrily.*)

MARY—You mustn't mind Edmund, James. Remember he isn't
well. (EDMUND *can be heard coughing as he goes upstairs.* She
adds nervously.) A summer cold makes anyone irritable.

JAMIE (*genuinely concerned*)—It's not just a cold he's got. The
Kid is damned sick. (*His father gives him a sharp warning look
but he doesn't see it.*)

MARY (*turns on him resentfully*)—Why do you say that? It *is*
just a cold! Anyone can tell that! You always imagine things!

TYRONE (*with another warning glance at* JAMIE—*easily*)—All
Jamie meant was Edmund might have a touch of something else, too,
which makes his cold worse.

JAMIE—Sure, Mama. That's all I meant.

TYRONE—Doctor Hardy thinks it might be a bit of malarial fever
he caught when he was in the tropics. If it is, quinine will soon cure
it.

MARY (*a look of contemptuous hostility flashes across her face*)—
Doctor Hardy! I wouldn't believe a thing he said, if he swore on
a stack of Bibles! I know what doctors are. They're all alike.
Anything, they don't care what, to keep you coming to them. (*She
stops short, overcome by a fit of acute self-consciousness as she
catches their eyes fixed on her. Her hands jerk nervously to her*

hair. She forces a smile.) What is it? What are you looking at? Is my hair—?

TYRONE (*puts his arm around her—with guilty heartiness, giving her a playful hug*)—There's nothing wrong with your hair. The healthier and fatter you get, the vainer you become. You'll soon spend half the day primping before the mirror.

MARY (*half reassured*)—I really should have new glasses. My eyes are so bad now.

TYRONE (*with Irish blarney*)—Your eyes are beautiful, and well you know it. (*He gives her a kiss. Her face lights up with a charming, shy embarrassment. Suddenly and startlingly one sees in her face the girl she had once been, not a ghost of the dead, but still a living part of her.*)

MARY—You mustn't be so silly, James. Right in front of Jamie!

TYRONE—Oh, he's on to you, too. He knows this fuss about eyes and hair is only fishing for compliments. Eh, Jamie?

JAMIE (*his face has cleared, too, and there is an old boyish charm in his loving smile at his mother*)—Yes. You can't kid us, Mama.

MARY (*laughs and an Irish lilt comes into her voice*)—Go along with both of you! (*Then she speaks with a girlish gravity.*) But I did truly have beautiful hair once, didn't I, James?

TYRONE—The most beautiful in the world!

MARY—It was a rare shade of reddish brown and so long it came down below my knees. You ought to remember it, too, Jamie. It wasn't until after Edmund was born that I had a single gray hair. Then it began to turn white. (*The girlishness fades from her face.*)

TYRONE (*quickly*)—And that made it prettier than ever.

MARY (*again embarrassed and pleased*)—Will you listen to your father, Jamie—after thirty-five years of marriage! He isn't a great actor for nothing, is he? What's come over you, James? Are you pouring coals of fire on my head for teasing you about snoring? Well then, I take it all back. It must have been only the foghorn I heard. (*She laughs, and they laugh with her. Then she changes to a brisk businesslike air.*) But I can't stay with you any longer, even to hear compliments. I must see the cook about dinner and the day's marketing. (*She gets up and sighs with humorous exaggeration.*) Bridget is so lazy. And so sly. She begins telling me about her relatives so I can't get a word in edgeways and scold her. Well, I might as well get it over. (*She goes to the back-parlor doorway, then turns, her face worried again.*) You mustn't make Edmund work on the grounds with you, James, remember. (*Again with the*

Bradford Dillman, Jason Robards, Jr., Florence Eldridge an

Fredric March in "Long Day's Journey into Night"

strange obstinate set to her face.) Not that he isn't strong enough, but he'd perspire and he might catch more cold. (*She disappears through the back parlor.* TYRONE *turns on* JAMIE *condemningly.*)

TYRONE—You're a fine lunkhead! Haven't you any sense? The one thing to avoid is saying anything that would get her more upset over Edmund.

JAMIE (*shrugging his shoulders*)—All right. Have it your way. I think it's the wrong idea to let Mama go on kidding herself. It will only make the shock worse when she has to face it. Anyway, you can see she's deliberately fooling herself with that summer cold talk. She knows better.

TYRONE—Knows? Nobody knows yet.

JAMIE—Well, I do. I was with Edmund when he went to Doc Hardy on Monday. I heard him pull that touch of malaria stuff. He was stalling. That isn't what he thinks any more. You know it as well as I do. You talked to him when you went uptown yesterday, didn't you?

TYRONE—He couldn't say anything for sure yet. He's to phone me today before Edmund goes to him.

JAMIE (*slowly*)—He thinks it's consumption, doesn't he, Papa?

TYRONE (*reluctantly*)—He said it might be.

JAMIE (*moved, his love for his brother coming out*)—Poor kid! God damn it! (*He turns on his father accusingly.*) It might never have happened if you'd sent him to a real doctor when he first got sick.

TYRONE—What's the matter with Hardy? He's always been our doctor up here.

JAMIE—Everything's the matter with him! Even in this hick burg he's rated third class! He's a cheap old quack!

TYRONE—That's right! Run him down! Run down everybody! Everyone is a fake to you!

JAMIE (*contemptuously*)—Hardy only charges a dollar. That's what makes you think he's a fine doctor!

TYRONE (*stung*)—That's enough! You're not drunk now! There's no excuse— (*He controls himself—a bit defensively.*) If you mean I can't afford one of the fine society doctors who prey on the rich summer people—

JAMIE—Can't afford? You're one of the biggest property owners around here.

TYRONE—That doesn't mean I'm rich. It's all mortgaged—

JAMIE—Because you always buy more instead of paying off mortgages. If Edmund was a lousy acre of land you wanted, the sky would be the limit!

TYRONE—That's a lie! And your sneers against Doctor Hardy are lies! He doesn't put on frills, or have an office in a fashionable location, or drive around in an expensive automobile. That's what you pay for with those other five-dollars-to-look-at-your-tongue fellows, not their skill.

JAMIE (*with a scornful shrug of his shoulders*)—Oh, all right. I'm a fool to argue. You can't change the leopard's spots.

TYRONE (*with rising anger*)—No, you can't. You've taught me that lesson only too well. I've lost all hope you will ever change yours. You dare tell me what I can afford? You've never known the value of a dollar and never will! You've never saved a dollar in your life! At the end of each season you're penniless! You've thrown your salary away every week on whores and whisky!

JAMIE—My salary! Christ!

TYRONE—It's more than you're worth, and you couldn't get that if it wasn't for me. If you weren't my son, there isn't a manager in the business who would give you a part, your reputation stinks so. As it is, I have to humble my pride and beg for you, saying you've turned over a new leaf, although I know it's a lie!

JAMIE—I never wanted to be an actor. You forced me on the stage.

TYRONE—That's a lie! You made no effort to find anything else to do. You left it to me to get you a job and I have no influence except in the theatre. Forced you! You never wanted to do anything except loaf in barrooms! You'd have been content to sit back like a lazy lunk and sponge on me for the rest of your life! After all the money I'd wasted on your education, and all you did was get fired in disgrace from every college you went to!

JAMIE—Oh, for God's sake, don't drag up that ancient history!

TYRONE—It's not ancient history that you have to come home every summer to live on me.

JAMIE—I earn my board and lodging working on the grounds. It saves you hiring a man.

TYRONE—Bah! You have to be driven to do even that much! (*His anger ebbs into a weary complaint.*) I wouldn't give a damn if you ever displayed the slightest sign of gratitude. The only thanks is to have you sneer at me for a dirty miser, sneer at my profession, sneer at every damned thing in the world—except yourself.

JAMIE (*wryly*)—That's not true, Papa. You can't hear me talking to myself, that's all.

TYRONE (*stares at him puzzledly, then quotes mechanically*)— "Ingratitude, the vilest weed that grows"!

JAMIE—I could see that line coming! God, how many thousand times—! (*He stops, bored with their quarrel, and shrugs his shoulders.*) All right, Papa. I'm a bum. Anything you like, so long as it stops the argument.

TYRONE (*with indignant appeal now*)—If you'd get ambition in your head instead of folly! You're young yet. You could still make your mark. You had the talent to become a fine actor! You have it still. You're my son—!

JAMIE (*boredly*)—Let's forget me. I'm not interested in the subject. Neither are you. (TYRONE *gives up.* JAMIE *goes on casually.*) What started us on this? Oh, Doc Hardy. When is he going to call you up about Edmund?

TYRONE—Around lunch time. (*He pauses—then defensively.*) I couldn't have sent Edmund to a better doctor. Hardy's treated him whenever he was sick up here, since he was knee high. He knows his constitution as no other doctor could. It's not a question of my being miserly, as you'd like to make out. (*Bitterly.*) And what could the finest specialist in America do for Edmund, after he's deliberately ruined his health by the mad life he's led ever since he was fired from college? Even before that when he was in prep school, he began dissipating and playing the Broadway sport to imitate you, when he's never had your constitution to stand it. You're a healthy hulk like me—or you were at his age—but he's always been a bundle of nerves like his mother. I've warned him for years his body couldn't stand it, but he wouldn't heed me, and now it's too late.

JAMIE (*sharply*)—What do you mean, too late? You talk as if you thought—

TYRONE (*guiltily explosive*)—Don't be a damned fool! I meant nothing but what's plain to anyone! His health has broken down and he may be an invalid for a long time.

JAMIE (*stares at his father, ignoring his explanation*)—I know it's an Irish peasant idea consumption is fatal. It probably is when you live in a hovel on a bog, but over here, with modern treatment—

TYRONE—Don't I know that! What are you gabbing about, anyway? And keep your dirty tongue off Ireland, with your sneers about peasants and bogs and hovels! (*Accusingly.*) The less you say about Edmund's sickness, the better for your conscience! You're more responsible than anyone!

JAMIE (*stung*)—That's a lie! I won't stand for that, Papa!

TYRONE—It's the truth! You've been the worst influence for him. He grew up admiring you as a hero! A fine example you set him! If you ever gave him advice except in the ways of rottenness, I've never heard of it! You made him old before his time, pumping him full of what you consider worldly wisdom, when he was too young to see that your mind was so poisoned by your own failure in life, you wanted to believe every man was a knave with his soul for sale, and every woman who wasn't a whore was a fool!

JAMIE (*with a defensive air of weary indifference again*)—All right. I did put Edmund wise to things, but not until I saw he'd started to raise hell, and knew he'd laugh at me if I tried the good advice, older brother stuff. All I did was make a pal of him and be absolutely frank so he'd learn from my mistakes that— (*He shrugs his shoulders—cynically.*) Well, that if you can't be good you can at least be careful. (*His father snorts contemptuously. Suddenly* JAMIE *becomes really moved.*) That's a rotten accusation, Papa. You know how much the Kid means to me, and how close we've always been—not like the usual brothers! I'd do anything for him.

TYRONE (*impressed—mollifyingly*)—I know you may have thought it was for the best, Jamie. I didn't say you did it deliberately to harm him.

JAMIE—Besides it's damned rot! I'd like to see anyone influence Edmund more than he wants to be. His quietness fools people into thinking they can do what they like with him. But he's stubborn as hell inside and what he does is what he wants to do, and to hell with anyone else! What had I to do with all the crazy stunts he's pulled in the last few years—working his way all over the map as a sailor and all that stuff. I thought that was a damned fool idea, and I told him so. You can't imagine me getting fun out of being on the beach in South America, or living in filthy dives, drinking rotgut, can you? No, thanks! I'll stick to Broadway, and a room with a bath, and bars that serve bonded Bourbon.

TYRONE—You and Broadway! It's made you what you are! (*With a touch of pride.*) Whatever Edmund's done, he's had the guts to go off on his own, where he couldn't come whining to me the minute he was broke.

JAMIE (*stung into sneering jealousy*)—He's always come home broke finally, hasn't he? And what did his going away get him? Look at him now! (*He is suddenly shamefaced.*) Christ! That's a lousy thing to say. I don't mean that.

TYRONE (*decides to ignore this*)—He's been doing well on the paper. I was hoping he'd found the work he wants to do at last.

JAMIE (*sneering jealously again*)—A hick town rag! Whatever bull they hand you, they tell me he's a pretty bum reporter. If he weren't your son— (*Ashamed again.*) No, that's not true! They're glad to have him, but it's the special stuff that gets him by. Some of the poems and parodies he's written are damned good. (*Grudgingly again.*) Not that they'd ever get him anywhere on the big time. (*Hastily.*) But he's certainly made a damned good start.

TYRONE—Yes. He's made a start. You used to talk about wanting to become a newspaper man but you were never willing to start at the bottom. You expected—

JAMIE—Oh, for Christ's sake, Papa! Can't you lay off me!

TYRONE (*stares at him—then looks away—after a pause*)—It's damnable luck Edmund should be sick right now. It couldn't have come at a worse time for him. (*He adds, unable to conceal an almost furtive uneasiness.*) Or for your mother. It's damnable she should have this to upset her, just when she needs peace and freedom from worry. She's been so well in the two months since she came home. (*His voice grows husky and trembles a little.*) It's been heaven to me. This home has been a home again. But I needn't tell you, Jamie. (*His son looks at him, for the first time with an understanding sympathy. It is as if suddenly a deep bond of common feeling existed between them in which their antagonisms could be forgotten.*)

JAMIE (*almost gently*)—I've felt the same way, Papa.

TYRONE—Yes, this time you can see how strong and sure of herself she is. She's a different woman entirely from the other times. She has control of her nerves—or she had until Edmund got sick. Now you can feel her growing tense and frightened underneath. I wish to God we could keep the truth from her, but we can't if he has to be sent to a sanatorium. What makes it worse is her father died of consumption. She worshiped him and she's never forgotten. Yes, it will be hard for her. But she can do it! She has the will power now! We must help her, Jamie, in every way we can!

JAMIE (*moved*)—Of course, Papa. (*Hesitantly.*)   Outside of nerves, she seems perfectly all right this morning.

TYRONE (*with hearty confidence now*)—Never better. She's full of fun and mischief. (*Suddenly he frowns at* JAMIE *suspiciously.*) Why do you say, seems? Why shouldn't she be all right? What the hell do you mean?

JAMIE—Don't start jumping down my throat! God, Papa, this ought to be one thing we can talk over frankly without a battle.

TYRONE—I'm sorry, Jamie. (*Tensely.*)   But go on and tell me—

JAMIE—There's nothing to tell. I was all wrong. It's just that last night— Well, you know how it is, I can't forget the past. I can't help being suspicious. Any more than you can. (*Bitterly.*) That's the hell of it. And it makes it hell for Mama! She watches us watching her—

TYRONE (*sadly*)—I know. (*Tensely.*)   Well, what was it? Can't you speak out?

JAMIE—Nothing, I tell you. Just my damned foolishness. Around three o'clock this morning, I woke up and heard her moving around in the spare room. Then she went to the bathroom. I pretended to be asleep. She stopped in the hall to listen, as if she wanted to make sure I was.

TYRONE (*with forced scorn*)—For God's sake, is that all? She told me herself the foghorn kept her awake all night, and every night since Edmund's been sick she's been up and down, going to his room to see how he was.

JAMIE (*eagerly*)—Yes, that's right, she did stop to listen outside his room. (*Hesitantly again.*) It was her being in the spare room that scared me. I couldn't help remembering that when she starts sleeping alone in there, it has always been a sign—

TYRONE—It isn't this time! It's easily explained. Where else could she go last night to get away from my snoring? (*He gives way to a burst of resentful anger.*)   By God, how you can live with a mind that sees nothing but the worst motives behind everything is beyond me!

JAMIE (*stung*)—Don't pull that! I've just said I was all wrong. Don't you suppose I'm as glad of that as you are!

TYRONE (*mollifyingly*)—I'm sure you are, Jamie. (*A pause. His expression becomes somber. He speaks slowly with a superstitious dread.*) It would be like a curse she can't escape if worry over Edmund— It was in her long sickness after bringing him into the world that she first—

JAMIE—She didn't have anything to do with it!

TYRONE—I'm not blaming her.

JAMIE (*bitingly*)—Then who are you blaming? Edmund, for being born?

TYRONE—You damned fool! No one was to blame.

JAMIE—The bastard of a doctor was! From what Mama's said, he was another cheap quack like Hardy! You wouldn't pay for a first-rate—

TYRONE—That's a lie! (*Furiously.*) So I'm to blame! That's what you're driving at, is it? You evil-minded loafer!

JAMIE (*warningly as he hears his mother in the dining room*)— Ssh! (TYRONE *gets hastily to his feet and goes to look out the windows at right.* JAMIE *speaks with a complete change of tone.*) Well, if we're going to cut the front hedge today, we'd better go to work. (MARY *comes in from the back parlor. She gives a quick, suspicious glance from one to the other, her manner nervously self-conscious.*)

TYRONE (*turns from the window—with an actor's heartiness*)— Yes, it's too fine a morning to waste indoors arguing. Take a look out the window, Mary. There's no fog in the harbor. I'm sure the spell of it we've had is over now.

MARY (*going to him*)—I hope so, dear. (*To* JAMIE, *forcing a smile.*) Did I actually hear you suggesting work on the front hedge, Jamie? Wonders will never cease! You must want pocket money badly.

JAMIE (*kiddingly*)—When don't I? (*He winks at her, with a derisive glance at his father.*) I expect a salary of at least one large iron man at the end of the week—to carouse on!

MARY (*does not respond to his humor—her hands fluttering over the front of her dress*)—What were you two arguing about?

JAMIE (*shrugs his shoulders*)—The same old stuff.

MARY—I heard you say something about a doctor, and your father accusing you of being evil-minded.

JAMIE (*quickly*)—Oh, that. I was saying again Doc Hardy isn't my idea of the world's greatest physician.

MARY (*knows he is lying—vaguely*)—Oh. No, I wouldn't say he was, either. (*Changing the subject—forcing a smile.*) That Bridget! I thought I'd never get away. She told me all about her second cousin on the police force in St. Louis. (*Then with nervous irritation.*) Well, if you're going to work on the hedge why don't you go? (*Hastily.*) I mean, take advantage of the sunshine before the fog comes back. (*Strangely, as if talking aloud to herself.*) Because I know it will. (*Suddenly she is self-consciously aware that they are both staring fixedly at her—flurriedly, raising her hands.*) Or I should say, the rheumatism in my hands knows. It's a better weather prophet than you are, James. (*She stares at her hands with fascinated repulsion.*) Ugh! How ugly they are! Who'd ever believe they were once beautiful? (*They stare at her with a growing dread.*)

TYRONE (*takes her hands and gently pushes them down*)—Now, now, Mary. None of that foolishness. They're the sweetest hands in the world. (*She smiles, her face lighting up, and kisses him gratefully. He turns to his son.*) Come on, Jamie. Your mother's right to scold us. The way to start work is to start work. The hot sun will sweat some of that booze fat off your middle. (*He opens the screen door and goes out on the porch and disappears down a flight of steps leading to the ground. JAMIE rises from his chair and, taking off his coat, goes to the door. At the door he turns back but avoids looking at her, and she does not look at him.*)

JAMIE (*with an awkward, uneasy tenderness*)—We're all so proud of you, Mama, so darned happy. (*She stiffens and stares at him with a frightened defiance. He flounders on.*) But you've still got to be careful. You mustn't worry so much about Edmund. He'll be all right.

MARY (*with a stubborn, bitterly resentful look*)—Of course, he'll be all right. And I don't know what you mean, warning me to be careful.

JAMIE (*rebuffed and hurt, shrugs his shoulders*)—All right, Mama. I'm sorry I spoke. (*He goes out on the porch. She waits rigidly until he disappears down the steps. Then she sinks down in the chair he had occupied, her face betraying a frightened, furtive desperation, her hands roving over the table top, aimlessly moving objects around. She hears EDMUND descending the stairs in the front hall. As he nears the bottom he has a fit of coughing. She springs to her feet, as if she wanted to run away from the sound, and goes quickly to the windows at right. She is looking out, apparently calm, as he enters from the front parlor, a book in one hand. She turns to him, her lips set in a welcoming, motherly smile.*)

MARY—Here you are. I was just going upstairs to look for you.

EDMUND—I waited until they went out. I don't want to mix up in any arguments. I feel too rotten.

MARY (*almost resentfully*)—Oh, I'm sure you don't feel half as badly as you make out. You're such a baby. You like to get us worried so we'll make a fuss over you. (*Hastily.*) I'm only teasing, dear. I know how miserably uncomfortable you must be. But you feel better today, don't you? (*Worriedly, taking his arm.*) All the same, you've grown much too thin. You need to rest all you can. Sit down and I'll make you comfortable. (*He sits down in the rocking chair and she puts a pillow behind his back.*) There. How's that?

EDMUND—Grand. Thanks, Mama.

MARY (*kisses him—tenderly*)—All you need is your mother to nurse you. Big as you are, you're still the baby of the family to me, you know.

EDMUND (*takes her hand—with deep seriousness*)—Never mind me. You take care of yourself. That's all that counts.

MARY (*evading his eyes*)—But I am, dear. (*Forcing a laugh.*) Heavens, don't you see how fat I've grown! I'll have to have all my dresses let out. (*She turns away and goes to the windows at right. She attempts a light, amused tone.*) They've started clipping the hedge. Poor Jamie! How he hates working in front where everyone passing can see him. There go the Chatfields in their new Mercedes. It's a beautiful car, isn't it? Not like our secondhand Packard. Poor Jamie! He bent almost under the hedge so they wouldn't notice him. They bowed to your father and he bowed back as if he were taking a curtain call. In that filthy old suit I've tried to make him throw away. (*Her voice has grown bitter.*) Really, he ought to have more pride than to make such a show of himself.

EDMUND—He's right not to give a damn what anyone thinks. Jamie's a fool to care about the Chatfields. For Pete's sake, who ever heard of them outside this hick burg?

MARY (*with satisfaction*)—No one. You're quite right, Edmund. Big frogs in a small puddle. It is stupid of Jamie. (*She pauses, looking out the window—then with an undercurrent of lonely yearning.*) Still, the Chatfields and people like them stand for something. I mean they have decent, presentable homes they don't have to be ashamed of. They have friends who entertain them and whom they entertain. They're not cut off from everyone. (*She turns back from the window.*) Not that I want anything to do with them. I've always hated this town and everyone in it. You know that. I never wanted to live here in the first place, but your father liked it and insisted on building this house, and I've had to come here every summer.

EDMUND—Well, it's better than spending the summer in a New York hotel, isn't it? And this town's not so bad. I like it well enough. I suppose because it's the only home we've had.

MARY—I've never felt it was my home. It was wrong from the start. Everything was done in the cheapest way. Your father would never spend the money to make it right. It's just as well we haven't any friends here. I'd be ashamed to have them step in the door. But he's never wanted family friends. He hates calling on people, or receiving them. All he likes is to hobnob with men at the Club or in a barroom. Jamie and you are the same way, but you're not to blame. You've never had a chance to meet decent people here. I know you both would have been so different if you'd been able to associate with nice girls instead of— You'd never have disgraced yourselves as you have, so that now no respectable parents will let their daughters be seen with you.

EDMUND (*irritably*)—Oh, Mama, forget it! Who cares? Jamie and I would be bored stiff. And about the Old Man, what's the use of talking? You can't change him.

MARY (*mechanically rebuking*)—Don't call your father the Old Man. You should have more respect. (*Then dully.*) I know it's useless to talk. But sometimes I feel so lonely. (*Her lips quiver and she keeps her head turned away.*)

EDMUND—Anyway, you've got to be fair, Mama. It may have been all his fault in the beginning, but you know that later on, even if he'd wanted to, we couldn't have had people here— (*He flounders guiltily.*) I mean, you wouldn't have wanted them.

MARY (*wincing—her lips quivering pitifully*)—Don't. I can't bear having you remind me.

EDMUND—Don't take it that way! Please, Mama! I'm trying to help. Because it's bad for you to forget. The right way is to remember. So you'll always be on your guard. You know what's happened before. (*Miserably.*) God, Mama, you know I hate to remind you. I'm doing it because it's been so wonderful having you home the way you've been, and it would be terrible—

MARY (*strickenly*)—Please, dear. I know you mean it for the best, but— (*A defensive uneasiness comes into her voice again.*) I don't understand why you should suddenly say such things. What put it in your mind this morning?

EDMUND (*evasively*)—Nothing. Just because I feel rotten and blue, I suppose.

MARY—Tell me the truth. Why are you so suspicious all of a sudden?

EDMUND—I'm not!

MARY—Oh, yes you are. I can feel it. Your father and Jamie, too—particularly Jamie.

EDMUND—Now don't start imagining things, Mama.

MARY (*her hands fluttering*)—It makes it so much harder, living in this atmosphere of constant suspicion, knowing everyone is spying on me, and none of you believe in me, or trust me.

EDMUND—That's crazy, Mama. We do trust you.

MARY—If there was only some place I could go to get away for a day, or even an afternoon, some woman friend I could talk to—not about anything serious, simply laugh and gossip and forget for a while—someone besides the servants—that stupid Cathleen!

EDMUND (*gets up worriedly and puts his arm around her*)—Stop it, Mama. You're getting yourself worked up over nothing.

MARY—Your father goes out. He meets his friends in barrooms or at the Club. You and Jamie have the boys you know. You go out. But I am alone. I've always been alone.

EDMUND (*soothingly*)—Come now! You know that's a fib. One of us always stays around to keep you company, or goes with you in the automobile when you take a drive.

MARY (*bitterly*)—Because you're afraid to trust me alone! (*She turns on him—sharply.*) I insist you tell me why you act so differently this morning—why you felt you had to remind me—

EDMUND (*hesitates—then blurts out guiltily*)—It's stupid. It's just that I wasn't asleep when you came in my room last night. You didn't go back to your and Papa's room. You went in the spare room for the rest of the night.

MARY—Because your father's snoring was driving me crazy! For heaven's sake, haven't I often used the spare room as my bedroom? (*Bitterly.*) But I see what you thought. That was when—

EDMUND (*too vehemently*)—I didn't think anything!

MARY—So you pretended to be asleep in order to spy on me!

EDMUND—No! I did it because I knew if you found out I was feverish and couldn't sleep, it would upset you.

MARY—Jamie was pretending to be asleep, too, I'm sure, and I suppose your father—

EDMUND—Stop it, Mama!

MARY—Oh, I can't bear it, Edmund, when even you—! (*Her hands flutter up to pat her hair in their aimless, distracted way. Suddenly a strange undercurrent of revengefulness comes into her voice.*) It would serve all of you right if it was true!

EDMUND—Mama! Don't say that! That's the way you talk when—

MARY—Stop suspecting me! Please, dear! You hurt me! I couldn't sleep because I was thinking about you. That's the real reason! I've been so worried ever since you've been sick. (*She puts her arms around him and hugs him with a frightened, protective tenderness.*)

EDMUND (*soothingly*)—That's foolishness. You know it's only a bad cold.

MARY—Yes, of course, I know that!

EDMUND—But listen, Mama. I want you to promise me that even if it should turn out to be something worse, you'll know I'll soon be all right again, anyway, and you won't worry yourself sick, and you'll keep on taking care of yourself—

MARY (*frightenedly*)—I won't listen when you're so silly! There's absolutely no reason to talk as if you expected something dreadful! Of course, I promise you. I give you my sacred word of honor! (*Then with a sad bitterness.*) But I suppose you're remembering I've promised before on my word of honor.

EDMUND—No!

MARY (*her bitterness receding into a resigned helplessness*)—I'm not blaming you, dear. How can you help it? How can any one of us forget? (*Strangely.*) That's what makes it so hard—for all of us. We can't forget.

EDMUND (*grabs her shoulder*)—Mama! Stop it!

MARY (*forcing a smile*)—All right, dear. I didn't mean to be so gloomy. Don't mind me. Here. Let me feel your head. Why, it's nice and cool. You certainly haven't any fever now.

EDMUND—Forget! It's you—

MARY—But I'm quite all right, dear. (*With a quick, strange, calculating, almost sly glance at him.*) Except I naturally feel tired and nervous this morning, after such a bad night. I really ought to go upstairs and lie down until lunch time and take a nap. (*He gives her an instinctive look of suspicion—then, ashamed of himself, looks quickly away. She hurries on nervously.*) What are you going to do? Read here? It would be much better for you to go out in the fresh air and sunshine. But don't get overheated, remember. Be sure and wear a hat. (*She stops, looking straight at him now. He avoids her eyes. There is a tense pause. Then she speaks jeeringly.*) Or are you afraid to trust me alone?

EDMUND (*tormentedly*)—No! Can't you stop talking like that! I think you ought to take a nap. (*He goes to the screen door—forcing a joking tone.*) I'll go down and help Jamie bear up. I love to lie in the shade and watch him work. (*He forces a laugh in which she makes herself join. Then he goes out on the porch and disappears down the steps. Her first reaction is one of relief. She appears to relax. She sinks down in one of the wicker armchairs at rear of table and leans her head back, closing her eyes. But suddenly she grows terribly tense again. Her eyes open and she strains forward, seized by a fit of nervous panic. She begins a desperate battle with herself. Her long fingers, warped and knotted by rheumatism, drum on the arms of the chair, driven by an insistent life of their own, without her consent.*)

CURTAIN

A VERY SPECIAL BABY

A Play in Two Acts

By Robert Alan Aurthur

[Robert Alan Aurthur *was born in Freeport, Long Island, and educated there and at the University of Pennsylvania. During World War II he joined the Marine Corps, rose to become a first lieutenant, and wrote a history of the Third Marine Division. After contributing to magazines, he broke into television, writing two shows for the NBC Playhouse that won awards and two that were turned into movies (one of them "Edge of the City"). He has also written a novel, "The Glorification of Al Toolum," and was among the founders of the original Playwrights '54.*]

A CROSS-SECTION of the Casale Long Island home shows a rather massive dwelling, heavily and even expensively furnished, verging on the plain ugly.

Part of the backyard, with a large tree encircled by a bench, is beyond the modern kitchen. Next to the kitchen, indoors, is a thickly carpeted living room, with a baroque-style breakfront, much too over-stuffed furniture, a TV set and a swivel chair.

The hall stairs lead to an upstairs hall off which only Joey's bedroom is visible. In this room, too, there is massive furniture: but this combination bookshelf-TV-Hi-Fi cabinet-desk is Joey's pride and handiwork.

Anna, Joey's still handsome forty-six-year-old sister, coming into his room to waken him, refuses to take "no" for an answer. He can't sleep all this afternoon: his friend Carmen is coming.

That does it. Swinging out of bed, Joey yells: "Holy Mackerel, Carmen'll be here on the one-fourteen." Then, as if he were a child, and not a hulking, balding, thirty-four-year-old veteran of two wars, Joey complains of the socks Anna holds out to him and the colored shirt she had chosen for him. Told not to dawdle,

"A Very Special Baby": Copyright © 1957 by Robert Alan Aurthur. Copyright © 1955 by Robert Alan Aurthur. Reprinted by permission of the author and of Dramatists Play Service, Inc., 14 East 38th Street, New York 16, N. Y.

Joey tackles a shirt he likes and says: "Dawdling? Who held the Nassau County record for the hundred yard dash, Class 'A' high schools, the season 1937-1938?" "You did," replies Anna. "Who won the Individual Big Apple championship, Mineola Theater, winter, 1936?" "I forgot about that," laughs Anna; "what a crazy dance!" "Well," asks Joey, "who won it?" Anna, humoring him, says he did. And, according to Joey, he's the guy who is now going to set the American record for making a million bucks.

Their father, Casale, back from a shopping spree, yells for Anna. A self-made millionaire of sixty-seven, he has, as usual, been indulging himself. He carries a new set of golf clubs, a brand-new suitcase, several boxes, and a couple of riotously colored caps perched on his head for laughs.

Coming into the kitchen, Anna takes in the headgear and tells Casale he looks beautiful.

CASALE (*crossing quickly to* ANNA *and kissing her, then sniffing appreciatively and holding her at arm's length*)—And you smell like a French kept lady.

ANNA (*pleased but pretending disapproval, pulls away*)—When was the last time you smelled a French kept lady?

CASALE—I see them on television, and you just know they gotta smell good. Hey, there's something wrong with my car. It started to miss bad coming home. You think there's somebody who don't want me to go to Florida or something? Every year it's the same thing. The top will go up by itself if it starts to rain, but drive, it won't.

ANNA (*setting table for* JOEY's *breakfast*)—If you would only take the train. Theresa keeps saying you could always use the Cadillac. It just sits down there, because she's got her Thunderbird.

CASALE—Why should I drive a black Cadillac when I got my own red Chrysler? Well, what's bad, Anna? Did you call Augie and George about the meeting this afternoon?

ANNA—They'll be here at one.

CASALE—I still don't understand why we have to have a special meeting.

ANNA—Because I want a special meeting.

CASALE—So I called one. Okay? I don't even know why you bother me. This is your house, and you can do what you want with it. You're the queen. Right, Anna?

Only interested in Florida, Casale picks up the phone to call ⁿhe garage. He shouts that his car is on the fritz; he has to have it by tomorrow. If it is fixed right by then, he'll make the garage man independently wealthy.

Thinking of her real reason for the family meeting, Anna in a roundabout way tries to speak to her father, but he's hard to pin down.

ANNA—You're going to Florida Monday, aren't you? Won't you be seeing Mrs. Fisari?

CASALE—No, Anna. I have not seen her for six months, and I will never see her again.

ANNA—Oh, that's right. Of course. She doesn't need you any more. You made her independently wealthy when you left her, didn't you?

CASALE—Oh, boy! Enough, Anna. She's a good woman, and she never gave me any trouble.

ANNA—Do I give you trouble, Pop?

CASALE—No. No, Anna, you never have. You're a wonderful woman, Anna. More than that, you're a saint. I'm a lucky man. I got my home. I got you and Joey.

ANNA—Well, listen, Pop, it's not really that simple.

CASALE—Nothing's simple, Anna.

ANNA—I mean, Carmen's coming today . . . and when they go into business together, Joey will leave and I'll be alone.

CASALE—Carmen this, Carmen that—Carmen this-that-and-the-other. I been hearing about this genius Carmen for three years. There ain't no such person. If there was, he'd be president of the world, he's so great, and I never heard of Carmen Russo outside of Joey. That Joey! What's he do up there? (*He goes out.*)

Joey, in a lather over Carmen's arrival, comes down to his late breakfast. He is persnickety about the way Anna does his eggs, and he listens to her no more than his father did. Anna insists that he listen: "We're having a special meeting today about the house. At one o'clock." "One o'clock!" Joey reacts. "I'm supposed to meet the one-fourteen." Anna wants him to know that, having already corraled the votes of her other two brothers, she intends to sell the house. Joey, startled, says she's crazy, and asks if Pop knows her plan. Not yet, says Anna.

JOEY—Anna . . . What the hell are you trying to do to Pop? He loves this house more than anything else in the world.

ANNA—He's hardly ever here. It's for his own good, believe me. I'll take better care of him if I don't have this big house to worry about.

JOEY—You can't do that!

ANNA—What do you mean I can't? I'm going to do it!

JOEY—But . . .

ANNA—Joey, you're leaving this house, aren't you?

JOEY—So?

ANNA—So you're getting what you want. What am I supposed to do? Sit here in this big house all alone? No, thank you.

JOEY—Okay, Anna, you do what you want. Only I'm not gonna start nothin' like that with Pop. Count me out.

When Casale has dealt with the mechanic and the Chrysler, he and Joey have some good-natured horseplay. They pose for each other in the garish new caps; they arm-wrestle; they joke about Joey's strenuous sex life. But with each mention of Carmen's name, Joey's father seems less good-natured. Finally snapping at Joey to remove the cap, Casale tells him he looks like hell in it. Joey protests but obeys, and obligingly totes his father's purchases for him. By the time he has reached the hall steps, Joey is his usual cocky self. "What makes you such a big shot all of a sudden?" Casale asks. "I don't know," answers Joey on his way upstairs; "I just feel confident."

Anna still has trouble catching her father's ear. Casale now goes into a sad story about a former neighbor, who though younger than he is, has become an old man. Casale seems to attribute this aging to his friend's moving into a two-room city apartment and eating cafeteria food. Having told his distressing tale, Casale settles down comfortably in his swivel chair and turns on the TV. Anna begs him to listen. Casale comments: "I'll have to talk to Joey about this set." "That's what I wanted to talk to you about," says Anna. "Carmen is coming today." "You already told me that," Casale answers, glued to the television. "Channel Two always looks like it's coming through oatmeal." "Well," Anna persists, "they're going to have a store. They have the location and a lease ready to be signed, and when the deal goes through Joey will be leaving the house." "Joey ain't going anywhere until he fixes Channel Two," Casale tells her.

Her voice rising, Anna insists that her father stop fooling with television and pay attention to her. She'll be forty-seven on her next birthday, and there is only one thing that she wants: she wants to go to Florida with Casale. Not believing his ears, Casale asks who would take care of Joey? Anna repeats: "When Joey goes away . . ." Casale rises: "You dream as much as he does. There isn't a chance in hell of him going anywhere. He's a kid yet. He has lots of time."

Casale then tries to talk Anna out of this idea: there's nothing for Anna to do in Florida. She'd do what he does, Anna replies. She'd go to the race track and the nightclubs, and she wouldn't mind the vulgarity. "Look," Casale warns her, "you won't find a man, I'm telling you." "You mean," Anna says, "there are no bachelors and widowers in Florida?"

CASALE—Anna, all the widowers like 'em under thirty, and the bachelors all got old mamas with the mink coats.

ANNA—I'll have my own mink coat. Pop, promise me. When Joey goes away, I want to go to Florida with you. Pop, I can't be alone.

CASALE—Okay. When Joey goes away, you can go to Florida. When Joey goes away, you can do anything you want.

ANNA—You mean it?

CASALE—I make you a deal.

ANNA—I can go to Florida with you?

CASALE—I'll buy you an adjoining suite at the Fontainebleau.

ANNA—Pop!

CASALE—That's where I'm staying this year. I figure, what the hell, if a man doesn't swim in clover-leafed swimming pools before he dies, life just hasn't been worth living. They got two, I hear. You take one, I'll take the other.

Overjoyed and relieved, Anna goes off to the kitchen. But Joey, returning to the living room, has another run-in with his father. When he reminds him that he must meet Carmen at the one-fourteen train, Casale exclaims: "Carmen! He's caused me more trouble for one day than I've had all year. Now you want to skip a meeting." And he vents his irritation on Joey's attempt to get a clearer picture for him on Channel Two.

JOEY—I'll fix it. I went to television school, didn't I? (*He fiddles with the knobs, kneels and places himself squarely in front of the picture tube.* CASALE *cranes to see around him.*)

CASALE—So I also sent you to dental school, but that doesn't mean you can pull teeth. That's good enough, Joey.

JOEY—It's still a little dark.

CASALE—I said that's good enough.

JOEY—The whole set could use some adjustment.

CASALE—For Christ's sakes, Joey!   Will you get away from there!
JOEY—Pop, I'm only trying . . .
CASALE—Just get away from it.
JOEY (*angrily*)—Okay, okay, Pop!   (*He rises and gets out of
the way.*)
CASALE—I know, you were only trying to get it good.   Well, I
told you it was good enough.   You don't have to make a five-year
contract out of everything.

Having heard the raised voices, Anna begs Joey to take it easy
this week-end.   Joey just hopes everyone else comes out of this
week-end as well as he will.
The rest of the family—Augie, the lawyer brother, and George,
the doctor brother—now arrive for the one o'clock family meeting.
When Casale sees that everyone is present, he asks that they get
on with this afternoon's business, which is to be about the house
and nothing else.
Joey, raising his hand, asks to be excused.   He has to meet Carmen's train.   Casale tells Augie to proceed.   Joey protests: "But,
Pop, I vote anything you vote for."   Casale tells him to wait.   Anna
comes to Joey's aid.   She reminds her father that this is important
to Joey.   Augie and George also urge their father to excuse him.
"Four still gives us a quorum," Augie points out, and Anna adds:
"Joey already said he votes on your side, Pop."

JOEY (*rising*)—Pop, I'm going.
CASALE—Sit down!
JOEY (*crossing to the door*)—I'm going, Pop.
CASALE (*rising*)—And I said sit down!
JOEY—Any other day, okay, Pop.   But today is different.   Today
I'm meeting my friend Carmen.   (*He exits.*)
GEORGE—Well, it looks like a minor revolu—   (CASALE *turns,
cutting him off.*)
CASALE—All right.   Let's get on with the goddam meeting.

SCENE II

No one else is about when Carmen at last arrives with Joey at
the house.   The place overwhelms him.   "My pop built it," Joey
explains, "with his own two hands, no help.   He even put in the
wiring."   As Carmen wanders about looking appreciatively at everything, Joey calls up for Anna to come meet his friend.   Carmen
finds it hard to believe that Joey and Anna live here all alone.

Joey says that they're alone a lot of the time: "My Pop is supposed to live here. I mean, he keeps a room and some clothes here, but most of the time . . . Carmen, maybe you won't believe this, but just in the past ten years he's been shacked up with four different broads." "Takes after his son," Carmen answers. Joey just hopes that he's that good at sixty-seven. "Boy," cries Carmen, "if my wife Rose saw this place as opposed to our lousy little four rooms, she'd have a heart attack." "Go on," says Joey, "inside of two years you'll have a better house than this. Why, for crying-out-loud, with our store and then a chain of stores . . ."

But Carmen is scared to death of starting *one* store. His suitcase is bulging with all the facts and figures he's lined up while Joey has been busy lining up two broads for ten o'clock that night. "Listen, buddy," Carmen protests, "you got the wrong guy. I'm so married it hurts." "When did that ever stop you?" Joey asks; "remember that night in Tokyo—the four lady acrobats?" "That wasn't me," says Carmen, "that was you." But they're laughing their heads off as Anna comes downstairs.

Introduced to Carmen, Anna has a moment alone with him while Joey goes off for beer. She is very earnest as she looks him over. Peering at him closely, Anna says to Carmen: "I wondered why you didn't come sooner. Joey's been waiting for you for three years." Carmen says that all that time he's been working and saving his money for the store. He asks: "Will I do?" "I hope so," says Anna; "you're married, aren't you?" "Married and three kids," answers Carmen, "and I'm thirty-five, been in two wars like Joey, met Joey in the second one, and I've lived in Chicago all my life except for the two wars." "I'm sorry," Anna apologizes, "I guess I sound like I'm prying. It's just that you're coming here . . . well, it could change things for everybody." "You mean it matters to you, too, what happens to Joey and me?" Anna answers: "It matters."

Coming back with the beer, Joey is mildly curious about the family confab, but more concerned over having walked out on it. Anna, saying that "it all ended up in a kind of mess," assumes the blame. Having business downtown, she leaves the men together.

Carmen asks the question that's been very much on his mind. "You been working, Joey?" Joey's evasive "here and there" answer disturbs him. "Where?" Carmen wants to know. "Well," Joey sashays, "I went to school for a while. Just like you told me I should do. To learn TV." What Carmen wants to know is how did he live? how did he make money? "I don't *have* to make money,"

Joey says, "I . . . I get an allowance. Hey, listen, Carmen . . ."
"An allowance," says Carmen, "Jesus!"

Carmen asks has Joey any idea of what it means to have a store.
Carmen has worked out the overhead to the last penny—even to
the electric bill. Dismissing this lightly, Joey claims to have put in
three solid months in his car, selecting the store site. "Three
months looking for a location," repeats Carmen. "Why weren't you
working?" "I told you!" Joey cries. "I was waiting for you."

Carmen asks does Joey realize it will take eleven thousand dollars
just to open the doors. He has his fifty-five hundred dollars.
"Where's yours?" Carmen asks. "Is money all you're worried
about?" says Joey. "That's the easiest. All I have to do is bring
it up with the family."

Having slaved away to save this money, Carmen tries to give
Joey the facts of life: ". . . I don't go to meetings where I raise my
hand and put in a chit for fifty-five hundred bucks or a new Olds."
Joey doesn't understand why he's so sore. "Joey," Carmen says,
"I came out here ready to talk business, all set to go. But I'm
scared. What happens if I blow the fifty-five hundred?" "The hell
with fifty-five hundred," says Joey, "I'll get up the whole amount.
I'll pay it all."

But in Carmen's book, if they do this they do it as partners.
Joey now has to persuade Carmen, and suddenly realizes that he
somehow has to prove himself to his friend, when what he wanted
was to prove himself to his family. He lists the rest of his family's
accomplishments and possessions. "Joey, those things aren't so important," Carmen says. "Maybe they're not important when you
have them," Joey says; "but the thing is, Carmen, they act like the
family ran out of something when it got to me."

CARMEN—C'mon, Joey, quit it.

JOEY—I'm only telling you these things so you'll know how important this is to me, so you'll see why you can't back out. All the
time I *planned,* Carmen. It can't all go down the drain. Please!
Let me put in more money. We'll get a better store.

CARMEN—No! It's fifty-fifty, or it's no deal.

JOEY—Then it's a deal, isn't it? Isn't it, Carmen?

CARMEN—Christ, Joey, I need this as much as you do. If this
doesn't go through . . . I've counted on this, too, Joey.

JOEY—Then say it's a deal.

CARMEN—Will you work hard?

JOEY—My sacred word.

CARMEN—In the army you were a reasonable guy. You didn't

take three months to find a place to park the radar truck. Can you be like that again? Can you do it?

Joey promises him that he can do anything. Not only did he show sense in the army, but when he was twelve years old he did the impossible. He got a car for four dollars from a junk heap, took it apart, put it together, and it ran. And what's more, he polished it up and rewired the whole system, and on Sunday took his whole amazed family in it to Mass—and it ran for three years after that. "Then," says Joey, "it got smashed when some bastard hit me coming out of his driveway without looking. Smashed all to hell, and when I came home, and I was crying because it was gone, all gone, smashed to hell, Pop said: 'What're you crying for, it only cost four bucks.'"

As Casale comes down the stairs carrying his overcoat, Joey is making a final, desperate plea to Carmen: "I can do anything. Anything in God's green world if I set my mind to it. Say it, Carmen. Just say it's a deal." As Casale comes in, Carmen shakes on the deal.

Joey, overjoyed, introduces his father and his friend. Casale remarks that Carmen doesn't look like such a genius. Carmen comes right back that Casale doesn't look like a man with two million dollars. Delighted, Joey says: "You two. You're a lot alike, you know?" He predicts that he and Carmen will make four million, two million apiece. "No. No more," says Casale straight at Carmen, "you ain't got guts no more to make a million dollars. To make a million you gotta do it with your hands and your guts. To make my million I hadda carry a million tons of bricks on my back. I hadda lift buildings up with my bare hands. You wouldn't do that. You young kids. . . . I got two sons, professional men, very well known in their own circles, but they're afraid to get their hands dirty. I got two daughters in Florida right now, they gotta live in a cloud of French perfume in case maybe they smell the common people. My daughter Anna she never even got married, and Joey here, he's the youngest, and he's been a baby all his life."

"I don't know," says Carmen, "he looks pretty grown up to me."

Casale orders Joey to show Carmen to his room, then come right back down. He wants to talk to him. Joey, on his return, asks his father if he's sore at him for the way he left the meeting. "You look at me like I'm a Mussolini or something," says Casale, "and just walk out like that. Joey, what's the matter between us?" Joey repeats he just had to meet the train.

Casale, seating himself on the couch, makes friendly overtures.

Casale—Do I act like a Mussolini, Joey? Now don't laugh.

Joey—I wasn't laughing at you, Pop. I was just thinking how ridiculous that thought is. I mean, you're the nicest guy in the world.

Casale—We yell at each other.

Joey—All my fault, Pop. I just gotta do something about my lousy temper.

Casale—Come to Florida with me.

Joey—What!

Casale—Pack a few things in a bag and come to Florida.

Joey—Pop, you just met Carmen, and you know . . .

Casale—I'll take you to the track, the jai alai . . .

Joey—I've just made a deal, and you know I've been waiting three years.

Casale—The deal can wait.

Joey (*rising*)—Ahhh, Pop . . . You know, you're the biggest character in town. Here for years I'd've given my left arm to go to Florida with you, and there was always some reason you wouldn't take me. Now you ask me, and *I* can't go. Boy, that's ironic fate, you know?

Before warming up to his next argument, Casale sees whether Anna is around. Hearing that she's gone, Casale tells Joey the reason for the family meeting: "Joey, you shouldn't have left the meeting. After you left I found out they want to sell the house." Joey says: "Well, maybe we should. It's getting pretty old, and you don't spend much time here . . ." "This house is a shrine to your mama!" Casale screams. "You know that!"

Stressing his point, Casale reminds Joey that he decided to build it the day Joey was born, thirty-four years ago. Then, in detail, Casale describes Joey's mother's death in giving birth to him. He recites his conversation with the doctor: ". . . You can't let my wife die. 'I got to save the baby. It would be a sin if we didn't save the baby.' No, I got five kids, five wonderful kids, but I only got one sainted wife. 'We got no choice, no choice,' he said. 'So be prepared, Angelo.' And he left me."

Casale—I started to yell, like . . . like a maniac. Save her! Save my wife! but nobody heard. I got down on my knees and prayed for a miracle. God didn't hear me. There was no miracle. She died with no pain, they said. No pain. You know her last words to me, Joey? (Carmen *comes down somewhere in this scene. Unable to escape, though unseen, he overhears.*)

JOEY—What, Pop?

CASALE—"Bless the baby, Angelo. Watch over him always. He's a very special baby." Joey, did I ever do anything to you to break my promise to your mama?

JOEY—Never, Pop.

CASALE—Then what's wrong?

JOEY—Pop, it's always been me. I'm the guy who's always failed. But from now on I'm going to be the son you always wanted. I'll never disappoint you again, Pop. Just you wait. In a couple of years, Carmen and I'll be so loaded I'll be taking you to the track and the jai alai. I promise. I'll make it up to you.

CASALE (*seeing* CARMEN, *he rises and starts toward the kitchen, picking up his coat*)—Sure, Joey.

JOEY—Pop, I promise. (*He follows* CASALE, *helping him to put on his coat.*) I swear on her sacred memory. Just bless me now, Pop, and I'll be the happiest guy in the world.

CASALE—You know you have my blessing.

JOEY—Don't go to the country club, Pop. Stay here with me and Carmen. Help us plan. (*They're in the kitchen now.*)

CASALE—I've got to go.

JOEY—Please, Pop . . .

CASALE—Augie and George are waiting for me.

JOEY—But if you'd only stay you'd see what a special kind of a guy Carmen is. You know what I mean?

CASALE—Yeah, Joey. I know what special means. (*He goes out into the yard.*)

JOEY—Pop! (CASALE *disappears.* JOEY *is left alone. He looks after his father, then, deeply disturbed, he turns toward* CARMEN.)

ACT II

That night Joey and Carmen, seated on the tree bench in the yard, are examining Joey's store model. Anna, as she goes back and forth, is their sympathetic listener.

Joey basks in Carmen's approval of his model: he has worked hard over it; he is full of good ideas. "Genius, Joey, you're a pure genius," Carmen tells him. "Never mind the genius," says Joey; "hard work, buddy. That's why I spent so much time looking for a location. The lay-out of the store had to fit my general plan . . ." Now they have to have a slogan, says Joey. "You know, for the truck. When it rides around the neighborhood it's gotta have a slogan on it. I'm good at slogans. And names. We have to have a great name for the store. Let's see . . . Carmen. Boy, I'm beginning to get excited. You know, there's a lot of things I've been wanting to do once I'm on my own. I'll take a little apartment and start looking for that redhead. Boy, I have *never been so excited in my life.*" Grabbing Anna, he whirls her around. "You hear that, Anna? You hear that? We're in, Sis, we're in."

Joey's delight turns to disapproval as he notices the brand of charcoal Anna has provided. He also notices that there are no hickory chips. To Carmen's utter bewilderment, he says "Bye" and starts to run off. "Where are you going?" Carmen shouts at him. "For the greatest charcoal on the Eastern Seaboard and the greatest hickory chips in the history of the world." "But what for?" Carmen protests; "this fire looks fine." Pausing only briefly, Joey says: "Carmen, can't you get used to the idea? . . . You're dealing with the very *last* of the high livers. Next to me, Nick the Greek is a bum."

Anna pacifies Carmen: "When Joey is on a wild kick like that I just let him go. Besides, the store's only a couple of blocks away. He'll be right back." Underneath, she assures Carmen, Joey is very serious. "I know Joey," Carmen tells Anna. "In the army—well, I never knew a better soldier, Anna. And I was in two wars, and I knew a lot of soldiers. Joey was the best. The most conscientious, the hardest-working. Only . . ." Comes the refrain: *why hasn't Joey been working?* Anna can only guess that he's been waiting for Carmen.

Both of them are now shivering. They go indoors for coffee. Joey's idea of a cook-out in October threatens to put Carmen in an early grave. But Anna is comforting to be with, and very reassuring about tomorrow's meeting. "It's just a formality," she says. "He'll get the money. Don't worry, Carmen." Carmen doesn't worry about Joey; he is worried for himself. His wife didn't want him to come: she thinks he's chasing a dream. Showing Anna pictures of his children, Carmen repeats that this business can't fail: "I can't, don't you see? I got to have a chance, that's all I ask. The only thing a guy can do is have kids and make them into good human beings. A guy and his wife, see, they have like three kids, and they raise these kids so they don't have to go to a head doctor, so they don't hate anybody, so they think straight, and that's all a guy can do at this time. Then some day, maybe a thousand years from now, all these descendants of guys who started this will look around and to their surprise it'll be paradise. That's the only answer. Me, Carmen Russo, I send three people into the world, good people, and I've done my job. *Boy,* I'm hungry. Old charcoal or not, I'm starting this steak." But he can't resist asking just once more: "Anna, Joey says you're the power in this family. Nothing can go wrong, can it?"

Anna not only promises that nothing will go wrong; she proposes that Carmen buy this house for his family. The money problem could be worked out with a mortgage, and she's sure his wife would love the house. Anna, wanting to sell it, would also like to choose who should live in it.

With the house so easily disposed of, Anna has all sorts of other dreams. Rather timidly, she tells Carmen that she might like to be a saleslady. And with such an encouraging audience, she practices a little on him. Carmen tells her that she'd be a great salesman. He makes her very happy. She believes him.

Joey rushes in, dumps huge bags of charcoal on the ground and pays no further attention to the fire. It's now to hell with the charcoal, he has the name for the store. "Listen!" he cries, "I got the flash driving in the car. How's this for the name? The C & R Appliance Mart. Casale and Russo—C & R. What do you think of it, Carmen?" Carmen considers it. "It could be the R & C," says Joey, "but I honestly think C & R sounds better because of the slogan." Carmen and Anna both signify approval. Anna would like to hear the slogan. "It's great," says Joey, "I mean, once you buy the name of the store, the slogan has got to be great. Ready?" Joey closes his eyes and proclaims, "Your dollar goes far at the C & R." He waits anxiously. "Wonderful!" says Carmen. "Really wonderful, Joey," says Anna.

Joey—Nothing. Nothing, really. Just the old brain going click-click every second. "Your dollar goes far at the . . ." Carmen, for crissakes, what're you doing?

Carmen—Cooking steak. Maybe you feed on your genius, but us ordinary people have to eat.

Joey—You've got too much flame, Carmen. It should be wet down.

Carmen—You see anything wrong with this steak?

Joey—It's getting burned. It should cook slowly so that the heat is evenly distributed, and . . . (Carmen *is staring at him coldly, and* Joey *subsides.*) But you do it any way you want, Carmen. You're the boss.

Settling down to enjoy themselves, the three, keyed up and happy about their future, are interrupted by Casale. Calling them crazy to freeze out there, Casale says: "Anna, from him I expect lunacy, but you should have more brains. Anna, I want to talk to you."

And he wants her, not after she eats, but this instant. Carmen offers Casale some steak. "No," says Casale curtly, "I got sick at the country club. You got too much flame there. You should wet it down. The steak is burning." "It's better that way, Pop," says Joey quickly, "much better. You ruin it if you wet it down." Carmen is his authority.

With another cold look, Casale says that if Carmen is such an expert at everything, perhaps he'll help Joey fix a few things around here: the whole place looks like hell. Casale finds fault with one thing after another: the lawn, the storm windows, the shrubs that Joey was to have wrapped for the winter. "So it isn't winter yet, it's only October," Joey answers back. "Listen, Pop . . . will you get off my back! There's nothing really wrong around here. I defy you to find one thing wrong. Just find one thing. We'll put it to an impartial judge like Anna." Casale wiggles out of it by saying his car is still missing and tells Joey to take it to Kelly's to be fixed right. Casale's look indicates that they can't eat yet—the car comes first. Telling Anna to keep the steak warm, Joey and Carmen go.

Ordering Anna into the house, Casale bursts out: "I got sick at the country club! I met a man there, Reilly. You know Reilly, Anna? He's a real estate man. On the Sunrise Highway." Anna knows him, she was going to tell her father. "Well, *he* told me," says Casale, "Reilly the real estate man. Kelly the garage man, Harmon the builder. *Goddamit,* aren't there any more Italians in this world? 'Hey, Casale, you're sellin' the house, hah?' and I said, 'What're you talking about, selling the house, what house?' And he said, 'Your house. Your daughter Anna was in today and listed it. Nice woman, your daughter, and nice house, too. I can get a good price for you, Angelo,' and I said, 'You goddam right it's a nice house, but you ain't gettin' *no* price for it.' So you listed the house with Reilly, Anna." "With Mr. Reilly, with Mr. Harrison, with Jones and Weber, and if it will make you feel any better, with Anthony Minelli and Son. That's two Minellis and the cousin Masconi who also works in the office. And for your sake, I hope Minelli sells it."

Casale, in a rage, says that this is his home and Anna is not going to take it away from him. "Pop," cries Anna, "what're you talking about? Didn't you tell me today that I could do anything with the house I wanted if Joey went away? Didn't you tell me that I could go to Florida with you? *Didn't* you? . . . Are you telling me now I can't?" "What makes you think Joey's going anywhere?" says Casale. Anna asks him not to sell Joey short—with the proper direction Joey can do things very well. "So why hasn't Joey ever done anything if we gave him every chance?" retorts Casale. "I'll tell you why. *Because he can't!*" . . . And he lists all Joey's previous family-backed ventures that failed. The Fire Island bar that burned; the fishing boat that sank. "Everything for Joey sinks!" cries Casale. Then, his tone becoming soft once more, Casale tells Anna that Joey isn't going to make it, and when he comes crawling back what will he crawl to? "Who will be there to take care of him?" he asks. "All the time before when he cried in the night someone was there to take care of him." "Someone?" cries Anna. "You mean I was there. It's never been anyone but me, Pop." Why is this her job? What about Florida? Doesn't she have any choice?

CASALE—Choice? You want a choice? Who in this life really has a choice? You grab what you can get. I loved your mama, God bless her sacred memory, but she was taken from me. Did I have a choice? I came to this country like everybody else thinking it would all be beautiful and the gold would be in the streets and I would do what I wanted. I would have a farm and a vineyard and live like a king. But I soon found out I was just another dumb guinea who had to live in a cold-water flat six flights up and carry bricks. Where was my choice? Anna, I started with nothing, but I ain't going back to nothing.

ANNA—All right, I'll stay with you. Pop, I'll always stay with you. That's why I want to go to Florida. To be with you. So why can't I go? Because of Mrs. Fisari? Or Mrs. Whatever the next one will be?

CASALE—Enough!

ANNA—Sure, enough. A man of sixty-seven. You should be ashamed, Pop, you make me sick.—Pop, why do I have to stay here? Why can't I go to Florida with you?

CASALE—Because in Florida I don't need you. Here I need you—in this house, my home. And Joey needs you.

ANNA—But he's going to leave.

CASALE—Is he?

ANNA—I can't keep him if he wants to go. And if he goes I'll be alone. And I told you, I can't be alone.

CASALE—Say what you want, do what you want. I don't care. But if Joey leaves, you will be alone. It's up to you, Anna. Monday call Reilly and those others. Tell them the house is not for sale. Good night.

SCENE II

Upstairs, on Joey's bed, Carmen and Joey are once more going over the store plans and figures; downstairs, Casale stares into the television set, as Augie and George arrive for the family meeting.

George, with Joey on his mind, thinks it would be great if it would happen, great for everybody if Joey would realize his potential. "Pop," he says, "you know . . . Joey could make it this time." George is curious about Carmen. Casale says smoothly: "Seems very talented." George repeats: "Then maybe they can make it, eh?" "Any reason why they shouldn't?" asks Casale.

"Anna," Casale calls, "it's time for the meeting. Augie, why don't you go out and help your sister? Why the hell does she have to do everything around here?" While Augie goes to the kitchen for the coffee tray, George calls for Joey.

Joey and Carmen, in a high state of nervousness, their heads full of figures, come down to meet the family. Joey takes his tension out in clowning. George, coming to Carmen's rescue, says: "I think we'd better get the meeting started." "Right now," says Casale; "the ball game starts in twenty minutes. Joey, the picture is still fuzzy." Joey, promising to fix the TV later, gets permission to turn off the set. Then Augie suggests that, there being other family business than Joey's store, Carmen go into the kitchen for a little while, to which Carmen agrees.

After further family joking, Augie as chairman pulls some papers from his briefcase and gets down to business. Joey's affairs come last on the agenda. First comes brother-in-law Lenny's request for a loan: Lenny wants $10,000 for store expansion. He thinks it fair that the family fund be given the six percent interest instead of a bank. "How much in the family fund now, Augie?" asks Joey with concern. "Latest figures," reports Augie, "ninety-two thousand, five hundred twenty-eight dollars and sixty-six cents. That's cash. I have a full report of the other holdings here." "Oh. Good," says Joey, much relieved.

Lenny's request is voted unanimously; so is some brokerage business; so is Anna's request for her Navaho school. After a report of Casale's successful business is passed around, Casale says: "Is that all? The ball game comes on in a couple of minutes." Joey waves frantically. Augie reminds his father: "There's still Joey's business."

Joey, fetching Carmen, sits him in uncomfortable full view of everybody. Then standing beside him, Joey takes a deep breath and starts his speech. He directs it squarely at his father, who pays less and less attention. Desperately aware of this, Joey only struggles the harder. He tells of what a good influence Carmen has been on him, how serious Carmen is, how well informed he is, how hard he has worked for his fifty-five hundred. Joey makes little nervous jokes, and somehow finally finishes: "All I have to do is come up with my fifty-five hundred . . . and that's what I want." Joey now asks confidentially for questions. He and Carmen handle George's question about the store location, and there would seem to be no others. Then Casale breaks in: "Wait a second."

Ordering Carmen once more out of the room, Casale has a few questions that Joey alone can answer. He applies the screws. He asks Anna to report on Joey. With a pleading look in Joey's direction, Anna says he's been fine. Casale then says that Joey could at least find two minutes to fix the squeak in his swivel chair. Augie intervenes: "Pop, I think . . ." "I have the floor," says Casale. "Joey, why ain't you been working? . . . You wait for Carmen, you wait for a dream. You're still a baby, Joey. You still dream." Over Joey's protests, he draws in George. He drags in Augie. He compares Joey to his two brothers. He dredges up everything from Joey's infancy to his flunking English at dentistry college. Joey is bewildered. "Sure," he says, "so I made a mistake. So I was wrong. I was only eighteen then. Are you going to kill me for a mistake I made at eighteen?"

AUGIE—No one wants to kill you, Joey. What Pop is talking about is still a question of maturity. At eighteen George and I had the same problem and we solved it. I mean, it's no great thing what we did, and neither George nor I expects any medals, but we were mature enough to know what we wanted and to go out and get it.

GEORGE—Joey, we *have* been worried about you. We've done a lot of talking about your problem down through the years, but because of Pop's insistence, and we've all agreed, nobody's made you do anything. If you wanted to sit around on an allowance, that's what you could do. But I think the reason we're all sitting around here weighing this latest thing is that you've gone off on some hare-brained schemes before, and you can't expect us to quickly reach a decision just on the basis of Carmen's being your buddy during Korea.

JOEY—George, you're kidding.

GEORGE—Why should I kid you?

JOEY—George, in September, didn't I rush over one night and fix your TV set so the kids could watch Sid Caesar in his first show of the season? Didn't I take your car radio out three weeks ago and take it apart and fix it? You know I'm good at that stuff, George. (*Pause.*) Jesus, *c'mon*, George, what're you doing to me here? All right, so for setting me up in business maybe you have to put me through the mill, but enough. Enough! (*He stares at* GEORGE *who suddenly grins.*)

GEORGE—I'm sorry, Joey, but I guess maybe the pattern around here is to pour it on a little . . .

Augie guesses that's it. It's okay with Augie and George. Joey, relieved, wants to get Carmen, when Casale plays his ace: "We got to hear from Anna. She is the one who loses the most if you leave." Only Anna understands this: "It's up to you, Pop, like it's always been. I'm not the queen any more, I never was. It's up to you."

Casale says that for Joey's own good he thinks he shouldn't go into this thing. Getting to their feet, Augie and George protest. Augie says: "Pop, we voted. George, Joey, and I. You can't do that. You can't override the vote." Casale suddenly shouts: "I can't! I can't what!"

Unbelieving, Joey, kneeling at his side, pleads with him. Casale rises and gives a flat "No." George and Augie are shocked; Joey is beside himself. Carmen, hearing the loud voices, comes into the house.

Casale throws the book at Joey. He accuses him of wanting to go off, of leaving his sister, of wishing to sell the house, of desecrating this shrine to his mother.

ANNA—Stop that, you hear me? She's dead. She's been dead thirty-four years. She can't be an excuse any more.

CASALE—Shut up! You . . .

JOEY—Pop, I don't want to do any of those things. Listen, please. I'll change. For my own good, this is the *only* thing, the only thing. This store. And Carmen. Honest-to-God, Pop, I know what I'm saying. If I don't get this I've got nothing. Maybe I haven't been the best son in the world, maybe I haven't been as good as Augie and George, but I did my best. I'll do better. I promise you on my sacred word. I'll do better. Just this one thing. Please, Pop, please. I'll be the son you always wanted me to be. Please. Just give me the money.

CASALE—Give you the money! I'll give you nothing! Nothing, you hear me? For what you did to me I'll give you nothing. You want to leave me alone. Alone! It's your fault I'm alone. (*Rising, he grabs* JOEY *by the lapels.*) You hear me—your fault. You son-of-a-bitch, you killed my wife. (*Then, almost in a scream.*) You hear me? You killed my wife!

He thrusts Joey away. After a moment of deathly silence, Joey goes after his father. Augie and George restrain him, and Joey dashes brokenly upstairs to his room with Carmen running after him. Joey tells him to go away. It's no good. "Please," Carmen pleads. "No." Joey says, "I'll see you around, Carmen. See you around." Carmen leaves the room. Breaking down, Joey suddenly wails: "Mama!—Mama!"

Scene III

There is an oppressive silence throughout Casale's house. Augie and George will have none of their father and go upstairs to pull Joey together. Joey begs them to tell Casale it wasn't his fault. "Joey," George says, "you can never make up for something you didn't do. You can kill yourself trying, but you can never make it. Pack your stuff, you're getting out of here." "Good," says Augie, "the sooner the better. He can come to stay with me, or he can stay with you until he gets a place of his own." "C'mon, Joey, move," says George; "start packing." When Joey says nothing, George starts doing it for him—"But goddamit, you're getting out of here."

Augie—Here, I'll help. (*He pitches in with* George.)

George—Carmen is still here. We'll go over to my place and talk this whole thing over.

Joey—I could never look Carmen in the face again.

George—You can work a job for a while and then find your own store. You and Carmen will still make it.

Joey—I can't hold a job, George. I get sick.

George—You get out of here, away from Pop, and maybe you won't get sick. (*Crossing to* Joey.) Here's a tie. Put it on. (Augie *closes the suitcase.*)

When Joey cries, "Why couldn't he love me like he loves Anna?" George advises him to take another look at what Anna has. George offers to carry his bags. Augie says: "We'll stand on each side of you and hold you up if necessary. It's only a door, Joey. *Please, Joey.*" Joey, needing a little time, promises to think it over. Augie and George give up and leave.

Casale hopes they talked some sense into Joey. They hope so, too, and start to go. "Dammit," cries Casale, "you're leaving me alone with this mess. You can't do that." "Why can't we, Pop," says George; "does your liver hurt?" "What're you talking about?"

Casale says. "Or is somebody suing you?" George asks. "You crazy?" says Casale. "Then you don't need us," George finishes. "Have a good time in Florida, Pop." Augie and George depart.

Carmen is the next to leave. Before he goes, he calls up to Joey's window from the yard. He tells Joey that his train doesn't leave for an hour; Joey must come with him; Carmen promises to get him a job in Chicago. "I don't care if you don't have any money," he calls out. "Money isn't the important thing. We're friends, Joey, you hear me, friends!" Casale yells at Carmen to go. Having made his plea, Carmen turns on Anna and Casale: "When he was a little baby, why didn't you drown him in his bath all at once and get it over with? Or did you enjoy it more the slow way?"

Anna, left with her father, now turns on him. But, responding as always to the deep emotional ties between them, she gives in all over again, and resigns herself to being nothing and having nothing. She goes to Joey's room as her father bids her.

Joey will have nothing to do with her. Why didn't she help him? Was she lying to him all that time? If she wasn't lying, why didn't she help him down there? Anna cries: "He said he'd leave me alone! Joey, I can't be alone." She promises that things will be all right, they won't be as bad as he thinks. "No?" says Joey; "it can only get worse, Anna." Joey advises her to take her money and get out. He doesn't need it; he only needs what Carmen had for him. He goes down to talk things over with his father.

Casale says they'll talk about it later. He offers him a trip to Florida, money even for a business. All through this, Joey fusses first with the TV set, then with the swivel chair. Casale cries: "Dammit, Joey—stop it!" and knocks him aside. That does it. Joey, knowing he has to get away, yells up to Anna. Anna takes his suitcase and starts with it down the stairs.

From now on, Joey tells his father, he wants no favors. Casale says that he gave him everything he wanted. "Yeah," says Joey, "and what have I got—nothing. I thought I had something. When Carmen came I thought I had a lot of things up to about an hour ago."

Casale—Carmen! I can buy you ten Carmens.

Joey—No. No you can't, Pop. You can't buy what Carmen had for me. You can't even buy it for yourself, and you've tried. Boy, how you've tried! But Carmen . . . he was the only one who really knew me. You never knew me, Pop, because from the day I was born you put me up against Augie and George.

CASALE—Yeah, sure. (ANNA *comes downstairs.*)

JOEY—I'm not Augie and I'm not George, and I couldn't have been a dentist if I tried for a hundred years. I'm not Augie and I'm not George. I'm Joey, and I'm good with my hands, God gave me that gift. I'm not a doctor or a lawyer, but I can fix television sets, and what's so bad about that? Pop, listen, I was a good corporal in the army, maybe one of the best, and I didn't have you standing over me telling me corporal wasn't so great, you've gotta be an officer. I *liked* being corporal, because Carmen was my sergeant, and he knew me only as Corporal Joey Casale without you putting me up against two big smart brothers to make me look like nothing. He liked *me,* Pop. *Me* he liked. Pop, I've got to get out of here. Don't you understand?

CASALE—I understand. Everybody's right. I'm wrong. I was wrong for making a home, giving you everything you ever wanted. Keeping a promise to your mama. All right. You want to go? You want to leave me? You go. Go. Leave me. But don't you come crawling back!

ANNA—Joey. (*She holds out the suitcase;* JOEY *takes it.*)

JOEY—When I've made it, I'll let you know, Pop.

Joey leaves. Anna turns on the TV set, adjusts the swivel chair for her father, and goes into the kitchen. Casale sinks into the chair.

CANDIDE

A Musical in Two Acts

(Based on Voltaire's Satire)

Book by Lillian Hellman

Score by Leonard Bernstein

Lyrics by Richard Wilbur

Other Lyrics by John Latouche and Dorothy Parker

[FRANÇOIS MARIE AROUET (*self-styled*) VOLTAIRE (*1694-1778*). *This French author, critic and dramatist was born in Paris and educated by the Jesuits at the Collège Louis-le-Grand. During his lifetime he was the wealthiest, most celebrated and active man of letters in the world. "Candide" is his most famous—today perhaps his only famous—work.*

LILLIAN HELLMAN *was born in New Orleans and educated in New York. She was a book reviewer and play reader before beginning her notable career as playwright. Her first play, "The Children's Hour," ran for 691 performances. Her other plays include "Days to Come," "The Little Foxes," "Watch on the Rhine" (which won the Critics Circle Award), "The Searching Wind," "Another Part of the Forest," "The Autumn Garden" and "The Lark."*

LEONARD BERNSTEIN *was born in Brookline, Mass., in 1918. After attending Harvard he came to New York to give music lessons and was later appointed assistant conductor of the New York Philharmonic-Symphony Orchestra. From there his rise was rapid. He has conducted the New York, Boston and Philadelphia orchestras. A remarkably gifted and versatile musician, he composed, in addition to his serious compositions, the music for the Broadway hits "On the Town" and "Wonderful Town."*

RICHARD WILBUR *was born in 1921, graduated from Amherst College in 1942 and received his M.A. from Harvard in 1947. In 1954*

"Candide": Book by Lillian Hellman, lyrics by Richard Wilbur, John Latouche and Dorothy Parker. Copyright © 1957 by Lillian Hellman. Copyright © 1955, 1957, by Leonard Bernstein. Copyright © 1957 by Richard Wilbur, John Latouche and Dorothy Parker. Reprinted by permission of Random House, Inc., New York, N. Y.

he was awarded the Prix de Rome fellowship of the American Academy of Arts and Letters. This spring he received the National Book Award in poetry as well as the Pulitzer Prize for "Things of This World." Earlier he had been given a Guggenheim Fellowship. He is professor of English at Wesleyan University, Middletown, Conn.]

ACT I

THE sun shines bright on the splendors of Westphalia. Outside the castle of Baron Thunder Ten Tronch, Doctor Pangloss tells us that the sun shines on all wedding days—excepting, of course, when it doesn't; that the women of Westphalia—who now appear—are very pure women. . . . "I am told there are women in this world who are not pure, but the uneducated say a great many foolish things, don't they?" As the men of Westphalia come to the castle, Pangloss credits them with great bravery in the war just won. Next, he introduces the King of Hesse, Westphalia's hereditary enemy, and just now their prisoner. And last, Doctor Pangloss, tutor in the Baron's house, introduces himself with all his degrees in philosophy and metaphysics from Heidelberg, Leipsig and Würzburg. His glad-eye lights on a passing girl. "Good morning, Gretchen," says Doctor Pangloss. "You owe me money," Gretchen replies.

"Ah, well," philosophizes Pangloss, "if she didn't think of money, she wouldn't think at all. Which," he concludes, "certainly proves that all is for the best in this best of all possible worlds." He sings to make his point:

"Look at this view! Mountains and towers!
Green meadows, too, bursting with flowers!
This is the heart of the best of all possible worlds.
Much the best part of the best of all possible worlds."

The gala crowds sing their agreement, and Pangloss signals the approaching wedding in song:

"All hail the groom
And bride, of whom
Our hearts could not be fonder.
The love that reigns in Heaven above
Is mirrored in the marriage of—
(CANDIDE *and* CUNEGONDE *enter*)
"Candide and Cunegonde!"

Doctor Pangloss is ready to answer any questions the young couple may ask. Lovely Cunegonde sings:

"Dear master, I am sure you're right
That married life is splendid.
But why do married people fight?
I cannot comprehend it."

CHORUS—
She cannot comprehend it.
PANGLOSS—
The private strife
Of man and wife
Is useful to the nation:
It is a harmless outlet for
Emotions which could lead to war
Or social agitation.
CHORUS—
A brilliant explanation! ◀

Pangloss finds marriage blest in this best of all possible worlds, and is ready for the next poser. Candide asks respectfully:

"Since marriage is divine, of course,
We cannot understand, sir,
Why there should be so much divorce.
Do let us know the answer."

Pangloss finds this easy:

"Why marriage, boy,
Is such a joy,
So lovely a condition,
That many ask no better than
To wed as often as they can,
In happy repetition."

CHORUS—
A brilliant exposition!
PANGLOSS, CANDIDE, CUNEGONDE—
Wherefore and hence, therefore and ergo . . .
CHORUS—
Wherefore and hence, therefore and ergo . . .
PANGLOSS—
All's for the best in this best of all possible worlds. . . .

The Baron enters to greet his daughter on her wedding day. And, in this best of all possible worlds, he immediately finds fault with his medal-bedecked son, Maximillian. The Baron would like to know where he got those medals. Maximillian evasively claims a headache. "Have you had a headache for three years?" asks the Baron. "Why didn't you join the army when I sent for you?" Using his adopted son, Candide, as an example, the Baron says that Candide earned his medals. Maximillian pleads a sprained ankle and soft bones. "Candide," says the Baron, "didn't worry about his bones. He worried about mine." "He has strong bones," retorts Maximillian. "Lower-class bones."

Pangloss presents the marriage contract, a record for history, written in Latin, Greek and Westphalian dialect. Maximillian, showing how poor a pupil he is of Pangloss, not only protests his sister's marrying a man of unknown birth, but the price she paid for her wedding dress. Candide shows what a good pupil he is by asking, as a favor, that the King of Hesse join the wedding feast. Then, at Pangloss' purring behest, Candide repeats unhesitatingly the golden rules of a high-minded Westphalian man: "The heart of mankind is a generous heart; the honor of a man is all he needs on life's journey; the poor must be respected and so must the rich since they are always with us; the beauty of noble thought; the treasure that is sweet, sacred womanhood—" Pangloss interrupts to greet a passing pretty girl: "Good morning, Paquette." "You owe me money," says Paquette.

Cunegonde, when asked, repeats her lesson, but not unquestioningly: "The honor of a woman is all she needs on life's journey. Dr. Pangloss, is that really all a woman needs?" Reassured, Cunegonde immediately thinks of other things such as clothes and curls. The Baron asks: "And how's my pretty daughter? Nervous as a bride should be?" "No, Father," she answers, "I am not nervous." "Oh, my God," says the hastily departing Baron. "Neither was your mother."

Left alone, Candide and Cunegonde have a last minute before the wedding. Candide, having no honeymoon to offer, no house nor anything else to give, promises to work and die for her. "Darling, darling," protests Cunegonde, "we've said all this before. I don't want houses or dresses or jewelry—they'll all rather vulgar, aren't they? I'll live in this dress the rest of my life. These shoes will last me until death. I want nothing. Absolutely nothing but you." It turns out, as they sing a duet, that while Candide dreams of a modest little farm, Cunegonde is counting on a yacht. Happily side by side, they sing of simplicity and worldly pleasures, of family life and high life:

CUNEGONDE—
   . . . Oh, won't my robes of silk and satin
   Be chic! I'll have all that I desire.
CANDIDE—
   Pangloss will tutor us in Latin
   And Greek, while we sit before the fire.
CUNEGONDE—
   Glowing rubies.
CANDIDE—
   Glowing logs.
CUNEGONDE—
   Faithful servants.
CANDIDE—
   Faithful dogs.
CUNEGONDE—
   We'll round the world enjoying high life;
   All will be pink champagne and gold.
CANDIDE—
   We'll lead a rustic and a shy life,
   Feeding the pigs and sweetly growing old.
CUNEGONDE—
   Breast of peacock.
CANDIDE—
   Apple pie.
CUNEGONDE—
   I love marriage.
CANDIDE—
   So do I.
Cunegonde, and then both, sing:

> "Oh happy pair!
> Oh happy we!
> It's very rare
> How we agree."

The crowds, including the King of Hesse, foregather. Candide hopes the King can forget old battles on this happy day. The King is delighted to: he hates war.

But Hesse's General has come stealthily to the feast. Unnoticed, he taps the King on the shoulder; the King orders him away. "We will not pay your ransom," the General persists. "We have been in conference all night and have decided it is cheaper to fight." The King, sick of war, wants none of him. But the Hessian General, swiftly substituting *honor* for money, says that the *honor* of Hesse demands the destruction of Westphalia.

In the midst of the wedding ceremony, the rape of Westphalia gets off to a good start. Cunegonde is carried away by the General. As bodies fall every which way, and women shriek and towers crumble, Pangloss announces that the whole thing is "unsporting."

Rushing back from battle, Candide finds Maximillian, the Baron, Cunegonde and Pangloss now staggering about, now collapsing in various dying positions. Pangloss cries to Candide: "Cunegonde is dead. Westphalia is destroyed. Don't cry, don't stay to mourn us. The world is beautiful—go forth and see it." "My Cunegonde—" cries Candide. "Yes, I know," says Pangloss rather cheerfully. "But think of it this way: If she hadn't died she'd never have been born. There is some sweetness in every woe. The world will be good to you, kind to you. Go now."

SCENES I-A AND II

The world couldn't be more unkind to Candide: it shuts every door in his face and spits upon him. Candide tries hard to hold onto what Pangloss has taught him, but by the time he reaches Lisbon, he is so weak from hunger he hardly can stand.

In the Lisbon marketplace there are many things to be bought, but nothing is given away. And the dissatisfied poor of Lisbon hate foreigners just on principle. Candide stumbles over a man as ragged and weak as himself. It turns out to be Pangloss, as logical as ever and delighted at their reunion. Pangloss (who hadn't died but merely fainted in Westphalia) is starving. "The emptier the stomach," he adds, "the more power in the brain. Starved, I am at my very best. . . ."

Suddenly, in the crowded marketplace, appears a procession with all the panoply of the Inquisition. The two old Inquisitors are wheeled in, seated in thronelike chairs. Their brisk young lawyer follows. It is to be an open-air court. Pangloss, waiting for the Inquisition to begin, thinks it will be a pleasure to watch such wise men settle current public problems.

Yawning, the very old Inquisitor remarks: "The witch and wizard stuff again?" The lawyer offers awards to any informers who will step forth and testify. A street Arab's wild, drunken creature, straight from a cage used in his soothsayer's act, pushes forward. She offers to point out the wizard. She identifies Candide. "He creep here this morning," she says. "In his bag he carry earthquake germs. You

Conrad Bain, Robert Rounseville and Max Adrian in "Candide"

open bag and you find germs. He bring danger." Police, grabbing Candide, corroborate this dire evidence. Pleasant and undisturbed, Pangloss comes forward with the reminder that though this is most interesting entertainment, things must not go too far. But they have: he is immediately arrested as a spy.

Pangloss, the teacher, asks Candide to tell these gentlemen his beliefs. Still the obedient pupil, Candide repeats: "I believe that the heart of mankind is a generous heart. The honor of a man is all he needs on life's journey. . . ." "Guilty," says the very old Inquisitor. "Take them away."

PANGLOSS—Gentlemen, this joke is becoming oppressive. It is necessary to understand the scientific fact that if the earth did not quake from time to time, a man would grow too confident of his sense of balance, and if a man becomes too confident of his sense of balance, he will forget how to fall without injury to his head bones. I will be happy to share with you all German scientific knowledge—

VERY, VERY OLD INQUISITOR—We condemn you to death.

PANGLOSS—Oh, you have a right to your opinion, sir. But that's a rather important opinion. Why do you disapprove of me?

VERY, VERY OLD INQUISITOR—You're a foreigner. You're a bore. You're a German scientist. You're a danger. Take him off.

CANDIDE—But we have done nothing.

VERY, VERY OLD INQUISITOR—That's the hardest way to die. The guilty die easier than the innocent. They have a normal sense of accomplishment. Take them away. (CANDIDE *and* PANGLOSS *are made ready for the hangings.*)

VERY OLD INQUISITOR (*addressing the crowd*)—I declare now an hour of private mourning and meditation. Go and gather the proper donations.

VERY, VERY OLD INQUISITOR—In gold. All donations are tax-deductible.

VERY OLD INQUISITOR—See to it that you fast until dinnertime.

VERY, VERY OLD INQUISITOR—And remember to give thanks that you have been saved from an earthquake. The danger is over. (*The earth quakes. People are thrown to the ground, the buildings rock back and forth and all is darkness. When the earthquake is over, in the dim light we see* PANGLOSS *on the gibbet, a noose around his neck.*)

PANGLOSS—Candide . . . The world is beautiful, my son. Go forth and see it. There is some sweetness in every woe.

SCENE II-A

Escaping from Lisbon, Candide—on the road to Paris—is a little shaken. He sings to himself:

> "My master told me
> That men are loving-kind;
> Yet now behold me
> Ill-used and sad of mind.
> Men must have kindness I cannot see.
> It must be me. It must be me. . . ."

So far, he has found that food or help of any kind seems to be offered only by atheists, beggars and whores.

Scenes III and III-A

In Paris, people are dancing in the ballroom of a great house. Beggars, with Candide among them, peer at the scene from the garden, while the co-hosts, a Marquis and a Sultan, wait impatiently outside their "niece's" boudoir.

An old woman carrying a jewel casket tells the waiting men to be patient. "This girl," the Old Lady says, "has come from the cloisters, pure and innocent. You've been very lucky, you boys."

MARQUIS (*to* SULTAN)—We've been very lucky, us boys.

SULTAN—I'm going to break down the door.

MARQUIS—No, no, cousin. We cannot go into her room unless she invites us.

SULTAN—We pay for this house, you and I, and we've been in that room before.

OLD LADY—That's different. She's not getting undressed. She's getting dressed.

The Marquis thinks that charming women should be permitted their own rules. *"Charming!"* shouts the Sultan. "In one generation you have learned to talk like these people. Such words. Charming. She's a woman. You and I are cousins and so it is sensible to split the expense. We are partners in this woman as we are partners in business. Has nothing to do with charm. So please remember to observe the proper hours and days. And do not fall in love, as you usually do with these women."

In the boudoir, the Old Lady finds Cunegonde rather disconsolate: "I've told you over and over again that I am Cunegonde, Baroness Thunder Ten Tronch of Westphalia." "Then," snaps the Old Lady, "how come I found you in a Paris gutter?" Last night, says Cunegonde, she dreamt of her wedding; the war arrived on the day of her wedding.

OLD LADY—Is that so? Ah, well, that's the way it happened to most of us. Sometimes war. Sometimes the man changed his mind. Where's the bridegroom?

CUNEGONDE—Dead. Trying to save me from rape . . .

OLD LADY—Died to save you from rape? Oh, aren't men silly? (*She exits from boudoir.*)

CUNEGONDE—Here I am in Paris. I don't even know how I got here. My heart is broken. And yet I am forced to glitter, forced to be gay—

> "Glitter and be gay,
> That's the part I play.
> Here I am in Paris, France,
> Forced to bend my soul
> To a sordid role,
> Victimized by bitter, bitter circumstance. . . ."

Itemizing the jewels purchased at such *awful* cost, Cunegonde decks herself out in her badges of sin until she's half-hidden by them. Suddenly bright again as she tops this display with two enormous bracelets, she sings:

> "And yet, of course, these trinkets are endearing, ha ha!
> I'm oh, so glad my sapphire is a star, ha ha!
> I'd rather like a twenty-carat earring, ha ha!
> If I'm not pure, at least my jewels are!

(Puts on three more bracelets.)

> "Enough, enough!
> I'll *take* their diamond necklace
> And show my noble stuff
> By being gay and reckless!

> "Ha ha ha ha ha . . .

> "Observe how bravely I conceal
> The dreadful, dreadful shame I feel.
> Ha ha ha ha ha ha . . .

(Puts on a giant diamond necklace.)

> "Ha!"

The Old Lady enters at the end of the aria and immediately begins to rip off the jewels.

CUNEGONDE—No! No! I'm cold.
OLD LADY—Only married women can afford to look like whores.

Unadorned, Cunegonde enters the ballroom. As the Sultan and the Marquis race for their prize, Cunegonde—catching sight of Candide among the beggars—screams and re-enters her boudoir. The hosts dismiss the guests and the Old Lady dismisses the hosts and beckons to Candide. Paralyzed with disbelief, Candide sings: "Oh.

Oh. Is it true?" Cunegonde, appearing, echoes: "Is it true?" They cry each other's names and over the Old Lady's warning, sing together: "Oh—my—dear—love!"

CANDIDE—
    Dearest, how can this be so?
    You were dead, you know.
    You were shot and bayonetted, too.
CUNEGONDE—
    That is very true.
    Ah, but love will find a way.
CANDIDE—
    Then what *did* you do?
CUNEGONDE—
    We'll go into that another day.
    Now let's talk of you.
    You are looking very well.
    Weren't you clever, dear, to survive?
CANDIDE—
    I've a sorry tale to tell.
    I escaped more dead than alive.
CUNEGONDE—
    Love of mine, where did you go?
CANDIDE—
    Oh, I wandered to and fro . . .
CUNEGONDE—
    Oh, what torture, oh, what pain . . .
CANDIDE—
    Holland, Portugal and Spain. . . .

Candide, who would have undergone anything to find Cunegonde, thinks it fair that she account for the presence of the Marquis and Sultan, who have returned from the garden. When he demands that they immediately leave the house, whosesoever and whatever house this is, he comes smack up against the Marquis' sword. Anxious not to fight, Candide, with a sword slipped into his hand by the Old Lady, backs away. He wants to take Cunegonde away with him in peace, but the Old Lady pushes him at the Marquis, who promptly falls to the ground. The Sultan leaps sword in hand to avenge his cousin: "Our family, despite occasional bickerings and law suits, are as one. Do you know," he says, dueling, "that you have killed the President of the Western division of the Far Eastern section of the banking house of—" The Old Lady trips him; he falls on Candide's sword and drops to the ground. Candide cries that without knowing why or how, he has killed two men. The Old Lady, picking up the furs and the jewel casket, urges them to escape at once. Candide, ever willing to pay the penalty, would still like an accounting from Cunegonde.

Saying that it's all an accident, that she was starving and these men had given her "a little food," Cunegonde catches the jewel box expertly as the Old Lady pitches it to her. She explains nervously that these are her mother's jewels. "What are you saying?" Candide cries. "Your mother had a little silver comb, nothing more." While Cunegonde argues with Candide and a police whistle gets uncomfortably near, the Old Lady, espying a Pilgrim procession at the end of the garden, decides they must join the Pilgrim band.

Pushing a petulant, unwilling, jewel-clutching Cunegonde before her, the Old Lady and her charges arrive at a dock where the Pilgrim ship is about to set sail. Bartering furs for passage with the shifty Captain, the Old Lady, Cunegonde and Candide manage (along with the unsuspecting Pilgrims) to be carried off to Buenos Aires on a slave ship, instead of to North American rocks and freedom.

SCENE IV

At Buenos Aires, everyone is taken off the boat in chains. Below the balcony of the Governor's palace, the ship's Captain tells the local street cleaner, Martin, why there are no black slaves: "Times are hard. I take what I can get. I won't get much for this lot. White slaves are impractical—they show the dirt." He goes about his business.

MARTIN (*to* PILGRIMS)—You're not the first he has brought this far afield. This miserable dump is called Buenos Aires. That's the Governor's palace. The Captain is about to put you up on the auction block. . . . Oh, don't carry on so loud. All men are in slavery in this worst of all possible worlds. We choose it for ourselves.

CANDIDE—Who are you?

MARTIN—A foreigner. A scholar. A beggar. A street cleaner. A pessimist.

CANDIDE (*puzzled*)—Once I knew a man—he looked very like you, sir. He was a great man, kind and wise. He was an optimist and yet he used almost the same words that you . . .

MARTIN—If he was an optimist, he was neither kind nor wise . . . as you must know from the chains around your wrists.

CUNEGONDE—Chains. Chains. I who was born in a castle, daughter to a baron. We had seven German meals a day. I'm hungry. My mother had a sponge bath whenever she called for it, with three maids to do the soaping and one for odds and ends. My brother was white and blond. . . .

OLD LADY—I don't believe a word you say. I never have. Your German stable would not have served as stables for my father's falcons. Ask me who I am. Ask me. I am the daughter of the Princess of Palestrina and a man so highly placed, of such piety, that even now I cannot disclose his name. I was beautiful, very spiritual, yet in my sixteenth year, from Constantinople to Odessa, round and round the Crimea, up and down the Black Sea . . . (*Screams.*) Ask me what happened to that lovely little princess . . .

CUNEGONDE (*very angry*)—A princess! (*To others.*) She's my servant. I picked her out of a Paris gutter. . . .

OLD LADY (*very, very angry*)—Where you were lying next to me until two rich men came along and took you to their house.

CANDIDE (*softly*)—Cunegonde, every hour of this long voyage I have asked you to tell me how it was that I found you in Paris dressed in jewels, living in that great house. I know you are a virtuous woman, but please explain to me . . .

OLD LADY—Oh, what a foolish man you are. Here we are about to be sold into slavery and you think of nothing but her virtue. Virtue. (*She laughs loudly.*) Well, that was my last laugh.

CUNEGONDE (*shrieking*)—You crone. You filth. You misery. (CUNEGONDE *and the* OLD LADY *fight.*)

MARTIN—I've seen so much evil in my life that simply to keep my balance I am sometimes forced to believe there must be some good in this world. (*Bows to ladies.*) I am grateful to you for reminding me there isn't.

And yet Martin frees them all with the key he steals from the Captain. The Pilgrims run for freedom; Candide and Cunegonde hide from the Governor's officers, the fanciest of whom now appears to be Maximillian.

Cunegonde's blond brother, Maximillian, had arrived from Westphalia by very easy gigolo stages: under the constant protection of sundry amorous old ladies. At the moment, the Governor of Buenos Aires finds Maximillian amusing, acts as his "protector," and indulgently takes orders from him. "Call your servants to attend my lady sister," Maximillian tells the Governor imperiously. "Have the largest rooms prepared to suit her station. . . ." Looking down from his balcony at the filthy Cunegonde, the Governor laughs: "Most certainly. Bring this . . . Bring her in." And as he is about to leave the balcony—"Have your sister bathed," he suggests, "three or four times. Then have her peeled and painted."

Maximillian extends his hand and charity to Candide, too. But a moment later, hearing that lower-class Candide still plans to marry his aristocratic sister, Maximillian threatens Candide with the slave block, or worse—the jungle. He advances haughtily on Candide, prepared to slap him with his glove. Candide, taking the glove away, attempts to slap him. Before he is touched, Maximillian drops to the ground.

The Old Lady, done up fantastically in feathers and jewels, saunters out to discover the latest casualty. "I have killed him!" cries Candide. "Killed him?" yelps the Old Lady. "He was our protector. The situation here was obvious, although nothing is ever obvious to you. . . ." With Martin's help, the Old Lady has Candide hide behind the palace. A moment later the Governor appears.

Crossing casually to examine Maximillian's body, the Governor calls: "Street cleaner! Tidy up here, please." Martin covers the body with canvas as Cunegonde, elegantly and shiningly clean, makes her presence felt. She wonders where her brother is. Martin, dragging Maximillian off, says: "Excuse me, madame, I have a message for you. Your brother has been called away. But you will meet him again . . . in the end."

The Governor has a proposition for Cunegonde. But Cunegonde simply won't understand; Cunegonde is very innocent. Noting the Governor's impatience, the Old Lady comes to his aid: "I think I understand. You are offering this girl a wing of your heart. . . ." "Yes," says the Governor, "because my heart has wings and flies about. I think it best to tell you that now." "I don't understand, sir," says Cunegonde. "I'll try once more," the Governor says, and sings:

> "Poets have said
> Love is undying, my love;
> Don't be misled;
> They were all lying, my love.

> "Love's on the wing,
> But now while he hovers,
> Let us be lovers.
> One soon recovers, my love.

> "Soon the fever's fled,
> For love's a transient blessing.
> Just a week in bed,
> And we'll be convalescing . . ."

Cunegonde is deeply hurt when the Old Lady says: "His Excellency is asking for your hand." The Old Lady tries again: "The great gentleman is proposing marriage." The Governor laughs too loudly, "I should like you to be my wife," and leaves her to think it over. Cunegonde says something about her love for Candide. The Old Lady maintains this is the way to help Candide.

CUNEGONDE—But I don't love this man and I don't want to be unfaithful. . . .

OLD LADY—Look. Think of it this way. Marrying another man is no more unfaithful than sleeping with another man.

CUNEGONDE—Ooooh! Is that true? You are so worldly.

OLD LADY—You have to live. You have to get along as best you can.

The Old Lady sings and begins dancing to the music of a tango.

"I was not born in Buenos Aires.
My father came from Rovno Gubernya.
But now I'm here . . . I'm dancing a tango:
    Di dee di!
    Dee di dee di!
I am easily assimilated.
I'm so easily assimilated.

"I never learned a human language.
My father spoke a High Middle Polish.
In one half-hour I'm talking in Spanish:
    Por favor!
    Toreador!
I am easily assimilated.
I'm so easily assimilated.
It's easy, it's ever so easy!
I'm Spanish, I'm suddenly Spanish! . . ."

Crowds of *señores* join in the singing and dancing. Even Cunegonde catches the spirit. She decides this time to be Spanish: "I will save Candide. My heart breaks." She runs gaily into the palace.

Having a real sense of accomplishment, the Old Lady, now more madam than maid, gets rid of Candide. Telling him that Cunegonde is safe as reading companion to the Governor, she urges Candide to make his fortune and then return. She leaves him to Martin, who also advises him to be off.

CANDIDE—Where shall I go?

MARTIN—What difference does it make where anybody goes? Be on your way, boy.

CANDIDE—There is no place for me. Wherever I go I am beaten and starved. I mean no harm to anybody and yet I have murdered three men in the name of love. I am alone now. . . .

MARTIN—So are we all. It is the worst of all possible worlds, and if it wasn't, we would make it so.

CANDIDE—No, no. Although I have seen a great deal of evil, it is my conviction that man is . . . (*He chokes on the words*) honest and kind and . . . well . . . and . . . well, there must be a place where he is honest and kind and good and noble and . . .

MARTIN—There is such a place. And if I thought you believed that foolishness I would send you there. They would like you.

CANDIDE—I do believe that foolishness. I mean, I do believe what I believe, but I don't believe there's such a place in this world. I mean there is such a place, of course, but I haven't found it. (*Almost in tears.*) Oh, I am tired. And I don't understand anything any more.

Martin describes the country from which he comes: *Eldorado.* It sounds like Paradise to Candide. "No, no," says Martin. "Not Paradise. They would think Paradise a dream for children." Candide asks why he ever left such a place. "They put me out," says Martin. "They said I was the first man ever born there who wasn't happy. They said I was diseased and could not stay with them. They asked me to go. Perhaps they were right. I don't believe that man is honest, or kind, or good." But saying that Eldorado will accept any man who comes in peace, Martin provides Candide with directions and a compass.

As the Governor, flanked by Cunegonde and the Old Lady, comes out on the balcony, Candide sings of his hopes and Eldorado. Then simultaneously singing, Cunegonde praises her self-deception, the Old Lady brags of her successful management, the Governor claims that marriage is awful, and Candide calls farewell to his love:

CUNEGONDE—
    Though it may seem I am
        discarding Candide,
    Truly my scheme is for safe-
        guarding Candide.
    Though I abhor this loveless
        connection—
    Farewell to my love
    Farewell to my love
    Farewell to my love
    Farewell to my love.

OLD LADY—
    Haven't I got brains?
    I'm devilishly witty.
    We were just in chains,
    And now we're sitting pretty.
    You've got to have brains
    You've got to have brains
    You've got to have brains to
        live.

GOVERNOR—
Why should I wed?
Marriage is awful, you know;
Passion is dead once it is lawful, you know.
Women are awful after the first fling—
No, no, I'll not wed
No, no, I'll not wed
No, no, I'll not wed, no.

CANDIDE—
Though that Eden may well be,
Though it shines however brightly,
What bright yonder can delight me?
Farewell to my love
Farewell to my love
Farewell to my love.

ACT II

Three years later, boredom has settled oppressively over the Governor's palace. The Old Lady can't stand this soft living any longer: "I'm homesick for everywhere but here," she says, and sings—

"No doubt you'll think I'm giving in
                        To petulance and malice,
But in candor I am forced to say
That I'm sick of gracious living in
                        This stuffy little palace.
And I wish that I could leave today.
I have suffered a lot
And I'm certainly not
    Unaware that this life has its black side.
I have starved in a ditch,
I've been burned for a witch,
    And I'm missing the half of my backside.
I've been beaten and whipped
And repeatedly stripped,
    I've been forced into all kinds of whoredom;
But I'm finding of late
That the very worst fate
    Is to perish of comfort and BOREDOM. . . ."

"Quiet," speaks the Governor. Cunegonde, still prating about her virtue, demands an early marriage—or threatens to leave. The governor, determined to get "QUIET!" and delighted to have them leave, has his officers bundle off Cunegonde and the Old Lady in heavy sacks.

At this moment, Candide, laden with gold and jewels, re-appears from Eldorado. He scatters largess among the peons, thanks Martin, and singing of Eldorado, confesses that he left that place of beauty and goodness—"that sweetly blessed place"—for love of Cunegonde.

The Governor, appearing on his balcony, observes the generosity of this rich stranger, hears that he has come for Cunegonde, and quickly asks: "Allow me the honor of joining you." He goes back into the palace.

CANDIDE—That's funny talk. It's no honor to join me.

MARTIN—That's the way the rich talk to the rich.

CANDIDE—The people of Eldorado made me very rich with gold and jewels. But I won't ever talk like that. I am a simple man—

MARTIN—Yes, you are. But His Excellency is not simple. I advise you to take care.

CANDIDE—Nothing to take care about. As soon as Cunegonde joins us, we will all take ship for home. Life will be good for us now—

MARTIN (softly)—You will take me with you?

CANDIDE—You are my friend and my benefactor. What I have is yours, now and always.

MARTIN (deeply upset)—Are you a man who remembers those who helped you? Are you a kind man, are you a just man?—(Screams in pain.) If you are a good man, I don't want to know you. It's too late, I am too old. I don't want to start thinking all over again—

The Governor, bearing a tray of wine, hardly pauses before swindling Candide. He tells Candide that Baroness Cunegonde has gone to look for him in Europe, and for a huge sum of gold and jewels sells him a leaking shell of a ship. Then, waving him and Martin off, he sings "Bon Voyage":

". . . I'm so rich that my life is an utter bore:
There is just not a thing that I need.
My desires are as dry as an applecore,
And my only emotion is *greed*.
Which is why, though I've nothing to spend it for,
I have swindled this gold from Candidi-di-di-di-dide,
    Poor Candide!"

And looking out to sea, the Governor exclaims: "Oh, dear, the water's up to his neck—well, there goes his head." And then he sings—

"But I never would swindle the humble poor,
For you can't get a turnip to bleed.
When you swindle the rich you get so much more,
Which is why I have swindled Candide.
    Oh, dear, I fear
He's going down, he's going to drown!
Ah, poor Candide!"

The crowd now sings—

"Bon voyage, best wishes.
Seems to have been a bit of sabotage.
Things don't look propitious,
Still from the heart we wish you bon voyage.
Bon voyage!!!!"

Scene I-A

Starving on a raft in the middle of the ocean, Candide rows hard, wanting very much to survive. He is still convinced that there is as much good as evil in this world and wants to find the good in others and in himself. Martin, fishing with a strip of cloth, repeats: "As much good as there is evil. In a world where men march across continents to kill each other without even asking why. Where the scientist strives to prolong life and at the same minute invents weapons to wipe it out. Where children are taught the rules of charity and kindness until they grow to the age where they would be considered insane if they put the rules into practice. Where half the world starves and the other half diets—" Martin admires a shark that pokes its head near the raft. Candide admits: "Yes, much of what you say is true, and many of my dreams have faded. But I still believe in the essential goodness of the human heart." "The human heart," sneers Martin, "is cowardly and hypocritical, and is not a heart at all: it is more vicious than the monsters of the sea that rise around us now. We would be safer in the arms of a shark than in the arms of a brother—" The shark obligingly yanks him from the raft.

Unaware of this mishap, Candide confesses to not being the optimist he once was. "But," says he, "we'll live quietly when we find my Cunegonde, and you'll feel better when you hear the laughter of my babies." Only then does Candide discover that he is alone. His shouts end when Pangloss clambers onto the raft.

"Dr. Pangloss!" cries Candide in amazement. "I left you in Lisbon. I thought you were dead." Hearing that Pangloss was saved only to become a galley slave for many years, Candide promises him safety and all that he can eat. Pangloss, on the raft, wants more. He wishes Candide to repeat the rules that he taught him. Candide balks. "You break the heart of an old man," says Pangloss. Dutifully Candide struggles: "The heart of mankind is a generous heart. The honor of a man is all he needs on life's journey. The poor must be respected, and so must the rich since they are always with us—"

SCENE II

In an elegant Venetian gambling house, the Old Lady, hired as a shill by Ferone, the owner, ineffectually gulls the fashionable players. Losing money for the house, she is threatened with loss of her job. She sings—

> "I have always been wily and clever
> At deceiving and swindling and such,
> And I feel just as clever as ever,
> But I seem to be losing my touch.
> Yes, I'm clever, but where does it get me?
> My employer gets all of my take;
> All I get is my daily spaghetti,
> While he gorges on truffles and steak.

> "What's the use?
> What's the use?
> There's no profit in cheating,
> It's all so defeating
> And wrong,
> Oh, so wrong!
> If you just have to pass it along. . . ."

In a vicious ronde, Ferone bewails what he has to pass on for protection to the Prefect of Police; the Prefect of Police bewails the Fat Man who shakes him down; the Fat Man, in turn, bewails the system at roulette that loses him the whole boodle. "What's the use?" they all sing. The Old Lady finishes with—

> "Of this cheating and plotting
> You end up with notting!"

The Old Lady goes to soak her feet. In a room off the salon, Cunegonde, a mere scrub woman, brings a foot bath. Dreaming of the nest egg she'll have in a few weeks, the Old Lady says that in this world you do the best you can.

Candide's search for Cunegonde has brought him to the gambling den. Elegantly masked and accompanied by Pangloss, he would go unnoticed in such a well-dressed crowd, if Pangloss didn't inform Ferone of Candide's great wealth.

While Ferone hastily marshals the Old Lady and Cunegonde to take Candide for all he's got, Pangloss happily starts throwing away Candide's money at the tables.

Masked and desperately energetic, the Old Lady and Cunegonde go to work on Candide. In the ensuing scuffle, masks are knocked off. Candide recognizes the thieves. "Cunegonde," he says softly. "My pretty, my sweet, my pure Cunegonde. My whole life has gone trying to find you." Taking his bags of gold, he throws them down. And saying, "This is what you want; I give it to you," Candide turns on his heel and leaves. Ferone grabs the money bags, kicks out the Old Lady and disappears along with all the crowds in the gambling rooms.

Pangloss, deserted by his erstwhile gambling companions, realizes sadly that he's been robbed—and that what he wasn't robbed of and didn't squander on young things, he lent to a nice couple who have somehow disappeared.

Scene III

In the wilds of Westphalia, Candide, Pangloss, the Old Lady and Cunegonde meet again: Maximillian had arrived a bit earlier. They come back to the ruins of their lives, to bickering and accusations, and bring with them nothing but their uselessness.

Candide, after not speaking for weeks, now turns on Pangloss. He says quietly: "You were my master, and I loved you, and you taught me lies. I was a stupid boy, and you must have known it." With great force, he thrusts forth: "A man should be jailed for telling lies to the young." To each in turn Candide, delivering his pointed remarks, says "Get out." No one but Cunegonde hesitates.

Cunegonde complains of hunger. Candide is unmoved. "I followed you around the world, believing every foolish tale you told me, killing men for something called your honor." He wants no more nonsense; he wants to live. "So go away," he tells her, "and let me live."

But one by one they return, each in his fashion trying to prove his worth. Pangloss summons a little practical knowledge and brings forth a fish. Candide puts a pot on the fire. The Old Lady, bowed under a huge pile of firewood, returns with Maximillian under her wing. Maximillian has a broom in his hand, though he has no idea what to do with it. Cunegonde, having made a real effort to clean up, and looking once more nearly pretty, contributes poisonous mushrooms to the stew. That not being enough, she upsets the pot.

As the Old Lady shrieks, Cunegonde sinks to the ground in shame. Candide smiles for the first time. Appreciating Cunegonde's humility, he asks her to marry him.

CUNEGONDE—It's too late. I'm not young, I'm not good, I'm not pure.

CANDIDE—And I am not young, and not worth much. What we wanted, we will not have. The way we did love, we will not love again. Come now, let us take what we have and love as we are.

PANGLOSS—I'd love to do a ceremony. I had three weeks of divinity school in the Würzburg Gymnasium. Now you must say after me, "Love between men and women is the highest order of love between men and women. Thus we promise to think noble and do noble . . ."

CANDIDE (*with force*)—No. We will not think noble because we are not noble. We will not live in beautiful harmony because there is no such thing in this world, nor should there be. We promise only to do our best and live out our lives. Dear God, that's all we can promise in truth. Marry me, Cunegonde. (*He sings.*)

"You've been a fool and so have I,
But come and be my wife,
And let us try before we die
To make some sense of life.
We're neither pure nor wise nor good;
We'll do the best we know;
We'll build our house, and chop our wood,
And make our garden.
And make our garden grow. . . ."

A CLEARING IN THE WOODS

A Play in Two Acts

By Arthur Laurents

[Arthur Laurents *was born in New York in 1918 and graduated from Cornell University. He began his career by writing radio scripts, which he continued to do even after joining the Army. His first play, "Home of the Brave," brought him a $1000 grant from the American Academy of Arts and Letters. He wrote "The Bird Cage," produced in 1950, and the popular "The Time of the Cuckoo," produced in 1952.*]

THE figures of three girls are barely discernible as darkness turns to foggy light on a clearing in a wood. One, a child, sits against some cottage steps; another, somewhat older, sits in an old deck chair; the third, the oldest, leans relaxed against a tree.

A woman's voice hullooing in the distance draws closer. Darting together, the girls join hands as though in a pact, then vanish into the darkness of the trees. As the light in the clearing becomes day-bright, a woman, wearing a soft, flowing negligee, rushes on.

The Woman—Hello—who? Hello, me. How are you? Fine! Oh, so very fine now! I'm back, back where I always ran to catch my breath. And I *can* breathe now! I'm here, I'm— (*Suddenly stops, looking around.*) But it isn't as pretty as it was. It isn't very pretty at all. (*Going to the cottage.*) Am I back? Where am I? Who was I calling? (*Mounting the steps.*) Andy? (*Calling.*) Andy? (*Silence. Then, with a wry smile.*) No Andy. Which fact she knew, but knowing never yet killed hope.

(*Summer morning sunlight is drifting through the trees as the* Young Girl *appears. About seventeen, she wears attractive clothes which are somehow slightly odd.*)

"A Clearing in the Woods": By Arthur Laurents. Copyright © 1957 by Arthur Laurents. Reprinted by permission of Random House, Inc., New York. All inquiries should be addressed to author's agent: Harold Freedman, c/o Brandt & Brandt, New York, N. Y.

THE WOMAN—Caught in the act of conversing with an old enemy: me.

YOUNG GIRL—Oh, I do it all the time!

THE WOMAN—Do you interrupt yourself with yourself?

YOUNG GIRL—Naturally!

THE WOMAN—Then we must interrupt ourselves with each other sometime. Good evening.

YOUNG GIRL—Good evening—and welcome, welcome home!

She doesn't know, the Young Girl tells the Woman, how glad they all are that she finally came back.

The Little Girl, a bespectacled child of nine or ten, neatly but again somewhat oddly dressed, comes from behind the cottage. Everything the Young Girl says, she questions. Told to be still, she asks: "Why?" When she asks for a reason, the Young Girl says the reason is: she's older. "Old, old, old," cries the Little Girl. "See?" She appeals to the Woman: "Nobody ever explains, not a single thing. 'Do as I tell you,' that's all. Well, when I grow up, I'm going to do what *I* tell *me!*" "Bravo!" cries the Woman.

The child, too, is so glad that she's back. "Why," the Woman wonders, "are you both so glad I'm back?" "Now you'll take care of us," the Young Girl cries . . . because "He's too old to do it," and (says the Little Girl) "He never did anyway." What's more, the Young Girl says, "He doesn't like us." The Little Girl cries: "But you do, don't you?" "Like you?" the Woman answers. "I don't even know you." The girls look at each other and laugh.

Jigee, the Little Girl, asks Nora, the Young Girl, "What's the matter with her? . . . You're acting very peculiar," she tells the Woman. "I'm just tired," the Woman answers. "It's a long drive from town. Why are you here? I came back to be alone. But how can you be alone where you have been before?"

Jigee and Nora wish the Woman to take care of them. "Please say yes, Virginia," the Little Girl begs. But though Virginia smiles brightly, it is obvious that she wants to be rid of them.

A lean, tanned, crew-cut older man, wearing casual clothes and a bright tie, and swinging a gold club, comes into the clearing. Virginia greets him emotionally: "Daddy! Oh, Daddy, I—" "You cry too quickly," Barney says. Virginia is just so happy to see him. "Where'd you think I'd be?" Barney answers. "At the club," interrupts Nora, and she is right. Barney is already late for a date but wanted to welcome his only child. "Say more than welcome," begs Virginia, as he looks at his watch: "Stay. Permission is granted to enter the sacred circle." Barney draws a blank, then as Virginia describes a "circle" in the clearing, ending with her arms upstretched to him, Barney goes to her. "Really, Virginia," he says, "that was only a silly child's rule." "It isn't silly," Nora intervenes. "Even a child wants a place of her own."

Jigee now has a run-in with Barney because she has taken off her specs. He says they are meant to be worn so when she is grown up she won't need them and will be pretty. "Why do I have to be pretty?" Jigee asks. "Because you're a girl," answers Barney. "But why?" Jigee persists. "Because I say so," Barney finishes amiably. "*That* again!" explodes Jigee.

He next tangles with Nora when he tells her that she'd be happier if she'd keep in line with what other people think. "Just yesterday," Nora tells Virginia, "he said: Learn to think for yourself and stand on your own two feet." "Can't you do both?" Barney asks. "Oh, yes," cracks Virginia, "with two heads." This gets a laugh from the girls. Barney, grinning, takes a swing with his club. "Fore," he cries to Jigee—"I never could be a winner around here, baby."

Barney has the idea that pretty girls make out better than smart girls, unless they can be both. He tells the girls: "Your mother would never let anyone but me see her reading."

VIRGINIA—Yes, Daddy, I know.

BARNEY (*poking at her negligee with his golf club*)—She was partial to things soft and floating, too. Of course, I don't exactly recall her wearing one down here.

VIRGINIA—Oh. Well, I didn't know where I was going to wind up when I left town last night. I—suddenly needed some place to unwind. Overworking, hard work. . . . Well, not really. Parties have become the hardest, whether giving or going. Last week, I cooked a complete East Indian dinner for ten people and left in the middle. Of course, Mother— Well, this is soft and cool, and it was too hot for sleeping in town last night. . . . Well, I didn't know where I was heading. I said that. (*Finally.*) No, Mother would not have made the error of wearing this.

Nora approves completely of her costume. Barney says what's the difference, so long as Virginia stays and they can have a good long talk. Nora knows what this means: as usual there's a reason for his being glad she's there. Virginia shoos the girls away.

"I don't have a reason," Barney says; "you're just always suspicious." "I would only be suspicious," Virginia says, "if you had no reason. Even strangers seem to know that." Barney wants to know what she means by "strangers." Virginia refuses to enlarge on the remark. ". . . Everything has a meaning, but look for the meaning in everything and you can lose your reason. Lose yours, Daddy. Your reason for being glad to see me." Barney wonders if she is ill. Virginia says that what she needs is a good friend.

BARNEY—You know that property I gave you as a wedding present? You're divorced now, you're not doing a thing with the land—
VIRGINIA—Those girls were right: you did have a reason.
BARNEY—It wasn't my idea, you understand, but my lawyers suggested—
VIRGINIA—Barney, I don't care about lawyers and property!
BARNEY—You'd better begin to care. Prices are going up, sky-high. You don't understand these things the way your mother did, but—
VIRGINIA—What prices are going up sky-high, Barney? Golf balls or whisky?
BARNEY—That is unfair. I ration my drinks now and you know it. I am merely trying to provide for our needs—
VIRGINIA—That need, I can provide for myself.

"An executive assistant makes—" Barney retorts: "Fancy title for secretary." "You think that," Virginia cries, "because I'm a woman!"
A young woman of about twenty-six, wearing a terry robe over her wet bathing suit, comes up the path, drying her hair. Virginia is happy to see her. The Young Woman is glad that she's come back. "I'm Ginna," she says.

VIRGINIA—Oh . . . Of course.
GINNA—Has he been upsetting you? (*Turns to* BARNEY.) Sly comparisons to a mother who was perfection—or has he been belittling your work?
VIRGINIA—The lady knows you well, Barney.
BARNEY—Her understanding of men is on a par with yours.
GINNA—I understand you.
BARNEY—As you do your husband.
GINNA—No. Pete is not quite as simple.

Barney and Ginna now do battle as she asks him to give up a moment of his "athletic" time to Virginia. He cracks about *her time:* "Another day, another cause . . ." Ginna rushes to defend her useful life. "Now, Ginna, I don't mean to run down these do-good organizations—" Barney answers. "Then don't reduce people who are trying, to a snide little country club phrase! And don't ridicule my work because I'm a woman. The work I am doing may not matter fifty miles from here, but I am not sitting at a bridge table!" Barney remarks that Virginia has a real job now. She won't be satisfied, he tells Ginna, until she's different from "us ordinary people." "Now," says Ginna, "I thought you were the one who always said: Be an individual. Either you—" (VIRGINIA *joins in*)— "stand on your own two feet or—" They stop. Ginna laughs: "Oh, dear, oh, dear, the echoes. Maddening, aren't they?" She drifts up the path.

Virginia would like to know if the woods are full of them. "They swing in and out like doors!" she cries. "Memories do," Barney answers. "I meant those girls," says Virginia.

Barney asks what's bothering her. "You could tell me," Barney says, "but you never do. You never come to see me. After your divorce, you moved out and you haven't spent one night here since."

Fearful, Virginia is sure that someone is listening—one of those girls. It makes no difference to Barney. He asks her if she doesn't like them. About to say she doesn't even know them, Virginia suddenly stops. She admits that she's met them, that they remind her of things she used to do: "They're confusing, slightly irritating, but nothing terrible." A moment later, she asks quietly: "Well, Doctor?"

Barney, grinning, says: "Well, madam, speaking impersonally—" "Please," says Virginia, "don't." Barney is reminded of her beau, the Doctor, whom he liked. Virginia hasn't seen Andy in two years. Barney had the impression that Andy was going to be husband number two. "Your impression was wrong," answers Virginia.

BARNEY—All right. I'm just trying to explore all the avenues. Logically. Now it isn't love, so . . . it must be overwork. Virginia, I'm sure that all you need is a good night's sleep.

VIRGINIA—But does sleep need me? What happens to the night when I am not in it? My bed has sprawled unmade for a week; my apartment has gone to weed; the extra room remains unfurnished. I loathe that apartment and yet I cannot get myself to move out. It's like being unable to open that office door: I want to but— (*He looks at his watch. She laughs.*) You're late for your game.

BARNEY—You ask for help only to expose my inadequacy. God wouldn't satisfy you! (*She picks up his club and hands it to him.*) I recognize your ailment because I, too, suffered from it. Just one more birdie, I'd say, then no more drink. I never made the birdie—

(*Grins*) so I always took the drink. Until I realized I was never going to make it.

VIRGINIA—Then you gave up trying: you quit.

BARNEY—You *would* look at it that way.

VIRGINIA—And you still drink.

BARNEY—Realistically! And I did not quit trying! I merely faced my limitations like a mature individual.

Even her fears are crazy—her feeling like a zero. Even the *problems* of other people don't satisfy her, Barney snaps. As usual, she has to be different. He repeats again that they're ordinary, the same as everyone else. Virginia hotly denies this: "I'm not! Nor will I be!" Ending on this wrangling note, Virginia tells him to be off to his nine holes of golf. "I'm still good for eighteen—and you be damned!" he yells, striding off into the woods.

Jigee, dashing on with a pair of shears, cuts up the tie Barney had dropped on the ground. He was mean to Virginia, she says as she snips. Telling her to stop, grabbing the pieces, Virginia says she's a bad little girl and to go home. "Oh, Virginia," Jigee cries, "I *am* home." She begs Virginia to love her and take care of her, and not to tattle on her. As the child darts away, Virginia crams the pieces of tie into her pocket. The piece she misses, she covers quickly with her foot. Barney, returning for his good-luck tie, picks up the shears. "Years ago," he says, "I had a new pair of plus-fours. Someone cut them to shreds . . . What's under your foot?" He throws the shears to the ground. Virginia, moving her foot, says that she did not cut the tie. "Then who did?" Barney asks. "Who could you care enough about to protect?" Jigee, with a cry of "Me!" comes to Virginia's aid. Virginia in turn protects Jigee from Barney's wrath: "Barney, she's a child!" "A bad child," says Barney. Jigee cries that he doesn't care if she loves him or not. "Not when you're bad, no," answers Barney. "Not ever! Never!" Jigee cries, running into the trees. "She's *not* bad," Virginia insists. "She cut the tie only to get attention." "Next time," Barney grins, "she'll cut my throat. That'll get a lot of attention."

Not caring for his jokes, Virginia recalls (there is nostalgic music and the light turns hazy here) that years ago, when she was as little as Jigee, not long after her mother died, she was in love with Barney. She wrote him a letter. He took it as a joke. "Dearest Daddy," she had written. "You never want me around because I'm not pretty. Therefore, I am a stepchild and so I am running away. Your loving daughter, Virginia." Coming back to a house full of laughing people, and a maid who greeted her with, "I thought you were running away," Virginia had answered: "Just because he wants me to, I won't." "I was watching," Barney says, "from behind the curtains. I wouldn't have let you get very far." "Why didn't you say something when I came in? Why didn't you even look at me? Why did you laugh?" Virginia asks. As the music ends, she says: "That night, I cut your new trousers."

As Barney, still bewildered, leaves for his golf game, he promises to surprise her someday.

Ginna, now wearing a simple summer dress and carrying a man's athletic sweater, asks Virginia if she feels better. As though she doesn't hear, Virginia says to herself: "I should have told him long ago or not at all. What is the good of telling someone too old to change?" "It would have been kinder," says Ginna, "to rid yourself of it through someone else." "But," Virginia answers, "they would know me, then." "And not like you," Ginna adds.

Virginia now admits to being terrified of all three girls—just as a shot makes them whirl in fear. "Pete!" cries Ginna. "Andy!" cries Virginia. Two more shots have Ginna disappearing into the woods, while Virginia cries out: "I didn't mean it, Andy!"

A virile, slick, sophisticated man, armed with gadgets, knapsack and gun, arrives in the clearing. They have met before, he assures Virginia: he's George. "Dear Virginia," he says, "you needn't be polite. I have an iron ego. You don't remember, but we drank great quantities, then ducked out to dinner, which we drank, then back to my place where—" "Oh," interrupts Virginia, "I'm afraid you could be several people." "Oh," answers George, "I'm afraid I am—"

They settle themselves down on the ground for the cocktail hour. Virginia wants George to help her forget everything up to the present minute. "Enjoyment isn't forgetting," says George, "it's making a happy memory. Of love, for example." He starts things moving. "You believe in love," says Virginia. He does not: he believes in Nothing. That's his secret. Believe in Nothing and one can never be disillusioned or disappointed.

Virginia, checking her kisses and embraces, sits up to accuse George: "They put you up to it. You are a warning of what can happen to me! I can die of nothingness!" A moment ago she was listening for a secret; now she knows that there is none except the one you find for yourself.

George, coolly picking up his knapsack, says Virginia didn't like his answer; he disappointed her: "Is this how you always react when people don't stand as tall as you've decided they should?"—Cut them down to pygmy or insect size? "No," cries Virginia, "I did *not* try to cut you down, Andy!" "I don't think you could, and the name," says George, "is still George." He is an optimist: the woods are full of girls.

Following him to the edge of the clearing, Virginia begs for another chance, just as Ginna reaches out her arm towards a young man who comes into the clearing. Frozen with fear, Virginia tries to ward off the sight of him, and with a sudden cry of "Wait!" follows George into the woods.

The young man, wearing tennis shoes and an unbuttoned shirt, picks up his cardigan as Ginna, in a dressing gown, joins him.

GINNA—But you never want to talk about any problem we have. What happened isn't so very terrible. Or even so very unusual.

PETE—Ginna—

GINNA—It happens to most men.

PETE—*How often?* And afterwards, the politeness of silence in the dark, acting asleep—

GINNA—There is no need to—

PETE—And the excuses for the morning: Gee, I was awfully tired last night; gee, I was awfully drunk last night. When we both know—

GINNA—Don't you know it's humiliating for me, too? (*Now he looks at her.*) To know that I don't excite you any more. That you don't find me attractive any more.

PETE—I do. It isn't that.

GINNA—Then, what is it?

PETE—All I know is that I've disappointed you.

It is he who is disappointed in her, Ginna asserts. She asks why he, the biggest man on campus—Man of the Year—wanted to marry her. She can remember how, in reflected glory, she was somebody, too.

PETE—Ginna, I'm drowning! Maybe you think you're helping me to shore, but you can't swim yourself. You keep telling me you fell in love with the biggest man on campus. Well, school's out and the world's in. I'm nothing.

GINNA—That's not so!

PETE—Help me get started to being even a little something.

GINNA—I don't know what to do any more—I've tried, I have—

PETE—But you've given up. Just as you have with—with what I suppose I was really talking about. With making love.

GINNA—I have not! . . . I told you: it's just as bad for me . . .
It's no different for a woman.

PETE—Yes, it is. You can fake.

And when he fails, he thinks that Ginna is glad. Pete asks her not
to evade the truth. Ginna, crying "The heart and mind are strangers," doesn't know the truth any more. Pete wants a divorce, and
Ginna, out of pride, refuses to remonstrate. "How can you have
pride and still be in love?" asks Pete. . . . Ginna calls after Pete.
He has gone. George materializes in his place, followed by Virginia.

Ginna tries to prevent Virginia from taking George into the cottage. Asking for silence, Virginia hears the sound of an axe. "No,
not yet, Virginia," Ginna tells her. "You're jumping time—that
comes later, in a little while." But Virginia and George have shut
the door of the cottage.

Nora, a rebellious adolescent accompanied by her chum, arrives
with blanket, basket and spiked drinks for a picnic. Settling themselves in the clearing, Nora pours out drinks and lights up. Listening critically to her friend's chatter, Nora says: "One summer in
Nashville three years ago is no excuse for that accent." "If you
can arbitrarily change your name to Nora," says the girl, "I can
certainly change my accent." Nora, pointing out that she has
named herself after Ibsen's first emancipated woman, trains her
glasses on a distant woodchopper and finds him really very cute.

Nora, determined never to be ordinary—determined always to be
different—offers the twenty-year-old woodchopper a drink from their
thermos. He is pleasantly surprised with the drink and asks for a
cigarette, then asks Nora to stick around awhile.

Shooing her dismayed friend home and asserting that she can take
care of herself, Nora goes off into the woods with the boy. Distressed
by the young couple's disappearance, Virginia dashes wildly out of
the cottage after them.

George, his shirt-tails flapping loose, follows her. "Don't come
out like that!" Virginia cries. "Are you that sorry?" George asks
her. "Why do what you don't enjoy?" "I thought I would . . .
I wanted to," she says. But, she admits, "I couldn't: I kept hearing
her, then."

Virginia now accuses "them" of raking up old things, of driving
her into ways she hates. "They do, Andy," she cries. George asks
why she keeps calling Andy. Virginia says she can't remember.

George's place in the clearing is taken by Ginna. Virginia now
accuses Ginna of pushing her toward George. "What?" cries Ginna.

VIRGINIA—By telling me not to do it. You *do* know me, you know that's all I need to make me go ahead. I wouldn't have if it weren't for you! I wouldn't have finally hurt my father if it weren't for Jigee! You drive me into doing things, all three of you! Deliberately! Is that your method of winning me over to like you? Interfering, driving me to do what I don't want, driving me to remember what I hate? Why must you keep bringing back and bringing back and bringing back— (JIGEE *steps into the light in the clearing from another part of the woods. She holds the garden shears in front of her.* VIRGINIA *stares at them. Then—*) I didn't want to hurt you, Daddy. I wanted to make you *see* me. I wanted— (*Stops. Looks around for* BARNEY, *then at the girls.*) Someone help! (*Silence; then—*) Don't come any nearer. You lied when you said you welcome me home. This nightmare imitation is not home. You lie when you say you want me to take care of you. You want something terrible to happen to me. I do *not* know who you are, but I know you are evil! I will not let anything more happen. You are getting out of here at once, immediately! I'm not asking you now, I'm telling you, ordering you: go away and stay away. (*The girls do not move.*) Very well. I shall get my father to help.

Ginna says that she's a fool. "It's you," she says, "and us." And always has been. Virginia starts for the trees, but is blocked by Ginna, then by Jigee holding the shears straight out, and finally by Nora.

"You can't do this!" Virginia cries. "You have no right to be here. I live here. This is my home." The voices echo back, as Nora, Jigee and Ginna cry: "I live here!" "I *do!*" cries Virginia. The echoing voices answer: "I do!" "*I* do!" Virginia cries; "I am Virginia!" The three cry: "*I* am Virginia—" "*I* am!" Virginia calls out. The "I am!" of the girls drowns out Virginia. Music plays as, in a panic, Virginia turns from one to the other, and with a scream tears through them into the cottage.

ACT II

Virginia, her heart beating so loud that it can be heard, has tried in vain to bolt the door of the cottage against the girls. They swarm all over it. Virginia, trying to hold onto her sanity, in desperation does arithmetic sums. The girls taunt and bedevil her, grab at all her clothes, and then start bickering among themselves over who should wear what.

Nora grabs a hat that Jigee wanted to wear. "That's mine!" cries Jigee. "It's hers," says Nora. "Girls—" interrupts Ginna. "Well, I'm her," reasons Jigee. "So am I," Nora says. "But," clinches Jigee, "I was her first and I took it first. . . ."

In a sudden fury, Virginia hurls herself upon them and throws clothes in all directions at them. They know who they are, she shrieks: Ginna's only a nickname for Virginia, and what was Nora before she was Nora, except a name she couldn't pronounce and so twisted it? But they are not her. She has been sick, and driven half-mad by these "three white nightmares"—that don't exist. Ginna thereupon topples over a chair, saying: "We exist, as long as you exist," and adding: "We belong to you as you belong to us."

VIRGINIA—*I belong to no one!* (*She runs down into the clearing.*) I will be held down by no one! I *don't* like you. You're weak, defiant, destructive, *unloved!* You have settled for the second rate because that's what *you* are!

GINNA (*caustically*)—We're willing to settle for you.

VIRGINIA—I will not be settled for! Nor will I settle! I have never accepted what is less than I want and I will not accept you!

And just to show them, Virginia, with an enormous act of will, thrusts out her hands and pushes the girls out of her mind. The girls disappear; the cottage resumes its original position in the scheme of things; and Virginia, bathed in a happy light, is determined to start anew.

Andy, older than Virginia, steps from the trees with quiet assurance. Virginia, knowing that by bringing Andy into the magic circle all their ugly clashes will have vanished, announces that it's a clean new day. "Our wedding," says Andy, "two years late."

Andy urges her to hurry: he has to get back to the lab. "Last time we hurried," says Virginia; "not now. It's not raining. It's a clean new day and I'm a new girl. That's quite apparent, isn't it?" "Some change is apparent," agrees Andy, "but you'd better tell me just where." "Inside," answers Virginia; "I've driven them out."

Andy listens amiably to her talk of their new apartment. He laughs with her, then says, after a kiss: "I really have to get back to the store."

Virginia offers her car; Andy says they'll take his. She gives in, but says the hospital can wait. "You're a new man," Virginia cries. "Yes, that's it. You're a very important man now! You got the new appointment!" Andy tells her he didn't and that she knows he didn't. Virginia says that he might still get it. Ginna's voice from the trees says: "He won't and you know it." Virginia insists that he will. "Why," Andy asks, "is it so terribly important to you? What are you afraid of?"

Evasively Virginia tries once more to lead Andy back into the magic circle. It doesn't work. She repeats herself about the apartment. "I didn't get the appointment," Andy says. She tries to avoid any mention of it, but Andy realizes how disappointed she is. Virginia manages a "No." "Liar!" comes from the trees. Crying that she's not disappointed, that she's angry, Virginia blames the loss of the appointment on politics. As far as Andy goes there were no politics. "The other man," he remarks, "was better." Ginna's catty voice is heard. He takes no pleasure in admitting it, says Andy, but the other man *is* better. "I know you: you're brilliant," Virginia insists; "you've a wonderful mind and a wonderful talent, and you work so hard—you are the best!" "Virginia," Andy says, "I am not the best . . . I'm good; I'm working hard to be better. And I think I will be. But that fantasy of yours of a near-genius— Virginia, that I am not, nor will I ever be." Ginna's voice offers: "Translation: mediocre."

Virginia hopes that he hasn't stopped trying, that he hasn't settled for being less than he can be. Ginna and Nora make pointed comments. Andy has had about enough: ". . . Now I am not ordinary. Nor have I settled for anything but the knowledge of what my limitations are. I'm old enough to accept them and that makes life a helluva lot happier. People who don't, Virginia, those people draw and quarter themselves. And if they keep at it too long, there is no thread strong enough to stitch them back together. . . . I tried for that appointment—hard. I always try—and you know that. . . ."

He knows, too, the only possible reason for her being angry: his failure. Forced to admit this, she confesses to having thought that if Andy knew this he would stop loving her. That if he knew she cared so much about success—about outward appearances . . . Andy interrupts: "But you know me now. And you said if I knew you, I couldn't love you. No, look at me. LOOK AT ME! . . . Don't you know that *loving is knowing someone and still loving?*" He sees that it doesn't mean that to her. Andy wonders if Virginia can feel—can feel anything. "Yes!" Virginia cries savagely. "Hatred of me! I am the enemy. I hate that I demand you be extraordinary, and yet I demand it! I hate that I demand *I* be, and yet I demand it! I hate that because you are not, I don't love you. But I don't, I can't! And if I cannot love you— *You*— The riddle is unriddled! The joker is pulled out and the card house falls in! I cannot love you because I—*cannot—love—anyone!* The truth came out of your anger; how do you like the sound of it? *I cannot love!*" *He* loves *her,* and he wishes to help her, but what Virginia hears instead is the girls playing cards on the porch. Andy has faded away.

The girls talk, while playing, and laugh. Virginia, from her isolation, comments: "Laugh. Nothing destroys like laughter. Nothing hurts like laughter. Nothing is as safe as laughter."

Ginna says casually: "If laughter destroys . . . why doesn't she laugh at us?" "She'd rather kill in an uglier way," says Nora. "Gas, for example." This sets their minds to work. Jigee comes up with: "I know how she can get rid of all three of us at once! With only those pills!" She wants it understood that it's her idea. Ginna is sure Virginia will give her full credit. Now they hope that Virginia's happy. "Have you anything to live for?" Ginna asks. Is there anyone she'd hurt, or anyone who'd care? The girls go through the lists: Barney—they don't think so. George? The Georges care only about themselves. Andy might care. That's not enough. Jigee ventures that *they* really care. Nora says: "She doesn't care whether we care or not."

Ginna puts the pills in Virginia's hand. Virginia's breathing comes harder and faster. She stares at the pills, brings them closer. There's a wild moment—the girls rush across the clearing. The lights play tricks, in a confusion of sound and color. Then, suddenly, Virginia realizes that She cares.

She sits down and the girls join her tenderly. She cares about them; she asks them to help her see their other side. She really wants to like them. Ginna thinks of getting someone who has really liked them to help: but who has really liked them? Nora says caustically: "A witness—to prove we're worth being liked despite what we are." "No," answers Virginia, "a witness to prove you're what I hope you are."

Andy, appearing not as a witness, but because he knows who all three girls are, has come back to make sure that Virginia listens.

Nora is frightened off by their first witness, the woodchopping boy. It gradually becomes clear, despite his youthful bumptiousness and conceit, he has returned in Nora's behalf because she was proud enough to finish what she had started. Having thus testified, he leaves a paper bag full of flowers for her. "And I thought," says Virginia, "that someone had just thrown them away." As she looks at Nora clutching the little bouquet, she says: "But that boy is—" "Ordinary?" answers Nora defiantly. "He isn't," says Andy, "and what if he were, Virginia?"

Pete, now in uniform, comes back as Ginna's witness. He had liked her because she made him alive. "A few have something special, inside them," explains Pete. "I don't know what it is. But somehow they make the same things everyone else does, they make the ordinary—exciting. They give life color. . . ."

Virginia, noting the ring on Pete's finger, finds that he has married again and has children. She is glad. Andy tells Ginna: "You didn't destroy him." Ginna is pleased: "No, Virginia, he made out all right." "Did he?" says Virginia, "I'd heard he was back in uniform, back in a world of boys." "But," says Andy, "if that's his place—"

GINNA (*To* VIRGINIA)—What would be enough for you? The moon? (*On this,* BARNEY *enters; gay, tipsy;* JIGEE *is leading him by the hand.*)

BARNEY—Oh, no, the moon is too available! The universe!

JIGEE—Ssh!

BARNEY (*shakes her off*)—All astronomical stations from Integrity to Brilliance. With local stopovers at South Charm, West Beauty, North—

Jigee didn't know that he'd be like that. Virginia tells her that she should have known by now. He's her witness, but Jigee doesn't dare ask him the question while he's like that. Virginia urges her to take the chance. Slowly going to Barney, Jigee asks: "Daddy . . . do you like me?" "A man is a father," Barney answers; "a man likes his daughter." Virginia cries that that is no answer.

All the girls pile into Barney. Does he love any of them? Andy adds: "Or Virginia?" "Yes," Ginna agrees, "the answer is for all of us."

VIRGINIA—Do you love me, Daddy?

BARNEY (*looks at her, then away: to* GINNA)—I loved you as much as you loved me. (*To* NORA.) And you—as much as you'd let me. (*To* JIGEE.) And you . . . (*Lamely.*) Your mother was a woman who—needed much attention. There are times when a child needs more love than a parent can give.

JIGEE (*ripping off her glasses*)—You just think I'm a bad girl!

ANDY—No, he doesn't.

JIGEE—Then *he's* bad.

ANDY—Not "*bad.*" Just not—

VIRGINIA—Just not perfect.

BARNEY—No. By your standards, I failed. Well, maybe I did a

little with her. (*Points to* Jigee, *then turns to* Nora.) But what about you? (*To* Ginna.) And you? (*To* Virginia.) And above all, *you*. There are times when a parent needs more love than the child gives! Did you all have to pass your anger along like a sickness? Did you have to let it turn you colder and colder with resentment? (*To* Virginia.) Do you have to let it freeze you into your grave?

All the girls snap back angrily. Andy asks Virginia not to listen to them. "But they know him and you don't," she answers. As the girls continue to tear into Barney, Andy asks him: "Are they what you want?"

Ginna—Are *you* what she wants?
Virginia—*Let me be!*
Andy—*No*. Not this time. Don't you know why you ask for more? Because you ask more of them.
Virginia—All because of them?!
Andy—Yes.

They now ask Virginia to like them, to belong to them. "And I can belong!" Virginia cries. According to Andy, the choice is hers. Then, Virginia realizes, this was the terrible thing that was going to happen. "Why terrible?" Andy asks.

Virginia—A choice should include something you want: a dream. Somehow, it never does. Somehow, it is always a choice of beggars. Why must I either fight them or take them as they are? Why must I take them at all? Why can't I be rid of them, be free, so free I could soar over those trees? That's what I dream! That's what I really choose.
Andy—Only the stars can get up there, Virginia. Most of us aren't capable of being stars, only of refusing *not* to be. Most of us aren't even meteors. Most of us never get off the ground. . . . It's not very sweet to accept that you're just another groundling.
Virginia—I don't want to! I don't want to stop trying!

Andy, turning to go, says: then keep fighting. ". . . Anything you think, you'll think out of anger. Anything you do—you'll do out of defiance. Any hand that's offered you, you'll slap." Virginia begs *his* hand. Since she can't know whether she'll be content with him till she has accepted "them," Andy goes. But he has never, he says, been very far away.

Virginia now asks for her father's hands. Embarrassed, Barney says that they are touched with whisky and always will be. Virginia doesn't care. "I'm too old to change," says Barney. "I'm not, Daddy," Virginia answers. "I meant," he says in defeat, "I'm too accustomed to you as a stranger." He goes quickly into the trees.

Jigee tries to keep from crying. Nora, putting her arm around her, comforts her. But Virginia asks them to weep for Barney instead. He's alone, while they at least have one another.

Accepting them, as they are, means that Virginia can never be what she dreamed. Though, as Ginna says, an end to dreams isn't an end to hope. "Come," cries Virginia, "it's time for us to go!" "All of us?" asks Jigee. "All of us together!" Virginia cries.

She climbs the cottage steps. The light is fading fast. She calls the girls. They are gone.

Suddenly summer light bathes the trees. Virginia, looking around like a delighted child, finds: "It *is* pretty here!" Laughing a little, she walks out of the clearing, up the path through the trees.

THE WALTZ OF THE TOREADORS

A Comedy in Three Acts

By Jean Anouilh

Translated by Lucienne Hill

[Jean Anouilh *was born in Bordeaux in 1910 and has been an increasingly prominent figure since 1932, when his first play "L'Hermine" was a success. A year later he wrote "Mandarine." This was followed by, among others, "Eurydice" (done here as "Legend of Lovers"), "Antigone," "Cry of the Peacock," "Ring Round the Moon," "Mademoiselle Colombe" and "The Lark."*

Lucienne Hill *is an English writer and also the adapter of Anouilh's "Thieves' Carnival," done last year at New York's Cherry Lane Theatre with great success.*]

THE time is 1910. The study of retired General St. Pé, adjoining his invalid wife's bedroom, is decorated with the booty and exotic trophies of a long military career. The General, despite the shrill, shrewish questions that keep coming from the bedroom, continues to write at his desk. What is he doing? of what is he thinking? the grating voice persists. "You," the General answers, without bothering to look up.

Voice—Liar. You are thinking about women being beautiful, and not feeling all alone in the world for a while, you told me so once.

General—I haven't the faintest recollection of it. Go to sleep, my love. You will be tired later.

Voice—I am only tired, only ill, because of you! Ill with thinking, always thinking of all the things I know you're doing!

General—Come now, my love, you exaggerate, as usual. The whole time you have been ill, and that makes years now, I haven't

"The Waltz of the Toreadors": By Jean Anouilh, translated by Lucienne Hill. Copyright © 1953 by Jean Anouilh and Lucienne Hill. First American edition published by Coward-McCann, Inc., New York, 1957. Reprinted by permission of the publishers.

left this room, sitting here glued to this chair dictating my memoirs, or pacing about like a bear in a cage, and well you know it.

VOICE—I feel ill with thinking of all the things you are busy doing in your head while you pretend to comfort me. Admit, it, hypocrite! Where were you just now in your head? With what woman? In which kitchen, tumbling Heaven knows what drab that scrubs away there on all fours? And you creep up on her, like a great tomcat. Leon, you make me sick!

GENERAL—By Hades, Madam, you are dreaming! I am sitting at my desk, writing to M. Poincaré.

VOICE—He's a good excuse, Poincaré! . . . Stop it, Leon!—if you don't want my death on your conscience. Have you no shame, man, no refinement?

GENERAL—Will you let me finish my letter in peace?

VOICE (*whimpering*)—But inside! Inside your head! Why won't you let me inside your head, just once—just for a minute?

GENERAL—Confound it, Madam, my head is out of bounds! It's the one spot where I can have a bit of peace, I want it to myself.

VOICE—I shall get into it one day. I shall come upon you there when you least expect it and I shall kill you!

Over her shrieks, the General closes the bedroom door. He is muttering that he won't put up with her whims forever, as his young and innocent male secretary enters. The General immediately addresses himself to the young man's sex life. The secretary considers himself far too young for such things. "Yes," retorts the General, "and in a flash you'll be too old. You'll be sitting at your desk dictating your memoirs. And between the two, pouff—a game of dice. You must feel the urge sometimes though?" the General inquires hopefully. "No, sir," says the secretary. "I have not long left the seminary. I am still chaste." "Good," the General answers. "Sad though. Life without women, my boy, what hell! There's another problem M. Poincaré will never solve. Now then, to work. Where were we?"

They are on the thirty-first chapter—dealing with the high points of the Moroccan Campaign—when they are interrupted by the General's appalling twin daughters. These grotesque twenty-year-olds, dressed in clothes they've long outgrown, have come to plead for new dresses for Corpus Christi. Bidding them put on last year's dresses for his inspection, the General orders them away. "My God, aren't they ugly?" he exclaims as they go. "To think that I, with such a soft spot for a pretty face, could have brought those into the world." The secretary says primly: "The Mademoiselles St. Pé are full of the finest moral qualities." "All sorts," corrects the General, "but not the right sort. Heigh-ho—where were we?"

Giving the secretary the benefit of an off-the-record version of his African experiences, the General has the poor boy panting for a sexy finale. He lets him down, however, with a thudding anti-climax, in time to greet his wife's physician, Doctor Bonfant. The secretary is dismissed.

The men go through their daily ritual. How is the patient? asks the Doctor. How is the medicine? asks the General. Apparently both are the same, as always, though of science the Doctor does say: "We have found other terms far less vague than the old ones to designate the same complaints. It's a great advance linguistically—" But Mme. St. Pé's paralysis has nothing vague about it to Doctor Bonfant. He knows she won't walk so that the General won't leave her. "You must have led her a dance to have brought her to that, General." "Not to that extent, Doctor, not to that extent," the General answers. "I loved my wife very much at first. Yes, it seems as odd to me now as my craze over a stamp collection at fifteen. But it's a fact, we had a few happy years—well, when I say happy. . . . Before lapsing into bigotry and fruit-bottling, Emily had quite an amorous disposition. My wife was an opera singer, you know. She bellowed her way through Wagner as a Valkyrie. I married her and made her give up the theatre, to my eternal cost. She was to go on acting for myself alone. A performance at his own expense, lasting for more than twenty years, tends to wear out your spectator. So I set about finding my fun elsewhere, naturally. Chambermaids, waitresses, whatever hole-and-corner capers a man dares to indulge in, who is very closely watched. And I grew old, little by little. First a shade too much stomach, then the paunch advancing as the hair recedes, and the sleeve wound round with more and more gold string. And beneath this fancy dress the heart of an aged youngster still waiting for a chance to give his all. But who's to recognize me underneath the mask?"

As the Doctor, whose own marriage is not an unqualified success, goes to take the invalid's too-normal blood pressure, the General escapes for one of his quick turns around the garden. A maid ushers in a lady visitor. Mlle. de Ste-Euverte, swathed in traveling veils and decked out in furs and feathers, greets the dumfounded General on his return.

According to Mademoiselle, she has arrived "with head held high." She assures him that she is untouched and unsullied despite the hazards of the train ride. A man in her compartment had the temerity to ask her the time. "But," Mlle. de Ste-Euverte tells the adoring General, "I gave him such a look that he took the hint immediately. He even said thank you as if I really had told him the time. . . ." Mademoiselle, however, was perfectly calm, for she was armed. She shows the General a little revolver. The General is touched: "Ghislaine, you have it still?" "Had he made one false move," says Ghislaine, "had he so much as touched the hem of my dress I would have slain him first and myself afterwards—I had to get to you intact," she cries.

Mlle. de Ste.-Euverte has kept herself "intact" these past seventeen years, since the Garrison Ball at Saumur, though not a moment has passed when she was not awaiting the General. Now, with certain evidence in her reticule, she is sure that their long wait is at an end. Romance and sentiment engulf the General; he relives every detail of their meeting at the ball.

GHISLAINE—Oh, the strange enchantment of that waltz, Leon!
GENERAL—The Waltz of the Toreadors.
GHISLAINE—Tra la la, la la la.
GENERAL—Mademoiselle, may I have the pleasure?
GHISLAINE—But sir, you are not on my card.
GENERAL—I will inscribe myself on it officially. Major St. Pé. We have not been introduced but I feel that I have known you all my life.
GHISLAINE (*coyly*)—Why, Major, how bold you are!—Then you took me by the waist and all at once your hand burned me right through your gloves and my dress. From the moment your hand touched my back I no longer heard the music. Everything whirled. . . .

As the couple whirls into a waltz, the General's daughters break into the room. Caught red-handed, the General blusters about his having a dancing lesson. The girls get their new dresses and go off happily; Ghislaine, in altered tones, wonders whether she has aged as much as those once-darling little babies. The General advises her not to add up the years and, taking her hand is his, remembers their meeting seven years ago. "No," corrects Ghislaine, "you're wrong. The whole of 1904 we couldn't meet at all. It was the beginning of her attacks."

A maid next shatters their mood. She comes to announce the latest replacement in chambermaids. "Suffering catfish!" yells the General. "Can't you see I'm busy? I haven't time to go on choosing chambermaids. . . ." But after a second's pause, he asks what she looks like. "A fine-looking girl, sir," the maid assures him, "dark and a little on the plump side." "A little on the plump side . . ." The General savors this last dreamily. "Engage her."

Once more alone with the General, Ghislaine breaks the news that she has come to stay. Armed with love letters written by the General's wife to a man, Ghislaine is sure that this evidence of betrayal will finally enable them to be together. She throws herself on his bosom. "We are free, Leon!" she cries.

GENERAL—Who is it? I demand to know his name!

GHISLAINE—Doctor Bonfant. (*The* DOCTOR *enters, beaming.*)

DOCTOR—General, I am happy to be able to tell you that she is much better today. We chatted for a while and that appeared to soothe her. You see how wrong you are to poke fun at doctoring. It all depends on the doctor, and the way one goes about it.

GENERAL (*icily*)—No need to labor the point, sir. There is a young lady present.

DOCTOR (*turning to Ghislaine in mild surprise*)—I do beg your pardon. (*Bowing.*) Madame.

GHISLAINE (*with infinite nobility*)—Mademoiselle. But not for very long now!

(*The* DOCTOR *straightens, astonished.*)

SCENE II

The General is howling for the Doctor's blood; the Doctor refers to the General's high blood pressure. This distracts him, but the next minute he is all for slapping the Doctor's face. The Doctor thereupon promises to return the slap, and since he is in far better shape than the General, it will be a much harder slap. To make his point, the Doctor lowers his trousers and has the General feel his flat stomach. Touching it, the General says grudgingly: "You're pulling it in." "No," the Doctor answers. "Feel it, it's quite natural. Now look at yours." Undoing his trousers, the General examines his paunch. "Holy Moses!" he exclaims, just as Ghislaine appears in the doorway. "Oh, my God," she cries at this sight, "you're wounded!" Both men hastily pull up their trousers, and the General, clutching his with one hand, propels Ghislaine with the other to the morning room.

Alone again, the two men button themselves and settle down. It is now the General's turn to explain.

GENERAL—Mlle. de Ste-Euverte—a lady descended from one of the noblest houses of Lorraine—is the love of my life, Doctor, and I am hers. I met her at the annual Ball of the Eighth Dragoons at Saumur in 1893, seventeen years ago. She was a girl of the best society, I was a married man. Anything between us was quite out of the question. At the time, owing to my career and the children, I dared not contemplate divorce. And yet we could not give up our love. Seventeen years that's been going on! Mlle. de Ste-Euverte is still a maiden and I am still a prisoner.

DOCTOR—But dammit, General, your career is established, your daughters are grown up, what in Heaven are you waiting for?

GENERAL—I'll tell you a secret, Doctor, a miserable secret. I am a coward.

DOCTOR—Stuff and nonsense, General. You wanted to run me through a minute ago. And what about your oak-leaves and your eighteen wounds?

To the General, battles are simple; but life is different. The Doctor, though sympathetic, advises quick action before it is too late. Ghislaine, feeling the same way, pops back into the room, causing the General to cry edgily: "Dammit all, Ghislaine, you've waited seventeen years, surely you can contain yourself for an extra ten minutes!"

Having borne Emily's cruelty so long, Ghislaine is adamant. Should the General hesitate further, Ghislaine threatens to use the pearl-handled revolver: "I shall end this life within the hour, without ever having known more of love than your vain promises, Leon." Playing for time, he asks her to go back to the morning room, where there are magazines. "Magazines!" cries Ghislaine. "Like at the dentist's! You have wounded me for the first time, my dear." Protesting that he adores her, the General shoves her once more through the door.

All courage gone, the General asks the Doctor to break the ice with his wife. The Doctor reminds him of those letters. Pulling himself together, the General enters his wife's room. She is not there. "What!" exclaims the Doctor. "Is there another way out?" "Through the window," answers the General, "by hanging on to the wisteria." Apparently Emily's condition was no deterrent. She left a letter behind: "I heard everything. Men are all cowards. Whatever they may have said to you, Leon, I have never loved anyone but you. I can walk when I want to. I am going. You will never hear of me again."

The men are alarmed. The Doctor thinks immediately of the railroad crossing where the train will pass any minute; the General thinks of the pond. They both rush out. And Ghislaine, who has overheard everything, thinks of her little pearl-handled revolver.

Calmly dabbing away at a tear or two, Ghislaine first pens a note for the General and props it up among his papers. Then unhurriedly extracting the revolver from her reticule, she presses it to her head and pulls the trigger. Nothing happens. Surprised, Ghislaine snaps it again, blows daintily into the muzzle, and fires. After seventeen years, the revolver has conked out. Throwing it casually to one side, Ghislaine glances at her watch. "Too late for the train," she decides. Since she does not choose to die in the same spot as Emily, she dismisses the idea of the pond. Happily, the window catches her eye, and taking a run for it, she swings over the sill and drops. The secretary, who has been singing in the garden below, hiccups loudly.

A minute later, the secretary enters with the unconscious form of Ghislaine in his arms. Placing her on the couch, he examines her to see whether she has broken any bones. The unconscious Ghislaine, delighted with the touch of his hands, orders: "Leave your hands, Leon—caressing me—or I feel I shall swoon again—your hands quickly—I'm going—" In something of a panic, the secretary obliges readily. Next, finding Leon's hands even gentler than at the Saumur Ball, Ghislaine orders him to kiss her. Though considerably confused, the secretary obliges again. The General, coming in with his unconscious wife slung over his shoulder, finds them tangled in an embrace. Rooted to the spot, he demands an explanation, which proves far from satisfactory. Then foisting his limp rag-doll wife on the secretary, the General throws himself down beside Ghislaine. She does not like his hands; she will not accept his kiss nor accept him as Leon. . . . "Leon kissed me just now, at long last. He is twenty years old. I forbid you to touch me. No one may touch me but him. I am keeping myself."

GENERAL'S WIFE (*coming to, in the* SECRETARY'S *arms*)—Leon!

GENERAL (*picking up* GHISLAINE)—That's done it. The other one will come to in a minute. She mustn't see her here. She'd kill herself a second time.

GENERAL'S WIFE (*clinging to the* SECRETARY'S *neck and screeching*)—Leon, hold me! Kiss me, Leon! You can see I'm dying. Kiss me quickly before I am quite dead!

SECRETARY (*yelling in his panic after the* GENERAL, *who is carrying* GHISLAINE *away*)—This one wants to be kissed before she dies as well! ! ! What am I to do?

GENERAL—You must be out of your mind, my boy. Can't you see they're both delirious? Put Madame down in her room. I am taking this young lady in here.

(*They both go out with their unconscious burdens. The* MAID *comes in with the coffee.*)

ACT II

Having placed both ladies under a sedative, the Doctor and the General exclaim about how peaceful it all is. The General wishes that science would find a way of keeping women permanently asleep —except, perhaps, for a brief spell at night.

The Doctor ascribes the General's woman problem to his having that rare thing, a soul. The General ascribes them to his perpetual fears of loneliness.

GENERAL—My bits of fun, even, do you think they amuse me? They bore me to death. It is my terror of living which sends me scampering after them. When you see them swinging by with their buttocks and their breasts under their dresses you feel I don't know what wild hope surge inside you. But once the dress is off and you have to get down to it! The only thing is that with all these philanderings you get to my age realizing that you have never in your life made love. It's wrong of me to make fun of my secretary. I am an old virgin, Doctor.

DOCTOR—No. You have the sickness, General, that's all.

GENERAL—Which one? I've had them all.

DOCTOR—Those sicknesses are nothing. They can be treated. We have a soul, General. I long denied the phenomenon. I was one of the old school. We did not bother with that subject in my day. I wanted to stick to abscesses and cancers. But now I know. It's in the soul the trouble lies, in nine cases out of ten.

The General would like to know what his soul is demanding of him. The only time that he is not afraid is in the presence of Mlle. de Ste-Euverte. In the sight of his fraud of a wife, his soul so floods him with pity that he is rooted to the spot.

At the door of the morning room, the General murmurs dreamily: "Dear Ghislaine! Dear, sweet, patient Ghislaine! Dear little soldier on half pay! Dear widow! . . . Give her a little less gardenal than the other one, will you?" he begs of the Doctor. "I should so like to console her." Agreeing, the Doctor advises him to take advantage of the arrangement and rehearse his lines for the big scene.

In a rollicking mood, the General now plans to dictate one last chapter to his secretary before taking final and permanent leave of his wife. His daughters, entering with dresses and dressmaker, provide a minor skirmish along the way. "Why, Mme. Dupont-Fredaine!" cries the General. "I'm delighted to see you. Lovely and tempting and swish-swishing as ever!" Kissing her hand, the General continues: "By Jove, what a figure! What allure! Mme. Dupont-Fredaine, you are the loveliest woman in the neighborhood." Mme. Dupont-Fredaine asks him to look at his girls' new dresses, but as the girls simper around, the General sidles up to her: "These repeated refusals are absurd, you know, Emma." "Stop it now," Madame answers, "you are a wicked old wolf. My husband is a friend of yours." "Exactly," finishes the General. "Nobody would take the least exception. Charming! Charming! I really must have a serious talk with you about the cost of these fal-lals, dear lady! Do come for a little stroll around the garden, won't you? I shall present you with a rose. We won't be a moment, girls. Gaston, I leave them in your care, my boy."

The girls, left with the secretary, profess to be madly in love with him. Gaston excuses himself from kissing either one of them, for fear of offending the other. The girls then proceed—for love of him—to pull each other's hair and tear each other's dresses. The secretary yowls for help.

The General, red in the face and annoyed at being interrupted, comes back with Mme. Dupont-Fredaine. Thoroughly impatient with his daughters' confessions of love (and with the secretary, of all people!) he decides things are beginning to get out of hand in his household. Madame, ordered to leave with the girls, defends them: "It's love, General." "That's rich!" he roars. "Love isn't an excuse for everything." With a surreptitious parting slap, Madame retorts: "Naughty fibber! You just told me the very opposite! Good-bye for the moment." With an answering wink, the General murmurs: "See you later, Emma."

The General intends to take Gaston to task for sowing confusion among the young women of his family, and, above all, for kissing Mlle. de Ste-Euverte. The secretary pleads that Mademoiselle mistook him for someone else; she kept calling him "Leon."

GENERAL (*easily*)—Leon? What a coincidence! The name of her intended, no doubt?

SECRETARY—But all the same it was to me she said it.

GENERAL (*bursting out laughing*)—Ha ha, that's a good one! That's very good! So you think one falls in love like that, do you? At first sight and for always? Fiddlesticks! You must gorge yourself on cheap novels!

SECRETARY—No, sir, on the classics, exclusively. But the course of events is frequently quite similar. (*With dignity.*) In any case I intend to confess to this lady when she is once more herself, and offer to make amends.

GENERAL—Confess? Confess what? You will do no such thing. I will not have you confuse the wits of this unfortunate girl. Am I going to have to teach you, by roundly boxing your ears, just what a young girl's honor means? I've seen you already, my lad, with that last little maid we had here. Don't deny it. I tell you I saw you!

SECRETARY—It was she who pursued me, sir. I avoided her. She was always coming up behind me in the passages—

GENERAL—Oh, the little bitch!

SECRETARY—She said she was fed to the teeth with this dump— I quote, of course—and that she absolutely had to have a young one.

The General proposes, as a father might, to instill some necessary principles in Gaston. He first treats of honor. "Honor" is the key to the lengthy parable he tells, of which Gaston completely misses the point. The General resigns himself; he scraps honor quickly and settles for "keeping up appearances." Substituting down-to-earth simile for high-flown parable, the General compares life to a long, tedious, formal family lunch, at which one does one's duty and resists pinching the maid's bottom. There's nothing much left of principle as he concludes: "But the coffee once drunk, down the backstairs and the best of luck! The law of the jungle comes into its own. Dammit, there's no need to be a complete fool. . . ."

Aware that this last might appear as "middle-class hypocrisy," he rounds off his lecture with a few words on "ideals." Using a buoy as the ideal, and the ocean with its dangerous currents as life, the General directs the secretary to use the regulation breaststroke in swimming towards it—to keep the buoy always in his sight. No one will expect more of him than that.

So much for ideals. "But does one never reach the lifebuoy, General?" asks the secretary. "Never," says the General, conceding that a few fanatics try, and deluge everybody in their attempt. Finally the secretary has something to say: "I would rather try to go fast and drown." Overwhelmed by memories of Lieutenant St. Pé, the General agrees completely, and feeling he was only doing his duty in counseling otherwise, now urges the secretary to wait for the right girl—and, having found her, for them to go at once toward the lifebuoy side by side. . . . "The only proper way to swim is two by two." And sensing that he himself may well drown, the General goes to the wife who has been screaming for him.

The secretary, bearing in mind the General's "at once," departs for the arms of Mlle. de Ste-Euverte.

Scene II

Determined to thrash things out, the General enters his wife's bedroom. From her quilted bed, with its masses of pillows to bolster her up, his wife hurls back epithets and accusations. Referring to her attempt at suicide, the General says that, like everything else she does, it was absurd. At that, she shrieks of how ill she is, and he tells her: "One has to be an idiot like myself, Madam, to go on believing in your aches and pains by this time. As for your poor ailing legs, thank God we'll hear no more of those for a bit. I strongly suspect you of stretching them in your room every night. They helped you keep your balance mighty well down the wisteria and over to the railway line this morning." Not in the least disconcerted, Madame launches an attack of her own. She demands of the General what he has to complain of: "While I lie here, racked with pain, you who can wander fancy free on your great fat legs, where do you go, eh?" "From my study to the garden," he answers, "at your beck and call every ten minutes." "And what," she hoots, "is there in the garden? Answer me that, you pig, you satyr, you lascivious goat!" But Madame needs no answer: she supplies it herself. On the other side of the privet hedge are the breasts of Madame Tardieu as she leans over her flower beds; and at the bottom of the garden, there are little convent girls passing by.

GENERAL—You're wandering, Madam. They say good morning to me and I say good morning back.

WIFE—And what about prize-giving day, at which you always manage to officiate, you old faun? When you kiss them, red as a lobster in your uniform!

GENERAL—It's the custom.

WIFE—What you're thinking about isn't the custom and you know it! You tickle their bosoms with your decorations as you lean over them. Don't say you don't. I've seen you.

GENERAL—If nothing worse happens to them as they're growing up we'll make May Queens out of them!

WIFE—Queens of the May, indeed! You've always been ready to officiate on May Day too. Last year's one, that hussy, as you kissed her, you whispered something in her ear. It was reported to me.

GENERAL (*chaffingly*)—I whispered something? You don't say so?

WIFE—You arranged to meet her, I know.   Besides I've seen her since.   She's pregnant.

GENERAL—Nonsense, she's put on weight, that's all.

WIFE—My maids are putting on weight too, one after the other.

The General changes the subject to the love letters that his wife has written.   She twists his words; when the General manages to get down to the letters again, Madame accuses him of ransacking her drawers.   She demands to see the letters; when she fails, she flops back on her pillows.   "Very well," she says, "if you really have those letters in your wallet, there can be nothing more between us but an ocean of contempt.   You may go.   I am sleepy. I'm asleep."

His wife lies with her eyes closed, and nothing will make her open them.   The General begins to lose his head.   He shakes her, he slaps her, he forces her eyelids up.   "Come to your senses, damn you!" he cries.   "What new game are you playing now?"   She's not beyond mentioning her heart.   Though dismissing this as the nonsense she uses only for big scenes, the General drops to his knees and forages frantically among her storehouse of bottles for the right heart medicine.   Finding a bottle with no dropper, he starts pouring it down her throat.   "Unclench your teeth, my love," he pleads, "unclench your teeth, damn you.   It's dripping all over you. . . . What's the matter with you?   Your pulse is all right.   There's no getting away from that.   I'll give you your injection."

Madame plans a deathbed scene with her children about her. The General, half beside himself, is ready to call the Doctor.   His wife remembers how he used to take her—his "little girl"—naked in his arms and bite her all over.   Madame is plaintive.   The General is more and more embarrassed.   He pleads his years and loss of teeth.   Up Madame bounces.

WIFE—You've teeth enough for others, you mealy-mouthed old fraud!   You can talk about those letters which were never even sent.   I have evidence of another sort, in a trinket box underneath my mattress, letters both sent and received, where there's no question of your having lost your teeth.   Letters in which you play the young man for another's benefit—and there you flatter yourself incidentally, my poor Leon—for apart from your summary prowess with the maids, you needn't think you're capable of much in that line either—

GENERAL—Be quiet, Madam!   What do you know about it?

WIFE—I know as much as all women left unsatisfied.   Learn first

Mildred Natwick and Ralph Richards

"The Waltz of the Toreadors"

to satisfy one woman, to be a man in her bed, before you go scampering into the beds of others.

GENERAL—So I have never been a man in your bed, Madam, is that it?

WIFE—Soon weary, my friend, soon asleep, and when for a wonder you had a little energy, soon replete. We would both close our eyes in the bed, but while you performed your little task picturing the Lord knows whom, you don't imagine, do you, that it was you I thought about?

GENERAL—How vulgar you are, Madam—vulgar and shameless. However, if that was so, why the reproaches and the scenes, why so many tears for so long?

WIFE—Because you belong to me, Leon! You are mine like my house, mine like my jewels, mine like my furniture, mine like your name.

GENERAL—And is that what you understand by love?

WIFE (*in a great and frightful cry, standing on her bed in her nightshirt, a nightmarish figure*)—Yes!

He will never escape her. Even in death, Madame is determined to pursue him. She is his wife. "I hate the sight and sound of you!" the General cries. "And I'll tell you something else that's stronger even than my hatred and disgust. I am dying of boredom, Madam, by your side."

Madame is just as bored, Madame hates him just as much. She is about to embark on the sacrifices she has made for this creature who bores her, when he demands a divorce. The General tells an incredulous Madame of the lovely creature who has waited for him for seventeen years. "I stayed out of respect for your grief," he says, "and pity for your illness, which I long took to be genuine, Madam." With a horrendous whoop, his wife screams: "What a fool you are! Do you think I couldn't dance if I wanted to?" Demanding him to look at her, she leaps out of bed; and dancing a few steps, invites him to come dance with her. "Let me go! You're mad," he cries, "go back to bed." But dancing her ghoulish dance, his wife asks if he can remember the ball at Saumur seventeen years ago. While the General was waltzing to the Waltz of the Toreadors, his wife left the ball. She was escorted home by a strange young man who became her lover.

GENERAL—What? You have had a lover, Madam, and it was at that Saumur Ball that you made his acquaintance? A man who had merely helped you find our carriage, a complete stranger?—

I won't even ask you his rank. How horrible! But I'd like to believe that you had a few doubts, dear God, a few misgivings, before taking such a step. I fondly hope you did at least wait a little?

WIFE—Of course, my dear. I was a respectable woman. I waited.

GENERAL—How long?

WIFE—Three days.

GENERAL (*exploding*)—Holy suffering rattlesnakes, I waited seventeen years, Madam, and I'm waiting still!

WIFE—And when that one was posted, I forget where—to the devil, to the Far East—I took another just as handsome, and another, and again another, and so on before I grew too old and there would only be you left who would have me.

GENERAL—But dammit, if you were untrue to me why the tears and the reproaches—why the immense heartaches and the torment —why this illness?

WIFE—To keep you, Leon. To keep you for always because I am your wife. For I do love you, Leon, on top of everything. I hate you for all the harm you did to me, but I love you—not tenderly, you fool, not with seventeen years of waiting and letter-writing—not for the bliss of being in your arms at night—we have never made love together, you poor wretch, and you know it—not for your conversation—you bore me—not for your rank either, nor your money—I've been offered more—I love you because you are mine, my object, my thing, my hold-all, my garbage bin—

She starts pursuing him. "No!" the General keeps shrieking. "Yes!" his wife keeps answering. "Come now, darling, dance with me. The Waltz of the Toreadors, the last waltz, with me this time." He cringes in a corner, then suddenly stretches out his arms and grips her throat: "Phantasmagoria!!" he cries.

ACT III

The Doctor reports that not only is the General's wife far from dead, she is far from giving up. As an old hand at opera, she found her husband's violence perfectly correct in the situation; she is even somewhat flattered.

To add to his misery, the General has discovered that Mlle. de Ste-Euverte and his secretary had wandered off, hand in hand, two hours before; and hearing of this, his two daughters had gone off to drown themselves. This last so little disturbs the General that he sends his gardener to see how they are doing. But the total glum effect has the General feeling that his life is tumbling about his ears. "Dear God," he cries, "how will it all end?" The Doctor tells him: "As in real life—or in the theatre, in the days when plays *were* plays—a contrived dénouement, not too gloomy on the face of it, and which really doesn't fool a soul, and then a little later—curtain. I speak for you as well as myself. Your blood pressure's up to 250 and my gall bladder is a bag of stones. Make way for the young! May they commit the self-same follies and die of the same diseases."

Whereupon a maid announces that dinner is being ruined, and Father Ambrose who is waiting to see the General has already drunk far too much wine. What the Father has to say is for the General's ears alone. "It's a secret," the maid says, "between Providence and him." "Well," snaps the General, "tell them both to wait."

Ghislaine and the secretary enter presently with news of their own. "Courage, Lieutenant!" says the Doctor as he leaves the room. "Something tells me this is going to be your last campaign." With remarkable self-assurance, Gaston exits, allowing Ghislaine a moment alone with the General.

As at the Saumur Ball, Ghislaine has fallen in love at first sight, but with a difference. The secretary has made love to her; she now belongs to him. From now on, no one else may touch her. And the General should know, Ghislaine reminds him, how faithful she can be. Gaston's touch, his jealousy, his companionship, all thrill and please her. Gaston has wit, too. "He told me," says Ghislaine, "that we must swim abreast towards the ideal as if towards a lifebuoy, and that the proper way to swim is two by two."

GENERAL—I might have known it! Did he also tell you that life was one long family lunch, with napkin rings, forks of different shapes and sizes, and a bell-push under the table?

GHISLAINE—What are you suggesting, spiteful? He says poetic things. He says life is but a holiday, a ball. . . .

GENERAL (*with an involuntary cry of pain*)—A ball!

GHISLAINE—Yes, isn't that a sweet idea? A ball of a night, and we must make haste, he says, before the lamps go out. I loved him from the very first, I told you so, but I had got so into the way of thinking love was nothing but one endless vigil, that when he asked me to be his I wanted to cry—later! Tomorrow! Do you know what he said?

GENERAL (*in a strangled voice*)—No.

GHISLAINE (*triumphantly*)—He said, "At once! At once, my

darling!" Now who but he would say a thing like that? At once!
It's wonderful. I never guessed that one could have something at
once!

The minute is up. Gaston and the Doctor return. The General
is after Gaston's blood. He demands immediate action. To pull
his crossed swords off the wall, the General piles up furniture and
climbs to the top. There is a hitch; the swords can't be budged.
The Doctor cries: "General, it would be murder. He's a child."

GENERAL (*still struggling to get the swords down*)—There are no
children any more. If he's a child let him go and play with his
hoop. Holy suffering bloodstained billicans, who's the double-dyed
blockhead who put up these swords! ! ! (*Calling unthinkingly.*)
Gaston!
SECRETARY (*running up*)—Yes, sir?
GENERAL—Give me a hand, my boy.

Discovering Gaston beside him on the chair, the General yowls
for him to get down. Then, swordless, the General thinks of a simpler solution: he will have Gaston's guardian prevent the marriage.
The twenty-year-old can't marry without the curé's consent.

The summoned Father Ambrose comes into the room bursting
with news. He manages to tell the General his secret: In 1890, in
Montauban, lived a dressmaker named Lea. In 1890 the Eighth
Dragoons were on maneuvers, and a dashing, fickle captain took
over Lea. "My dear fellow," interrupts the General, "why of course!
Lea! A ravishing girl, Doctor. A dark-haired filly with eyes a man
could drown in—reserved, prudish almost, but in bed of an evening
—oh, my dear fellow . . . !"

All that was twenty years and nine months ago, and Gaston, exactly twenty in strawberry time, may claim the General as his father.
While Gaston throws his arms about the General, Ghislaine rhapso-
dizes from the sidelines. The General's dripping daughters now enter to meet their new brother. Finding the role he has been playing untenable, the General gives up: he grants the young couple
permission to marry and dismisses the whole crowd.

Only the Doctor remains. The General cries softly: "Lieutenant
St. Pé. I want to live. I want to love. I want to give my heart
as well, dear God!" "General," the Doctor advises, "nobody wants
it any more. Let it unswell quietly, that old over-tender sponge.
You should have sown fewer wild oats and had the courage to hurt
while there was still time. Life should be led like a cavalry charge,
General. They ought to have told you that at Saumur. My poor

old friend, shall I tell you the moral of this story?   One must never understand one's enemy or one's wife.   One must never understand anyone for that matter, or one will die of it.   Heigh-ho, I must go home to Madame Bonfant and her scenes.   I think you will do very nicely on your own."   And the Doctor goes.

Mme. St. Pé screeches at the General not to do anything while she naps.   He answers automatically, then in the gathering twilight reaches for his service revolver.   "Lieutenant St. Pé.   Graduated second from Saumur!   Take aim!   Steady!   Fire!"   Out of the dusk comes the new maid.   The revolver is replaced in its holster, and the General puts his arm around the girl instead.   With a promise of a rose from the garden, he murmurs: "That's a good girl.   It's nicer like this, don't you think?   Not that it means anything, but still, one feels less lonely, in the dark."   The absurd couple walks into the garden.

THE POTTING SHED

A Play in Three Acts

By Graham Greene

[Graham Greene *graduated from Oxford University and then worked briefly on the Nottingham Journal. He later became sub-editor of the London Times and while working there wrote his first novel, "The Man Within." The same year he became a Catholic and married a Catholic girl. Many of his novels, including "The Orient Express," "This Gun for Hire," "Confidential Agent" and "The Third Man," have been made into motion pictures. His works are usually religious in theme and somewhat unorthodox in treatment. His play "The Living Room" (produced on Broadway in 1954) was hailed by British reviewers as "the best first play of a generation."*]

IN the outmoded, book-lined living room of "Wild Grove," a one-time country house now overpowered by a neighboring factory, a fussy elderly man paces back and forth. He is rehearsing a passage from the eulogy he has written.

Thirteen-year-old Anne slips in unnoticed through the garden window and watches Dr. Baston. ". . . unworthy of him if, if—" Dr. Baston consults his pages, looks around, picks up an ashtray from a table, and continues—"we did not recognize that these ashes that at his request I now resign to the river and the fields and the earth he loved—" Dr. Baston swings the ashtray—"are all that remains. . . . Now that the immense spaces of the empty universe, of uninhabited planets and cooling stellar systems have taken the place of the Christian God, we have Callifer to thank for a human life worthy of courageous Man. To the Christian superstition of eternal life, he bravely countered with the truth, Eternal Death." Curious, Anne inquires if her grandfather has died. She not only startles Dr. Baston, but is asked in turn a number of questions she does not wish

"The Potting Shed": Copyright © 1956, 1957, by Graham Greene. Reprinted by permission of The Viking Press, Inc., New York, N. Y. All rights strictly reserved. All inquiries should be addressed to author's representative: Monica McCall, Inc., 667 Madison Avenue, New York 21, N. Y.

to answer. Anne warns the doctor to be careful: "You see, I've made a vow that for one month I'll speak the exact truth. A lunar month, not a calendar. There are still eighteen days to go." Baston would like to know what happens afterwards. "I shall tell lies again like everybody else," Anne says. She repeats: "Is grandfather dead yet?" "He's making a wonderful fight," Baston says. "So would you, wouldn't you?" Anne retorts. "It can't be very nice, being dead. . . ."

Anne's grandmother, Anne's father, and the doctor are all with the dying man upstairs, while her Aunt Sara, according to Anne, is "sniveling" outside in the garden. Whether this is for the dying man or lost love, Anne cannot decide. She also cannot understand why this ex-aunt should be sent for when her Uncle James was not. Having been given the telegrams to send off, she knows there was none for him. She asks Dr. Baston if her Uncle James was criminal, wicked, or mad. Baston answers impatiently: "Of course not." Anne is glad then that she sent a telegram to Uncle James herself.

She has upset and shocked Dr. Baston. He feels he must warn her grandmother. Anne ponders the word "warn." "He's not wanted here," Dr. Baston says. "Nobody wants him here." Sara, entering from the garden, wouldn't mind his coming: this good-looking, though disappointed, woman of thirty-six feels that James has the right to see his father. Sara can't understand why they have always hated James so. She, his ex-wife, doesn't.

BASTON (*hedging*)—It's not hate. They never got along, that's all. Even when he was a boy . . .

SARA—I would have loved a child of mine whatever he did. (*A pause.*) Do you know, they only got fond of me after the divorce? They wrote to me so kindly then. But as long as James and I were together I was infectious. A mother generally defends her son, doesn't she?—but when I left him, I won his mother's approval.

BASTON—I shan't tell Mrs. Callifer yet. Perhaps he'll have the sense to keep away. For your sake, too, it would be painful.

SARA—Would it? I suppose so. It's very bitter when a man leaves you for nothing. I wouldn't have minded so much if he'd been in love with another woman. I could bear being beaten by someone younger, someone lovely. But I was beaten by a bed-sitting room in Nottingham. That's all he left me for.

Unwarned, Mrs. Callifer enters. Her handsome, erect figure suggests complete control, though the strain she is under shows in her restless manner. She glances, much to his embarrassment, at Baston's eulogy. "It reads very well, Fred," Mrs. Callifer says. . . . "Cooling stellar systems."

BASTON—Those are *his* words.

MRS. CALLIFER—We had a royalty statement last week. They only send them once a year now. They'd sold three copies of *The Cosmic Fallacy* for export.

BASTON—Anyway it's in print still.

MRS. CALLIFER—Oh, yes. At that rate it will be in print longer than we shall be. Christianity is the fashion now.

BASTON—A passing fashion.

MRS. CALLIFER—Of course. But how he hated those sentimental myths, virgin births, crucified Gods. (*She is thinking of something else and talks to distract herself.*) Just now, from Henry's room, I thought I heard a dog barking. Did you?

Mrs. Callifer has always detested dogs: "Parodies of men and women. I hate parodies. We both always hated parodies." Making an effort to be detached, she comments favorably on Sara's flower arrangements, complains that the *Times* hasn't rung up, and dismisses the *Rational Review* that has. She allows herself the hope that her husband may become conscious just once more, and then see all the faces he has loved. "You, Fred, especially," says Mrs. Callifer. This being too near emotion, she veers away. Picking up Baston's papers, she mentions how she appreciates his taking all this trouble, how she had tried to persuade her husband to alter his will about the ceremony. "The River Wandle is not how he remembers it. Too much pollution from the dye factory, and the housing development has ruined the fields." Baston assures her that he and John found a spot where only the chimneys can be seen. Mrs. Callifer tries to say that it doesn't really matter. "It's just a gesture, scattering ashes. People are so sentimental sometimes—about death —wishing to be buried together." She can't quite manage this; her voice breaks; she begins to rearrange the flowers in a vase.

Sara, breaking the silence, is sure that she too heard a dog. Mrs. Callifer starts talking of slipcovers and flower shows when Anne, sliding through the garden window, grabs at the first book that comes to hand and hopes she won't be noticed.

The old question of *where has she been* pops up again. Trying as usual to avoid it, she tells her grandmother sullenly that she has been to the potting shed. And, if they must know why, she was shutting up a secret dog that, if they must know that too, belongs to Sara's ex-husband, James.

John, Anne's solid-looking widower father, now enters: he has seen

James. Mrs. Callifer says stiffly: "If he's here, well—of course—naturally—he's welcome."

Appearing nervous and ill as ease, James comes through the garden window. Though a good five years younger than John, he might be the elder. He is a shabbily dressed stranger in his own home. When Mrs. Callifer says she's glad he's come, James says: "I didn't mean to be a nuisance. I just thought if Father—" "Of course you're not a nuisance," his mother answers. "We telegraphed for you." James knows better even before his mother refuses him permission to see his father. After an unhappy pause, and a few stilted remarks, Mrs. Callifer, John, and Dr. Baston find excuses to leave.

Left alone with Sara, James blurts out: "It wasn't true. I had the true story from Anne. I was to be left out. Why? One's father's death is usually supposed to be important." Sara suggests that it might not be very important if you believe in nothing afterwards.

James implores her to tell him what is wrong with him, why they keep him away. He concedes that he wasn't much of a husband—but he wasn't bad. He wasn't bad, Sara admits readily, he just wasn't interested. . . . "You pretended very well and very kindly. Even in bed you pretended. I used to think there was another woman somewhere—" But then she discovered there was nobody, and thought how bored James had been.

SARA—I took a lover after you went. He didn't pretend. And then one night I woke and saw him sleeping beside me, content—and I remembered you with your eyes open, thinking of something else, and I didn't want him any more. I didn't love him any more.

JAMES—What's the good of talking importantly about love? It doesn't last like a book or a tune. It goes out with the breath, and we can always snuff that out, can't we? We're not worth loving.

SARA—Then nothing is.

JAMES—And I love nothing.

SARA (bitterly)—You do indeed. In the night you'd wake love Nothing. You went looking for Nothing everywhere. When you came in at night I could see you had been with Nothing all day. I was jealous of Nothing, as though it was a woman; and now you sleep with Nothing every night.

James had hoped that if he saw his father now, at the end, he would tell him what was wrong. Sara thinks she knows. When Mrs. Callifer heard James was coming, she appeared afraid. "Afraid of what I'd do?" James asks. "Afraid of what you are," Sara answers. According to James, he is simply a middle-aged newspaperman who goes regularly to the office on the night shift and shares.

lodgings with a fellow reporter and the dog he brought along here today. He had forgotten that his mother hated dogs, but, after all, seeing her so seldom, how should he remember?

James, in fact, can remember nothing. "Absolutely nothing. Until I was ill, just before they sent me away to school at fourteen. Lying in bed with a sore throat. A dim light burning, and a nurse —a very kind nurse—bringing me soup. I thought she was an angel. I'd seen a picture of one once, I suppose, in a shop."

Sara, loving him, says softly that she would come to live with him in Nottingham. "Sara," James says, coming behind her and putting his hands over her eyes, "I could always talk to you better in the dark. Sara, I simply don't know what love is. What is it?" "It's what I feel now," she answers. "But," James tells her, "if I took my hands away and we saw each other, I'd see—a want. Isn't there a love that just exists and doesn't want? My father's dying. He has nothing to hope for, any more, for ever. When he looks at me, don't you think I might see—just love? No claim, no hope, no want. Whisky taken neat."

James is not to see his father. Mrs. Callifer, calling for all the others to go quickly to her husband's bedside, again refuses James permission. "He mustn't have a shock—now," Mrs. Callifer says. Bracing herself for the plain truth, his mother tells James: "I don't want you to see him." He starts for the door, saying he is going to anyway, but Mrs. Callifer shuts it and stands blocking it.

MRS. CALLIFER—I don't want to be harsh. That's why I wanted to let you know afterwards. But he's got to die in peace.

JAMES—Why should I destroy his peace?

MRS. CALLIFER (*pleadingly*)—I love him, James. I want so much to see the last of him. Promise me you won't move from here.

JAMES—No! (*He shakes his head.*)

MRS. CALLIFER—Then I stay. (*She leans wearily against the door.*)

JAMES—Mother, if you love me—

MRS. CALLIFER—I love him more.

JAMES—Give me one reason. (*She doesn't answer, but she is crying.*) All right. You've won, Mother. I promise not to come. (MRS. CALLIFER *goes through the door, leaving her son behind.*)

SCENE II

Two evenings later, the men are gathered, whisky in hand, around a table, going over the odds and ends that Henry Callifer had collected. Anne is occupied in outstaying her bedtime.

A large number of books on the table appear to be visitors' books, filled with such names as Wells, Bertrand Russell, and Dr. Baston. The particular names don't catch James' eye so much as the general sense of the past. "August third to eighth, 1919. Do you remember that visit?" he asks Dr. Baston. James can recall nothing of the cricket game with his father that Dr. Baston remembers so happily. Picking up another book, James tries another date: "Nineteen twenty-five—that was the year I was ill, the year I went away to school. Who's William Callifer?"

BASTON—Don't you even remember your own uncle?

JAMES—No. Didn't he get a telegram either—or is he dead? (ANNE *looks up sharply*.)

JOHN—Father never had much to do with him.

JAMES (*turning the pages*)—He was here for three days that autumn.

BASTON—It was the last time. He behaved rather badly.

JOHN—It was bad enough to have a convert in the family. But when he became a priest . . .

JAMES—I'm glad I'm not the only pariah among the Callifers. (*He puts the book down*.)

JOHN—Bertrand Russell again. I hope he was worth his meal ticket. (ANNE *closes her book and comes over*.)

Reminding James to take water to his dog, Anne says her goodnights. Obviously uneasy, James tries in turn to have Anne go to the potting shed for him. She has splendid reasons for refusing. "Good-night, Anne," says Dr. Baston. "It's a good thing when a sad day ends." It didn't seem so very sad to Anne. She thought it downright amusing when James' dog, looking for his master, disrupted the ceremony in the Long Meadow. She thought it funny that a startled Dr. Baston dropped the ashes before he could consign them to the river. Dr. Baston is not amused.

After Anne leaves, James thinks of bed, but is loathe to put down the book with William Callifer's name in it. He wonders at Callifer's being a priest. Dr. Baston informs him that William Callifer is a very drunken priest. "How unlike a Callifer!" says James. "Well, I'm going to bed." Again he is told to take water to the potting shed; again he seems strangely evasive. This time he decides that the dog can do without water until morning. The dog's howl has John cry, "Oh, for God's sake, James, do something. He'll keep everybody awake." As James goes unwillingly into the hall, John comments: "He hasn't changed. Always difficult . . ."

Taking a last glance at the names of Henry Callifer's distinguished guests before discarding them as of no great value, John and Dr. Baston look up to see Mrs. Callifer enter. Dressed for bed, but unable to sleep, she has come in search of a book to make her drowsy. She chooses one of Dr. Baston's, dedicated to Henry Callifer, "a great leader and a great friend." For Mrs. Callifer, this doesn't ring true any longer.

BASTON—I don't follow you.

MRS. CALLIFER—How could you, Fred? But for nearly fifty years I've looked after his laundry, I've seen to his household. I've paid attention to his—allergies. He wasn't a leader. I can see that now. He was someone I protected. And now I'm unemployed. Please go to bed, both of you, and leave me alone.

JOHN (*standing up*)—You have your family, Mother.

MRS. CALLIFER—You don't need protection, John. You're like me, a professional protector. It wasn't what I intended to be. But men either form us with their strength or they form us with their weakness. They never let us be.

BASTON—Mary, you mustn't—

MRS. CALLIFER—Poor James had to suffer. We did him a great wrong, Henry and I. Why shouldn't he know—as much as we know?

JOHN—You've never told me anything.

MRS. CALLIFER (*ignoring him*)—I don't want your empty spaces, Fred. I don't want anything except Henry. Henry alive. Somehow. Somewhere.

Not yet strong enough to listen to sympathy, Mrs. Callifer asks them to leave her to herself. She would like to wait a while before facing that large, empty room upstairs. Baston kisses her and, going out, says absentmindedly that he will look in on Henry. He stops aghast. Mrs. Callifer reassures him that something much the same had happened to her.

BASTON—Mistakes like that are a kind of immortality. You remember Samuel Butler's sonnet:

> "Yet meet we shall, and part, and meet again,
> Where dead men meet, on lips of living men."

As long as there are you and I—and his books.

MRS. CALLIFER—Yes, three copies for export. There was once a Callifer Club, do you remember?

BASTON—Yes, Mary, I was going to write to Macmillan's and suggest a biography, an intimate biography with letters. . . .

Mrs. Callifer advises him to wait till he's asked. Baston remembers that after Henry Callifer's first bad illness they had suggested a biography. That, Mrs. Callifer remarks, was thirty years ago.

Mrs. Callifer sits on in the dark except for the reading lamp by her chair. Finding it impossible to concentrate, she drops the book to her lap as James enters through the garden window.

In the semi-darkness a certain gentleness comes over both mother and son, as if both had shed thirty years. James, putting down the bowl of water which out of fear he had been unable to give to the dog in the shed, comes to sit at her feet. He tries to tell her what happened: "I didn't want to go. I was frightened before I left the house, just as though I knew someone was waiting for me, among the laurels, on the path to the potting shed." "My poor James," says Mrs. Callifer.

The constraint between the two seems to have melted away, and yet, when James begs her to tell him what he did all those years ago that was so horrible, Mrs. Callifer replies: "You are imagining things." The truth will have to be found elsewhere. Mrs. Callifer insists that she is too old to help with it. James says that he's already looked for it in some very strange places: he has been making weekly visits to a doctor for injections of methedrine, to make him talk.

MRS. CALLIFER—What good does that do?

JAMES—None yet. I tell him how my marriage broke and about my childhood, all I can remember. How my parents avoided me. Don't we have to learn love from our parents, like we learn to walk? You taught me to walk, but I've no idea what love is.

MRS. CALLIFER—You're wrong, James. You had love, so much love, my dear, until—(*She stops.*)

JAMES—Until what?

Mrs. Callifer pleads being tired, that it's been buried now so long that she doesn't know what it would look like, that she still must protect Henry: "Can't I be loyal to him for a few hours?" "It won't affect him," James says. "How do we know?" asks Mrs. Callifer. "I don't," snaps James, "I thought you did. . . ." The old bitterness has come back. James gets to his feet, demanding why the child doesn't deserve the same protection as the father. In the accusation he hurls at his mother's bowed and weeping head, James associates something with a toy spade. With a whimper of pain, Mrs. Callifer says that he was six when he had the toy spade, that he was so happy with it. . . .

Excited, but also fearful, James realizes that he has never remembered anything as far back as that before. Just as the door to his memory might open, Mrs. Callifer asks his permission to leave. "We can talk again—one day," she says.

Mulling over his small discovery, James has company. In her self-appointed role of detective, Anne has been outside, listening to everything. She confesses that she, too, was afraid to take the water to the potting shed. Her fear is based on something that she "overheard" the gardener say one day: "He was talking about Potter, the gardener they used to have here years ago. He said, 'I always thought Mr. Callifer was pleased when old Potter passed on.' He meant died, you know. The other man said why, and Willis—he's the gardener now—said, 'I reckon it was because he was here when that thing happened. He saw it all. Right here. Something shocking, it was.'" "Something shocking," James repeats. Anne expects it was hushed up.

JAMES—But it needn't have anything to do with me. I couldn't have done anything very terrible. Not at that age.

ANNE—He said, "Poor Master James."

JAMES—I remember nothing. Nothing. I don't look like someone who'd do anything as shocking as that, do I?

ANNE (*looking at him carefully before replying*)—No. You don't look like that, but I don't suppose people usually do. Everything is possible, isn't it?

ACT II

A month later, Dr. Kreuzer has hurried to James' barren, dreary Nottingham lodgings in search of his patient and the pills he had taken from his office. Deeply concerned over James' state of mind, Dr. Kreuzer is trying to find out where he may be from his roommate, Corner. To the doctor's great relief, James returns.

Obviously still excited from the methedrine injection, James fences with the doctor. Corner gives him a telegram announcing that his mother and Anne will stop in between trains. Saying, "She always makes me feel like a cub reporter," Corner gets out of the way.

Dr. Kreuzer and James are left alone. After a short silence, the doctor confesses: "I had a sense that I failed you today." James wishes no further questioning: "I've talked myself dry. Six months of talking. It hasn't got us far. Perhaps what I really need is action." He plays deliberately with the pills, his new toy. "There's no point in the spade," James says. "Every child has one. Or so I've read. I've read a lot about childhood. It helped to fill the gap."

James responds, however, to Dr. Kreuzer's careful questioning.

He tells of the imaginary childhood he had made up for himself, but his word associations lead from pictures on imagined seed packets straight to the potting shed. "In what book did you read about the potting shed?" Dr. Kreuzer asks. Agitated, James admits that it might be a real potting shed: "And a month ago I began to walk down the laurel path towards it. It was dark. I was carrying water for my dog. And I didn't have the courage even to come within sight of the door. Father, can't you tell me?" "You called me father," says Dr. Kreuzer. "So I did," James says, "but he's dead and he'll never tell me now."

Kreuzer believes that there is nothing human which somehow, with patience, can't be recalled.

JAMES—And do you believe in anything that isn't human?
DR. KREUZER—No, I don't believe. Sometimes I doubt my disbelief.
JAMES—What could have happened that was so terrible it wiped out all memory? I was a boy, doctor. What a boy can do is very limited.
KREUZER—Perhaps it was something done to you.
JAMES—Then why the disgrace? Oh, I know some parents make a fuss about the little sexual games children play. Not my parents, though. It can't have been anything like that. They were never worried by anything human.
KREUZER—That word human again.
JAMES—Well, God was taboo. My father had killed that superstition for his generation. Poor Father! I'm glad he didn't realize how it was beginning to return. Like memory. We were not allowed ghost stories, either. Do you believe in ghosts, Doctor?
KREUZER—No.
JAMES—Or the soul?
KREUZER—I've never understood what the word means.

James is sure that if he had a child, he wouldn't forbid fairy stories; they might develop the sense of hope. James had never wanted children. "To have a child you need hope," he tells Kreuzer. If he were only able to settle for the simple kind of hope all around him . . . Why isn't that enough for him? What happened to him in the potting shed?

For six months Kreuzer has been trying to help him answer that question, and James hasn't furnished him a simple clue. They always get to the door of the shed and can't get through it. Once more Kreuzer asks him to improvise, to tell any story and mention anything that comes into his head.

This time James tells of the dark walk and the door that was never painted and how he kept his spade in there among the real spades, so that it seemed no longer a toy. "But that was years before," he says. "Something made a pattern on the path as I walked, like a snake crawling beside me." He reaches the potting shed door and his unhappiness leaves him. He's only frightened. But what was waiting for him, he doesn't know. The door shuts it all out. Kreuzer asks him: "And when you came out again?" "I don't believe," says James, "I ever came out. Sometimes I think I'm still lying there."

Since James is afraid to remember, Kreuzer says he can't cure him: he can only cure the irrational, and James may have good, if unremembered, reason for his melancholia. James seems to jump at this opportunity of giving up, but Kreuzer refuses to give up a patient, ever.

The doorbell rings below. James knows that his mother has arrived. Kreuzer holds out his hand; James pretends to be perplexed. "You acted very quickly," says Kreuzer. "I suppose it was when I turned to my telephone. I forgot to examine my desk before you left. My tablets, please." "Suppose I won't give them to you?" James asks. As casually as possible, Kreuzer remarks that he will only get a stomach ache: the tablets are not poisonous. "Then why did you follow me here?" says James. Kreuzer tells him: "I couldn't allow a patient to leave me ever again in that state of mind."

As Corner shows in Mrs. Callifer, James hands back the bottle.

Mrs. Callifer, rather upset from losing Anne at the station, feels she is interrupting. She hopes her son is not ill.

JAMES—He's not that kind of doctor. He makes me talk, that's all.

MRS. CALLIFER—Is that supposed to be a good thing nowadays?

KREUZER (*picking up his case*)—Your generation believed in letting sleeping dogs lie, Mrs. Callifer.

MRS. CALLIFER—Was that so wrong?

KREUZER—You were clever at keeping them asleep, but sometimes they wake up your children.

Kreuzer adds as he goes: "Mrs. Callifer, if only you would help him."

"What did he mean? How could I help?" asks Mrs. Callifer. "What were you talking about before I came?" "About a potting shed," James answers, "where something happened. Mother, why did you leave my uncle out as well as me when my father died?"

Saying that there was a quarrel years ago, Mrs. Callifer wishes he would stop digging into the past; she wants to be let alone.

The truant Anne now arrives, doing her best to slip in unnoticed. This is not her day to answer questions either. But she has something up her sleeve: she's been playing detective again. Yesterday, Anne sent another one of her telegrams. This was addressed to Mrs. Potter, gardener Potter's widow. It read: "Dying. You can relieve a mind in torment. Come teatime Thursday." She had signed it "Callifer."

The bell rings. Mrs. Callifer doesn't want it answered. James is trembling. The bell rings three times. Corner announces the woman and is told to bring her in. James offers to send Mrs. Potter away if his mother will reveal the truth herself. "Can't I keep a promise to the dead?" repeats Mrs. Callifer, as the scared old lady comes into the room.

Mrs. Potter answers James' questions. She remembers Father Callifer as a fine young man. "You and he were very close," she says. "That is, before—" Mrs. Potter stops, hedges, says she promised Potter she never would tell and never has. If his mother doesn't want him to know . . . "Weren't we friends in those days, Mrs. Potter?" James asks. "You were always my favorite, Master James," she replies. "It wasn't any fault of yours what happened. You were a dear boy to me. If your father had let you alone . . ."

Suddenly Mrs. Callifer is ready to talk about it all. James had an accident in the potting shed: "You slipped and fell. You were unconscious when Potter found you. And afterwards—it made you strange." "Mad?" James asks. "Not exactly mad. You didn't get on with your father. Family life wasn't good for you," Mrs. Callifer says. "Is that all?" James asks. "All except Potter's fairy stories," says Mrs. Callifer.

That does it. An angry Mrs. Potter insists that what Mr. Potter spoke was the truth. "How could it be?" Mrs. Callifer argues.

MRS. POTTER—It's not the first time. There was Lazarus. They buried *him*.

ANNE—Who was Lazarus?

MRS. CALLIFER—Someone in a book.

MRS. POTTER (*angrily*)—A book you Callifers aren't allowed to read. All right. I'll tell you how it was, Master James. It was dinnertime. Potter was late. Near two o'clock. I knew something was wrong as soon as he came in. He had a coffin face. It was bad for Potter because he found you first.

JAMES—He found me?

MRS. POTTER—He lifted you down, poor boy.

JAMES—Lifted me . . . (*He sits down at the desk.*)

MRS. POTTER—You were hanging there, sir. You'd used a cord from the playroom. He cut you down.

There was no life in him. Potter did all he could, but James' heart had stopped. "Potter left the door open," Mrs. Potter continues, "and he looked up and saw your uncle was there. 'Master James has killed himself,' Potter said. You were stretched out there on the ground and you had no more breath, Potter said, than a dead fish." Mrs. Callifer cries out that it was all a mistake: "You don't take this seriously, James?"

JAMES—What's your story, Mother? You've kept it dark a long while.

MRS. CALLIFER—There was no story to tell. We didn't want you to remember how foolish you'd been. You were in a coma from shock. When the doctor came he revived you.

MRS. POTTER—Not the doctor. Potter left you with your uncle, Master James.

MRS. CALLIFER—Potter did better than he knew. Perhaps he did save your life.

MRS. POTTER—Potter never thought that. He was beyond human aid, Potter said.

JAMES—Mother, where's my uncle now?

Mrs. Callifer wouldn't tell him if she knew. At once Anne offers to trace him. James cries: "No! Leave this to me."

SCENE II

James, arriving at Father Callifer's East Anglian presbytery, has a difficult time getting past the hard-bitten housekeeper. He is unwilling to reveal either his identity or his errand; she is unwilling to have him see the Father. "You should have come in the morning," Miss Connolly says, "he's best after breakfast." Leaving James in the dark, unlighted hall, she shuts the door on him, crosses the barren living room in search of Father Callifer. There is a strange similarity between the homeless quality of this room and that of James' "digs" in Nottingham. The only difference is the extra hideous touch contributed by religious pictures.

His housekeeper at his heels, Father Callifer comes into the sitting room. His face stubbly and worn, his eyes bloodshot, his Roman collar a mussed handkerchief twisted above his shirt, he places his hands on the mantlepiece for support.

Before fetching the visitor, Miss Connolly is determined, for Father Callifer's own sake, to have it out with him.

CALLIFER—Miss Connolly, you've looked after a lot of priests. You take it as your right to speak your mind to them. And me —you expect me to serve you, all of you, every day for twenty-four hours. I mustn't be a man. I must be a priest. And, in return, after Mass you give me coffee and eggs (in all these years you've never learnt how to make coffee) and you made my bed. You keep my two rooms clean—or nearly. (*He runs his finger along the mantlepiece.*) I don't ask you for any more than you are paid to do.

MISS CONNOLLY—The people here have a right to a priest with the faith.

CALLIFER—Faith. They want a play-actor. They want snow-white hair, high collars, clean vestments (who pays the cleaner?— not their sixpence), and they want a voice that's never husky with the boredom of saying the same words day after day. All right. Let them write to the Bishop. Do you think I want to get up every morning at six in time to make my meditation before Mass? Meditation on what? The reason why I'm going on with this slave-labor? They give prisoners useless tasks, don't they, digging pits and filling them up again? Like mine.

MISS CONNOLLY—Speak low. You don't understand what you are saying, Father.

CALLIFER—Father! I hate the word. I had a brother who believed in nothing, and for thirty years now I have believed in nothing too. I used to pray, I used to love what you call God, and then my eyes were opened—to nothing. A father belongs to his children until they grow up and he's free of them. But these people will never grow up. They die children and leave children behind them. I'm condemned to being a father for life.

MISS CONNOLLY—I've never heard such words before out of a priest's mouth.

CALLIFER (*after a pause*)—You wouldn't have heard them now if the bottle you found hadn't been empty.

MISS CONNOLLY—They say your breath smells in the confessional.

CALLIFER—And so do theirs. Of worse things. I'd rather smell of whisky than bad teeth.

MISS CONNOLLY—You're full of it now.

CALLIFER—Oh no, I'm empty. Quite empty.

Having listened to this long enough, James, opening the door, introduces himself as Callifer's nephew.

The old priest, unused to playing the host, makes a real effort. He welcomes his nephew, insists that he spend the night and that Miss Connolly provide him with dinner. "Where are my manners?" says Callifer. "I forgot to introduce the two of you. This is my housekeeper, Miss Connolly. My nephew, John." Letting this pass uncorrected, James says that what he could use is a drink. He has already had his dinner.

Very grudgingly Miss Connolly supposes she might find some altar wine. Callifer tells her to bring along a jug of water too. That rouses her suspicions. Callifer says that he just wants to temper the wine. As she goes out, Callifer asks James how the bank is. James says that he works on a newspaper.

CALLIFER—Oh, I was thinking . . . but I haven't kept up. Were you at your poor father's funeral?

JAMES—Yes, but I wasn't invited.

CALLIFER—Nor was I, but you— (*He looks at him sharply.*)

JAMES—For the same reason. I'm James, Uncle, not John. A strange meeting, isn't it?—the first since that potting shed.

Miss Connolly, having brought in the water and wine, is dismissed for the night. Callifer wonders if James remembers how close they used to be, and appears glad that James doesn't and so can't notice the change in his uncle.

James admits that he overheard the wrangling with Miss Connolly. Relieved that he needn't pretend further, Callifer—removing his bottle of whisky from its hiding place (Volume II of the Catholic Encyclopedia)—pours two very large drinks. He welcomes James to his home—one rather different from Wild Grove. "But then," Callifer adds, "your father and I followed different ways. They say you can tell a man's character from his furnishings." James looks about the room.

CALLIFER—Yes, you can see mine standing all around you for yourself. What sort of rooms have you got, I wonder? They'll have told you at Wild Grove that I'm overfond of this. (*He raises his glass.*) But I do my job. Nobody can deny I do my job. Look at the pictures, the books. I keep up appearances, don't I? We are intelligent men, you and I. Look at that picture of the Sacred Heart. A Christmas card made out of a medical text-book. (*He takes another long drink of whisky.*) Does John drink?

JAMES—A glass of wine with his meals.

CALLIFER—A lucky man. How does it go? 'They scoff at scars who never felt a wound.'

JAMES—What's your wound, Uncle?

CALLIFER—My wound? Nothing serious. It's a difficult thing, though, practising a faith, day in, day out, when you don't believe one jot of it. Do you know that at night I still pray—to nothing, to that. (*He indicates the crucifix with his glass.*) I was teaching you to believe in that when your father interfered. How right he was.

JAMES—Right?

CALLIFER—He was a very clever man. Older and cleverer than I was. He took everything I told you and made fun of it. He made me a laughing stock before you. I had taught you about the Virgin birth and he cured you with physiology.

JAMES—Was that why I tried to kill myself?

CALLIFER—So you know about that, do you? He was a bit too rough. (*A pause.*) Fill your glass. We have to get through this bottle by twelve.

JAMES—Why by twelve?

CALLIFER—I have to say Mass in the morning. I abide by the rules. It's the least I can do.

JAMES—For who?

CALLIFER—For myself. (*He gives an unhappy laugh.*) I caught you there. You thought you had squeezed out a small drop of faith. But there isn't one drop.

Carrying the alarm clock set for six, Miss Connolly discovers them at the whisky. James takes full blame. Her harshness gone, Miss Connolly, with a look at the old man drooping in his chair, asks James to see him soon to bed. "He works hard in his way," she says. "Do you know what he called himself just now? A convict. He said he was in prison. I'm the warder, I suppose. He hasn't any love or gratitude in him for the years he has been looked after." "It's a terrible thing to have nothing in you," James replies.

When she is once out of the room, Callifer rouses himself, and reminded of what they had been talking about, remembers only too clearly finding James' body. He remembers that he as well as Potter thought him dead. But now he repeats what the doctor said: it was just a coma. James wonders whether Potter couldn't have been right.

CALLIFER—If you were dead, it would have been a miracle, and if it were a miracle God would exist. That hideous picture there would have a meaning. But if God existed, why should He take away His faith from me? I've served Him well. I go on serving

Him. The saints have dark nights, but not for thirty years. They have moments when they remember what it felt like to believe.

JAMES—Do you remember nothing?

CALLIFER—I don't want to remember. You shouldn't have come.

Unwillingly, Callifer thinks back to the shed: "I prayed. I was a model priest, you see, with all the beliefs and conventions. Besides, I loved you. Yes, I remember now, how I loved you. I couldn't have a child and I suppose you took his place. Let me have one more drink." He pours out a drink but does not drink. "When I had you on my knees I remember a terrible pain—here. So terrible I don't think I could go through it again. It was just as though I was the one who was strangled—I could feel the cord round my neck. I couldn't breathe, I couldn't speak, I had to pray in my mind, and then your breath came back, and it was just as though I had died instead. So I went away to bury myself in rooms like this." James wants to know what he prayed for. Callifer does his best to change the subject, but slips back to it himself.

CALLIFER—I'd have given my life for you—but what could I do? I could only pray. I suppose I offered something in return. Something I valued—not spirits. I really thought I loved God in those days. (JAMES *gets up and walks around the room. He stands for a moment under the hideous picture.*) I said—I said, "Let him live, God. I love him. Let him live. I will give you anything if you will let him live." But what had I got to give Him? I was a poor man. I said, "Take away what I love most. Take—take—

JAMES—"Take away my faith but let him live"?

CALLIFER—Did you hear me?

JAMES—Yes. You were speaking a long way off, and I came towards you through a cave of darkness. I didn't want to come. I struggled not to come. But something pushed me to you.

CALLIFER—Something?

JAMES—Or somebody. (CALLIFER *begins to weep.*) Uncle, can I help?

CALLIFER—I even forgot what I said to Him, until you came. He answered my prayer, didn't He? He took my offer.

JAMES—Do you really believe . . .

CALLIFER—Look around you. Look at this room. It makes sense, doesn't it, now? (*He sweeps a glass onto the floor.*) You must forgive me. I'm tired and a little drunk. I haven't thought about that day for thirty years. Will you see me to my room? It's dark on the landing. (*He gets up, and then pauses and looks up at the hideous picture.*) I thought I had lost Him forever.

ACT III

It is Christmas at Wild Grove. Sara is decorating the room with holly; John is taking Anne, much against her will, to a holiday children's party. Mrs. Callifer bribes her: "If you stay as long as your father thinks polite you can have a glass of wine when you come home." "Thank you, Grannie. Now I can spurn the fruit cup." She goes with her father.

Mrs. Callifer says that they celebrate only because of Anne. "Henry had his own name for the day. He called it Children's Day. He never approved of the word Christmas."

SARA (*ironically*)—Why shouldn't we celebrate the great Palestinian religious leader?

MRS. CALLIFER—Oh, you know, dear, Christmas existed long before him.

SARA—Did your husband mind holly?

MRS. CALLIFER—No. That belonged to the ancient pagan festival —so he said.

An unexpected visitor comes in. Dr. Kreuzer had hoped to find James, who has disappeared. "I am very anxious," he tells Mrs. Callifer. "You see, I know that he had suicide on his mind." Dr. Kreuzer eventually pries from Mrs. Callifer the fact that James had had a wild notion of visiting his uncle, William Callifer.

KREUZER—Mrs. Callifer, your son is in a very dark place. We in Europe have had experience of dark places. I know a man who lived five days in a sewer without food. The manhole was in the pavement just in front of his home. All day he heard the voices of strangers and at night there were the footsteps of policemen. He stayed there, just under the manhole, waiting for his mother to speak to him and tell him it was safe to come out. He couldn't trust even his father.

SARA—I suppose she never came.

KREUZER—She came.

SARA—Perhaps in Europe they breed mothers.

Kreuzer tells Mrs. Callifer that her son is in great danger; it is time for her to tell what she knows. "It's no good, Dr. Kreuzer," Sara says. "You're working on a false assumption. Mothers don't necessarily love their children." Mrs. Callifer insists that she loves him. "Who? Henry?" says Sara. "I don't suppose James told

you this, Dr. Kreuzer. It was always Henry. What suited his
stomach (not string beans), his mind, his reputation. William Callifer didn't suit it. He had to go. And then her son. If I had a
son, I wouldn't sacrifice him for my husband. Why do we have
to sacrifice people? Why can't we just let each other be?"

Sara, leaving the room, asks Dr. Kreuzer to drive her back to
town. She refuses to sit here waiting for James to die. Mrs. Callifer inquires of Dr. Kreuzer whether he too thinks her a monster.
"No," Dr. Kreuzer answers, "but perhaps I've been treating the
wrong patient."

Having seen Sara, Baston bursts in: "What's this about James
attempting suicide again?" "Again?" asks Kreuzer. "When he was
fourteen he tried to hang himself," Baston explains. Dr. Kreuzer
wishes that he had known about this. Baston is sure of what must
be done: the time has come to commit James. He says: "We have
to deal with facts. At fourteen he tried to kill himself. Since then
he has suffered from all kinds of delusions. Melancholia . . ."

James walks in while Baston, unaware of his presence, pursues his
theme. Sorry to interrupt, James says: "I don't suppose you would
care for my opinion, but I've never felt saner in my life." "Trying to kill yourself again—that wasn't exactly sane," Baston retorts.

For James, all this belongs to the past. He is sure that he no
longer needs the care of a doctor. He has filled in the gap. He
knows: "I killed myself in the potting shed." "You see, Dr. Kreuzer?" asks Baston.

Sara comes in to James. Baston says to her: "Sara, you'd better know this right away. I want to have James certified."

SARA—Certified? But that's nonsense.
BASTON—He's completely irresponsible.
SARA—But those pills—after all, they weren't dangerous.
BASTON—We are dealing with something worse than pills. James
has just told us he killed himself in the potting shed and was—
resurrected. By the prayers of his uncle, I suppose.

Sara protests that he couldn't have said that. But James agrees
that Baston has quoted him quite accurately. An attempted suicide,
Kreuzer interposes, isn't necessarily serious; only the suicides that
succeed. Baston says irritably that people may succeed through in-
experience. "You can hardly gain experience in killing yourself,
Dr. Baston," Kreuzer answers. His irritation is getting the best of
him. Baston asserts: "He succeeded the first time." "He what,
Dr. Baston?" asks Kreuzer. Baston backtracks, but Kreuzer now

says he would like the opinion of the doctor who was here at the time. "Dr. Baston was the doctor," Mrs. Callifer remarks.

Under Dr. Kreuzer's questioning, Baston says that it had been too late for any treatment. "He was already conscious when I arrived."

KREUZER—Oh, I see.

BASTON—The layman can't recognize death. He thinks just because a mirror doesn't fog or a leaf on the lips move—

KREUZER—They tried that?

BASTON—If such a test for death was infallible, and it never could be, even then I would not accept a miracle. I would simply say we had to redefine our terms—the concepts, life and death.

MRS. CALLIFER—Henry told himself that too. The trouble was he didn't believe the argument.

BASTON—What on earth are you suggesting, Mary?

MRS. CALLIFER—Henry believed that Potter's story was true. He never spoke of it, but I knew.

BASTON—That's nonsense, Mary.

MRS. CALLIFER—Why do you think I was afraid to let James see him when he was dying? Henry could forget so long as he wasn't reminded. If you are guilty, you want to forget. (*To* JAMES.) You loved your uncle. You half believed—but your father had a wicked tongue and all the arguments. Oh, it was my fault too. I didn't know how deeply he cut. A child can't stand confusion.

BASTON—Mary, we aren't concerned with trivial mistakes in a child's upbringing. You can't pretend Henry believed that ignorant gardener's story.

MRS. CALLIFER—James, I never wanted to tell you this. I wanted to forget too. Sleeping dogs, Dr. Kreuzer, sleeping dogs. Henry was a fake.

BASTON—You appall me. I always thought you loved him.

MRS. CALLIFER—You know I loved him. One can love a fake. Perhaps it's easier than loving rectitude. All his life he'd written on the necessity for proof. Proof, proof, proof. And then a proof was pushed under his nose, at the bottom of his own garden. Fred, I saw his face. We always knew each other's thoughts. I could hear him saying to himself, "Must I recall all those books and start again?" But I was trained to my job. I began to protect him— my husband, not my son.

John and Anne return from what Anne calls "the most hideous party of the year." Mrs. Callifer, wanting to get rid of her quickly, puts off the promised glass of wine until the next day. James tells

Anne he has a present for her and will come up with it to say good-night. "Thank you, Uncle James," says Anne, "I can trust your promises. All right. I'll go. But I've got hideous suspicions." Her father drags her away.

Since James came to see her, Sara wants to be alone with him. Baston refuses to take the responsibility. "Then I will," says Mrs. Callifer.

Alone together, James asks Sara if she too thinks him mad. Sara doesn't know. "Is everyone who believes in a god mad?" he asks. "Of course not," Sara says. "I suppose I believe in Him—in a way —on Sundays if the music's good. But James, I'm in such a fog. I don't know what I think. It would have been such a useless miracle. It ruined us. It gave you thirty empty years, and your uncle . . ." "I don't understand either," James replies. "But I couldn't believe in a god so simple I could understand Him."

James wants to marry Sara, wants to try again. He had no idea of love in the days of their marriage. Now, when he looks at Sara, he sees someone who will never die forever. This is too difficult for Sara: she doesn't want eternity. "Darling," she pleads, "please try to understand. Even if there was a miracle, I want to forget it." Not for his father's reasons, but because she hates big things. She is scared. "Suppose this time I failed you," says Sara. "No, don't speak. You've got to understand me. I don't want to lose you again, but I'd rather lose you than fail you—and if you're look-ing for someone important, I won't come up to the specifications, that's all." She wants a little time to think. She promises not to go away.

Meeting Mrs. Callifer as she goes, Sara apologizes: "I was so smug, wasn't I, condemning you? At least you were trying to pro-tect someone you loved. And here I am just trying to protect my-self. Good-night, Mother. Good-night, James."

Mrs. Callifer thinks James' God is cruel. "Perhaps He had no choice," James answers. "God is conditioned, isn't He? If He's all-powerful, He can't weaken. If He knows everything, He can't forget. If He's love, He can't hate. Perhaps if someone asks with enough love, He has to give." People are asking all the time, Mrs. Callifer answers. James questions this. "But your uncle doesn't believe," she argues. "Oh, yes, he does," James says. "I left him praying."

Mrs. Callifer, like Sara, asks him for time; he has spoilt their certainties: "It seems such an enormous supernatural act. But then our certainties—they were pretty big too. It was all right to doubt the existence of God as your grandfather did in the time of Dar-win. Doubt—that was human liberty. But my generation, we didn't doubt, we *knew*. I don't believe in this miracle—but I'm not sure any longer. We are none of us sure. When you aren't sure, you are alive. . . ."

James tells of his simple hope—marrying Sara. He too has lived with the complex long enough. When Mrs. Callifer now looks at her son, she sees neither a madman nor a miracle, but all the happy, ordinary life they had before it happened. She has had his old room made ready. James wants to stay, and hoping that Anne is still awake, goes to give her the promised toys.

Kreuzer, about to leave and finding that he has lost Sara as a passenger, tells Mrs. Callifer how pleased he is about things. Mrs. Callifer finds she can talk to Dr. Kreuzer now.

MRS. CALLIFER—I went down to the potting shed. And suddenly I wasn't frightened. There was nothing ghostly there. The ground wasn't holy. There were no voices and whispers and messages. Only the boxes of seeds and the gardening tools, and I thought perhaps even miracles are ordinary. There was a girl in the village once they thought had died—do you think perhaps things like that are happening all the time everywhere?

KREUZER—I don't know. I don't much mind one way or the other.

MRS. CALLIFER—I thought you wanted the truth. You are a scientist.

KREUZER—I only want a relative truth to make life tolerable.

MRS. CALLIFER—That's not very brave, is it?

KREUZER—Courage can be a very difficult neurosis.

James reports that Anne isn't in her room. By a process of elimination, he finds her sound asleep behind the drawn curtains of the window seat. "The detective asleep at her post," murmurs Mrs. Callifer.

ANNE (*stretching and yawning*)—Oh, I've had such a funny dream. I was going down the path to the potting shed, and there was an enormous lion there fast asleep.

JAMES—What did you do?

ANNE—I woke it up.

MRS. CALLIFER—Did it eat you?

ANNE—No, it only licked my hand.

VISIT TO A SMALL PLANET

A Comedy in Three Acts

By GORE VIDAL

[GORE VIDAL *was born at the United States Military Academy, West Point, N. Y., in 1925. He enlisted in the Army following his graduation from Exeter. He wrote his first novel, "Williwaw," when he was 19; some of his subsequent novels are "In a Yellow Wood," "The City and the Pillar" and "A Search for the King." During the past few years he has very successfully written television scripts and film scenarios.*]

THE time is the year after this one, the scene the Virginia living room of a well-heeled television commentator named Roger Spelding. Roger's old classmate from the Harvard Business School, Major General Tom Powers, is giving a distraught account of recent political goings-on in the Pentagon.

POWERS— . . . and I'm in charge. It's all mine. All of it. The whole insane mess. Of course, when it first broke it was strictly Strat. Air's baby. Nobody could get near it. Cover them with glory, they thought. Ha! But yesterday Lieutenant General Claypoole decided it was too hot for him to handle, so while my back was turned with the new Laundry Project—something really exciting, by the way. (ROGER *offers* POWERS *a cigar.*) Thank you, Rog. Strat. Air tosses it to Major General Spotty McClelland— he's Com. Air Int. now—who lobs it straight at me; so by the time I get back from luncheon, I find I've been TD'd C.O.S. Priority-1A the hell and gone out of Interserv. Strat. Tac. into Kangaroo Red with the whole bloody UFO deal dumped right in my lap. (ROGER *lights* POWERS' *cigar.*) Thank you, Rog. *While* Lieutenant General Claypoole *and* my good friend Major General Spotty McClelland are sitting there in the Chief of Staff's air-conditioned office sucking

"Visit to a Small Planet": Copyright © 1956, 1957, by Gore Vidal. Reprinted by permission of the publishers, Little, Brown & Company, Boston, Mass.

up to those damned civilians: "Yes, Mr. Secretary. No, Mr. Secretary. It's only an invasion from Mars or something, Mr. Secretary." So why not let good old Tom Powers handle it? Of course, if he goofs, he can always go back to Panama! (*Gets a grip on himself.*) Sorry, Roger. I shouldn't be talking like this. But they mean to destroy me. (*He pours himself a large drink at the bar and belts it down.*)

ROGER—It's okay, Tom boy. I didn't understand a word you said. *What* has been dumped in your lap?

POWERS—UFO. You know, U.F.O.—Unidentified Flying Objects. Flying saucers. . . . Claypoole knows damn well I come up for promotion to permanent B.G. in January and . . .

ROGER—A *flying saucer?* Oh, come off it, Tom boy. As I prove to my television audience tonight, there "jest" ain't no "sech" animal. No, sir. No "sech" animal.

POWERS (*officially*)—Two days ago an unidentified object appeared in the earth's atmosphere. For the last twelve hours it has been observed over Washington and this part of Virginia.

This, according to Powers, is no Air Force stunt; it registers on radar. Roger, thinking of his program on television, is willing to buck the United States government and tell all to this "free country." Powers, his strength renewed after a stiff drink, threatens his old classmate with the revised Espionage Act.

Roger's gray-haired wife, Reba, breezing in, gives Powers the once-over and decides he's so filled out in his "Admiral's" outfit that she would never have recognized him. Through his teeth, and down his chin, Powers volleys: "Gosh, it's grand to see you, Reba, really grand. Why, Roger, this little lady hasn't changed one iota in twenty years." Reba wouldn't go so far: "Remember my hair?" she asks; "well, *look!* It's so much longer now. . . ." She invites him for dinner. Powers grinds out: "Tell you what I'll do, Reb . . . I'll do my best. Roger, it's grand seeing you, but remember—this flying saucer business is *top secret.*" "Flying saucers!" Reba interrupts. "Oh, but there aren't any flying saucers; Roger says there aren't. In fact, tonight he's going to prove it's all in the mind . . ."

As the three walk out to the terrace, Powers points almost proudly high up and out: "Will you just come out here, folks? . . . You see? Way up there? To the left of that tree? . . . That's it." Roger, with his reading glasses, can't see a thing. Reba is curious. "An unidentified flying object," says Powers. "*Yes,*" Reba agrees, "of course. That's exactly what it looks like." "And," says Powers in doom-ridden tones, "it's mine . . . all mine. And I was so happy in the Laundry Corps at Interserv. Strat. Tac. Well, that's the way the ball bounces." He goes.

Reba is more concerned with whether her daughter Ellen is sleeping with her next-door farmer friend, Conrad, than with unidentified flying objects; while Roger, agonizing over how to kill tonight's untenable broadcast, wonders if—"Maybe I could get them to run an old film. One of my 'Open Letters to the American Mom' . . . or one of those damned 'Tolerance' things. . . ." Reba thinks if Roger showed more interest in his daughter, if he talked to her— "She could hear me on television three nights a week, if she'd take the trouble," he snaps. "It can't be a flying saucer. It just can't."

REBA—*My* father always talked to me. He used to read aloud, too. You *never* read aloud.

ROGER—This is going to be another Thomas E. Dewey. I can feel it coming. Oh, when you've got a Trendex like mine, you've got enemies, waiting for you to fall on your face; nine years and they still haven't forgotten. (*Shudders at the memory.*) Millions of people heard that broadcast: "Congratulations," I said, "congratulations, President Dewey!"

Reba is left with her knitting, while outside on the terrace Ellen and Conrad try to make up for last night's fiasco: Conrad had taken Ellen to a Virginia motel in such a flustered state that he forgot to bring a suitcase, neglected to make reservations and signed the motel register, "Mr. and Mrs. Ulysses Simpson Grant and wife." As a result, they were thrown out. Finding him sexually attractive, Ellen would like to share a motel bed with Conrad but balks at marrying him. She wants her degree from Bryn Mawr, money, a diamond tiara—and momentarily longs to save the world. "Honey," says Conrad, kissing her, "'be simple." She is willing to be that, too.

In the midst of their next kissing bout, Reba comes out on the terrace, and with no thought that three's a crowd, chatters on about Admiral Powers and his spaceship. "It seems," she says, "there is one, after all. It's way up there. See," she points, "right above that tulip tree, the one the woodpeckers killed. Pretty, isn't it?"

Conrad sits up in alarm. But having once pointed out the thing, Reba promptly forgets it; and while she lectures Ellen on no marriage before graduation, the flying saucer slips away. Ellen, perversely, thinks now that her destiny lies in breeding: "A broad pelvis. Out in the fields. Then, an hour later, back to the plow, carrying my newborn child on my back . . . or do they just leave it in the fields?" "Ellen!" says her shocked mother. "If you're going to talk like that, go some place where smart talk's appreciated. Go to a bar or . . . or to a bus station. And when I think of all the work I did with poor Margaret Sanger! The lectures we gave! The leaflets we distributed. Conrad, I appeal to you! . . ." She decides to produce some of Margaret's left-over pamphlets for Ellen's benefit. "She'll frighten you to death," Reba adds, "all those statistics . . ." After inviting Conrad for dinner at eight, Reba wonders if all that cod liver oil wasn't a mistake. As she goes back into the house she still wonders: "Cod liver oil for this, cod liver oil for that: children were stuffed with it and now look at them!"

Roger, coming out for a look at the spaceship, regards the tangled figures coldly and abruptly leaves the terrace. Stopping their necking long enough to plot tonight's assault on another motel, Conrad briefs Ellen that this time they're going to be armed with a telephone-book-filled suitcase and a reservation in the solid, dreary name of "Claude Ollinger."

Inside the house, Roger still wrestles with the problem of the flying saucer broadcast. "Venus is covered with ammonia," he assures himself. "And there's nothing but fungus on Mars. The Air Force is behind this. I knew it. I just knew it." He shouts to his family that it's seven o'clock and time to listen to him.

Ellen comes in with marriage on her mind; Reba joins them with one of poor Margaret's more shocking pamphlets. The television sound apparatus refuses to work. Roger, groaning, sits forward to gaze at himself even if he's wordless. Reba, looking at the screen, thinks Roger looks a little tired. He blames it on the new film. "I keep telling them," Roger says, "I look much better live . . . more vital. From now on I'm doing the shows right here at home. Well?" He waits. He's very much put out that no one notices anything. Ellen, with a whoop, discovers that her father's image is sporting a new toupée. Hurt by her hilarity, Roger needs Reba's reassurance before he's his old confident self.

For the last time, Roger wishes to hell he could hear what he's saying; for a moment later, Conrad, dashing in with his overnight bag, yells that the spaceship is landing. Ellen hastily hides the bag, while Roger makes weak noises that sound like "mass hysteria." But the others are too busy rushing to the terrace to notice or listen. They all watch the blindingly bright object land in Reba's rose bed.

Just as Roger hysterically phones the police and General Powers in Manassas, his TV voice bellows forth: ". . . I should like this opportunity to nail the subject down once and for all: there jest ain't no sech animal . . ." "Oh, shut up!" Roger snarls.

A side of the spaceship opens and Reba, seeing a man step out, is all ready with a dinner invitation. "How do you know," says Roger ominously, "it's a man? And not . . . not a monster?"

A very pleasant-looking man, dressed in 1860 fashion, enters the living room.

KRETON—I hope the battle hasn't begun yet.

ROGER—Battle? There's no battle here.

KRETON—Oh, good. Then I'm in time. Please take me to General Robert E. Lee. I have a message for him.

ROGER—There isn't any General Lee staying here. There's just us, and General Powers, who's in Manassas. He's on a mission. Maybe you mean him.

KRETON (*looking at* ROGER's *suit—then at the others; then at himself*)—Oh, dear! I *am* sorry. I seem to've made a mistake. I'd better go back and start all over again.

ROGER—But you've only just arrived! Come in, come in. I don't need to tell you what a pleasure this is, Mister . . . Mister . . .

KRETON—Kreton. Offhand I should say I was about a hundred years out of my way.

Looking around, Kreton is obviously delighted, however, with everything he sees. "A real house!" he exclaims. "In the year— now, don't tell me—don't tell me because I know this period intimately: 1935 A.D." Catching sight of the television, he makes another guess: 1965. "You're getting warmer; it's 1957," says Roger, "and you're in the state of Virginia, U.S.A." Nodding, Kreton says: "Virginia, near Manassas. Right place, wrong year." The year he had in mind was 1861; he was on his way to the Battle of Bull Run when something went wrong with his machine and he landed a hundred years out of his way. But he has a word of comfort for them: "Hitler will not conquer the world. He will be exiled to an island in the Atlantic." Set right, he admits he isn't very good at dates and is in rather a muddle after his trip; but he's very much pleased to be in the twentieth century.

Ellen's assumption that he is not an American tickles Kreton. Roger asks where he *is* from. "Another place," Kreton answers after a brief pause. "On this earth, of course," says Roger. "No, not on this planet," replies Kreton. Ellen suggests Mars. "Oh, dear, no!" laughs Kreton. "No one lives on Mars. At least no one *I* know!"

Roger itches to get a television interview from Kreton, who knows the authorities would never permit it. "They're frightfully upset as it is," Kreton explains. He knows, for instance, that in a few minutes members of the Army will arrive to question him. "Why did you come here?" asks Ellen. Kreton replies evasively: "Oh, just a trip, a pleasure trip, a visit to your small planet. I've been studying you for ages. In fact, one might say you're a hobby of mine . . . especially this period of your development." He rises and recites: "The planet Earth is the third planet of a 412 Sun K (and quite a nice sun it is!). Earth is divided into five continents with a number of large islands. It is mostly water. There is one . . . two? No, *one* moon. And at this particular moment civilization is just beginning." "Just beginning? My dear sir—" Roger breaks in. "I only meant," apologizes Kreton, "that the initial stages of any civilization are always the most fascinating. I do hope I don't sound patronizing."

Powers and his aide, marching into the room, look for the monster. On being introduced to Kreton, Powers asks scornfully, "Who's this joker?" Told Mr. Kreton is from another planet, Powers shows impatience. Cutting through Reba's batch of introductions and invitations, Powers sends his aide to check the spaceship. Then looking down his nose at Kreton, he says: "So *you're* from another planet." He would like to have a few matters cleared up: "Which planet you from?"

KRETON—None you have ever heard of.
POWERS—Where is it?
KRETON—I couldn't begin to tell you.
POWERS—Is it in the solar system?
KRETON—No.
POWERS—In another system?
KRETON—More or less.
POWERS—Look, friend, let's not play twenty questions. I just want to know where you're from. The Pentagon requires it.
KRETON—But, my dear . . . "friend," it would take me years and years to teach you all you would need to know, and by the time I'd finished, you would be dead, because you *do* die, don't you?
POWERS—Sooner or later, yes.
KRETON (*shuddering*)—Such a disagreeable custom; poor fragile

butterflies—a single brief moment in the sun, then: nothing. You see, we don't die.

POWERS—Well, you'll die if it turns out you're a spy or a hostile alien or something like that.

Powers' aide returns with technical information about the spaceship, which means, when boiled down, that the saucer has nothing, not even food, in it. Asked for the instrument panel, Kreton says he doesn't have one, that he has no idea how the thing goes; it just goes. Powers blusters; Kreton says that they all travel that way: "I suppose once upon a time I must've known how these little cars operate, but I've quite forgotten. After all, General, we're no mechanics, you and I. We mustn't clutter our minds with trivia. It just gets me there and it gets me back."

Escorted to the study by Powers, Kreton tries amiably to give simple answers about where he lives. "We live," he tells Powers, "now let me see, you have a crude word for it. Keep on thinking; that's right. Oh, there it is, bobbing around in your mind: *dimension*. We live in another dimension, in the suburbs of time, you might say." Letting this pass, Powers arranges blanks and an army of stamps on the desk before he proceeds with such forms as the Pentagon requires. It being his job to safeguard the security of this nation, Powers frankly regards Kreton as a spy sent here by an alien race to study us, preparatory to invasion. Kreton finds this delicious. He would love Powers to repeat it. "No, I will not say it again," Powers snaps. "And I suggest you get down to brass tacks, mister. If your people are thinking of invasion they should know that we're ready for them. We'll fight them with everything we've got. We'll fight them with the hydrogen bomb, with poison gas, with broken beer bottles if necessary; we'll fight them on the beaches; we'll fight them in the alleys; we'll fight them . . ." Kreton loves it all, but tells Powers that like so many things, he must take on faith that Kreton's people wouldn't dream of invasion. What's more, Kreton warns him that he can tell everything that is going on in Powers' busy mind. With a magic wave of his arm, Kreton plays back Powers' sound track, in which Lieutenant General Son-of-a-Bitch Claypoole looms large and persecution hovers. Consoling the now deflated figure, Kreton promises to do anything he can to help his career. Pulling himself together again, Powers manages efficiently to maneuver all his Pentagon stamps. "(a)—Are you the first of your race to visit the earth?" "Oh," says Kreton, "I should think so, and even this little visit of mine smacks of the impromptu. I'm a creature of impulse, I fear!" "(b)—" says

Powers, "Are there apt to be any more of you arriving in the near future?" "Goodness, no! No one would ever dream of visiting *you!* Except me. But then, of course, I'm a hobbyist. I love to gad about."

In the course of the interview, a phone call is received from the Chief of Staff, who would like above all to know whether Kreton is human. Powers asks Kreton if he is a mammal. "For all practical purposes," Kreton answers.

When Powers says that security requires dismantling Kreton's spaceship, Kreton displays extra-mammary powers. Though hating to be a spoilsport, he creates—with a gesture—an invisible wall around his ship, which in turn creates a buzz of excitement among the onlookers. The disturbed aide hotfoots it to the study.

"You're making us look damned silly, you realize that?" Powers yells. But the next minute, *sotto voce,* he asks a small favor of Kreton. Would Kreton let him in on what his West Point aide is thinking? Kreton obliges with a gesture: "Well," says the Captain's mind, "it sure looks like old Lead-Ass has got his hands full this time." Powers is again deflated.

Kreton, terribly sociable, joins his host, Ellen and Conrad in the living room while Powers, accompanied by his aide, goes off to reconnoiter the spaceship. Although originally put out because of arriving at the wrong "address," Kreton now tells Conrad that he's sure he will have a really *nice* visit. Ellen hopes that after all that traveling in space, these Virginians won't prove too dull. Things may, however, prove a bit cooped up: Powers returns with an order that "Anybody who knows about this joker must remain here under military surveillance. If word leaked out now, there'd be an international panic." Instead of going to the motel, Conrad now has to bunk with Roger; Ellen with her mother; Kreton in the spare room; while guards stand at all the doors.

Unable to communicate with the outside world, Roger dabbles about, among other things starts an off-the-record interview with Kreton.

ROGER—Now, you know I like to level with people and, well, we're afraid you belong to a . . . to a hostile race.

KRETON—And I've assured General Powers that my people are not remotely predatory. In fact, except for me, no one is interested in you. Oh, dear, I shouldn't have said that! Anyway, *I* adore you and that's all that matters. *You are my hobby.* I love you.

POWERS (*heavily*)—That's certainly decent of you.

ROGER—So you've come down here for an on-the-spot visit, sort of going native.

KRETON—What a nice turn of phrase. Exactly. I am going native.

POWERS—Well, it is my view that you have been sent here by another civilization for the express purpose of reconnoitering prior to invasion.

KRETON—That would be your view! The wonderfully primitive assumption that all strangers are hostile. Oh, General, you're almost too good to be true.

POWERS—You deny your people intend to make trouble for us?

KRETON—I deny it.

ROGER—Well, then are they, ah, interested in establishing trade, communications?

KRETON—But we've always had communication. And as for trade, well, we just do not trade; it's an activity peculiar to *your* social level. (*Quickly.*) Which I'm not criticizing, mind you! I love all the things you do!

ROGER—In any case, you have no plans to, well, to dominate the earth? We have your solemn assurance of that?

KRETON (*blandly*)—No. I'm sorry, but you haven't.

ROGER—We haven't? I thought you said your people weren't interested in conquest.

KRETON—They're not, but *I* am.

Kreton, it turns out, expects to make the whole world his. Powers yells for his men to grab Kreton, only for an invisible wall immediately to block them. Kreton is having such fun; but what with his long day's journey, he feels the need of a little nap.

REBA—I'll show you to your room.

KRETON—Don't bother. I know the way. (*Touches his brow.*) Such savage thoughts! My head is vibrating like a drum. I feel quite odd, all of you thinking at once. (*He gestures and we hear, in order—*)

ROGER'S MIND—I realize, ladies and gentlemen, that the Nobel Prize you have just given me . . .

REBA'S MIND—Since Mr. Kreton isn't eating, that leaves just enough chicken for everybody . . .

CONRAD'S MIND—Ellen, honey, I'm here. Right in the house . . . with *Daddy.*

ELLEN'S MIND—This is all a dream. It's been a hot, muggy day and I've fallen asleep in the swing.

POWERS' MIND—This joker can't take over the world. Napoleon couldn't. Hitler couldn't. I can't.

KRETON—You see? Quite overpowering. And so good night, children, dear *wicked* children. Tomorrow will be a wonderful day for all of us. Sleep tight!

ACT II

Kreton, an unusual house guest in an elaborate Prince-Albert dressing gown, whiles away the time finding out what's on the Spelding cat's mind. Ellen, bringing in the breakfast, is wide-eyed at their rapport. When Kreton, answering the cat's request, turns over his "horribly real" twentieth-century breakfast to the animal (Kreton never eats), Ellen asks if he really can see inside the cat's mind too. "Oh, yes," Kreton nods. "Exactly the same principle. Same raw, blazing emotions . . . though somewhat one-track. Not unlike General Powers, actually."

Ellen's mind seems to be running on one track. Kreton wishes to "unmix" her sex life for her. "Offhand," he says, "I should say your problem, essentially, is one of housing. Conrad must stay here. So far so good. *But,* unhappily for your purposes, he has elected to sleep in your father's room." Ellen tries to "unmix" *him* on that idea: Conrad doesn't like her father; her father despises Conrad. This is a bit complex for Kreton, but not insoluble. "Now," says he, "there are three bedrooms. I occupy one. The four of you must occupy the other two, in pairs. Threes, I gather, are taboo. Very well. Let us be logical. Methodical. Two must go into Room A. And two into Room B. Since the present combination is unsatisfactory, I propose—now listen closely—that Mr. and Mrs. Spelding *together* occupy Room A while you and Conrad—oh, this is brilliant—occupy Room B!" Ellen, saying that she and Conrad aren't married, perplexes Kreton. "Neither were Mr. and Mrs. Claude Ollinger," he answers, fascinated. Where he comes from, people don't tangle at all, having given up sex with the appendix and fifth toe.

Where Kreton comes from, there is no need for multiplying. "You see," he explains, "we have ourselves, and since we don't die, we don't need any more of us! So we gave it up. . . . I sometimes wonder if we weren't rather hasty."

With quickening anthropological zeal, Kreton wishes to be present the next time Ellen makes love. It is one of the things he *most* wants to see while on Earth. In fact, he wants her to get to work at once, and if Conrad—who is still asleep—is not available, Kreton proposes Powers' aide, the Captain, as a strapping substitute. Ellen is horrified.

KRETON (*bewildered*)—Oh? But . . . but it's on your minds so much I simply assumed it was quite public. I *am* sorry if I've put my foot in it. . . .

ELLEN—Of course I know you're from another planet and all and I guess we do *think* an awful lot about sex, but we're not supposed to talk about it and we only do it when nobody's looking.

KRETON—How ravishing! These primitive taboos. You revel in public slaughter: you pay to watch two men hit one another repeatedly, yet you make love secretly, guiltily and with remorse . . . too delicious!

ELLEN—You sound awfully superior.

KRETON—We are. But it was not easy. It took us ages to stamp out disease—scarlet fever, mumps, anxiety, the common cold and, finally, the great killer itself, the ultimate disease: passion!

ELLEN—Passion?

KRETON—Love, hate, that kind of thing. Passion—the Hydra-headed monster, so difficult to diagnose: love-nest slayings, bad temper, world wars, verse tragedies in five acts—so many variants. But at last success crowned our efforts. And now . . . we feel nothing. We do nothing. We are perfect.

ELLEN—That sounds terribly dull!

KRETON—How neatly you put it. And that's why I'm here. To escape the dreary company of Delton 4.

ELLEN—Delton 4?

KRETON—Yes, he's the most niggling. Though Deltons 1, 2 and 3 are hardly prize packages. In fact, I am afraid that in our perfection we have become intergalactic bores. Our continuum is rather a frost.

Conrad, still sleepy after a gruesome night listening to Roger grind his teeth, learns that Kreton has been reading Ellen's mind again. "Hearing it, actually," Kreton corrects. "Such a confused mind, no concentration." Accepting Kreton's remark as a challenge, Ellen shows off her powers of concentration by quickly memorizing pages from a book chosen at random. Conceding this to be a good performance for a lower primate, Kreton demonstrates how *his* level uses 100 per cent of the mind. With his finger pointed at a vase on the mantlepiece, Kreton wills it to rise in the air, then lowers it again to where it was. Ellen wants a crack at it. At first she has no luck; then, clearing her mind, contorting her face and tensing her body, she too wills the vase into the air and drops it back with a clatter. Conrad insists she has had some help. "No," says Kreton, "she did it all by herself. Oh, my dear, what a success you'll be at parties."

After all this fun, Ellen trusts that Kreton wasn't serious about controlling the world. "Of course I was serious!" he exclaims. In a gossipy fashion, he runs through various secret ways of doing it. Ellen wishes that before embarking on such a large project, he would at least think it through. "You sound exactly like Delton 4," complains Kreton. "It's not my fault I'm impulsive—heart rules the head and all that. . . ."

A casual reference to the vase trick now really gets Kreton going. He makes a sweeping gesture, and out on the terrace the Captain's rifle leaps from his hands and hangs high in the air. The Captain is a wreck: he knows he will be court-martialed. He does not know that every other rifle in the world now hangs in an identical position. Nor does he know, as his rifle drops back into his hands, that everywhere rifles are dropping back. Only Kreton, Ellen and Conrad share that secret.

Powers, full of top secrets of his own, barges in. He asks to be left alone with Kreton, and, as soon as the young couple depart, launches into what they're doing to him at the Pentagon. "I put it up to you, Mr. Kreton, as an impartial observer—I assume you're impartial—why should I be the one who has to carry the ball on this project: Operation Kreton? Not that I haven't enjoyed knowing you—I mean that's one of the great things about Army life; you get to meet all kinds of people, from different places, or, in this case, different *planets*. . . . But after all, Interserv. Strat. Tac.'s mission is a larger one, covering, as you know, saddle making, dry cleaning, hygiene and, of course, laundry. So why, I asked the Chief of Staff, why don't you toss this right back to Com. Air Int., where it belongs? I've held the fort, and so far I haven't goofed. Well, to make a long story short, I lost. So until the civilians make up their minds what to do with you, I remain in charge. Why? Because I am the innocent victim of conspiracy and intrigue. Ever since Korea, Claypoole has been trying to get my corner office with the three windows and the big waiting room, and I tell you, he'll stop at nothing to get it. . . . And Tom Powers is now expendable . . . but I don't want to bore you with my problems." "I love having you bore me," says Kreton. "You do it so beautifully." "Well, thank you, sir," says Powers.

Powers also would have Kreton forget this business of taking over the world. His argument is that Kreton is the U.S.A.'s newest weapon, and as such will be given "the best possible break, publicity-wise." Kreton, demurring, forbids Powers to let anyone know that he's here, or to print a word about him. "Mr. Kreton," says Powers, "just how do you think you're going to stop us?" Kreton starts to make magic gestures. Powers agrees hastily: "Just as you say. You're probably right. We announce we have you, then the damned Russians start claiming they've got one too . . . only better. . . . They haven't got one, have they?" Kreton reassures him on that score.

Before they can get down to writing an itemized laundry list of Kreton's unusual powers, Roger bursts in with the news as he sees it: "At eleven twenty-six this morning, every rifle in the free world was raised fifteen feet in the air for thirty seconds and then lowered again. It's the Russians, obviously." With a complete news black-out east of the Rhine, Roger is convinced *"this is it."* He and Powers are aghast at the extent to which Russia can use antigravity. Kreton eggs them on. His offhand remark that, once you get the hang of it, antigravity is quite a simple affair, inspires Roger to invite him to appear on tonight's TV show. Sidestepping politely, Kreton saddles Roger with Powers instead. With a murderous look, Roger goes off to arrange network clearance.

Unaware of Roger's distaste for him, Powers puts Kreton to work on his list. Kreton sits at the desk in the library. ". . . looks like we'll be using you sooner than we thought, eh?" says Powers. "You do know how to write, don't you?" "Oh, I love writing," Kreton answers as he makes painstaking Palmer-method flourishes. Glad to hear that Kreton isn't worried about that antigravity thing, Powers crows: "We'll give 'em the old (*imitates* KRETON's *gesture*), eh?" and goes off to bother Roger.

Kreton, practicing penmanship, confides to the cat how thrilling it all is: "One incident and the whole world is now aquiver! You found a mouse? Oh, how luscious. . . . Well, you have your hobby and I have mine. . . . Oh, I know you don't like people, but then, I don't like mice. *Chacun à son goût.* I simply dote on people. . . . Why? Because of their primitive addiction to violence, because they seethe with emotions which I find bracing and intoxicating. For countless ages I have studied them and now I'm here to experience them firsthand, to wallow shamelessly in their steaming emotions . . . and to have fun, fun, fun! . . . How? You *were* listening, weren't you? Well, I do believe I have started a war. At least, I hope so. After all, that's what I came down here to see!

Cyril Ritchard in "Visit to a Small Planet"

I mean, it's the one thing they do really well. Oh, I can't think what will happen next." Kreton crosses to a globe of the world, ponders it thoughtfully. "Rosemary, advise me. Do I dare? Yes? Well, then why not go whole hog? Metaphor!" Kreton gestures, and the library globe explodes. "Oh, dear! That was a bit much. . . . But very pretty!"

Scene II

That evening, Roger—surrounded by TV technicians and equipment—is introducing the foaming goodness of Cloverdale milk to the American public, along with news that will give it ulcers. He separates Powers from a highball to bring him to Mother and Father America's attention.

In his interview with Major General Tom Powers, Roger asks all the questions, provides all the answers, and leaves not even a second for Powers to slip in a word about the Laundry Corps.

After the TV technicians dismantle the equipment, say their good nights and depart, Powers manages a "Real treat to be on, Rog." "Well," blasts Roger, "it may be a treat for you, but it's a living hell for me! The first visitor from outer space right here in this house . . . and what do I do? I interview *you!*"

Kreton, indulging in his first bath, calls down from upstairs for a sponge. Powers hops to it. Roger, seeing Conrad and Ellen saunter in, cries: "While civilization crashes around our heads, Mr. Kreton takes a bath and you two are off Heaven knows where. . . ." As it happens, they've been enjoying a picnic. "Well," snarls Roger, "while you were lunching alfresco, the entire international situation was exploding. We are on the brink of another world war . . ." He advises Conrad to get into uniform, preferably by nightfall. Kreton now calls down for a mop. This time it's Roger's turn to oblige.

"The brink of another war?" Ellen asks. "What is my father talking about?" "Honey," answers Conrad, "according to your father, this makes the sixth world war we've had since Dewey was elected President." Taking no chances, however, Conrad urges immediate marriage. Ellen still balks. She does it on the sofa, in his arms. Kreton, decked out as a Confederate General, discovers them together. He is depressed that Conrad hasn't donned a uniform and rallies him to the colors. "Mr. Kreton, Conrad doesn't believe in fighting," Ellen explains.

KRETON—But . . . how will you answer your children when they ask, "Daddy, what did *you* do in the big war?"

CONRAD—Oh, no, not that one.

KRETON—Has that argument been propounded before?

CONRAD—Yes.

KRETON—It *seemed* emotionally correct. The pitch was perfect. Conrad, I don't entirely understand you. Do you love your country?

CONRAD—Uh-huh.

KRETON—Then don't you want to slaughter its enemies?

CONRAD (*shaking his head*)—Uh-huh.

KRETON—That is the wrong answer. That is not a proper mid-twentieth-century sentiment. Come now, Conrad, you know that deep down inside you're a warm, passionate human being like the

rest.   After all, the Jefferson Davis Motel, Cottage D . . . the
four telephone books . . .

CONRAD—That has nothing to do with it.

KRETON—Oh, yes, it does. Sex and aggression—exactly the same
thing. I'm sure in your heart you want to fight side by side with
your buddies.

ELLEN—No, Conrad's different.

KRETON—But surely he has the same patriotic responses as General Powers and your father and— (*Points to* AIDE *at terrace door*)
that young man there.

CONRAD—No, I just want to be let alone. I'm a peace-loving
man who grows English walnuts.

KRETON—Until emotional stimuli are applied. Such as the Dec-
laration of Independence. (*Recites.*) ". . . with malice toward
none . . ."; Mount Rushmore; Ars Gratia Artis. . . . Conrad,
aren't your hackles rising?

Nothing happens. Kreton is exasperated. Conrad believes in
self-control; nobody can rouse him to fight anybody. Kreton wants
a go at it. Ellen warns him: "Now . . . no tricks."

KRETON—No tricks. I shall stir him emotionally . . . in his
own terms. (*Clears his throat.*) Relax, Conrad. Better get your
hanky out. You will probably cry, but it's for your own sake. (*Begins to sing emotionally.*)

> There's a long, long trail a-winding
> Into the land of my dreams,
> Where the nightingales are singing
> And a white moon beams.

(*Goes to the telephone; sings.*)

> Hello, Central, give me No Man's Land.
> My daddy's there . . . my mamma told me.

(*Blends into—*)

> Over there, over there,
> Send the word, send the word over there,
> For the Yanks are coming, the Yanks are coming,
> With drums rum tumming everywhere!

(*Marches about; intones—*) Abraham Lincoln. Ann Rutledge.
"The world may little note nor long remember . . ." Barbara
Fritchie. (*Sings.*)

When Johnny comes marching home again, tra-la, tra-la,
When Johnny comes marching home again, tra-la, tra-la.

Having constantly checked Conrad's pulse and reactions, Kreton goes into the home stretch with "Comin' in on a wing and a prayer." Tears wet his cheeks. *"And,* Conrad," he says softly, "it's for Mother." "Then," says Conrad, "let Mother go fight."

Not being able to figure out what went wrong, Kreton admits sadly that he wasn't in good voice. Ellen tells him this wasn't so. "No, no, you're just saying that. It was an awful bust." *"I* thought it was wonderful, sir," weeps Powers' aide from the terrace door. Enormously perked up, Kreton exclaims: *"There* is a man . . ." and forthwith reveals what a *man's* mind thinks. The aide's mind, sounding like a staccato burst of a machine gun, is not original, yet for Conrad it packs a wallop. "This one's for me," says the aide's mind; "and this one's for that babe with the crazy build. Yeah, I been watching you shaking it around this house. And you been watching me, watching you, driving me mad." "Why," says Ellen, "he's thinking about *me!"* The aide's mind, in spite of the aide's resistance, continues aloud: "We don't need words, woman, not you and me. We both of us knew that night old Lead-Ass and me walked into this house and you gave me the eye. Bells rang. The earth moved. It was like there was nobody in the world, just you and me, and the black, burning night exploding like a thousand Roman candles . . ." Conrad becomes increasingly dangerous; Kreton is enchanted. Conrad takes a swing at the aide; the aide retaliates; they slug away and have a routine barroom fight. Kreton is overjoyed; Ellen jumps in to help Conrad, who needs any help he can get. Roger and Powers, with bucket and mop, arrive on the scene and break up the fight.

Roger knows in an instant that the fight was Conrad's fault; Powers, the stern militarist, demands discipline from his staff.

KRETON—I'm limp with excitement. It all started when I tried to appeal to this boy to join the Army in his country's hour of peril.

ROGER—Slacker is an ugly word, Conrad.

ELLEN—Conrad's a pacifist and he's willing to fight for it.

KRETON—A pacifist with a hard right, a stealthy left jab and a sly knee to the groin. . . . And may I add, that in his heart there was blood lust.

POWERS—Well, I can't let the troops rape and loot. Doesn't look right for the Laundry Corps, Captain!

Once more, Ellen has changed her mind. She is going to marry Conrad tonight. Revolted, Roger washes his hands of both of them and leaves the room. As the young couple, escorted by the aide, go off to be married, Kreton remembers he hasn't told them the good news. He lets Powers have it instead.

KRETON—War! I have arranged a sneak attack for tonight. The good ones always start with a sneak attack.

POWERS—*You* arranged this?

KRETON—Yes, in exactly forty-seven minutes. Zero hour. You see, I was so troubled by that antigravity, I couldn't sit still. And since no one else was doing anything except talk, I took the bull by the horns and launched the bombers myself.

POWERS (*taking a heavy drink*)—You? Well, at last the old eagle strikes. (*Sinks into a chair.*)

KRETON—Exactly. Isn't it thrilling?

POWERS—Yes, thrilling.

KRETON—I must say you don't seem awfully keen.

POWERS—Oh, no, I'm keen. . . . "Into the valley of death rode the six hundred," and all that.

KRETON—Your spirits are flagging. Oh, General, do buck up! (*Sighs.*) Well, here we go again. (*Singing.*)

> There's a long, long trail a-winding
> Into the land of my dreams. . . .

This time, Powers joins in Kreton's singing.

ACT III

To show just what the world may expect in seventeen minutes hence, Kreton conducts his own active war games. He employs toy bombers and fighters, designates Powers as the enemy and Powers' aide as radar. The aide beeps as Kreton swoops, and Powers, liquored up, buzzes off.

Kreton, needing ground troops, sends the aide off for toy soldiers. Alone with Powers, he asks his tippling friend how he likes his plan. "Am I to understand that this, ah, tactical demonstration is for real?" Powers wants to know. "Of course, 'for real.' I confess," says Kreton, "there were times today when I wanted to tell you, but then I thought: No! let it come as a wonderful surprise for the General."

Grasping his fifth drink and listening to the warlike news on the walkie-talkie, Powers accepts Kreton as a comrade-in-arms. "Buddies?" says Kreton. "Buddies," says Powers, and adds: "I suppose we're going to win *right away,* aren't we?" His buddy is evasive.

Kreton, making a bombing noise with one of the toy planes, upsets Powers badly. He never could stand loud noises! Kreton, thinking of him as a twentieth-century soldier leading his men through barbed wire, is perplexed: "You have fought, haven't you?" "Not in the field, no," Powers states. "You see, during the last war I got interested in laundry . . ."

KRETON—Laundry?

POWERS—Major logistical problem, laundry. Mobile units. Lots of big decisions to make in that area: kind of soap to use, things like that. Decided finally on Snow Chip Flakes. Fine lather. Good detergent. Doesn't harm the fabric *and* has bluing already built in, which cut down our expenditures by two million dollars. All my idea. . . . Then of course you've heard of the Powers Mobile Laundry Unit K.

KRETON—No. You see, I don't like laundry.

POWERS (*growing progressively drunker, begins to act out a Mobile Laundry Unit*)—Well, you'll like this. All my own design, too. Put the laundry here. Dirtier the better. Stuff it in this opening. Slam the door shut. Pull the lever. Whoosh. Feel that hot water circulating? Now—and get this, it's automatic—soap is *shot* through the water. Detonated. Like puffed wheat. Got the idea from a cereal box, believe it or not. Snap, crackle, pop. (*The walkie-talkie checks in, and* KRETON *answers it.*)

KRETON—Some Chinese students have just blown up the Burmese Embassy in Peiping!

POWERS—Always admired the Chinese, great little people, born laundrymen. Naturals . . .

After another drink, Powers hears some really horrible news over the walkie-talkie. He's sunk. Strat. Air and Com. Air Int. have been combined, as an emergency measure, under Claypoole. Powers has lost his office and waiting room. War is hell, all right, Powers tells Kreton: "I've seen it happen before too many times. Mr. Kreton, if there is one thing that destroys an army's morale and discipline, it is a major war. Everything goes to hell. Lose more damned sheets and pillow cases. Your laundry's a wreck!" Miserably, with another drink in hand, and his life in tatters, Powers mumbles his way up to bed.

Kreton is delighted when Ellen and Conrad, joined in matrimony, return in time for his sneak attack. "But you can't *want* a war . . ."

says Ellen, amazed. "Of course I want a war," says Kreton. "After all, I missed the Civil War, so the next best thing is to have one of my very own right here."

Conrad does his best to straighten him out. No one around here wants a war. He doesn't want to be killed, Ellen doesn't want to be killed. . . . "That tin-headed general does not want to be killed. Even Ellen's deranged father—"

ELLEN—Conrad!
KRETON—You see? That's the way it starts. A quarrel. The air vibrates. My dear children, don't you know what you are? What you all are? Savages, bloodthirsty savages. That's why you're my hobby. That's why I've returned to the Dark Ages of an insignificant planet in a minor system circling a small and rather chilly sun to enjoy myself, to see you at your most typical . . .

CONRAD—So maybe we're *not* vegetables like you.
KRETON (*stung*)—I am not a vegetable. I am a mammal. The optimum work of nature.

Alone with Kreton, Ellen turns on him with loathing. Quite unfazed, he jumps with joy at his dream coming true. "If only Delton 4 could see me now!" Kreton, knowing that there shouldn't be a war now, is delighted that all the history books will have to be rewritten. Delton 4, according to Kreton, will be livid.

Carefully, Ellen inquires if Delton 4 isn't looking for him. "Of course they are," says Kreton happily, "but the odds against being found *in time* are absolutely minuscule. Besides, knowing my passion for the Civil War, they'll look for me back in 1861, never dreaming I'm holed up in 1957. Practically one of the family." If he wishes, Ellen asks tactfully, how would he get in touch with them? He doesn't wish; but under her questioning, Kreton says: "Through the mind, like everything else. Concentration. . . ." Then, with a look at the clock, Kreton rushes off to get in his battle togs for zero hour and the dazzling "forest of mushroom clouds."

Wasting only a moment on a practice run with the vase trick, Ellen settles down to get in touch with Delton 4 by concentration. All the household activity swirling about her fails to distract her. She hears nothing. Even when Kreton, in campaign regalia, charges in brandishing a sword, she hears nothing. His cry, "Tippecanoe and Tyler too!" doesn't disturb her. She concentrates with her eyes shut. By the time Kreton notices what she is doing, it is too late.

The brilliant light of another flying saucer floods the terrace.

Rushing for the study, Kreton hides behind the desk there. Delton 4, in morning suit and bowler, with a quiet thank-you to Ellen, heads for the study, where he berates a sheepish Kreton in a language all their own. Kreton reluctantly removes his sword.

Following them, Ellen hopes that Delton 4 will stop the sneak attack. As it happens he has already stopped it and spoilt Kreton's fun. "'You see," Delton 4 explains, "Kreton is a rarity among us. He is morally retarded and, like a child, he regards this world as his plaything. . . . Come, Kreton." "Like a child!" Kreton sputters. "Now, really! Simply because I have given pleasure and employment to a number of savages . . . very sweet savages."

Delton 4, after finding Kreton gone from his nursery, had combed the last few hundred years and was only at Waterloo when he got Ellen's message. He tells Ellen that after their departure, time will bend back to the instant before Kreton's arrival. All will be forgotten.

Making his farewells, Kreton can't help envying his hosts' lovemaking and violence. "But don't worry," he promises, "I'll be back one bright day. One bright day in 1861. The Battle of Bull Run . . . Only," he tells Ellen, "next time I think it'll be more fun if the South wins!"

ORPHEUS DESCENDING

A Play in Three Acts

By Tennessee Williams

[Tennessee Williams *was born 43 years ago in Columbus, Mississippi, and named Thomas Lanier Williams. Disliking this name, he took his present one. He graduated from the State University of Iowa and has been a clerk in a shoe store, an elevator operator, a bellhop, a movie usher, a waiter and a teletyper. "Battle of Angels," the original of "Orpheus Descending," was his first long play to gain production, but did not get to Broadway. "The Glass Menagerie," however, did—and straightway won the Drama Critics Circle Award. In the season of 1947-48 his "Streetcar Named Desire" won this award and the Pulitzer Prize as well. Williams has also written "You Touched Me" (with Donald Windham), "Summer and Smoke," "The Rose Tattoo," "Camino Real" and in 1954-55 "Cat on a Hot Tin Roof," which also won both the Critics Circle Award and the Pulitzer Prize.*]

IN a Southern dry goods store, whose owners also have the adjoining "confectionery," a couple of middle-aged women are busily laying out a buffet supper. While putting the food on one of the tables moved in from the confectionery, they yowl for their husbands to get to the station.

The men, having played Jabe Torrance's slot machines, go to meet him at the train, leaving the women to gossip and snoop. Jabe, the proprietor of the store, is returning from having an operation in Memphis. The women assume it was useless: when they spoke of it to the doctor, he just shook his head.

Dolly—I guess he signed Jabe Torrance's death warrant with just that single silent motion of his haid.

"Orpheus Descending": Copyright © 1957 by Tennessee Williams. Selections reprinted by permission of the author and New Directions, 333 Sixth Ave., New York 14, N. Y. All inquiries should be addressed to author's agent: Audrey Wood, MCA Management, Inc., New York, N. Y.

BEULAH—That's exactly what passed through my mind. I understand that they cut him open— (*Pauses to taste something on the table.*)

DOLLY—An' sewed him right back up! That's what I heard . . .

After more sampling of the food, the women—curious as to where the rest of the welcoming committee is—decide that the Temple sisters are snooping around upstairs. "If Lady catches 'em," says Beulah, "she'll give those two old maids a touch of her tongue. She's not a Dago for nothin'!"

DOLLY—Ha, ha, no! You spoke a true word, honey. . . . Well, I was surprised when I wint up myself!

BEULAH—You wint up you'self?

DOLLY—I did and so did you because I seen you, Beulah.

BEULAH—I never said that I didn't. Curiosity is a human instinct.

DOLLY—Y'know what it seemed like to me up there? A county jail! I swear to goodness it didn't seem to me like a place for white people to live in! That's the truth . . .

BEULAH (*darkly*)—Well, I wasn't surprised. Jabe Torrance bought that woman.

DOLLY—Bought her?

BEULAH—Yais, he bought her, when she was a girl of eighteen! He bought her and bought her cheap because she'd been thrown over and her heart broken by David Cutrere . . . you know, Carol Cutrere's big brother. *Oh,* what a—*mmm,* what a—beautiful thing he was. . . . And those two met like you struck two stones together and made a fire! Well, he quit Lady the summer the Mystic Crew set fire to her father's wine-garden for sellin' liquor to niggers! And Lady's father was burned alive fightin' the fire.

DOLLY—Lawd have mercy!

BEULAH—Uh-huh, I second the motion. But after that happened, David Cutrere didn't want no further connection with Lady, and thrown her over . . .

"Speakin' of the Cutreres!" says Dolly as Carol Cutrere materializes out of the darkness of the confectionery. Carol's dead-white make-up calls for comment; the women provide it.

The thirty-year-old, strange, almost beautiful wraith crosses to the pay telephone. Needing coins, she rings open the cash register and helps herself.

One of the Temple sisters, coming down the stairs next to the phone, sidles past Carol timidly. She joins Carol's audience. "What she doin' barefoot?" whispers Eva Temple loudly. "The last time she was arrested on the highway," says Beulah, "they say that she was naked under her coat." The other Temple sister now slips down the stairs. "She a sight?" says Sister Temple. "Uh-huh! A sight to be seen!" Eva Temple answers.

Reaching her cousin Bertie in New Orleans, Carol, in her clear, childlike voice, tells him and all the eavesdroppers how she blackmailed her shocked sister-in-law. Carol has contrived to get monthly remittance money as long as she stays out of Two River County. She finishes her phone call, promising that unless she is "irresistibly delayed," she will meet him in New Orleans by morning. Hanging up the receiver, Carol hesitantly removes a revolver from her trench coat and crosses behind the counter to find some cartridges.

DOLLY—She don't have a license to carry a pistol.

BEULAH—She don't have a license to drive a car.

CAROL—When I stop for someone I want to be sure it's someone I want to stop for.

DOLLY—Sheriff Talbott ought to know about this when he gits back from the depot.

CAROL—Tell him, ladies. I've already given him notice that if he ever attempts to stop me again on the highway, I'll shoot it out with him. . . .

To add to the sisters' fright, an old, fantastically dressed Negro Conjure Man emerges from the gloom of the confectionery. As the women scream to get him put out, Carol goes up and asks what he's holding in his outstretched hand. "Oh," says she, "it's a bone of some kind. No, I don't want to touch it, it isn't clean yet, there's still some flesh clinging to it. You leave it a long time on a bare rock in the rain and the sun, till every sign of corruption is burned and washed away from it, and then it will be a good charm, Uncle." As the Negro bows and is about to leave, Carol begs him for a Choctaw cry. She starts the cry herself; he throws back his head and completes the barking wild noises.

As though fetched by the Choctaw cry, Val enters the store. He is a young man about thirty, whose wild beauty and odd snakeskin jacket seem not unlike the cry itself. Val, with the guitar he carries, attracts Carol's immediate attention. Rifling the cash register to pay off the Negro, she gets rid of the Conjure Man and smiles at Val. But he is not alone.

Vee Talbott, the heavy, vague wife of the county sheriff, coming in out of the sun's glare, is at first unable to see. But regaining her eyesight and her manners, she introduces Val to the gathered women:

"Mr. Xavier is a stranger in our midst. His car broke down in that storm last night and I let him sleep in the lock-up. He's lookin' for work and I thought I'd introduce him to Lady an' Jabe because if Jabe can't work they're going to need somebody to help out in the store." Vee and the women move off; Carol circles Val with childlike curiosity.

At first, concentrating on a belt buckle that needs fixing, Val ignores her. Carol, remembering him from a drinking bout in New Orleans and recognizing her cousin Bertie's Rolex Chronometer on his wrist, as well as the unforgettable snakeskin jacket, recalls even what she had said to him: "I said, what on earth can you do on this earth but catch at whatever comes near you, with both your hands, until your fingers are broken?" Val asks why she is so anxious to prove that he knows her.

CAROL—Because I want to know you better and better! I'd like to go out jooking with you tonight.

VAL—What's *jooking?*

CAROL—You know what that is? That's where you get in a car and drink a little and drive a little and stop and dance a little to a juke box, and then you drink a little more and drive a little more and stop and dance a little more to a juke box—and then you stop dancing and you just drink and drive and then you stop driving and just drink, and then, finally, you stop drinking . . .

VAL—What do you do then?

CAROL—That depends on the weather and who you're jooking with. If it's a clear night you spread a blanket among the memorial stones on Cypress Hill, which is the local bone orchard, but if it's not a fair night, and this one certainly isn't, why, usually then you go to the Wildwood cabins between here and Sunset on the Dixie Highway.

VAL—That's about what I figured. But I don't go that route. Heavy drinking and smoking the weed and shacking with strangers is okay for kids in their twenties, but this is my thirtieth birthday and I'm all through with that route. I'm not young any more.

CAROL—You're young at thirty—I hope so! I'm twenty-nine!

VAL—Naw, you're not young at thirty if you've been on a goddam party since you were fifteen.

Vee interrupts their swigging at Carol's pint of bourbon to say sharply: "Mr. Xavier don't drink." "Oh, ex-cuse me!" says Carol. Vee retorts: "If you behaved yourself better your father would not be paralyzed in bed!"

Lady, leading Jabe and his welcoming entourage into the store, appears exhausted. She could be anywhere from thirty-five to forty-five, and is near hysteria. Jabe, limping behind her, is a gray, wolfish, dying man. He hardly hears the women gushing and cackling over how well he looks. He only wants to get to bed; and yet his mean eye at once detects that Lady had moved the shoe department. Hostile and sarcastic, Jabe says: "Tomorrow I'll get me some niggers to help me move the shoe department back front." "You do whatever you want to, it's your store," answers Lady. "Uh-huh. Uh-huh," Jabe says, starting up the stairs, "I'm glad you reminded me of it."

As Lady sinks wearily into a chair at the table, Beulah is sure that man will never come down those stairs again. "Never in the world, honey," echoes Dolly. "He has the death sweat on him!" Beulah says. They crowd around Lady with morbid curiosity. A knocking from the floor above brings Lady to her feet with a startled laugh. Excusing herself to answer Jabe's summons, she leaves all their questions unanswered.

The knocking gives Carol a chance to invite Val for a ride in her car, with the thought that he inspect the knock in the motor. Since Val is waiting for a paying job in the store, Carol makes plain that she will pay him, too. The outraged women hang on every word. Carol asks Val what they are saying about her. "Play it cool," Val advises. "I don't like playing it cool," Carol says. "What are they saying about me? That I'm corrupt?" Asking why, if she doesn't want to be talked about, she makes up and acts up as she does, Val gets Carol's answer at great length. She is an "exhibitionist" who wants people to know that she is alive. "We don't go the same route—" Val says. Carol tells of the time when she was a *"benign* exhibitionist" who scattered her inheritance on the poor and oppressed and donned a potato sack for a barefoot march on the capitol. She was hooted and spat upon, and arrested. "Guess what for?" she asks Val. "Lewd vagrancy! Uh-huh, that was the charge, 'lewd vagrancy,' because they said that potato sack I had on was not a respectable garment. . . . Well, all that was a pretty long time ago, and now I'm not a reformer any more. I'm just a 'lewd vagrant.' And I'm showing the S. O. B.s how lewd a 'lewd vagrant' can be if she puts her whole heart in it like I do mine! . . . All right. I've told you my story, the story of an exhibitionist. Now I want you to do something for me. Take me out to Cypress Hill in my car. And we'll hear the dead people talk. They do talk there. They chatter together like birds on Cypress Hill, but all they say is one word and that one word is 'live.' They say, 'Live, live, live, live, live!' It's all they've learned, it's the only advice they can give—just live. . . ." Carol, opening the door, says: "Simple! A very simple instruction." She goes out, to a chorus of "Absolutely degraded . . . corrupt!" Val, repelled by these hissed words, suddenly gets up and follows.

Vee, coming back for Val, finds him gone. "You might as well face it, Vee," calls one of the women, "this is one candidate for salvation that you have lost to the opposition." The fighting starts, and ends with Vee rushing upstairs in a huff, and Dolly and Beulah, impatient at what they call her "hypocriticism," departing. The two weird sisters are left. Considering the others "common as dirt," they do a bit of light-fingered pinching. They take the vase and flowers off the table, pick up the remaining food and make off with all this. They do say they will give Jabe credit for this loot in the parish notes.

Sheriff Talbott, returning, cries: "Where in the hell is my wife? Vee!"

VEE (*from landing*)—Hush that bawling! I had to speak to Lady about that boy and I couldn't speak to her in front of Jabe because he thinks he's gonna be able to go back to work himself.

SHERIFF—Well, move along, Mama, quit foolin'.

VEE—I think I ought to wait till that boy gits back.

SHERIFF—I'm sick of you making a goddam fool of yourself over every stray bastard that wanders into this county.

As the car drives off, dogs bay in the distance.

SCENE II

Later that night, having been dropped off by Carol, Val comes back to the darkened store for his guitar. Lady, near hysteria, comes down the stairs in her bathrobe, turns on the light over the counter and does her best to have the telephone operator wake the druggist. She doesn't see Val, as she shrills over the phone that it is an emergency. "Oh, God," she mutters, "I wish I was dead, dead, dead . . ." "No, you don't, ma'am," Val says quietly. Seeing Val, Lady grabs a revolver from the cash register and threatens to shoot him.

Val reminds her that Sheriff Talbott's wife had brought him to the store for a job. He hadn't stayed because Carol Cutrere had taken him away to fix her car.

LADY—Did you fix it?

VAL—She didn't have no car trouble, that wasn't her trouble. Oh, she had trouble, all right, but *that* wasn't it. . . .

LADY—What was her trouble?

VAL—She made a mistake about me.

LADY—What mistake?

VAL—She thought I had a sign "Male at Stud" hung on me.

LADY—She thought—you—? (*Into phone, suddenly.*) Oh, Mr. Dubinsky, I'm sorry to wake you up but I just brought my husband back from the Memphis hospital and I left my box of luminal tablets in the—I got to have some! I ain't slep' for three nights, I'm going to pieces, you hear me, I'm going to pieces, I ain't slept in three nights, I got to have some tonight. Now you look here, if you want to keep my trade, you send over some tablets. Then bring them yourself, God damn it, excuse my French! Because I'm going to pieces right this minute!" Hanging up violently, she shivers.

Val gives her his snakeskin jacket to put over her thin wrapper. After examining it curiously, Lady puts it on. "It feels warm, all right," she says.

VAL—It's warm from my body, I guess.

LADY—You must be a warm-blooded boy . . .

VAL—That's right . . .

LADY—Well, what are you lookin' for around here?

VAL—Work.

LADY—Boys like you don't work.

VAL—What d'you mean by boys like me?

LADY—Ones that play th' guitar and go around talkin' about how warm they are . . .

VAL—That happens t' be the truth. My temperature's always a couple degrees above normal the same as a dog's. It's normal for me the same as it is for a dog, that's the truth.

They are smiling and laughing together; Lady has found Val pleasant, though odd. Still, she can't see giving any but local help a job: "I couldn't hire no stranger with a snakeskin jacket and a guitar . . . and that runs a temperature as high as a dog's." With another of her sudden, soft laughs, Lady takes off his jacket and advises Val to go. "I got nowhere to go," Val says. "Well," Lady answers, "everyone's got a problem and that's yours."

Caught by her voice, Val wonders if Lady's a foreigner. "I'm the daughter of a Wop bootlegger that was killed here," Lady replies. Then hearing Jabe's knock, she turns off the light and tells Val the door will lock behind him.

Instead of leaving, Val starts playing his guitar and singing. He breaks off to tell Lady he does electrical repairs and all kinds of odd jobs: "Ma'am, I'm thirty today and I'm through with the life that I've been leading." As dogs bay loudly in the distance, Val persists: "I've lived in corruption but I'm not corrupted. Here is why—" Holding up his guitar for Lady to see, Val maintains: "My life's companion! It washes me clean like water when anything unclean has touched me." Lady's attention is held; she wants to look at all the writing on his guitar. Val explains the autographs as people who are his "immortals": Leadbelly, King Oliver, and Bessie Smith— "That name of Bessie Smith is written on the stars! Jim Crow killed her, John Barleycorn and Jim Crow killed Bessie Smith. She bled to death after an auto accident, because they wouldn't take her into a white hospital. . . ." Lady, listening, is so close to Val that the guitar is all that separates their bodies.

Lady asks suddenly if Val has had any selling experience, and has any character references. Val digs a worn letter from the junk in his wallet. Lady reads aloud: "This boy worked for me three months in my auto repair shop and is a real hard worker and is good and honest but is a peculiar talker and that is the reason I got to let him go but would like to keep him—" Lady whoops, but concedes that what people say doesn't mean much, and if he can read shoe sizes and make change, she can use him. She has plans to open the confectionery, to serve set-ups and to compete for the night life of the county. She's going to redecorate, she tells him eagerly: "Artificial branches of fruit trees in flower on the walls and ceilings! It's going to be like an orchard in the spring!— My father, he had an orchard on Moon Lake. He made a wine-garden of it. We had fifteen little white arbors with tables in them and they were covered with grapevines . . . and we sold Dago red wine an' bootleg whiskey and beer. . . . They burned it up one summer."

VAL—Who burned it up?

LADY—An outfit in this county called the Mystic Crew rode out there one night with a blow-torch an' gallons of coal-oil and set the whole thing on fire, and I want you to know that not a single fire-engine in this county pulled out of the station that night. My Papa, he took a blanket and run up into the orchard to fight the fire single-handed. He burned alive in it . . . burned alive! I heard him scream in the orchard—I ran—I fell—I saw him run towards me with his clothes on fire! . . . Whenever I look at a man in this county, I wonder if he was one of 'em that set our orchard on fire! (*A figure appears at the door, knocks and calls: "Mrs. Torrance?"*) Oh, that's the sandman with my sleeping tablets. (*She crosses to the door.*) Thanks, Mr. Dubinsky, sorry I had to disturb you, sorry I— (*Man mutters something and goes; she closes the door.*) Well, go to hell then, old bastard. . . . (*To* Val.)   You ever have trouble sleeping?

Val—I can sleep or not sleep as long or short as I want to.

Lady—Is that right?

Val—I can sleep on a concrete floor or go without sleeping, without even feeling sleepy, for forty-eight hours.   And I can hold my breath three minutes without blacking out, I made ten dollars betting I could do it and I did it!   And I can go a whole day without passing water.

Lady (*startled*)—Is *that a fact?*

Val—That's a fact.   I served time on a chain-gang for vagrancy once and they tied me to a post all day and I stood there all day without passing water to show the sons of bitches I could do it.

Lady—I see what that auto repair man was talking about when he said, This boy is a peculiar talker!   Well—(*sitting at the table*) —what else can you do?   Tell me some more about your self-control!

Val (*grinning*)—Well, they say that a woman can burn a man down.   But I can burn down a woman.

Lady, laughing, knows of quite a few women around here who'd be delighted to put him to the test, but she's not one.   Val says quickly that he's done with all that: he's fed up.   "I'm telling you, lady, there's people bought and sold in this world like carcasses of hogs in butcher shops!"   He's not telling Lady anything new.   For Val, there are just two kinds of people—the ones that are bought, and the buyers; though of course there's that third category, bums like himself who have character references that describe them as crazy.   He doesn't want to have his feet on the ground; he'd like to rise above it.

Val says that he wants to be like one of those little sky-colored birds that live their whole life on the wing: "They fly so high in gray weather, the goddam hawks would get dizzy.   But those little birds, they don't have no legs at all and they live their whole lives on the wing, and they sleep on the wind, that's how they sleep at night, they just spread their wings and go to sleep on the wind like other birds fold their wings and go to sleep on a tree. . . . They sleep on the wind . . . an' never light on this earth but one time when they die!"   Lady, too, would like to be one of those birds, but she doesn't believe that any living thing can be that free.   She'd give this whole store and everything in it to be a tiny bird the color of the sky and, for one night, to sleep on the wind.

Jabe's knocking cuts short her fancies.   She remembers that she lives with a son-of-a-bitch who bought her at a fire sale, and in fifteen years she has not had a single good dream.

Ringing open the cash register, Lady hands Val a dollar for food and tells him to report back for work in the morning. It will be a straight business relationship; there will be no interest in Val's perfect functions. About to leave, Val gushes that she is the nicest person he has ever met. He promises to be the perfect worker and to help solve her sleeping problem: "A lady osteopath taught me how to make little adjustments in the neck bone and spine. It will give you a sound natural slee . Good-night!"

ACT II

Only a week later, Val is the source of complaints from women customers. Lady, too, is disturbed by his presence. His physical charms are too much in evidence. Everything he does, according to Lady, is suggestive. "Suggestive of what?" asks Val. "Of what you said you was through with—somethin'— Oh, shoot, you know what I mean. Why d'ya think I give you a plain, dark business suit to work in?" With a sigh, Val gives her back the suit jacket; he is ready to take off the pants and give up his job. Lady backtracks, apologizes, and grabs his guitar from the alcove so that he can't go.

LADY—I ain't dissatisfied with you. I'm pleased with you, sincerely!

VAL—You sure don't show it.

LADY—My nerves are all shot to pieces. Shake.

VAL—You mean I ain't fired, so I don't have to quit? (*They shake hands like two men. She hands him the guitar. Then silence falls between them.*)

LADY—You see, we don't know each other, we're—we're—just gettin' acquainted.

VAL—That's right, like a couple of animals sniffin' around each other . . .

LADY—Well, not exactly like *that*, but—!

VAL—We don't know each other. How do people get to know each other? I used to think they did it by touch.

But lately he thinks this has made them more strangers than ever. He thinks now that nobody ever gets to know *nobody:* "We're all of us sentenced to solitary confinement inside our own skins, for life! You understand me, Lady? I'm tellin' you it's the truth, we got

to face it, we're under a life-long sentence to solitary confinement
inside our own lonely skins for as long as we live on this earth!"

Lady won't agree to anything as sad as that, but she listens to
Val. From his earliest days, Val says, he has been looking for things
to make more sense. He found the make-believe answer—love. . . .
"It's fooled many a fool besides you an' me, that's the God's truth,
Lady, and you had better believe it." He first found it in a naked
girl on the bayou when he was fourteen. But afterwards the question wasn't any plainer than the answer, and at fifteen he went to
New Orleans in his snakeskin jacket, where it didn't take long for
him to learn the score.

VAL—I learned that I had somethin' to sell besides snakeskins and
other wild things' skins I caught on the bayou. I was corrupted!
That's the answer . . .

LADY—Naw, that ain't the answer!

VAL—Okay, *you* tell me the answer!

LADY—I don't know the answer, I just know corruption ain't the
answer. I know that much. If I thought that was the answer I'd
take Jabe's pistol or his morphine tablets and—

A woman bursts in to telephone the Cutreres that Carol is back
on the town and is honking her car horn for service at the woman's
gas station. Dolly and Beulah arrive to make the excitement general. They're all for calling the sheriff's office and organizing a boy-
cott against Carol. They start with Lady, but run into their first
refusal. Dolly next grabs the phone to make sure that Mr. Dubinsky won't wait on Carol, although Beulah doesn't think there's much
hope there: "Dubinsky'd wait on a purple-bottomed baboon if it
put a dime on th' counter an' pointed at something!"

DOLLY—I know she sat at a table in the Blue Bird Cafe half'n
hour last time she was here and the waitresses never came near her!

BEULAH—That's different. They're not foreigners there! You
can't ostracize a person out of this county unless everybody coop-
erates. Lady just told me that she was going to wait on her if she
comes here.

Lady, delighted that this wild girl is giving her brother so much
trouble, has no intention of refusing to wait on her. However, when
Carol suddenly appears, Lady soon grows impatient at the girl's
feverish air. Lady repeatedly asks her what she wants so that she
can get rid of her. Before she can find out, the phone rings to an-

nounce that Carol's brother is on his way for her. Lady blows up: *"David Cutrere is not coming in this store!"* Dolly and Beulah take it all in. Wheeling on them, Lady cries: "Beulah! Dolly! Why're you back there hissing together like geese? Why don't you go to th'—Blue Bird and—have some hot coffee—talk there!" "It looks like we're getting what they call the 'bum's rush,'" says Beulah. "I never stay where I'm not wanted," says Dolly, "and when I'm not wanted somewhere I never come back!"

After their huffy departure, Lady tells Carol that she'd better hurry up with her private message for Val before her brother gets here. Everyone knows what her private message is, and Lady warns her that this boy is not for sale in her store.

Left with Val, Carol delivers her piece. It meets with no surprise.

VAL—Who're you tryin' t' fool beside you'self? You couldn't stand the weight of a man's body on you. (*He casually picks up her wrist and pushes the sleeve back from it.*) What's this here? A human wrist with a bone? It feels like a twig I could snap with two fingers. . . . (*Gently, negligently, he pushes the collar of her trench coat back from her bare throat and shoulders, and runs a finger along her neck, tracing a vein.*) Little girl, you're transparent, I can see the veins in you. A man's weight on you would break you like a bundle of sticks.

CAROL (*startled by his perception*)—Isn't it funny! You've hit on the truth about me. The act of love-making is almost unbearably painful, and yet, of course, I do bear it, because to be not alone, even for a few moments, is worth the pain and the danger. It's dangerous for me because I'm not built for child-bearing.

VAL—Well, then, fly away, little bird, fly away before you—get broke.

He's through with her crowd and their hangouts. . . . "Take this Rolex Chronometer that tells the time of the day and the day of the week and the month and all the crazy moon's phases. I never stole nothing before. When I stole that it was time for me to get off the party, so take it back, now, to Bertie . . ." He tries to force the watch into Carol's fist. She is crying. Violently hurling the watch across the room, Val cries: "That's my message to you and the pack you run with!" Carol shouts that she runs with nobody, that Val is in danger here, now that he's changed his snakeskin jacket for a conforming blue suit. "The message I came here to give you," Carol cries, "was a warning of danger; I hoped you'd hear me and let me take you away before it's—too late."

Maureen Stapleton, Cliff Robertsa

nd Lois Smith in "Orpheus Descending"

Lady, who had loudly forbidden anyone to let David Cutrere in her store, changes her mind the minute she sees his handsome face. Rid of Carol, David stands miserably by as Lady pours out all the thoughts that have been bottled up fifteen years.

Seeing David for the first time since the Mystic Crew burned her father's place, Lady tells him that she carried his child that summer. After he deserted her, she had an abortion. David keeps saying miserably that he hadn't known. Lady accuses him passionately of making whores of them both. Her mood's mercurial: the good memories quickly take over. She talks of the nights in her father's wine-garden. David says these are his only memories. He starts to go. Lady shifts again: she is not asking for pity; she doesn't need it with this store and the confectionery that is going to be done over like her father's wine-garden. "The wine-garden of my father," she cries, "those wine-drinking nights when you had something better than anything you've had since!" David, his hand on the door, blurts out, *"That's true!"*—but leaves.

Left with Jabe's knocking, and sure that she's just made a fool of herself, Lady goes heavily up the stairs.

Vee Talbott, blinded by the setting sun, stumbles into the store. She wants Val to join her church and wishes to give one of her religious paintings to those non-churchgoers, Jabe and Lady. Val receives her sympathetically and listens as she explains that she can only paint when she has visions. Talbott, passing them on his way upstairs to Jabe, regards them suspiciously and orders Vee out to the car.

About to do as she is told, Vee reveals: "Since I got into this painting, my whole outlook is different. I can't explain how it is, the difference to me." Val suggests that she means existence up to then hadn't made sense; that as the wife of the county sheriff she had seen awful things. "Awful things!" Vee repeats. "Beatings!" says Val. "Yes. Lynchings!" cries Vee. "Runaway convicts torn to pieces by hounds!" says Val. "Chain-gang dogs!" cries Vee in horror.

In evangelical tones, Val talks to Vee about her painting, her visions, and slowly and gently lifts her hands to his lips. "You made some beauty out of this dark county with these two, soft woman hands," he says. Talbott, coming down the stairs, observes them. "Cut this crap!" Talbott yells. "Jabe Torrance told me to take a good look at you." Talbott looks Val up and down. "Well, now I've taken that look," he says and follows Vee out of the store.

Upset by the terrible things Jabe has been calling her, Lady joins Val, who, though ready to leave for the night, stays on for company's sake. Carol's warning has bothered him; he has never felt safe here. The sudden baying of chain-gang dogs intensifies their moods. The baying grows—as the dogs reach their quarry, an escaped convict—to a sustained, almost single, note of savagery. A shot at length brings quiet.

Again Val starts to go; again Lady stops him. She now suggests that he live here in the little alcove under the stairs. She promotes the notions that he would be saving rent and that she would feel safer. She is full of ideas for making him comfortable: she promises to install a hot and cold shower for him. Lady begs him to have a look at the alcove.

Val, having looked behind the curtain, says he can't resist something he gets for nothing. As a bachelor, however, he might miss being able to bring home girls. Lady becomes increasingly self-conscious.

To relax her, Val uses some tricks learned from the lady osteopath who had also sheltered him. He finishes this treatment by stroking Lady's neck: "Your skin's like silk," Val says, "you're light-skinned to be Italian." To cover her confusion, Lady starts chattering and going in for little outbursts of senseless laughter. Then she gathers courage to go for Val's bed linen.

As soon as she is out of sight, Val rings open the cash register, scoops out a fistful of money, picks up his guitar, and decamps. Returning to the empty room, Lady throws down the linen furiously. She heads immediately for the cash register to ring it open. Incensed at the theft, she cries, "Thief!" and grabs the telephone. In the act of calling the operator, she thinks better of it, and, frustrated, does nothing.

Scene II

Later that night, Val returns somewhat unsteadily to replace the money he'd lifted from the cash register. As if she had been waiting, Lady, wearing a white satin kimono and carrying a flashlight, hurries down the stairs.

They square for a fight and start having it out right away.

LADY—Why'd you open the cashbox when you come in?

VAL—I opened it twice this evening—once before I went out and again when I come back. I borrowed some money and put it back in the box an' got all this left over! (*Shows her a wad of bills.*) I beat a blackjack dealer five times straight. With this much loot I can retire for the season.

LADY—Chicken-feed! . . . I'm sorry for you.

VAL—You're sorry for me?

LADY—I'm sorry for you because nobody can help you. I was touched by your strangeness, your strange talk—that thing about birds with no feet so they have to sleep on the wind. . . . I said to myself, this boy is a bird with no feet so he has to sleep on the wind, and that softened my fool Dago heart and I wanted to help you. . . . Fool, me!—I got what I should of expected. You robbed me while I was upstairs to get sheets to make up your bed! I guess I'm a fool to even feel disappointed.

VAL—You're disappointed in me. I was disappointed in you.

LADY—How did I disappoint you?

VAL—There wasn't no cot behind that curtain before. You put it back there for a purpose.

LADY—It was back there! Folded behind the mirror.

VAL—It wasn't back of no mirror when you told me three times to go and—

LADY (*cutting in*)—I left that money in the cashbox on purpose, to find out if I could trust you.

VAL—You got back th'—

LADY—No, no, no, I can't trust you, now I know I can't trust you, I got to trust anybody or I don't want him.

VAL—That's okay, I don't expect no character reference from you.

LADY—I'll give you a character reference. I'd say this boy's a peculiar talker! But I wouldn't say a real hard worker or honest. I'd say a peculiar slew-footer that sweet-talks you while he's got his hand in the cashbox.

VAL—I took out less than you owed me.

LADY—Don't mix up the issue. I see through you, Mister!

VAL—I see through you, Lady.

LADY—What d'you see through me?

VAL—You sure you want me to tell?

LADY—I'd love for you to.

VAL—A not so young and not so satisfied woman, that hired a man off the highway to do double duty without paying overtime for it. . . . I mean a store-clerk days and a stud nights, and—

LADY—God, no! You—!

Invective fails her, so she uses her fists. He seizes her wrists, and after a slight struggle she collapses sobbing in a chair. Says Val, "It's natural. You felt lonely . . ." As he starts gravely to leave with his guitar, she dashes ahead and extends her arms across the door. She cries out passionately for him not to go; she needs him. After a moment Val, touched, goes to the alcove, looks back at her. Lady needs him, she says: *"To live . . . to go on living!!"*

ACT III

The trained nurse, believing that even the dying should be mobilized, encourages Jabe to survey his store and helps him, step by step, down the stairs. In the nick of time, Lady rouses Val from his alcove bed. Val just manages to be ready for Jabe's sneering inspection.

Assuming that young and old women alike are attracted by Val's looks, Jabe says that Lady is getting him cheap. Having had his look at Val, Jabe refuses to sit down, insists on going into the confectionery. The lights suddenly go on, and arbors, flowers, moon and juke box are flooded with color.

NURSE—Well, isn't this artistic.

JABE—Yeh. Artistic as hell.

NURSE—I never seen anything like it before.

JABE—Nobody else did either.

NURSE—Who done these decorations?

LADY (*defiantly*)—I did them, all by myself!

NURSE—What do you know! It sure is something artistic.

Jabe hears a calliope playing on the streets; Lady says excitedly that it's been hired to announce the opening of the confectionery. "I married a live one, Miss Porter," says Jabe savagely. "How much does that damn thing cost me?" Lady reluctantly confesses what she is paying by the hour. Jabe's ferocity becomes even more apparent.

JABE—Miss Porter, I married a live one! Didn't I marry a live one? (*He switches off the light in the confectionery.*) Her daddy, "The Wop," was just as much of a live one till he burned up. (LADY *gasps as if struck.* JABE *continues, with a slow, malignant grin.*) He had a wine-garden on the north shore of Moon Lake. The new confectionery sort of reminds me of it. But he made a mistake, he made a bad mistake one time, selling liquor to niggers. We burned him out. We burned him out, house and orchard and vines, and "The Wop" was burned up trying to fight the fire. . . .

Jabe suddenly is taken with a cramp. By the time the nurse gets him to his room, he's had a hemorrhage. The nurse tears down to telephone the doctor. Lady, unhearing, is indifferent, thinks only of what Jabe had said: "Did you hear what he said? He said, 'we' did it, 'we' burned house-vines-orchard—'The Wop' burned fighting the fire . . ."

SCENE II

Talbott, the sheriff, catches Vee and Val together again. Val, bathing Vee's blinded eyes, has been listening to her vision of the Resurrection as it had just appeared to her. Talbott has his bully boys cover Val as he hauls his wife roughly to the door. There are the preliminaries of a lynching. Spring-blade knives come from pockets; sadism is given full play. But suddenly, with Miss Porter's calling for Lady, Talbott suggests that his companions go up to Jabe while he straightens out Val.

Talbott, almost gently, tells Val that he's not going to hurt him or his guitar, but he's going to tell him something: "They's a certain county I know of which has a big sign at the county line that says, 'Nigger, don't let the sun go down on you in this county.' That's all it says, it don't threaten nothing, it just says, 'Nigger, don't let the sun go down on you in this county!'" He chuckles hoarsely. "Well, son? You ain't a nigger and this is not that county, but, son, I want you to just imagine that you seen a sign that said to you, 'Boy, don't let the sun rise on you in this county.' I said 'rise,' not 'go down,' because it's too close to sunset for you to git packed an' move on before that. But I think if you value that instrument in your hands as much as you seem to, you'll simplify my job by not allowing the sun tomorrow to rise on you in this county. . . ." Talbott hopes so, because he doesn't like *violence*.

SCENE III

As Jabe lies dying, the busy townswomen gather. His wife, however, was last seen entering the beauty parlor.

Finally, ablaze with nervous excitement, Lady comes home loaded down with favors for the confectionery opening, decked out herself in everything from a low-cut dress and pearls to a be-ribboned corsage. She taunts the women over their mournful voices. She brushes off their comments, kind or otherwise. She shouts for Val to help her. An unwanted Carol appears.

Lady says the confectionery is off-bounds to Carol. "Sheriff Talbott, the county marshall," says Carol, "suggested I get Val to drive me over the river since he'd be crossing too." Lady is incensed. Why does Carol have to bother that boy? "Why would he be leaving here tonight?" She shouts again for Val. This time the Conjure Man enters. Lady tries to shoo him away, but Carol bribes him to do the Choctaw cry. The cry produces a violent reaction, clearing the store of the women, and the men from upstairs who hustle the Negro out of the store. Val, as if summoned by the cry, appears in the alcove. Proclaiming that there is still something wild in the country, Carol goes outside to wait in her car.

Lady is pretty much hopped-up. She tries to get Val to put on his white jacket and shave ice for set-ups; she struggles to remember the amount of liquor needed, the restrictions on minors from buying it. Gasping and touching her diaphragm, she yells at Val not to goof. He simply can't get her ear. "Will you quit thrashin' around like a cat-fish?" Val asks.

VAL—You can't open a night-place here this night.

LADY—You bet your sweet life I'm *going* to!

VAL—Not *me*, not *my* sweet life!

LADY—I'm betting my life on it! Sweet or *not* sweet, I'm—

VAL—Yours is yours, mine is mine. . . . (*He releases her with a sad shrug.*)

LADY—You don't get the point, huh? There's a man up there that set fire to my father's wine-garden and I lost my life in it, yeah, I lost my life in it, three lives was lost in it, two born lives and *one—not*. . . . I was made to commit a murder by him up there! I want that man to see the wine-garden come open again when he's dying! I want him to hear it coming open again here tonight—while he's dying! It's necessary, no power on earth can stop it. Hell, I don't even want it, it's just necessary, it's just something's got to be done to square things away, to, to, to—*be not defeated!* You get me? Just to be not defeated! Ah, oh, I won't be defeated, not again, in my life! (*Embraces him.*) Thank you for staying here with me! God bless you for it. . . . Now please go and get in your white jacket . . .

With a sigh and a sad shrug, Val goes for his suitcase and snakeskin jacket. With or without wages, he's going to head south. He never gets to leave. Nurse Porter, who has been trying to get hold of Lady all day, comes downstairs. Her watchful eyes take everything in.

Lady makes the fatal mistake of asking the nurse if it isn't possible to help shorten a man's suffering. Nurse Porter gets huffy and Lady fires her. The nurse lashes out that—"The moment I looked at you when I was called on this case last Friday morning, I knew you were pregnant." Lady gasps. "I also knew," adds Miss Porter, "the moment I looked at your husband it wasn't by him." Lady is overjoyed. Miss Porter asks venomously why Lady doesn't have the clown and calliope announce it. "You do it for me, save me the money!" cries Lady. "Make the announcement all over!"

Knowing the nurse has gone to broadcast the news, Val, scared, asks if it's true. Lady, highly overwrought and knowing that Val should leave at once, thanks him: "You've given me life," she cries, "you can go!" In hysterical ecstasy, Lady grabs a paper horn and pipes the news up to Jabe.

She rouses Jabe from his deathbed. Revolver in hand, stumbling down the stairs, clutching at anything for support, he shoots Lady twice, but having no cartridges for Val, rushes at the door, shouting: "I'll have him killed! I burned your father and I'll have him killed!" In the street he cries: "The clerk is robbing the store, he shot my wife, the clerk is robbing the store, he killed my wife!"

Lady goes to die in the confectionery. The lynching starts in earnest: the mob closes in from all directions. Val is dragged off. The chain-gang dogs start their baying; a man calls for rope. Another answers: "Don't need no rope for that boy, they're gonna tear off his clothes an' throw the son-of-a-bitch to the chain-gang dogs!" Someone decides to rob the cash register, then rushes away.

Carol and the Conjure Man appear out of the dark. Carol sees the Negro carrying Val's snakeskin jacket and buys it off him. Shivering, she puts the jacket on: "Wild things," says Carol, "leave skins behind them, they leave clean skins and teeth and white bones behind them, and these are tokens passed from one to another, so that the fugitive kind can always follow their kind. . . ."

A MOON FOR THE MISBEGOTTEN

A Play in Four Acts

By Eugene O'Neill

[*For a biographical sketch of Eugene O'Neill, see "Long Day's Journey into Night."*]

THE Place: the Connecticut farmhouse of tenant farmer Phil Hogan. The time: from noon one September day in 1923 to sunrise of the following day. The farmhouse, a boxlike, unpainted clapboard horror, was originally built elsewhere, but moved to this barren site and then propped up on timber blocks. A homemade tarpaper annex, Josie's bedroom, with a separate entrance and a few wooden steps, has been tacked onto the box to add to the dismal effect. There are no shutters, no curtains, no shades at the windows—not even panes of glass in most of the frames. There is no "foundation planting"; the only thing that rises from the dirt is a big, flat-topped boulder close to the house.

It is almost noon when Josie helps her kid brother, Mike, run away from the farm. This oversized woman, more powerful than any but an exceptionally strong man (yet "all woman"), towers over her brother, a runty boy—a "New England Irish Catholic Puritan, Grade B."

In helping Mike with cash and a suitcase stolen from their father, Josie is obviously helping to rid herself and her father of an irritant. Mike, for his part, considers them two of a kind, and a bad kind. Josie, taking his waspishness good-naturedly, tells Mike that he can change into his Sunday suit in the can at the station or in the train.

JOSIE— . . . and don't forget to wash your face. I know you want to look your best when our brother, Thomas, sees you on his

"A Moon for the Misbegotten": By Eugene O'Neill. Copyright © 1952 by Eugene O'Neill. Reprinted by permission of Random House, Inc., New York, N. Y.

doorstep. (*Her tone becomes derisively amused.*) And him way up in the world, a noble sergeant of the Bridgeport police. Maybe he'll get you on the force. It'd suit you. I can see you leading drunks to the lockup while you give them a lecture on temperance. Or if Thomas can't get you a job, he'll pass you along to our brother, John, the noble barkeep in Meriden. He'll teach you the trade. You'll make a nice one, who'll never steal from the till, or drink, and who'll tell customers they've had enough and better go home just when they're beginning to feel happy. (*She sighs regretfully.*) Ah, well, Mike, you was born a priest's pet, and there's no help for it.

MIKE—That's right! Make fun of me again, because I want to be decent.

JOSIE—You're worse than decent. You're virtuous.

MIKE—Well, that's a thing nobody can say about . . . (*He stops, a bit ashamed, but more afraid to finish.*)

JOSIE—About me? No, and what's more, they don't. (*She smiles mockingly.*) I know what a trial it's been to you, Mike, having a sister who's the scandal of the neighborhood.

In spite of his over-virtuousness, Josie shells out a few stolen dollars as his going-away present: "Get along now, so you won't miss the trolley. And don't forget to get off the train at Bridgeport. Give my love to Thomas and John. No, never mind. They've not written me in years. Give them a boot in the tail for me."

MIKE—That's nice talk for a woman. You've a tongue as dirty as the Old Man's.

JOSIE—Don't start preaching, like you love to, or you'll never go.

MIKE—You're as bad as he is, almost. It's his influence made you what you are, and him always scheming how he'll cheat people, selling them a broken down nag or a sick cow or pig that he's doctored up to look good for a day or two. It's no better than stealing, and you help him.

JOSIE—I do. Sure, it's grand fun.

MIKE—You ought to marry and have a home of your own away from this shanty and stop your shameless ways with men. (*He adds, not without moral satisfaction.*) Though it'd be hard to find a decent man who'd have you now.

JOSIE—I don't want a decent man, thank you. They're no fun. They're all sticks like you. And I wouldn't marry the best man on earth and be tied down to him alone.

MIKE (*with a cunning leer*)—Not even Jim Tyrone, I suppose.

(*She stares at him.*) You'd like being tied to money, I know that, and he'll be rich when his mother's estate is settled. I suppose you've never thought of that? Don't tell me! I've watched you making sheep's eyes at him.

JOSIE (*contemptuously*)—So I'm leading Jim on to propose, am I?

MIKE—I know it's crazy, but maybe you're hoping if you got hold of him alone when he's mad drunk— Anyway, talk all you please to put me off, I'll bet my last penny you've cooked up some scheme to hook him, and the Old Man put you up to it. Maybe he thinks if he caught you with Jim and had witnesses to prove it, and his shotgun to scare him—

Controlling her anger, Josie tells him to shut up, and with a threatening swipe sends "the dirty tick" running. Washing her hands of him, Josie prepares to greet her father by arming herself with a sawed-off broom handle. "Not that I need it," she says, "but it saves his pride."

Hogan, her tough, small, fighting-cock of a father, appears in hot pursuit of Mike. Frustrated, he starts cussing, and Josie, with provoking calm, gives him back as good. She tells her father that Mike, like Thomas and John ahead of him, ran off to escape his slave-driving.

HOGAN (*baffled, sits on the boulder and takes off his hat to scratch his head; with a faint trace of grudging respect*)—I'd never dreamt he had that much spunk. (*His temper rising again.*) And I know damned well he hadn't, not without you to give him the guts and help him, like the great soft fool you are!

JOSIE—Now don't start raging again, Father.

HOGAN (*seething*)—You've stolen my satchel to give him, I suppose, like you did before for Thomas and John?

JOSIE—It was my satchel, too. Didn't I help you in the trade for the horse, when you got the Crowleys to throw in the satchel for good measure? I was up all night fixing that nag's forelegs so his knees wouldn't buckle together till after the Crowleys had him a day or two.

HOGAN (*forgets his anger to grin reminiscently*)—You've a wonderful way with animals, God bless you. And do you remember the two Crowleys came back to give me a beating, and I licked them both?

JOSIE (*with calculating flattery*)—You did. You're a wonderful fighter. Sure, you could give Jack Dempsey himself a run for his money.

HOGAN (*with sharp suspicion*)—I could, but don't try to change the subject and fill me with blarney.

JOSIE—All right. I'll tell the truth then. They were getting the best of you till I ran out and knocked one of them tail over tin cup against the pigpen.

HOGAN (*outraged*)—You're a liar! They was begging for mercy before you came. (*Furiously.*) You thief, you! You stole my fine satchel for that lump! And I'll bet that's not all. I'll bet, like when Thomas and John sneaked off, you— (*He rises from the boulder threateningly.*) Listen, Josie, if you found where I hid my little green bag, and stole my money to give to that lousy altar boy, I'll—

JOSIE (*rises from the steps with broom handle in her right hand*) —Well, I did. So now what'll you do? Don't be threatening me. You know I'll beat better sense in your skull if you lay a finger on me.

HOGAN—I never yet laid hands on a woman—not when I was sober—but if it wasn't for that club— (*Bitterly.*) A fine curse God put on me when he gave me a daughter as big and strong as a bull, and as vicious and disrespectful. (*Suddenly his eyes twinkle and he grins admiringly.*) Be God, look at you standing there with the club! If you ain't the damnedest daughter in Connecticut, who is? (*He chuckles and sits on the boulder again.*)

JOSIE (*laughs and sits on the steps, putting the club away*)— And if you ain't the damnedest father in Connecticut, who is?

After this excitement has died down, and Hogan has lit his pipe, he admits that he isn't sorry to have seen the last of Mike, whom he liked no better than his other sons. Hogan thanks God that Josie, at least, is like her mother and himself: "When I think your poor mother was killed bringing that crummy calf into life—I've never set foot in a church since, and never will—"

Josie's mother was the other who could put Hogan in his place, when he'd come home drunk. Hogan remembers appreciatively: "I only raised my hand to her once—just a slap because she told me to stop singing, it was after daylight. The next moment I was on the floor thinking a mule had kicked me. Since you've grown up, I've had the same trouble. There's no liberty in my own home."

Hogan asks what Mike's final sermon was. "Oh, the same as ever," Josie says airily; "that I'm the scandal of the countryside carrying on with men without a marriage license." Hogan, giving her a strange, embarrassed glance, looks away before saying casually: "Hell roast his soul for saying it. But it's true enough." Josie asserts her independence defiantly. But while wishing no preaching, she still wonders why a fighting man like her father never used her disgrace as an excuse to beat those men up. "Wouldn't I look a great fool," Hogan replies, "when everyone knows any man who tried to make free with you, and you not willing, would be carried off to the hospital? Anyway, I wouldn't want to fight an army. You've had too many sweethearts."

Josie now relays Mike's last bit of advice: that she should settle down. Since no decent man would have her, Mike advised catching an indecent man with money to steal. With another of his quick, probing side-glances, Hogan asks casually: "He meant Jim Tyrone?" "He did," Josie answers, "and the dirty tick accused you and me of making up a foxy scheme to trap Jim. I'm to get him alone when he's crazy drunk and lead him on to marry me." She adds scornfully: "As if that would ever work. Sure, all the pretty little tarts on Broadway, New York, must have had a try at that, and much good it did them."

As if misunderstanding, Hogan comments on the merits of Mike's scheme: it might work because it's so old that no one would suspect anyone's trying it. Telling him to shut up, Josie cries: "You like Jim and you'd never play a dirty trick on him, not even if I was willing." "No," says Hogan, "not unless I found he was playing one on me." Hogan's motto is never to trust anyone too far, not even himself. "You've reason for the last," Josie says. "I've often suspected you sneak out of bed in the night to pick your own pockets."

Hogan wouldn't drop Mike's idea, though. It might be a happy marriage, because since they're both disgraces, neither one could look down on the other. Josie knows her father: "You old divil, you've always a trick hidden behind your tricks, so no one can tell at times what you're after."

Hogan is sure Josie has a soft spot for Jim, who, he says, likes her, too. "Because he keeps dropping in here lately?" Josie asks. "Sure, it's only when he gets sick of the drunks at the Inn, and it's more to joke with you than to see me." Hogan thinks she should use her wits to catch him: "Who knows? With all the sweethearts you've had, you must have a catching way with men." Josie at once assumes her boastful manner, but subsides quickly: "Och, Father, don't play the jackass with me. You know, and I know, I'm an ugly overgrown lump of a woman, and the men that want me are no better than stupid bulls. Jim can have all the pretty, painted little Broadway girls he wants—and dancers on the stage, too—when he comes into his estate. That's the kind he likes."

Assuring Josie that Jim has taken in her fine points, he suggests that marrying Jim might be a way of bettering herself. Josie confesses that, married to Jim, she would cure him of drink even if she had to kill him. Hogan quickly gets on to the estate that Jim's inheriting. Josie knew he would be mentioning that, and says defiantly of course she'd love the money as much as anyone else, and, compared to the Broadway scum who'll pick him clean, she's decent and deserving. But, with sudden illogical anger, Josie asks her father to keep his mad scheming to himself.

Hogan wins back her attention when he brings their home, the farm, into the conversation.

HOGAN—Don't forget, if we have lived on it twenty years, we're only tenants and we could be thrown out on our necks any time. (*Quickly.*) Mind you, I don't say Jim would ever do it, rent or no rent, or let the executors do it, even if they wanted, which they don't, knowing they'd never find another tenant.

JOSIE—What's worrying you, then?

HOGAN—This. I've been afraid lately the minute the estate is out of probate, Jim will sell the farm.

JOSIE (*exasperated*)—Of course he will! Hasn't he told us and promised you can buy it on easy time-payments at the small price you offered?

HOGAN—Jim promises whatever you like when he's full of whiskey. He might forget a promise as easy when he's drunk enough.

JOSIE (*indignantly*)—He'd never! And who'd want it except us? No one ever has in all the years—

HOGAN—Someone has lately. The agent got an offer last month, Jim told me, bigger than mine.

JOSIE—Och, Jim loves to try and get your goat. He was kidding you.

HOGAN—He wasn't. I can tell. He said he told the agent to tell whoever it was the place wasn't for sale.

JOSIE—Of course he did. Did he say who'd made the offer?

HOGAN—He didn't know. It came through a real-estate man who wouldn't tell who his client was. I've been trying to guess, but I can't think of anyone crazy enough unless it'd be some damn fool of a millionaire buying up land to make a great estate for himself, like our beautiful neighbor, Harder, the Standard Oil thief, did years ago. May he roast in hell and his Limey superintendent with him!

What Hogan is afraid of is one of Jim's sneering, bitter drunks in which, if the price is big enough, he will sell the farm over their heads. Hogan persists that Jim has done a lot of mad things when he was drunk that he was sorry for afterwards. Not, of course, that Hogan suspects him, but he'd be a damned fool if he didn't fear the possibility and do something to guard against it.

Josie defends Jim in one breath, but in the next she's curious how Hogan plans to protect himself. Hogan, first of all, would have Josie be extra nice to Jim, and secondly, modify her rough talk around him. He doesn't like it. "I'll talk as I please," Josie says with a defiant toss of her head, "and if he don't like it he can lump it! I'm to pretend I'm a pure virgin, I suppose? That would fool him, wouldn't it, and him hearing all about me from the men at the Inn?" Getting to her feet, she changes the subject abruptly: "We're wasting the day, blathering.—If he ever went back on his word, no matter how drunk he was, I'd be with you in any scheme you made against him, no matter how dirty. But it's all your nonsense. I'd never believe it. I'll go to the meadow and finish Mike's work. You needn't fear you'll miss his help on the farm." She gets to her bare feet and takes up a pitchfork. Advising her to wait, Hogan points out Jim at the farm gate. Josie's face softens as she watches him in his blind hang-over. She notices pityingly what a bluff of smiling and straightening up he puts on when he knows he's observed. Then just as perversely, Josie decides to leave the men alone: Jim comes only to joke and drink with her father. She follows her father's advice, however, to go into the house and tidy up: "I'll go in the house," Josie says angrily, "but only to see the stew ain't burned, for I suppose you'll have the foxiness to ask him to have a bite to eat to keep in his good graces." "Why shouldn't I ask him?" retorts Hogan. "I know damned well he has no appetite this early in the day, but only a thirst."

Jim Tyrone, dressed like a well-groomed Broadway gambler, armed with enough morning pick-me-ups to steady his nerves, comes up the path. Though in his early forties, Tyrone's once fine physique has become soft and soggy from dissipation. In spite, however, of puffiness and bags under the eyes, he is still good-looking, and with his Irish humor and charm, still attractive to women.

TYRONE (*stands regarding* HOGAN *with sardonic relish while* HOGAN *scratches a match on the seat of his overalls and lights his pipe, pretending not to see him;* TYRONE *recites with feeling*)—

> "*Fortunate senex, ergo tua rura manebunt,*
> *et tibi magna satis, quamvis lapis omnia nudus.*"

HOGAN—It's the landlord again, and my shotgun not handy. Is it Mass you're saying, Jim? That was Latin. I know it by ear. What the hell insult does it mean?

TYRONE—Translated very freely into Irish English, something like this—(*He imitates* HOGAN's *brogue.*) "Ain't you the lucky old bastard to have this beautiful farm, if it is full of nude rocks."

HOGAN—I like that part about the rocks. If cows could eat them this place would make a grand dairy farm. (*He spits.*) It's easy to see you've a fine college education. It must be a big help to you, conversing with whores and barkeeps.

TYRONE—Yes, a very valuable worldly asset. I was once offered a job as office boy—until they discovered I wasn't qualified because I had no Bachelor of Arts diploma. There had been a slight mis-understanding just before I was to graduate.

Tyrone delights Hogan no end with details of his bawdy past; then changing his pace and manner, and sitting down on the steps, he says: "Slaving and toiling as usual, I see." "Hasn't a poor man a right to his noon rest," grumbles Hogan, "without being sneered at by his rich landlord?" " 'Rich' is good," says Tyrone; "I would be, if you'd pay up your back rent." "You ought to pay me instead, for occupying this rockpile, miscalled a farm," snaps Hogan, his eyes twinkling. "But I have fine reports to give you of a promising harvest. The milkweed and the thistles is in thriving condition, and I never saw the poison ivy so bounteous and beautiful." As Tyrone, laughing, says Hogan wins, Josie joins the men.

Tyrone starts to rise; Josie pushes him down again: ". . . sure, you know I'm no lady . . ." she banters; "how's my fine Jim this beautiful day? You don't look so bad. You must have stopped at the Inn for an eye-opener—or ten of them."

TYRONE—I've felt worse. (*He looks up at her sardonically.*) And how's my Virgin Queen of Ireland?

JOSIE—Yours, is it? Since when? And don't be miscalling me a virgin. You'll ruin my reputation, if you spread that lie about me. (*She laughs;* TYRONE *is staring at her. She goes on quickly.*) How is it you're around so early? I thought you never got up till after-noon.

TYRONE—Couldn't sleep. One of those heebie-jeebie nights when the booze keeps you awake instead of . . . (*He catches her giving him a pitying look.*) But what of it!

JOSIE—Maybe you had no woman in bed with you, for a change. It's a terrible thing to break the habit of years.

TYRONE (*shrugs*)—Maybe.

JOSIE—What's the matter with the tarts in town, they let you do it? I'll bet the ones you know on Broadway, New York, wouldn't neglect their business.

Josie's line of talk irritates and upsets Tyrone; he tells her to cut it out. She is startled, then resentful. He is annoyed at himself for his interest, and tells her to forget it. "Anyway," he says, "who told you I fall for the dainty dolls? That's all a thing of the past. I like them tall and strong and voluptuous now, with beautiful big breasts." Josie blushes; Hogan breaks in on her confusion: "There you are, Josie darlin'. Sure he couldn't speak fairer than that."

Tyrone, with Josie to give him encouragement, goes through a well-established routine of wheedling a drink from Hogan. Hogan, an equally practised hand at the routine, plays his part of skinflint to perfection. Tyrone is no nearer the drink than before until he plays his trump card: "I have it off the grapevine that a certain exalted personage will drop in on you before long." They may expect Mr. Harder, the Standard Oil millionaire, their neighbor, to stop by on his way home from a horseback ride.

At the Inn, Tyrone ran into Simpson, Harder's superintendent. The man had told his boss that the Hogans would be overwhelmed with awe if he deigned to come in person. And, Tyrone says: "For once in his life, Simpson is cheering for you. He doesn't like his boss. In fact, he asked me to tell you he hopes you kill him." The Hogans feel this is indeed a beautiful day.

Tyrone mentions that the Hogan pigpen is not far from the Harder icepond, that in some strange fashion the Harder fence has a habit of breaking down, and that Harder does not look forward to the taste of pig in next summer's ice water. "He must be delicate," crows Hogan; "remember he's delicate, Josie, and leave your club in the house."

Joy reigns at the Hogans. Josie kissing Tyrone laughingly on the lips, is suddenly stirred and at the same time frightened. She forces a scornful laugh: "O there's no spirit in you! It's like kissing a corpse."

Tyrone, beginning to have qualms over the excitement he's generated, wishes they wouldn't get too enthusiastic. Harder, he reminds them, has a big drag, and the Hogans would be arrested if he got beat up. "Sure," says Josie, passing the treasured whisky to Tyrone for another swig, "all we want is a quiet chat with him."

Spotting two horsemen on the road, Josie literally picks Tyrone up under the arms from the steps and offers him a grandstand seat at her window. "Go into my beautiful bedroom," she orders, "it's a nice place for you." "Just what I've been thinking for some time, Josie," Tyrone kids. "Sure, you've never given me a sign of it," Josie answers boldly. "Come up tonight and we'll spoon in the moonlight and you can tell me your thoughts." "That's a date, remember now," Tyrone answers.

Harder, in gentleman's riding clothes, approaches the shanty alone. It would be hard to find anyone less equipped to spar with the Hogans who, far from greeting him respectfully, hardly bother to notice that he's alive.

The Hogans aren't interested when he announces who he is. "Sure," says Josie, "who in the world cares who the hell you are." She declines an introduction to anyone with such a silly sheep face. She has no use, either, for jockeys and wagers this one is no damned good to a woman. Tyrone's whoop of laughter from the bedroom contributes to Harder's discomfort. Hogan is warming up; he doesn't allow Harder to finish a sentence. Harder, seeing the bottle on the boulder, affects tolerance of drunken behavior and tries to make good his escape. As the man turns to go, Hogan grabs his shoulder, spins him around, and goes into high gear.

Hogan—Wait now, my Honey Boy. I'll have a word with you, if you plaze. I'm beginning to read some sense into this. You mentioned that English bastard, Simpson. I know who you are now.

Harder (*outraged*)—Take your hands off me, you drunken fool. (*He raises his riding crop.*)

Josie (*grabs it and tears it from his hand with one powerful twist*) —Would you strike my poor infirm old father, you coward, you!

Harder (*calling for help*)—McCabe!

Hogan—Don't think McCabe will hear you, if you blew Gabriel's horn! He knows I or Josie can lick him with one hand. Josie! Stand between us and the gate. (Josie *takes her stand where the path meets the road. She turns her back for a moment, shaking with suppressed laughter, and waves her hand at* McCabe *and turns back.* Hogan *releases his hold on* Harder's *coat.*) There now. Don't try running away or my daughter will knock you senseless. You're the blackguard of a millionaire that owns the estate next to ours, ain't you? I've been meaning to call on you, for I've a bone to pick with you, you bloody tyrant! But I couldn't bring myself to set foot on land bought with Standard Oil money that was stolen from the poor it ground in the dust beneath its dirty heel—land that's watered with the tears of starving widows and orphans— (*He abruptly switches from this eloquence to a matter-of-fact tone.*) But never mind that, now. I won't waste words trying to reform a born crook. (*Fiercely shoving his dirty unshaven face almost into* HARDER's.) What I want to know is, what the hell do you mean by your contemptible trick of breaking down your fence to entice my poor pigs to take their death in your ice pond? (*There is a shout of laughter from the bedroom.*) Don't lie, now! None of your damned Standard Oil excuses, or be Jaysus, I'll break you in half! Haven't I mended that fence morning after morning, and seen the footprints where you had sneaked up in the night to pull it down again. . . .

Josie serves as Hogan's straight man as he tears into Harder for the murder of the Hogan pigs. Flabbergasted by this mad accusation, Harder only manages to sputter, "I've had enough," before Hogan goes into his climax: "Be God, I believe you! Look out now! Keep your place and be softspoken to your betters! You're not in your shiny automobile now with your funny nose cocked so you won't smell the poor people." He gives Harder a shake. "And," he says, "let me warn you! I have to put up with a lot of pests on this heap of boulders some joker once called a farm. There's a cruel skinflint of a landlord who swindles me out of my last drop of whiskey, and there's poison ivy, and ticks and potato bugs, and there's snakes and skunks! But be God, I draw the line somewhere, and I'll be damned if I'll stand for a Standard Oil man trespassing! So will you kindly get the hell out of here before I plant a kick on your backside that'll land you in the Atlantic Ocean!" Giving Harder a shove, he cries: "Beat it now!" Harder's retreat is a rout.

Tyrone, laughing so hard he has to hold his sides, joins the Hogans for further celebration. Then, sardonically, he points out that this rocky farm has become a gold mine. Harder, he explains, was the original bidder for the property because he loathed Hogan as a neighbor. He is now bound to triple his offer. Tyrone bets the sky will be the limit.

HOGAN (*gives* JOSIE *a meaningful look*)—I see your point! But we're not worrying you'd ever forget your promise to us for any price.

TYRONE—Promise? What promise? You know what Kipling

wrote: "There's never a promise of God or man goes north of ten thousand bucks."

HOGAN—Do you hear him, Josie? We can't trust him.

JOSIE—Och, you know he's kidding.

HOGAN—I don't! I'm becoming suspicious.

TYRONE (*a trace of bitterness beneath his amused tone*)—That's wise dope, Phil. Trust and be a sucker. If I were you, I'd be seriously worried. I've always wanted to own a gold mine—so I could sell it.

JOSIE—Will you shut up your rotten Broadway blather!

TYRONE (*stares at her in surprise*)—Why so serious and indignant, Josie? You just told your unworthy Old Man I was kidding. (*To* HOGAN.) At last I've got you by the ears, Phil. We must have a serious chat about when you're going to pay that back rent.

HOGAN (*groans*)—A landlord who's a blackmailer! Holy God, what next! (JOSIE *is smiling with relief now.*)

TYRONE—And you, Josie, please remember when I keep that moonlight date tonight I expect you to be very sweet to me.

JOSIE (*with a bold air*)—Sure, you don't have to blackmail me. I'd be that to you, anyway.

HOGAN—Are you laying plots in my presence to seduce my only daughter? Well, what can I do? I'll be drunk at the Inn, so how could I prevent it?

ACT II

Around eleven o'clock that moonlit night, Josie, dressed in her sober Sunday best, including the unaccustomed black stockings and shoes, rises from the doorstep. Tyrone hasn't kept their date. Lonely and humiliated, she goes indoors to light the kerosene lamp in the shanty's mangy sitting room.

When her father comes home from the Inn unusually early (a full hour before closing time), and drunker than Josie's ever seen him, she's ready to tackle him with club or without. She's in no mood for his wildly drunken behavior. Ready to turn in herself, Josie is going to let Hogan sit in the dark so he won't burn down the house. He doesn't seem to care if the house does burn down.

Such unheard-of indifference puzzles Josie. Hogan mumbles about the lying bastard who pretended he was their friend, and calls Josie a fool for defending Jim Tyrone. "You've had a good taste of believing his word," says Hogan, "waiting hours for him dressed up in your best like a poor sheep without pride or spirit—" "Shut up!" Josie cries. "I was calling him a lying bastard myself before you came, and saying I'd never speak to him again. And I knew all along he'd never remember to keep his date after he got drunk." "He's not so drunk he forgot to attend to business," says Hogan. With forced assurance, Josie answers: "Sure, I know what's happened as well as if I'd been there. Jim saw you'd got drunker than usual and you were an easy mark for a joke, and he's made a goat of you!"

Offended, Hogan asserts drunkenly he'll not say another word. From the chair in which Josie has dumped him, he mumbles: "It's too late. It's all settled. We're helpless entirely." Earlier he had had his suspicions about Tyrone, but Josie was so full of mush and love— "You'll tell that lie about my love once too often!" Josie shouts furiously, "and I'll play a joke on him that'll make him sorry he—" Hogan says: "He's agreed to sell the farm! Simpson came to the Inn to see him with a new offer from Harder. Ten thousand, cash." Josie, almost in tears, won't believe that Jim accepted it. "Don't then, be God," says Hogan, "you'll believe it tomorrow! Harder proposed that he meet with Jim and the executors in the morning and settle it, and Jim promised Simpson he would." Josie hopes desperately that Tyrone's so drunk he'll forget the whole thing. Harder, Hogan says, will pick Tyrone up in the morning to make sure of him. "Anyway," says Hogan, "don't think because he forgot you were waiting—in the moonlight, eating your heart out, that he'd ever miss a date with five thousand dollars, and all the pretty whores of Broadway he can buy with it." He has Josie, given the chance, in a mood to do anything.

Hogan suddenly remembers that Josie, of all people, has apparently ensnared Tyrone. Before Simpson arrived at the Inn, Tyrone was talking so much about Josie that Hogan began to have hope for Mike's first scheme. "He said," Hogan now tells her, "you had great beauty in you that no one appreciated but him." "You're lying," Josie says shakily. "Great strength you had," continues Hogan, "and great pride, he said—and great goodness, no less! But here's where you've made a prize jackass of him, like I said." He leers drunkenly: "Listen now, darlin', and don't drop dead with amazement." He leans towards her and whispers: "He believes you're a virgin!" Josie stiffens. "He does, so help me!" says Hogan; "he means it, the poor dunce! He thinks you're a poor innocent virgin! He thinks it's all boasting and pretending you've done about being a slut. A virgin, no less! You!"

Hogan says that Tyrone hadn't forgot the date; he wanted to leave Josie alone for her sake, because he loves her. Josie is stricken, but snapping out of her bewilderment, asks angrily: "But what's all his crazy lying blather got to do with him betraying us and selling the place?" Nothing, her father says, except she's had that much revenge. Aroused, Josie isn't ready to stop there. She'll humble her pride, and go and drag Tyrone right out of the Inn. "And," she says, "if he doesn't want to come I've a way to make him. I'll raise a scene and pretend I'm in a rage because he forgot his date. I'll disgrace him till he'll be glad to come with me to shut me up. I know his weakness, and it's his vanity about his women. If I was a dainty, pretty tart he'd be proud I'd raise a rumpus about him. But when it's a big, ugly hulk like me—" Josie falters, forces herself to go on: "If he ever was tempted to want me, he'd be ashamed of it. That's the truth behind the lies he told you of his conscience and his fear he might ruin me, God damn him!" She'll get him so drunk that he'll fall asleep. Then she will carry him to her bed.

Hogan offers to arrive at sunrise with his witnesses. He can't, however, think of any threat to use on Tyrone that he wouldn't laugh at. "Well, I can!" says Josie. "Do I have to tell you his weakness again? It's his vanity about women, and his Broadway pride he's so wise no woman could fool him. It's the disgrace to his vanity—being caught with the likes of me—my mug beside his in all the newspapers—the New York papers, too—he'll see the whole of Broadway splitting their sides laughing at him—and he'll give anything to keep us quiet, I tell you. He will! I know him! So don't worry—" She ends up on the verge of bitter tears.

Josie disappears into the next room to look at herself in the mirror. Hogan, abruptly sober, peering after her, says pityingly: "A look in the mirror and she's forgot to light her lamp! God forgive me, it's bitter medicine. But it's the only way I can see that has a chance now."

Before Josie has to put into practice her humiliating plan, Tyrone is at the gate. Josie tells her father quickly: "Pretend you're as drunk as when you came. Make believe you're so drunk you don't remember what he's done, so he can't suspect you told me."

Watching Hogan reel down the road, Tyrone seems vaguely surprised: "I've never seen him that stinko before. Must have got him all of a sudden. He didn't seem so lit up at the Inn, but I guess I wasn't paying attention."

Josie playfully makes Tyrone apologize for being late. He says he's damned sorry, though he could give a good honorable excuse. With a shrug, he tells Josie to forget it.

JOSIE—Holy Joseph, you're full of riddles tonight. Well, I don't need excuses. I forgive you, anyway, now you're here. (*She takes his hand playfully.*) Come on now and we'll sit on my bedroom steps and be romantic in the moonlight, like we planned to.

TYRONE (*mechanically*)—Had to get out of the damned Inn. I was going batty alone there. The old heebie-jeebies. So I came to you. (*He pauses, then adds with strange, wondering sincerity.*) I've really begun to love you a lot, Josie.

JOSIE (*blurts out bitterly*)—Yes, you've proved that tonight, haven't you? (*Hurriedly regaining her playful tone.*) But never mind. I said I'd forgive you for being so late. So go on about love. I'm all ears.

TYRONE—I thought you'd have given me up and gone to bed. I remember I had some nutty idea I'd get in bed with you—just to lie with my head on your breast.

JOSIE (*moved in spite of herself; but keeps her bold, playful tone*)—Well, maybe I'll let you— (*Hurriedly.*) Later on, I mean. The night's young yet, and we'll have it all to ourselves. But here's for a starter. (*She puts her arms around him and draws him back till his head is on her breast.*) There, now.

TYRONE—Thanks, Josie. (*He closes his eyes. . . . From far-off, HOGAN's mournful song drifts back through the moonlight quiet. TYRONE rouses himself and straightens up. He acts embarrassed as if he felt he'd been making a fool of himself, recites mockingly.*) "Hark, Hark the Donegal lark!" . . . "Thou was not born for death, immortal bird." Can't Phil sing anything but that damned dirge, Josie? (*She doesn't reply.*) Still, it seems to belong tonight —in the moonlight—or—in my mind— (*He quotes.*)

> "Now more than ever seems it rich to die,
> To cease upon the midnight with no pain,
> In such an ecstasy!"

Good God! Ode to Phil the Irish Nightingale! I must have the D.T.'s.

JOSIE (*her face grown bitter*)—Maybe it's only your bad conscience.

TYRONE (*starts guiltily and turns to stare into her face—suspiciously*)—What put that in your head? Conscience about what?

JOSIE—How would I know, if you don't? (*Forcing a playful tone.*) For the sin of wanting to be in bed with me. Maybe that's it.

TYRONE (*with strange relief*)—Oh. Forget that stuff, Josie. I was half nutty.

Tyrone, drawing away from her, asks Josie to lay off that line— at least for tonight. He'd like tonight to be different.

Almost as if he were ashamed, Tyrone admits liking the moonlight instead of the Inn. Josie repeats that he'll soon be back on Broadway with all the pretty little tarts to comfort him. "Oh, to hell with the rough stuff, Josie," Tyrone says, "you promised you'd can it tonight." "You're a fine one," Josie says, "to talk of promises!" Tyrone is surprised. To cover up, Josie offers to get a bottle of the best as proof that there are no hard feelings.

Left alone, Tyrone crying suddenly: "You rotten bastard!" springs to his feet. With a miserably guilty look on his face, he lights a cigarette with a trembling hand.

ACT III

Josie, returning with her father's best illegal bourbon, finds Jim looking as if he'd seen a ghost. Promising that the whiskey will keep the ghost in its place, Josie starts tending bar. "Hello!" Tyrone cries, noticing that she's poured herself one, "I thought you never touched it." Josie says glibly that she has no intention of being left out of the Harder victory, and anyway, a drink or two will make her better company.

She has trouble getting it down. Tyrone watches her critically. "I'm my father's daughter," Josie boasts, "I've a strong head. So don't worry I'll pass out and you'll have to put me to bed." "Nix on the raw stuff, Josie," Tyrone barks. "Remember you said—" "I'd be different?" Josie taunts him; "that's right. I'm forgetting it's your pleasure to have me pretend I'm an innocent virgin tonight." "If you don't look out," says Tyrone, "I'll call you on that bluff, Josie." And staring at her with a deliberate look that undresses her, Tyrone says: "I'd like to. You know that, don't you?" Equally deliberate, Josie leads him on.

With genuine passion, Tyrone grabs her to him, then quickly lets her go again. Again he begs her to cut it out. Josie merely pulls him down beside her on the steps.

Even in his cups, Tyrone notices that the drinks are coming too fast, and passes up one. He does his hazy best to change the conversation. He insists that Josie is beautiful: "You're real," he tells her, "and healthy and clean and fine and warm and strong and kind." He loves her a lot—in his fashion.

Josie gives him a quick, shy kiss. Aroused, Tyrone pulls her head down, and staring into her eyes, says: "You have a beautiful strong body, too, Josie—and beautiful eyes and hair, and a beautiful smile and beautiful warm breasts." He kisses her, and she, though frightened, returns the kiss. Again Tyrone breaks away: "Nix!

Nix! Don't be a fool, Josie," he cries, "don't let me pull that stuff."

He doesn't want Josie to be poisoned by him. Nor does he want her to drink. In strange disgust, he suddenly knocks the glass from Josie's hand. "I've slept with drunken tramps too many nights!" he shouts, but the next moment is apologetic and bewildered. Gulping down his own drink, he blurts out: "That fat blonde pig on the train—I got her drunk! That's why—" He's off on another tangent.

In his ramblings, Tyrone lectures Josie on appreciating her father, because Hogan worships the ground she walks on. "And," Tyrone adds, "he knows you a lot better than you think— As well as I do, almost."

Josie offers him yet another drink. Tyrone warns her to watch her step: "It might work—and then think of how disgusted you'd feel, with me lying beside you, probably snoring, as you watched the dawn come—" Take it from him, Tyrone goes on bitterly, he's seen too God-damned many dawns creeping grayly over too many dirty windows.

Once more Josie's bold talk angers him: "How about your not talking the old smut stuff to me? You promised you'd be yourself." In a blur he tells Josie: "You see, you don't get it. You see, she was one of the smuttiest talking pigs I've ever listened to." Josie asks if he means the blonde on the train. "Train? Who told you?" Tyrone replies sharply. "Oh—that's right—I did say." He asks vaguely: "What's the difference? Coming back from the Coast. It was long ago. But it seems like tonight. There is no present or future—only the past happening over and over again— now. You can't get away from it. Nuts! To hell with that crap." But Josie remembers he came back from the Coast about a year ago after his mother's death.

With another sudden switch, Tyrone is back on what a grand guy Phil is, and switching again, it occurs to him that Josie mentioned a while ago that he'd be leaving for New York soon. Pulling her hand away from his, Josie watches Tyrone as she asks: "You'll be taking a train back to your dear old Broadway tomorrow night, won't you?" According to Tyrone, Phil must have got the dates mixed. But according to Josie, Hogan was too drunk to tell her anything.

TYRONE—He was sober when I told him. I called up the executors when we reached the Inn after leaving here. They said the estate would be out of probate within a few days. I told Phil the glad tidings and bought drinks for all and sundry. There was quite a celebration. Funny, Phil wouldn't remember that.

JOSIE (*bewildered; not knowing what to believe*)—It is—funny.

TYRONE (*shrugs his shoulders*)—Well, he's stewed to the ears. That always explains anything. (*Then strangely.*) Only sometimes it doesn't.

JOSIE—No, sometimes it doesn't.

TYRONE (*goes on without real interest, talking to keep from thinking*)—Phil certainly has a prize bun on tonight. He never took a punch at me before. And that drivel he talked about owing me one— What got into his head, I wonder.

JOSIE (*tensely*)—How would I know, if you don't?

TYRONE—Well, I don't. Not unless—I remember I did try to get his goat. Simpson sat down with us. Harder sent him to see me. You remember after Harder left here I said the joke was on you, that you'd made this place a gold mine? I was kidding, but I had the right dope. What do you think he told Simpson to offer? Ten grand! On the level, Josie.

JOSIE—So you accepted?

TYRONE—I told Simpson to tell Harder I did. I decided the best way to fix him was to let him think he'd got away with it, and then when he comes tomorrow morning to drive me to the executors' office, I'll tell him what he can do with himself, his bankroll and tin oil tanks.

Relieved and overjoyed, Josie hugs Tyrone and kisses him: "I knew you'd never—I told him— Oh, Jim, I love you." Tyrone is grateful that she doesn't believe him a louse like everybody else does, but can't figure what got into Phil, who knew the farm was to be his. Josie is ready to use her club on her father.

Amused, Tyrone calls her bluff, not only about the club held over her father, but about her wanton ways with men. He asks if she plans to keep up this pretense with him. "You think I've never, because no one would—because I'm a great ugly cow—" Josie says feebly. Tyrone tells her gently: "You could have had any one of them. You kidded them till you were sure they wanted you. That was all you wanted. And then you slapped them groggy when they tried for more. But you had to keep convincing yourself—" Josie tries to stop him. Tyrone knows the whole picture: none of the guys at the Inn wanted to admit that he got a slap in the puss when he imagined the other guys had made it. "Phil," Tyrone adds, "is wise to you, of course, but although he knew I knew, he would never admit it until tonight." Josie can't wait to get her hands

Wendy Hiller and Franchot Tone in "A Moon for the Misbegotten"

on her father. She tells Tyrone almost hysterically to stop talking about him.

Tyrone again gives his shrug: "You have a hell of a license to be sore," he says; "he's the one who ought to be. Don't you realize what a lousy position you've put him in with your brazen-trollop act?" And not only Phil cares; Tyrone cares. Kissing Josie, he says he loves her.

JOSIE (*with pitiful longing*)—Do you, Jim? Do you? Then I'll confess the truth to you. I've been a crazy fool. I am a virgin. (*She sobs.*) And now you'll never—and I want you to—now more than ever—because I love you more than ever, after what's happened— (*Suddenly she kisses him with fierce passion.*) But you will! I'll make you! To hell with your honorable scruples! I know you want me! I couldn't believe that until tonight—but now I know. It's in your kisses. (*She kisses him again with passionate tenderness.*) Oh, you great fool! As if I gave a damn what happened after! I'll have had tonight and your love to remember for the rest of my days! (*She kisses him again.*) Oh, Jim darling, haven't you said yourself there's only tonight? (*She whispers tenderly.*) Come. Come with me. (*She gets to her feet, pulling at his arm; with a little self-mocking laugh.*) But I'll have to make you leave before sunrise. I mustn't forget that.

TYRONE (*a strange change has come over his face; he looks her over now with sneering cynical lust and speaks thickly as if he was suddenly very drunk*)—Sure thing, Kiddo. What the hell else do you suppose I came for? I've been kidding myself. (*He steps up beside her and puts his arm around her and presses his body to hers.*) You're the goods, Kid. I've wanted you all along. Love, nuts! I'll show you what love is. I know what you want, Bright Eyes. (*She is staring at him now with a look of frightened horror. He kisses her roughly.*) Come on, Baby Doll, let's hit the hay. (*He pushes her back in the doorway.*)

JOSIE (*strickenly*)—Jim! Don't! (*She pulls his arms away so violently that he staggers back and would fall down the steps if she didn't grab his arm in time. He goes down on one knee. She is on the verge of collapse herself.*) Jim! I'm not a whore.

Tyrone, ready to push off, says thickly that their moonlight romance seems to have been a flop. He won't see her before he goes to New York. He had hoped that tonight would be different, but she didn't get it. "Believe me, Kid," Tyrone says, "when I poison them, they stay poisoned."

Josie's maternal love comes to the fore. She calls Tyrone back, and pulls him down beside her on the steps. She hugs him gently to her breast. He closes his eyes, finally at peace.

The moonlight gives such a pale look to his face that Josie calls out in fright. Tyrone tells her simply: "You said I looked dead—well, I am." Josie hugs him, but he continues: "Ever since Mama died."

Suddenly the grief and guilt that have haunted him, pour from him. Tyrone tells Josie of his great love for his mother and how, because of it, he stayed sober for two years. But when she became fatally ill while they were out West, he felt she was deliberately leaving him forever. He took to drink again. On the train carrying his mother's body back East, he not only was drunk, but had a whore in his stateroom for the entire ride. And when he reached New York, he was too drunk to go to his mother's funeral.

Josie pulls away in horror, but then draws him back to her. She now knows that Tyrone has wanted all along to cry his heart's repentance on his mother's breast. She hugs him, sobbing, to her. She says that his mother hears, understands and forgives. When the exhausted Tyrone quiets down, Josie, looking at the pale face in her arms, speaks as she would to a child.

JOSIE—You're a fine one, wanting to leave me when the night I promised I'd give you has just begun, our night that'll be different from all others, with a dawn that won't creep over dirty windowpanes but will wake in the sky like a promise of God's peace in the soul's dark sadness. (*She smiles a little amused smile.*) Will you listen to me, Jim! I must be a poet. Who would have guessed it? Sure, love is a wonderful inspiration! . . . That's right. Sleep in peace, my darling. Oh, Jim, Jim, maybe my love could still save you, if you could want it enough! No. That can never be. God forgive me, it's a fine end to all my scheming, to sit here with the head hugged to my breast, and the silly mug of the moon grinning down, enjoying the joke!

ACT IV

Beneath the first, faint streaks of dawn, Josie, still hugging the middle-aged drunk to her bosom, presents a tragic picture. Hogan, sneaking guiltily into the yard, is startled by Tyrone's deathlike mask. Josie orders her father to be quiet: she doesn't want Tyrone to be awakened until the dawn has beauty in it.

Her feelings toward her father are grim. He has told for once just one lie too many. "Sure, if I'd brought the witnesses," Hogan finally blurts out, "there's nothing for them to witness that—" "No. You're right there," Josie replies, "there's nothing. Nothing at all. Except," she adds with a strange smile, "a great miracle they'd never believe, or you either." "What miracle?" Hogan asks. "A virgin," Josie answers, "who bears a dead child in the night, and the dawn finds her still a virgin. If that isn't a miracle, what is?" Hogan is definitely uneasy: "Stop talking so queer. You give me the shivers." Then attempting a joking tone, he asks: "Is it you who's the virgin? Faith, that would be a miracle, no less!" "I told you to stop lying," says Josie.

Josie's sorrowful air has Hogan deeply disturbed. Ordering her father to speak low, Josie says that Tyrone has done nothing to bring her sorrow. "It was my mistake," she tells Hogan. "I thought there was still hope. I didn't know he'd died already—that it was a damned soul coming to me in the moonlight, to confess and be forgiven and find peace for a night." Quickly becoming matter-of-fact, Josie says that Tyrone simply got drunk; got one of his crazy notions. He wanted to sleep this way, so she let him.

Then she tells off her father and his lies and schemes. Josie has been fooled once too often, and used once too often for his dirty money-grabbing plans. She wants no more talk from him. She has but one thing more to say: "I'm leaving you today, like my brothers left. You can live alone and work alone your cunning schemes on yourself."

She doesn't seem to hear Hogan's excuse: "I knew you'd be bitter against me, Josie, but I took the chance you'd be so happy you wouldn't care how—" She is thanking God that the dawn is beautiful and is praying that when Tyrone awakes he will remember only the one thing and forget the rest.

Josie orders her father into the house, then shakes Tyrone awake. Without opening his eyes, Tyrone mumbles that all dawns are gray. "Go to sleep, Kid," he says, "and let me sleep." Thinking bitterly that now he'll never notice this dawn, that she'll be simply the whore on the train, and that Tyrone won't remember what he should about last night, Josie gives him a good, rough shake. He comes to.

Offered an eye-opener, he doesn't seem to need the drink. For once, he has a nice, dreamy, peaceful hang-over. As Josie stretches and rubs at her numbed arms and legs, Tyrone says that she shouldn't have let him get away with it. "Oh, don't be apologizing," says Josie, "I was glad of the excuse to stay awake and enjoy the beauty of the moon."

Tyrone now remembers it *was* a beautiful night, but fishes around to find out what really happened. He remembers leaving the Inn and hopes that he didn't tell Josie the story of his sad life. He hopes that he didn't weep on her bosom. "There's nothing you said or did last night for you to regret," says Josie, "you can take my word for it." Tyrone feels strangely at peace. Turning to watch the sunrise, he is moved. He tries, however, to sneer it off. "God," he cracks, "seems to be putting on quite a display. I like Belasco better. Rise of curtain, Act-Four stuff." Josie is bitterly hurt. Tyrone adds quickly and angrily: "God damn it! Why do I have to pull that lousy stuff? God, it's beautiful, Josie! I—I'll never forget it—here with you." Her face clearing, Josie says simply: "I'm glad, Jim. I was hoping you'd feel beauty in it—by way of a token."

Tyrone has a question which he asks guiltily: "You're sure I didn't get out of order last night—and try to make you, or anything like that?" Reassured, he says he'd never forgive himself, and catching sight of the drink he's all the while been holding, downs it.

Memory returns, and with it, shame and anguish. Tyrone thinks he'll be running along. "See you later, Josie," he says. Josie is stricken. She pleads that, for his own sake, he remember only her love that gave him peace for a while. Defensively, Tyrone tries to say that he doesn't know what she's getting at. Josie accepts it the way he wants it, and turns toward the house.

"Wait, Josie." Tyrone comes to her. "I'm a liar! I'm a louse! Forgive me, Josie. I do remember! I'm glad I remember! I'll never forget your love." He kisses her repeatedly on the lips and says that he will always love her. Then with a "Good-bye" and "God bless you!" Tyrone goes off without a backward glance. Josie puts her hands to her face and sobs.

Hogan comes out of the house, bitterly angry. Josie manages to say she'll make his breakfast in a minute.

HOGAN—To hell with my breakfast! I'm not a pig that has no other thought but eating! (*Then pleadingly.*) Listen, darlin'. All you said about my lying and scheming, and what I hoped would happen, is true. But it wasn't his money, Josie. I did see it was the last chance—the only one left to bring the two of you to stop your damned pretending, and face the truth that you loved each other. I wanted you to find happiness—by hook or crook, one way or another, what did I care how? I wanted to save him, and I hoped he'd see that only your love could— It was his talk of the beauty he saw in you that made me hope— And I knew he'd never go to bed with you even if you'd let him unless he married you. And if I gave a thought to his money at all, that was the least of it, and why shouldn't I want to have you live in ease and comfort for a change, like you deserve, instead of in this shanty on a lousy farm, slaving for me? (*He pauses; miserably.*) Can't you believe that's the truth, Josie, and not feel so bitter against me?

JOSIE (*her eyes still following Tyrone; gently*)—I know it's the truth, Father. I'm not bitter now. Don't be afraid I'm going to leave you. I only said it to punish you for a while.

Making a gallant effort, Josie forces a teasing smile and her old breezy manner. Hogan enters joyfully into the spirit of their usual rough give-and-take. But with a sudden burst of rage, he curses Tyrone for the unhappiness he caused his daughter. Josie cries out with real anguish: "Don't, Father! I love him!" It was life,

Hogan says, that he was cursing— "And, be God," he adds, "that's a waste of breath, if it does deserve it—"

As Hogan bangs the door into the shanty, Josie turns a tender, pitying face for a last look down the road: "May you have your wish and die in your sleep soon, Jim, darling," she says; "may you rest forever in forgiveness and peace." She turns slowly and enters the shanty.

A GRAPHIC GLANCE

"Show Boat" at the Jones Beach Marine Theatre

with Paul Hartman and Geoffrey Holder

As Al Hirschfeld sees Al Capp's Dogpatch denizens

in a "Li'l Abner" rehearsal

*Four stars in summer revues: Mae West, Tallulah Bankhead,
Beatrice Lillie and Hermione Gingold*

In "Maiden Voyage," which failed to reach Broadway: Tom Poston, Mildred Dunnock, Melvyn Douglas, Valerie Bettis, Walter Matthau and Bryarly Lee

Carmen Mathews and Don Ameche in "Holiday for Lovers"

Judy Holliday and Sydney Chaplin in "Bells Are Ringing"

Jerry Lewis at the Palace

Menasha Skulnik in "Uncle Willie"

Martyn Green, Shirley Yamaguchi, Dennis King, Jack Cassidy

Alice Ghostley, Joan Holloway and Harold Lang in "Shangri-La"

Three busy "matchmakers" on Broadway: Ethel Merman, Charlotte Rae and Menasha Skulnik

Walter Slezak in "The First Gentleman"

Helen Wood, Beatrice Lillie, Harold Lar

d Billy De Wolfe in "Ziegfeld Follies"

Ethel Merman and Fernando Lamas, Virginia Gibson and Gordon Polk in "Happy Hunting"

PLAYS PRODUCED IN NEW YORK

PLAYS PRODUCED IN NEW YORK

June 1, 1956—May 31, 1957

(Plays marked "Continued" were still running on June 1, 1957)

SHANGRI-LA

(21 performances)

Musical in two acts, based on James Hilton's novel, "Lost Horizon"; book and lyrics by Mr. Hilton, Jerome Lawrence and Robert E. Lee; music by Harry Warren. Produced by Robert Fryer and Lawrence Carr at the Winter Garden, June 13, 1956.

Cast of characters—

Hugh Conway .... Dennis King
Chao-Li .... Kaie Deei
Robert Henderson .... Harold Lang
Rita Henderson .... Joan Holloway
Charles Mallinson .... Jack Cassidy
Miss Brinklow .... Alice Ghostley
Chang .... Martyn Green
Arana .... Carol Lawrence
Ti .... Edwin Kim Ying
The Little One .... Leland Mayforth
Lo-Tsen .... Shirley Yamaguchi
Rimshi .... Ed Kenney
High Lama .... Berry Kroeger
The Dancer Perrault .... Robert Cohan
    The People of Shangri-La:
    Singers: Edward Becker, Walter Farrell, George Lenz, Bob McClure, David McDaniel, Jack Rains, Ed Stroll, Ted Wills, Marvin Zeller, Jay Bacon, Sara Bettis, Elizabeth Burgess, Joan Cherof, Sylvia Fabry, Teresa Montes, Eileen Moran, Maggie Worth.
    Dancers: Ralph Beaumont, Michael DeMarco, Ray Dorian, Eddie Heim, Rico Riedl, Ed Stinnett; Dorothy Hill, Greb Lober, Ellen Matthews, Ilona Murai, Mary Ann Niles, Doris Wright.
    The action takes place in a patrol station on the Tibetan border, on the mountain plains of the Himalayas, and in the terraces and chambers of the Lamasery of Shangri-La.
    Staged by Albert Marre; production designed by Peter Larkin; costumes designed by Irene Sharaff; musical direction, choral arrangements and musical continuity by Lehman Engel; musical arrangements by Philip J. Lang; ballet music composed and arranged by Genevieve Pitot; additional dance arrangements by John Morris; dances and musical numbers staged by Donald Saddler; production manager, Robert Linden; stage manager, Ross Bowman; press representatives, Arthur Cantor and Robert Ganshaw.

Musical numbers—

ACT I

"Om Mani Padme Hum" .... Male Singers
"Lost Horizon" .... Entire Company

313

Dance of Welcome ....Robert Cohan, Edwin Kim Ying
Pole Boys ....Ray Dorian, Eddie Heim, Rico Riedl
Lotus Girl ....Ilona Murai
Tigers ....Ed Stinnett, Michael DeMarco
Tiger Tamer ....Ralph Beaumont
"The Man I Never Met" ....Shirley Yamaguchi
"Every Time You Danced with Me" ....Harold Lang,
Joan Holloway
Dance of Moderate Chasitity ....Alice Ghostley and Dancers
"The World Outside" ....Shirley Yamaguchi and Jack Cassidy
Requiem ....Singers and Dancers
"I'm Just a Little Bit Confused" ....Alice Ghostley
"The Beetle Race" ....Martyn Green and Ensemble
"Somewhere" ....Jack Cassidy
The Story of Shangri-La ....Robert Cohan and Dancers

ACT II

"What Every Old Girl Should Know" ....Alice Ghostley and
Martyn Green
"Second Time in Love" ....Harold Lang and Joan Holloway
"Talkin' With Your Feet" .....Harold Lang and Joan Holloway
"Walk Sweet" ....Shirley Yamaguchi
"Love Is What I Never Knew" ....Shirley Yamaguchi and
Jack Cassidy
"We've Decided to Stay" ....Alice Ghostley, Harold Lang
and Joan Holloway
Dance of Time ....Shirley Yamaguchi and Dancers
"Shangri-La" ....Dennis King

(Closed June 30, 1956)

NEW FACES OF '56

(220 performances)

Musical revue in two acts. Music and lyrics mostly by June Carroll, Arthur Siegel, Marshall Barer, Dean Fuller, Murray Grand, Matt Dubey, Harold Karr, Irvin Graham, Ronny Graham, Paul Nassau, John Rox and Michael Brown; sketches mostly by Paul Lynde, Richard Maury and Louis Botto. Produced by Leonard Sillman and John Roberts, in association with Yvette Schumer, at the Ethel Barrymore Theatre, June 14, 1956.

Principals—

Franca Baldwin	Bill McCutcheon
Suzanne Bernard	John Reardon
Jane Connell	Amru Sani
Billie Hayes	Bob Shaver
Johnny Haymer	Jimmy Sisco
Tiger Haynes	Maggie Smith
Ann Henry	Dana Sosa
T. C. Jones	Rod Strong
Johnny Laverty	Inga Swenson
Virginia Martin	

Entire production conceived and supervised by Leonard Sillman; musical numbers staged and directed by David Tihmar, assisted by Peter Conlow; sketches directed by Paul Lynde; settings by Peter

Larkin; costumes by Thomas Becher; lighting by Peggy Clark; orchestrations by Ted Royal, Albert Sendrey and Joe Glover; musical direction by Jay Blackton; production stage manager, Morty Halpern; stage manager, Leonard Auerbach; press representatives, Bill Doll and Robert Ullman.

Sketches and musical numbers—

ACT I

Opening (By Ronny Graham)	Entire Company
(Introduction)	T. C. Jones
Madame Interpreter (By Danny and Neil Simon)	
France	Maggie Smith
United States	Bob Shaver
Italy	Johnny Haymer
Great Britain	Bill McCutcheon
India	Amru Sani
Brazil	Virginia Martin
U.S.S.R.	John Reardon
Mme. Interpreter	Jane Connell

"What Does That Dream Mean?" (Lyrics and music by Matt Dubey and Harold Karr)

The Dreamer	Johnny Haymer
His Dreams	Franca Baldwin, Suzanne Bernard, Dana Sosa, Johnny Laverty, Jimmy Sisco, Rod Strong, Johnny Haymer, Ann Henry, Tiger Haynes, Bill McCutcheon, Virginia Martin, Billie Hayes

Stars in the Rough (By Paul Lynde)

Announcer	John Reardon
Soprano	Inga Swenson
Helen Hunt	T. C. Jones
Patty Potts	Dana Sosa
Old Lady	Jane Connell
Tony Taps	Johnny Laverty

One Perfect Moment (By Marshall Barer, Dean Fuller, Leslie Julian-Jones)

Woman	Maggie Smith
Violinist	Johnny Haymer
Lover	Bill McCutcheon

"Tell Her" (Lyrics and Music by June Carroll and Arthur Siegel)

Sung by	John Reardon
Danced by	Franca Baldwin and Jimmy Sisco

The Washingtons Are Doin' Okay .... Tiger Haynes
(By Michael Brown)
A Canful of Trash (By Louis Botto)

(Introduction)	Maggie Smith
Zelda	Virginia Martin
Manny	Bill McCutcheon
Moe	Johnny Haymer
Junk Man	Bob Shaver
1st Sanitation Man	Rod Strong
2nd Sanitation Man	Johnny Laverty

April in Fairbanks .... Jane Connell
(By Murray Grand)
"A Doll's House" (Lyrics and music by June Carroll and Arthur Siegel)

Nurse	Maggie Smith
Tina	Inga Swenson
Urchin	Suzanne Bernard
Father Doll	Jimmy Sisco
Mother Doll	Virginia Martin
Girl Doll	Dana Sosa
Princess Doll	Franca Baldwin
Prince Doll	Rod Strong
Sweeper Doll	Billie Hayes

And He Flipped ....Ann Henry
  (By John Rox)
Girls 'n' Girls 'n' Girls (By Irvin Graham)
  Mother ....Inga Swenson
  Johnny ....Johnny Laverty
  Father ....John Reardon
  Grace ....Franca Baldwin
  Ava ....Suzanne Bernard
  Marilyn ....Virginia Martin
I Could Love Him ....Billie Hayes
  (By Paul Nassau)
Steady Edna (By Paul Lynde)
  (Introduction) ....Virginia Martin
  Eric ....Johnny Haymer
  Edna ....Jane Connell
  Doc ....Bill McCutcheon
  Steffany ....Maggie Smith
  Father ....Johnny Laverty
  Native Chief ....Rod Strong
"Hurry" ....Amru Sani
  (Lyrics by Murray Grand and Elisse Boyd, music by Murray
  Grand)
"Isn't She Lovely" (Lyrics and music by Marshall Barer and Dean
  Fuller)
  (Introduction) ....T. C. Jones
  Production Singer ....John Reardon
  Ponies ....Franca Baldwin, Suzanne Bernard,
                                 Dana Sosa, Billie Hayes
  Chorus Boys ....Johnny Laverty, Bob Shaver,
                                Jimmy Sisco, Rod Strong
  The Boy Friend ....Bill McCutcheon
  Miss Bird Cage ....Virginia Martin
  Miss Blue Fish ....Inga Swenson
  Miss Orange ....Maggi Smith
  Miss Hat ....Jane Connell
  Moth of Desire ....T. C. Jones

ACT II

Entr'acte
  (Introduction) ....T. C. Jones
  "I Could Love Him" ....Johnny Laverty
  "Girls 'n' Girls" ....Dana Sosa
  "Blues" ....Jimmy Sisco
  "Don't Wait" ....Franca Baldwin
  "Tell Her" ....Rod Strong
Twenty Years in the Blackboard Jungle (By Terry Ryan and Barry
  Blitzer)
  (Introduction) ....T. C. Jones
  Teacher ....Billie Hayes
  Mahoney ....Jimmy Sisco
  Levine ....Tiger Haynes
  Kowalski ....Bob Shaver
  Roger ....Johnny Laverty
  Hairy Hilda ....Virginia Martin
  Girl Monitor ....Franca Baldwin
  Policeman ....Rod Strong
  Principal ....Bill McCutcheon
"Don't Wait 'Til It's Too Late to See Paris" (Lyrics and music by
  June Carroll and Arthur Siegel)
  Husband ....John Reardon
  Wife ....Inga Swenson
  Gamin ....Suzanne Bernard
  Ice Cream Vendor ....Jimmy Sisco
  Girl ....Dana Sosa
  Boy ....Rod Strong
Rouge ....Jane Connell
  (By Murray Grand)
Darts (By Phil Green and Paul Lynde)
  George ....Bill McCutcheon
  Harriet ....Maggie Smith
  Man ....John Reardon

"Scratch My Back" ....Ann Henry and Tiger Haynes
   (Lyrics and music by Marshall Barer and Dean Fuller)
"Boy Most Likely to Succeed" (Lyrics and music by June Carroll
   and Arthur Siegel)
Sung by ....Inga Swenson
Graduating Class ....Franca Baldwin, Suzanne Bernard,
                              Dana Sosa, Johnny Laverty, Bob
                              Shaver, Jimmy Sisco, Rod Strong
Principal ....Bill McCutcheon
Talent ....Virginia Martin
   (By Paul Nassau)
"The Broken Kimona" (Sketch and lyrics by Richard Maury, music
   by Robert Stringer)
(Introduction) ....Maggie Smith
Messenger ....Johnny Laverty
Bartender ....Jimmy Sisco
Bamboo Brothers ....Bill McCutcheon, John
                                          Reardon, Rod Strong
Daughter ....T. C. Jones
Broken Kimona ....Johnny Haymer
Water Color ....Tiger Haynes
Pura ....Maggie Smith
Caller ....Bob Shaver
Townspeople ....Franca Baldwin, Suzanne
                              Bernard, Billie Hayes, Dana Sosa
Filly ....Ann Henry
"La Ronde" (Lyrics and music by Marshall Barer and Dean Fuller)
(Introduction) ....Rod Strong
Roué ....Johnny Haymer
Jeune Fille ....Inga Swenson
Adolescent ....Bob Shaver
Femme du Monde ....Virginia Martin
"The White Witch of Jamaica" (Lyrics and music by June Carroll
   and Arthur Siegel)
Tourists ....Suzanne Bernard, Maggie Smith,
                              Johnny Laverty Bob Shaver
Native Man ....John Reardon
Native Woman ....Dana Sosa
Lola ....Franca Baldwin
Overseer ....Jimmy Sisco
"The Greatest Invention" ....Billie Hayes and Johnny Haymer
   (Lyrics and music by Matt Dubey, Harold Karr and Sid Silvers)
"Mustapha Abdullah Abu Ben Al Raajid" (Lyrics and music by
   Marshall Barer and Dean Fuller)
Mrs. Mustapha ....Amru Sani
Harem Houris ....Maggie Smith, Inga Swenson, Jane
                              Connell, Suzanne Bernard, Dana
                              Sosa, Franca Baldwin
Powers Below (By Paul Lynde)
(Introduction) ....T. C. Jones
Wife ....Jane Connell
Superintendent ....Johnny Haymer
Mrs. Carruthers ....Virginia Martin
"She's Got Everything" (Lyrics and music by Marshall Barer and
   Dean Fuller)
M. C. ....Johnny Haymer
Four Aristocrats ....Johnny Laverty, John Reardon,
                                          Bob Shaver, Jimmy Sisco
Hope Diamond ....T. C. Jones
Finale ....Entire Company

(Closed December 22, 1956)

SAINT JOAN

(77 performances)

Play in three acts by George Bernard Shaw. Produced by the
Phoenix Theatre (T. Edward Hambleton and Norris Houghton) at

the Phoenix Theatre, September 11, 1956—October 21, 1956. Return engagement November 27, 1956—December 9, 1956. Reopened at the Coronet Theatre December 25, 1956; produced by MBM, Roger L. Stevens and Jerome Friedman.

Cast of characters—

Robert de Baudricourt ....Dennis Patrick
Steward ....P. J. Kelly
Joan ....Siobhan McKenna
Bertrand de Poulengey ....Lee Richardson
Archibishop of Rheims ....Frederic Tozere
Duc de la Tremouille ....Chris Gampel
Court Page ....John Glennon
Gilles de Rais ....Paul Sparer
Captain La Hire ....Arch Johnson
The Dauphin ....Michael Wager
Duchesse de la Tremouille ....Janet Dowd
Dunois, Bastard of Orleans ....Earle Hyman
Dunois' Page ....Ralph Williams
Earl of Warwick ....Kent Smith
Chaplain de Stogumber ....Earl Montgomery
Peter Cauchon, Bishop of Beauvais ....Ian Keith
Inquisitor ....Thayer David
D'Estivet ....Lee Richardson
De Courcelles ....Richard Purdy
Brother Martin Ladvenu ....Dick Moore
The Executioner ....Paul Sparer
An English Soldier ....Peter Falk
A Gentleman of 1920 ....Richard Purdy
Ladies of the Court ....Joanna Hill, Jill Livesey, Betty Rollin
     Assessors, Courtiers, Soldiers: Ray Barbata, Bert Beyers, Walter Carlin, John Cullum, James Egan, William Francis, Tom Gilson, Sam Gorden, Edward Hastings, Geoffrey Johnson, Derk Kinnane, Arthur Le Ral, Robert Ludlum, George O'Halloran, Lawrence Spector, Don Spence.
     Act I.—Scene 1—The castle of Vaucouleurs on a fine spring morning in the year 1429. Scene 2—The throne room at Chinon in Touraine, March 8, 1429. Scene 3—The south bank of the Loire at Orleans, April 29, 1429. Act II.—Scene 4—A tent in the English camp. Scene 5—The ambulatory in the Cathedral of Rheims. Act III. —Scene 6—A great hall in the castle at Rouen, May 30, 1431. Epilogue—The bedchamber of Charles VII, June 14, 1456.
     Staged by Albert Marre; settings and lighting by Klaus Holm; costumes by Robert Fletcher; music by Caldwell Titcomb; production stage manager, Robert Woods; stage manager, Stark Hesseltine; publicity director, Ben Kornzweig; press associate, Robert Ganshaw.

Cast Changes in Return Engagements—

Steward ....Byron Russell
Bertrand de Poulengey ....James Neylin
Captain La Hire ....Tom Clancy
Dunois ....Lee Richardson
Peter Cauchon, Bishop of Beauvais ....Alexander Scourby
Inquisitor ....David J. Stewart
D'Estivet ....Robert Ludlum
Ladies of the Court....Jennifer Hill; (also Jill Livesey, Betty Rollin, from first-engagement cast)
     Assessors, Courtiers, Soldiers: Ray Barbata, Walter Carlin, John Cullum, William Francis, Sam Gorden, Edward Hastings, Geoffrey Johnson, Derk Kinnane, Arthur Le Ral, George O'Halloran, Don Spence (all from first-engagement cast), Taldo Kenyon, Paul Stoudt.

(Closed January 5, 1957)

PICTURES IN THE HALLWAY

(19 performances)

Stage reading, adapted by Paul Shyre from the second of six autobiographical volumes written by Sean O'Casey. Produced by the Playhouse at the Playhouse, September 16, 1956, for a series of special performances.

Principals—

Aline MacMahon	George Brenlin
Staats Cotsworth	Paul Shyre
Rae Allen	Robert Geiringer

As The Dubliners—

Johnny Casside	Old Biddy
Mrs. Casside	Mr. Greenberg
Archie Casside	Mr. Dyke
Young Kelly	Alice Boyd, the Presbyterian
Uncle Tom	Reverend Harry Fletcher
The Warder	Ayamonn O'Farrell
Mrs. Middleton	Mrs. Nearus
The Dung-Dodgers	The Doctor
Ella	Daisy Battles

Mr. Anthony Dovergull

Staged by Stuart Vaughan; flutist, Dorothy Tutt; stage manager, Robert Paschall; press representatives, Richard Maney and Martin Shwartz.

(Closed November 4, 1956)

AUTOBIOGRAPHY

(6 performances)

Program of dances by Irene Hawthorne. Presented at the Booth Theatre, October 2, 1956.

Stories and choreography by Miss Hawthorne; musical director, Kurt Adler; original music and arrangements by Dorothea Freitag; stage manager, Charles Bellin; publicity director, Robert Ganshaw.

Program

1. "Autobiography"
   "How many miles to Bostontown?
   Fourscore and ten.
   Can I get there by candlelight?
   Yes, and back again."
   Scene 1. I.
   Scene 2. Them.
   Scene 3. We.
   Piano .... Dorothea Freitag
   Percussion .... Joe Venuto
2. "The Boy Mozart"
   Overture .... Sonatina in C Minor,
                                      K. App. 229, No. 4
   Scene 1. The Composer's Room.
   Thunderstorm .... Contre danse, K. 534

The Canary .... German dance, K. 600
Nannerl's hoopskirt ....Minuet in D, K. 355
Higher Mathematics ....Gigue, K. 574
The Kingdom ....Piano Variations, K. 265
Scene 2. Olympus.
Mozart's Muse ....Piano Fantasy in D Minor, K. 397
Scene 3. The Composer's Room.
The Coronation ...."The Sleigh Bells,"
German dance, K. 605
Music by Wolfgang Amadeus Mozart
Kurt Adler at the Piano.
3. "La Borrasca"
In a crowded cafe a Spanish dancer suddenly recognizes in her
audience the man who murdered her family.
Music by Garcia Lorca and Joaquin Nin
Piano ....Lucy Brown
Guitar ....Steve Newberry

(Closed October 6, 1956)

THE LOUD RED PATRICK

(93 performances)

Comedy in three acts by John Boruff, suggested by Ruth McKenney's book of the same name. Produced by Richard W. Krakeur, Robert Douglas and David Wayne at the Ambassador Theatre, October 3, 1956.

Cast of characters—

Mrs. Gallup ....Mary Farrell
Rita Flannigan ....Renne Jarrett
Rosalie Flannigan ....Kimetha Laurie
Mary Flannigan ....Nancy Devlin
Maggie Flannigan ....Peggy Maurer
Patrick Flannigan ....Arthur Kennedy
Mr. Finnegan ....David Wayne
Ralph Penrose ....James Congdon
Richard ....James Karr
The entire action of the play takes place in the Flannigan living room, in Cleveland, Ohio, August, 1912. Act I.—Late afternoon. Act II.—Several days later. Act III.—The following day; early morning.
Staged by Robert Douglas; scenery, costumes and lighting by Paul Morrison; production stage manager, Jean Barrere; stage manager, Kermit Kegley; press representatives, Karl Bernstein and Glen Allvine.

Period piece laid (as it might have been written) in 1912, about a blustering Irish-American widower with four daughters whose brogue is worse than his bite. Beyond the camphorated didoes and old comic-strip commotions, there was never any sense of a real household or the least ghost of a story.

(Closed December 22, 1956)

HARBOR LIGHTS

(4 performances)

Play in three acts by Norman Vane. Produced by Anthony Parella at the Playhouse, October 4, 1956.

Cast of characters—

Gene	Peter Votrian
Marion	Linda Darnell
Roy	Paul Langton
Chris	Robert Alda
Jake	Pat Harrington
Willy	Ronn Cummins
Mike	Darryl Richard
Dolly	Joan Mann Carter
Margery	Albie Gaye

The action takes place in a back yard on Staten Island; the time is the present. Act I.—Scene 1—Late afternoon of a Saturday in August. Scene 2—Three o'clock the next morning. Act II.—Late afternoon that day. Act III.—One hour later.

Staged by Guy Thomajan; Miss Darnell's costumes by Jeanne Partington; settings by Perry Watkins; lighting by Lee Watson; production stage manager, Daniel S. Broun; stage manager, Brooks Clift; press representatives, David Lipsky and Jay Russell.

A sea-girt drama, about a boy's love for his worthless mariner father and dislike of his well-intentioned stepfather; also involved is the conflict of feelings, in the boy's mother, for her first and second mates. A lushly stark work, with (at one point) bright-purple lighting effects trying in vain to keep up with the prose.

(Closed October 6, 1956)

SIXTH FINGER IN A FIVE FINGER GLOVE

(2 performances)

Play in two acts by Scott Michel. Produced by Gertrude Caplin and Thelma Fingar at the Longacre Theatre, October 8, 1956.

Cast of characters—

Matt Holly	Jimmie Komack
Grandfather Holly (Voice)	Wyrley Birch
Uncle Harry (Voice)	Walter Fisher
Andy Barrett	Bill Zuckert
Erna Kuloc	Gladys Holland
Samuel Holly (Voice)	Michael Keene
Frank Castellano	Frank Campanella
Stu Norton	Charles Mendick
Edgar Pinnell, Jr.	Samuel Gray
Vincent Vanyard	Leopold Badia
Herb Ingersoll	Charles Campbell
Miss Ferguson	Salome Jens
Mayor Thomas E. Seller	Bruce Evans
Dr. Peter Hoenig	Conrad Bain
Dr. John Evans	Paul Huber

The action of the play takes place in Matt Holly's "Swap Shop" and living quarters back of the shop. Act I.—Scene 1—A mid-afternoon in May. Scene 2—That night. Act II.—Scene 1—The next morning. Scene 2—A week later; evening.

Staged by John Holden; setting and lighting by Paul Morrison; original music composed by Charles Strouse; stage manager, Richard Platt; press representatives, Samuel J. Friedman and Lewis Harmon.

(Closed October 9, 1956)

THE RELUCTANT DEBUTANTE

(134 performances)

Comedy in two acts by William Douglas Home. Produced by Gilbert Miller in association with Loew's, Inc., by arrangement with E. P. Clift, at Henry Miller's Theatre, October 10, 1956.

Cast of characters—

Jimmy Broadbent	Wilfrid Hyde White
Sheila Broadbent	Adrianne Allen
Jane	Anna Massey
Mabel Crosswaithe	Brenda Forbes
Clarissa	Christina Gillespie
David Bulloch	David Cole
David Hoylake-Johnston	John Merivale
Mrs. Edgar	Renee Gadd
A Telephone	Sloane 8479

The scene is laid throughout in Jimmy Broadbent's flat off Eaton Square, London, in June. Act I.—Scene 1—Breakfast time. Scene 2—Cocktail time the same evening. Act II.—Scene 1—Early the following morning. Scene 2—Breakfast time.

Staged by Cyril Ritchard; setting designed by Raymond Sovey; costumes supervised by Kathryn B. Miller; stage manager, Richard Bender; press representatives, Richard Maney and Martin Shwartz.

See "The Season on Broadway."

(Closed February 2, 1957)

TOO LATE THE PHALAROPE

(36 performances)

Play in three acts by Robert Yale Libott, from the novel by Alan Paton. Produced by Mary K. Frank at the Belasco Theatre, October 11, 1956.

Cast of characters—

Lieut. Pieter Van Vlaanderen	Barry Sullivan
Stephanie	Ellen Holly
Dick Vorster	Geoffrey Horne
Jakob Van Vlaanderen	Finlay Currie
Nella Van Vlaanderen	Laurinda Barrett
Frikkie Van Vlaanderen	Patrick Dewar
	Roy Barba, alternate
Tante Sophie	Ann Dere

Isak ....Cherokee Thornton
Sergeant Steyn ....George Tyne
Esther ....Estelle Hemsley
Herman Geyer ....Byron Russell
Japie Grobler ....Paul Mann
Anna Van Aardt ....Janine Manatis
Veronica Massingham ....Bronia Stefan
Dominee Stander ....Grant Code
Captain Massingham ....Alan Napier
Matthew Kaplan (Kappie) ....Joseph Boley
Johannes Maartens ....Kurt Cerf
Captain Jooste ....Ralph Sumpter
Native Policeman ....Roy Thompson
Party Guests ....Wesley Lau, Rudolph Adler, Joe Biviano,
                 Lindsay Bergen, Bruce Peyton, Marvin Goodis
Natives.................Robert Henson, Roy Thompson, Adelaide
                 Boatner, Bill Glover, Joseph Boatner
   The action of the play occurs during a single summer in and near
the town of Venterspan, in the southeast Transvaal, Union of South
Africa. The time is the present.
   Staged by John Stix; settings and lighting by George Jenkins;
costumes by Dorothy Jeakins; music composed and supervised by
Josef Marais; production stage manager, Seymour Milbert; stage
manager, Paul Leaf; press representatives, William Fields and
Reginald Denenholz.

See "The Season on Broadway."

(Closed November 10, 1956)

DOUBLE IN HEARTS

(7 performances)

Comedy in three acts by Paul Nathan. Produced by Barnard
Straus, Paul Vroom and Adna Karns at the John Golden Theatre,
October 16, 1956.

Cast of characters—

Henry Waterhouse ....William Redfield
Mack Daniels ....Lawrence Hugo
Dinah Lawrence ....Julia Meade
Nan Waterhouse ....Neva Patterson
   The entire action takes place over a period of about sixteen hours
in the New York apartment in the Fifties shared by Henry Water-
house and Mack Daniels. Act I.—Toward dusk of a Saturday early
in spring. Act II.—Scene 1—Eleven p.m. Scene 2—About eight-
thirty the next morning. Act III.—An hour later.
   Staged by John Gerstad; set by Sam Leve; costumes by Natalie
Walker; production stage manager, Adna Karns; assistant stage
manager, William Windom; press representative, David Lipsky.

(Closed October 20, 1956)

THE APPLE CART

(124 performances)

Comedy in three acts by George Bernard Shaw. Produced by Charles and Joseph Neebe at the Plymouth Theatre, October 18, 1956.

Cast of characters—

Pamphilius .... Norman Barrs
Sempronius .... George Turner
Bill Boanerges, President of the Board of Trade .... Mercer McLeod
King Magnus .... Maurice Evans
Princess Alice .... Patience Cleveland
Balbus, Home Secretary .... Guy Spaull
Nicobar, Foreign Secretary .... Jack Livesey
Crassus, Colonial Secretary .... Noel Leslie
Pliny, Chancellor of the Exchequer .... William Jackson
Joseph Proteus, Prime Minister .... Charles Carson
Lysistrata, Powermistress General .... Pat Nye
Amanda, Postmistress General .... Claudia Morgan
Orinthia .... Signe Hasso
Queen Jemima .... Katherine Hynes
Vanhattan, American Ambassador .... Raymond Bramley
    The time is the future. Act I.—An office in the royal palace.
Act II.—An interlude in Orinthia's boudoir; three-thirty the same
day. Act III.—The terrace of the palace; later in the afternoon.
    Staged by George Schaefer; settings and lighting by Robert
O'Hearn; costumes designed by Noel Taylor; stage manager, Richard
Grayson; press representatives, Leo Freedman and Abner D.
Klipstein.

(Closed February 2, 1957)

THE OLD VIC COMPANY

(95 performances)

Repertory of four dramas by William Shakespeare: "Richard II" (première October 23, 1956), "Romeo and Juliet" (première October 24, 1956), "Macbeth" (première October 29, 1956) and "Troilus and Cressida" (première December 26, 1956). Produced, under the management of S. Hurok, by Old Vic Trust Ltd. and the Arts Council of Great Britain at the Winter Garden, October 23, 1956.

RICHARD II

Cast of characters—

King Richard the Second .... John Neville
John of Gaunt, Duke of Lancaster,
    Uncle to the King .... Paul Rogers
Henry Bolingbroke, Duke of Hereford,
    afterwards Henry IV .... Charles Gray
Thomas Mowbray, Duke of Norfolk .... Jack Gwillim
Lord Marshal .... Ronald Allen
Duke of Aumerle, son to the Duke of York .... Jeremy Brett
Page to Richard .... Job Stewart
Herald to Bolingbroke .... Daniel Moynihan

Herald to Mowbray ....Peter Needham
Green ⎫   ⎧   Derek New
Bushy ⎬ favorites of King Richard ....⎨ James   Villiers
Bagot ⎭   ⎩   Alan Penn
Duke of York, uncle to the King ....Richard Wordsworth
Earl of Northumberland ....Ernest Hare
Queen to King Richard ....Claire Bloom
Lord Ross ....Bryan Pringle
Lord Willoughby ....Edward Harvey
Servant to the Duke of York ....Aubrey Morris
Henry Percy, surnamed Hotspur,
   son to Northumberland ....John Greenwood
Lord Scroop of Berkeley ....John Woodvine
Earl of Salisbury ....Timothy Parkes
Bishop of Carlisle ....Denis Holmes
Ladies attending on the Queen ....Margaret Courtenay, Jennifer
                                           Wilson, Sally Home, Marion
                                           Hood, Juliet Cooke
Gardeners ....Job Stewart, Keith Taylor
Sir Pierce of Exton ....Donald Homer
Servants to Exton ....Derek New, Keith Taylor
Groom of the King's Stable ....Aubrey Morris
Keeper of the Prison ....Graeme Campbell
   Soldiers, Commons, Officers, Attendants: Peter Bowles, Graeme
Campbell, Donald Homer, Fraser Kerr, Tom Kneebone, Aubrey Morris,
Peter Needham, Derek New, Timothy Parkes, Alan Penn, Keith
Taylor, James Villiers, Charles West, John Woodvine.
   The scene is England and Wales; three acts.
   Staged by Michael Benthall; decor and costumes by Leslie Hurry;
music composed by Christopher Whelen.

ROMEO AND JULIET

Cast of characters—

Escalus, prince of Verona ....Charles Gray
Paris, young nobleman,
   kinsman to the prince ....Jeremy Brett
Montague ⎫ Heads of two houses at   ⎧ Denis Holmes
Capulet ⎬ variance with each other ....⎨ Ernest Hare
Romeo, son to Montague ....John Neville
Mercutio, kinsman to the prince and
   friend to Romeo ....Paul Rogers
Benvolio, nephew to Montague and
   friend to Romeo ....Ronald Allen
Tybalt, nephew to Lady Capulet ....Richard Wordsworth
Friar Laurence, a Franciscan ....Jack Gwillim
Friar John, of the same order ....Daniel Moynihan
Balthasar, servant to Romeo ....John Woodvine
Sampson ⎫ servants to Capulet   ⎧ Aubrey Morris
Gregory ⎬ ....⎨ Bryan Pringle
Peter, servant to Juliet's nurse ....Job Stewart
Abraham, servant to Montague ....Peter Bowles
An Apothecary ....Edward Harvey
Page to Paris ....John Greenwood
Street Muscian ....Timothy Parkes
Lady Montague, wife to Montague ....Jennifer Wilson
Lady Capulet, wife to Capulet ....Margaret Courtenay
Juliet, daughter to Capulet ....Claire Bloom
Nurse to Juliet ....Wynne Clark
   Citizens of Verona, Kinsfolk of Both Houses, Maskers, Guards
and Watchmen: Graeme Campbell, Donald Homer, Fraser Kerr,
Tom Kneebone, Peter Needham, Alan Penn, Timothy Parkes, Keith
Taylor, James Villiers, Charles West, Sally Home, Marion Hood,
Derek New, Juliet Cooke.
   Singers ....Marion Hood and Charles West
   The action of the play takes place in Verona and Mantua; two acts.
   Staged by Robert Helpmann; costumes and decor by Loudon
Sainthill; music composed by Brian Easdale; fights arranged by
Bernard Hepton and John Greenwood.

MACBETH

Cast of characters—

Witches ....Richard Wordsworth, Wynne Clark, Job Stewart
Duncan, King of Scotland ....Denis Holmes
Malcolm } his sons ....{ Jeremy Brett
Donalbain } ....{ Peter Needham
Macduff } Noblemen of Scotland ....{ John Neville
Lennox } ....{ Charles Gray
A Sergeant ....John Woodvine
Ross, another Noble ....Ernest Hare
Macbeth } Generals in the King's army ....{ Paul Rogers
Banquo } ....{ Jack Gwillim
Fleance, son to Banquo ....Kieth Taylor
Seyton, servant to Macbeth ....Aubrey Morris
Lady Macbeth ....Coral Browne
A Porter ....Richard Wordsworth
A Doctor ....Edward Harvey
Murderers ....John Woodvine, Graeme Campbell
Apparitions ....Peter Needham, Sally Home, Juliet Cooke
Lady Macduff ....Jennifer Wilson
Son to Macduff ....John Greenwood
Gentlewoman, attending on Lady Macbeth ......Margaret Courtenay
Apparitions, Attendants, Messengers, Nobles, Soldiers: Ronald
Allen, Peter Bowles, Graeme Campbell, Fraser Kerr, Tom Kneebone,
Donald Homer, Daniel Moynihan, Derek New, Timothy Parkes, Alan
Penn, Bryan Pringle, Job Stewart, James Villiers, Charles West,
John Woodvine, Sally Home, Marion Hood, Juliet Cooke.
The scene is Scotland, with one scene in England; three acts.
Staged by Michael Benthall; costumes and decor by Audrey
Cruddas; music composed by Brian Easdale; fight arranged by
Bernard Hepton and John Greenwood.

TROILUS AND CRESSIDA

Cast of characters—

Trojans

Priam, King of Troy ....Keith Taylor
Hector } ....{ Jack Gwillim
Troilus } ....{ Jeremy Brett
Paris } his sons ....{ Ronald Allen
Deiphobus } ....{ Timothy Parkes
Helenus } ....{ Bryan Pringle
Aeneas, a Trojan officer ....Denis Holmes
Antenor, a Trojan captured by the Greeks,
  later returned to Troy in exchange for Cressida ....James Villiers
Pandarus, uncle to Cressida ....Paul Rogers
Cressida's Groom ....Aubrey Morris
Troilus' Servant ....John Greenwood
Helen, formerly wife of Menelaus ....Coral Browne
Andromache, wife of Hector ....Jennifer Wilson
Cassandra, daughter of Priam ....Margaret Courtenay
Cressida, daughter of Calchas ....Rosemary Harris

Greeks

Agememnon, in command of the Greek
  expedition to Troy ....Rupert Davies
Menelaus, his brother ....Edward Harvey
Ulysses } { Richard Wordsworth
Nestor } { Job Stewart
Ajax } officers in the expeditionary force...{ Ernest Hare
Achilles } { Charles Gray
Patroclus } { Derek New
Diomedes } { Donald Homer
Thersites, a civilian attached to
  the expeditionary force .... John Neville

Calchas, a refugee from Troy .... John Woodvine
Greek Officers .... Aubrey Morris, Peter Needham
    Sailors, Trumpeters, Myrmidons: Peter Bowles, Graeme Campbell,
John Flint, Fraser Kerr, Tom Kneebone, Daniel Moynihan, Alan
Penn, Bryan Pringle, Charles West
    The scene: Inside and outside besieged Troy; two acts.
    Staged by Tyrone Guthrie; costumes and decor by Frederick
Crooke; music composed by Frederick Marshall; fights arranged by
Bernard Hepton and John Greenwood.
    For entire series: Director of The Old Vic Company, Michael
Benthall; orchestra under direction of Arthur Lief; scenic super-
visor, Mordecai Gorelik; costume supervisor, Elizabeth Montgomery;
stage director, John Murphy; stage managers, Elizabeth Butterfield
and John Wayne; press representatives for S. Hurok, Martin
Feinstein and Michael Sweeley.

(Closed January 12, 1957)

SEPARATE TABLES

(251 performances)
(Continued)

Two plays by Terence Rattigan. Produced by the Producers
Theatre, in association with Hecht-Lancaster, at the Music Box,
October 25, 1956.

TABLE BY THE WINDOW

Cast of characters—

Mabel .... Georgia Harvey
Lady Matheson .... Jane Eccles
Mrs. Railton-Bell .... Phyllis Neilson-Terry
Miss Meacham .... May Hallatt
Doreen .... Helena Carroll
Mr. Fowler .... William Podmore
Mrs. Shankland .... Margaret Leighton
Miss Cooper .... Beryl Measor
Mr. Malcolm .... Eric Portman
Charles Stratton .... Donald Harron
Jean Tanner .... Ann Hillary
    The action takes place in the Beauregard Hotel, Bournemouth, a
seaside town on the south coast of England. The time is winter.
Scene 1—Dining room; dinner. Scene 2—Lounge; after dinner.
Scene 3—Dining room; breakfast.

TABLE NUMBER SEVEN

Cast of characters—

Jean Stratton .... Ann Hillary
Charles Stratton .... Donald Harron
Major Pollock .... Eric Portman
Mr. Fowler .... William Podmore
Miss Cooper .... Beryl Measor
Mrs. Railton-Bell .... Phyllis Neilson-Terry
Miss Railton-Bell .... Margaret Leighton
Lady Matheson .... Jane Eccles
Miss Meacham .... May Hallatt

Mabel ....Georgia Harvey
Doreen ....Helena Carroll
    The action takes place (as in the previous play) in the Beauregard
Hotel. The time is summer. Scene 1—Lounge; after tea. Scene
2—Dining room; dinner.
    Entire production staged by Peter Glenville; settings by Michael
Weight; lighting and supervision by Paul Morrison; production by
arrangement with Stephen Mitchell; production stage manager,
Frederic de Wilde; assistant stage manager, Howard Fischer; press
representative, Barry Hyams.

See page 77.

THE BEST HOUSE IN NAPLES

(3 performances)

Comedy in three acts by Eduardo de Filippo, adapted by F. Hugh
Herbert. Produced by Nick Mayo at the Lyceum Theatre, October
26. 1956.

Cast of characters—

Domenico Soriano ....Rino Negri
Alfredo ....Silvio Minciotti
Rosalia ....Esther Minciotti
Linda ....Leila Martin
Lucia ....Renee Rogers
Father Bonno ....Carlo De Angelo
Filomena Marturano ....Katy Jurado
Counsellor Nocella ....Mort Marshall
Ricardo ....Morris Miller
Umberto ....Yale Wexler
Antonio ....Loren Farmer
Mario ....Hope Rissman
    The action of the play, which is contemporary, takes place in
Naples. Act I.—A villa on a hill overlooking Naples; twilight on a
late summer evening. Act II.—The villa; the following morning.
Act III.—Scene 1—A chapel in the Church of the Madonna of the
Roses; several months later; twilight. Scene 2—Kitchen in the home
of Ricardo; night, several weeks later. Scene 3—The villa; a week
later, at night.
    Staged by Nick Mayo; assistant to Mr. Mayo, Michael Shurtleff;
scenery and lighting by Ralph Alswang; costumes by Jerry Boxhorn;
original music by George Bassman; lyrics by Benny Davis; production stage manager, Ross Bowman; assistant stage manager, George
Lenz; press representatives, Harvey Sabinson, Max Eisen and
Bernard Simon.

Tale of a painter's bordello-bred mistress who, after 23 years,
tricks him into marrying her and forthwith introduces three grown-up
sons. The whole thing, from the outset, was as tedious and non-
sensical as it was vulgar.

(Closed October 27, 1956)

MAJOR BARBARA

(232 performances)

Play in two acts by George Bernard Shaw. Produced by Robert L. Joseph and the Producers Theatre at the Martin Beck Theatre, October 30, 1956.

Cast of characters—

Morrison, butler to Lady Britomart ....John Astin
Footman to Lady Britomart ....Frank Gero
Maid to Lady Britomart ....Louise Latham
Lady Britomart ....Cornelia Otis Skinner
Stephen, Lady Britomart's son ....Frederic Warriner
Major Barbara of the Salvation Army,
    Lady Britomart's daughter ....Glynis Johns
Sarah, Lady Britomart's daughter ....Myra Carter
Adolphus Cusins, Barbara's fiancé ....Burgess Meredith
Charles Lomax, Sarah's fiancé ....Richard Lupino
Andrew Undershaft, husband to Lady Britomart ....Charles Laughton
Rummy Mitchems ....Sally Gracie
Snobby Price ....Walter Burke
Jenny Hill ....Nancy Malone
Peter Shirley ....Colin Keith-Johnston
Bill Walker ....Eli Wallach
Mrs. Baines, Colonel in the Salvation Army ....Patricia Ripley
    The action takes place in a fashionable section of London; in the slums of London; and in a garden city outside London in the year 1905.
    Staged by Charles Laughton; settings and lighting designed by Donald Oenslager, assisted by Klaus Holm; costumes by Dorothy Jeakins; production stage manager, Harry Young; stage manager, Joanne Taylor; press representatives, Karl Bernstein and Glen Allvine.

(Closed May 18, 1957)

AUNTIE MAME

(236 performances)
(Continued)

Comedy in two acts by Jerome Lawrence and Robert E. Lee, based on the novel by Patrick Dennis. Produced by Robert Fryer and Lawrence Carr at the Broadhurst Theatre, October 31, 1956.

Cast of characters—

Norah Muldoon ....Beulah Garrick
Patrick Dennis, as a boy ....Jan Handzlik
Ito ....Yuki Shimoda
Vera Charles ....Polly Rowles
Raymond ....Cris Alexander
Ralph Devine ....Grant Sullivan
Bishop Eleftharosees ....William Martel
M. Lindsay Woolsey ....John O'Hare
Auntie Mame ....Rosalind Russell
Mr. Waldo, a paper hanger ....Geoffrey Bryant
Mr. Babcock ....Robert Allen
Al Linden, the stage manager ....Wally Mohr

A Theatre Manager ....William Martel
Assistant Stage Manager ....Duane Camp
A Maid ....Kip McArdle
A Butler ....Paul Lilly
A Leading Man ....James Field
Lord Dudley ....Walter Riemer
A Customer ....Kip McArdle
A Customer's Son ....Barry Towsen
Mr. Loomis, a floor-walker ....Cris Alexander
Beauregard Jackson Pickett Burnside ....Robert Smith
Cousin Jeff ....William Martel
Cousin Fan ....Nan McFarland
Cousin Moultrie ....Frank Roberts
Sally Cato MacDougal ....Marian Winters
Emory MacDougal ....Barry Blake
Mother Burnside ....Ethel Cody
Fred, a groom ....Paul Lilly
Sam, another groom ....James Field
A Huntsman ....Cris Alexander
Dr. Shurr, a vet ....Geoffrey Bryant
Patrick Dennis, a young man ....Robert Higgins
Agnes Gooch ....Peggy Cass
Brian O'Bannion ....James Monks
Gloria Upson ....Joyce Lear
Doris Upson ....Dorothy Blackburn
Claude Upson ....Walter Klavun
Pegeen Ryan ....Patricia Jenkins
Michael Dennis ....Jan Handzlik
    And a great many friends of Auntie Mame.
    The action of the play takes place in Auntie Mame's Beekman
Place apartment and various other locales in which she becomes
involved during a period of years from 1928 to 1946.
    Staged by Morton DaCosta; production designed by Oliver Smith;
lighting by Peggy Clark; costumes by Noel Taylor; Miss Russell's
clothes by Travis Banton of Marusia; hair styles by Ronald DeMann;
incidental music by Saul Schechtman; production manager, Robert
Linden; stage manager, Duane Camp; press representative, Arthur
Cantor.

See "The Season on Broadway."

THE SLEEPING PRINCE

(60 performances)

Play in two acts by Terence Rattigan. Produced by the Producers
Theatre and Gilbert Miller at the Coronet Theatre, November 1,
1956.

Cast of characters—

The Major-Domo ....Ronald Dawson
The First Footman ....William Major
The Second Footman ....Martin Waldron
Northbrook ....Rex O'Malley
Mary ....Barbara Bel Geddes
The Butler ....Sorrell Booke
The Regent ....Michael Redgrave
The King ....Johnny Stewart
The Grand Duchess ....Cathleen Nesbitt
The Countess ....Nydia Westman
The Baroness ....Betty Sinclair
The Archduchess ....Margaret Neff Jerome
The Princess ....Elwin Stock
    The scene throughout is the Royal Suite of the Carpathian Lega-
tion in London. Act I.—Scene 1—Wednesday, June 21st, 1911,

about eleven-thirty p.m. Scene 2—Thursday, June 22nd, 1911, about eight a.m. Act II.—Scene 1—Thursday, June 22nd, 1911, about seven p.m. Scene 2—Friday, June 23rd, 1911, about one a.m. Scene 3—Friday, June 23rd, 1911, about ten a.m.

Staged by Michael Redgrave, assisted by Fred Sadoff; setting designed by Norris Houghton, assisted by Klaus Holm; costumes designed by Alvin Colt, assisted by Stanley Simmons; Miss Bel Geddes' gown by Valentina; words and music for "The Coconut Girl" by Vivian Ellis; production stage manager, James Gelb; stage manager, Michael Chase; press representatives, Richard Maney and Martin Shwartz.

See "The Season on Broadway."

(Closed December 22, 1956)

DIARY OF A SCOUNDREL

(25 performances)

Comedy in two acts, adapted by Rodney Ackland from the Russian of Alexander Ostrovsky. Produced by the Phoenix Theatre (T. Edward Hambleton and Norris Houghton) at the Phoenix Theatre, November 4, 1956.

Cast of characters—

Madame Glafira Gloumova	Ruth McDevitt
Styopka	Jerry Stiller
Yegor Gloumov	Roddy McDowall
Vassily Kourchaev	Bert Remsen
Golutvin	John Reese
Madame Babakina	Josephine Brown
Mamaev's Servant	Peter Falk
Neel Fedoseitch Mamaev	Howard da Silva
General Anton Kroutitsky	Mike Kellin
Madame Kleopatra Mamaeva	Margaret Hamilton
Ivan Gorodoulin	Robert Culp
Matriosha	Dee Victor
Lubinka	Doro Merande
Madame Sofia Tourousina	Blanche Yurka
Mashenka	Zohra Alton
Grigori	Jerry Morris
Poodle	Lorelei Lee
Pilgrim	Eugene Firsow

The action takes place in Moscow in the eighteen-sixties. Act I.—Scene 1—Gloumov's apartment; morning. Scene 2—Mamaev's house; evening, two weeks later. Scene 3—Madame Tourousina's country house; the next afternoon. Act II.—Scene 1—Gloumov's apartment; a week later. Scene 2—Madame Tourousina's country house; later the same day.

Staged by Alan Cooke; scenery and lighting by Klaus Holm; costumes by Alvin Colt; production stage manager, Robert Woods; stage manager, Melvin Bernhardt; publicity director, Ben Kornzweig; press associate, Robert Ganshaw.

(Closed November 25, 1956)

LONG DAY'S JOURNEY INTO NIGHT

(178 performances)
(Continued)

Play in four acts by Eugene O'Neill. Produced by Leigh Connell, Theodore Mann and José Quintero at the Helen Hayes Theatre, November 7, 1956.

Cast of characters—

James Tyrone .... Fredric March
Mary Cavan Tyrone .... Florence Eldridge
James Tyrone, Jr., their elder son .... Jason Robards, Jr.
Edmund Tyrone, their younger son .... Bradford Dillman
Cathleen, second girl .... Katherine Ross
 The action takes place in the living room of the Tyrones' summer home. Act I.—8:30 a.m. of a day in August, 1912. Act II.—Scene 1—Around 12:45 p.m. Scene 2—About a half-hour later. Act III.—Around 6:30 that evening. Act IV.—Around midnight.
 Staged by José Quintero; setting by David Hays; lighting by Tharon Musser; costumes by Motley; production stage manager, Elliott Martin; stage manager, George Petrarca; press representatives, Arthur Cantor and Louis Sheaffer.

See page 100.

THE TEAHOUSE OF THE AUGUST MOON

(14 performances)

Comedy in three acts by John Patrick, based on the novel by Vern Sneider. Revived by the New York City Center Theatre Company (Jean Dalrymple, Director) at the New York City Center of Music and Drama, November 8, 1956.

Cast of characters—

Sakini .... Rosita Diaz
Sgt. Gregovich .... Paul Davis
Col. Wainwright Purdy III .... John Alexander
Capt. Fisby .... Gig Young
Old Woman .... Naoe Kondo
Old Woman's Daughter .... Christal Kim
The Daughter's Children .... { Rosalind Gonzales / Rita Gonzales / Ronny Gonzales
Lady Astor .... Brandy
Ancient Man .... Yen Soo Kim
Mr. Sumata .... David Renard
Mr. Sumata's Father .... Jerry Fujikawa
Mr. Hokaida .... Man Mountain Dean, Jr.
Mr. Seiko .... Jim Russell
Mr. Oshira .... Tura Nakimura
Mr. Omura .... Karaji Seida
Mr. Keora .... Aki Aleong
Villagers .... Minoru Watanabe, Conrad Yama, Mark Satow, Leon Moore, Yoji Matsuoka
Miss Higa Jiga .... Shizu Moriya

Ladies League for Democratic Action ....Tafa Lee, Helen Lee,
                                           Anne Jung, Christal
                                           Kim, Naoe Kondo
Lotus Blossom ....Michi Kobi
Capt. McLean ....Bernard Hughes
    Staged by Billy Matthews; settings and lighting based on designs
by Peter Larkin; costumes by Noel Taylor; music composed and
conducted by Dai-Keong Lee; Miss Kobi's dance staged by Yuki
Shimoda; production stage manager, Herman Shapiro; stage manager,
Chet O'Brien.

The Teahouse of the August Moon was first produced by Maurice
Evans, in association with George Schaefer, at the Martin Beck
Theatre, October 15, 1953, for 1,027 performances.

(Closed November 18, 1956)

THAT GIRL AT THE BIJOU

(11 performances)

Revue in two acts by Iva Kitchell. Produced by Luben Vichey
at the Bijou Theatre, November 9, 1956.

Program—

Selections from the following character sketches and dances by
Miss Kitchell:
                                                    Music by
Bacchanale (As Seen at the Opera) ....Saint-Saëns
Chanteuse-Danseuse ....Pease, Nelson and Dodge
Dance Espagnol ....Bizet-Brown
Chorus Girl (Vintage of 1920) ....Fisher
Coloratura ....Harvey Brown
Dance & Encore ....Chopin
Growing Up ....Friedman-Gartner
Maisie at the "Moovies" ....arr. by Harvey Brown
Me-ow ....Alda Astori
Nocturne ....Rachmaninoff
Non-Objective ....No Music
Obsession ....Harvey Brown
Oriental Dance (by an Occidental Girl) ....Strickland
Pseudo-Voodoo ....Harvey Brown
Romance ....Friedman-Gartner
Salesman (with apologies to the
    Fuller Brush Man) ....Peter Paul Fuchs
Something Classic ....Beethoven and Schubert
    Scarf Dance—Garland Dance
Fantasy for Body and Piano ....Harvey Brown
Sonatina Rococco ....Harvey Brown
    Allegro Artifical—Andante
    Sentimental—Rondo con Esprit
Soul in Search ....No Music
Tale of a Bird ....Harvey Brown
The Gentleman Friend ....Harvey Brown
The Vert Bros. (Intro & Extro) ....Harvey Brown
Valse Triste ....Sibelius
When I Was Eight ....Gautier
Ze Ballet ....Ponchielli
    Staged by Gene Perlowin; costumes and choreography by Iva
Kitchell; composer-pianist, Harvey Brown; press representative, Gerald
Goode.

(Closed November 18, 1956)

CHILD OF FORTUNE

(23 performances)

Play in two acts by Guy Bolton, adapted from "Wings of the Dove" by Henry James. Produced by Jed Harris at the Royale Theatre, November 13, 1956.

Cast of characters—

Bennett ....Bert Bertram
Lionel Croy ....Martyn Green
Kate Croy ....Betsy von Furstenberg
Richard Denning ....Edmund Purdom
Milly Temple ....Pippa Scott
Mrs. Lowder ....Norah Howard
Susan Shepherd ....Mildred Dunnock
Sir Luke Strett, M.D. ....Stafford Dickens
Lord Marcus Annersley ....Peter Pagan
Eugenio ....Anthony Di Palazzo
Bianca ....Mary Foskett
    Act I.—Scene 1—The morning room in Mrs. Lowder's house in London; June. Scene 2—The same; July. Act II.—A sitting room in the Palazzo Leporelli in Venice; August. Act III.—Scene 1—The same; September. Scene 2—The same; October.
    Staged by Jed Harris; settings and lighting by Robert O'Hearn; costumes by William Pitkin; stage manager, George Greenberg.

See "The Season on Broadway."

(Closed December 1, 1956)

A VERY SPECIAL BABY

(5 performances)

Play in two acts by Robert Alan Aurthur. Produced by David Susskind at the Playhouse, November 14, 1956.

Cast of characters—

Joey ....Jack Warden
Anna ....Sylvia Sidney
Casale ....Luther Adler
Augie ....Will Kuluva
George ....Carl Low
Carmen ....Jack Klugman
    The setting is the Casale home in Wellport, Long Island. The time is the present. Act I.—Scene 1—Noon, Saturday. Scene 2—A half-hour later. Act II.—Scene 1—7 p.m., Saturday. Scene 2—2 p.m., Sunday. Scene 3—A few minutes later.
    Staged by Martin Ritt; setting and lighting by Howard Bay; costumes by John Boxer; associate producer, Michael Abbott; stage manager, Jose Vega; press representatives, Arthur Cantor and Walrath J. Beach.

See page 127.

(Closed November 17, 1956)

LI'L ABNER

(*226 performances*)
(Continued)

Musical comedy in two acts, with book by Norman Panama and Melvin Frank, based on the characters created by Al Capp; lyrics by Johnny Mercer; music by Gene de Paul. Produced by Norman Panama, Melvin Frank and Michael Kidd at the St. James Theatre, November 15, 1956.

Cast of characters—

Lonesome Polecat	Anthony Mordente
Hairless Joe	Chad Block
Romeo Scragg	Marc Breaux
Clem Scragg	James Hurst
Alf Scragg	Anthony Saverino
Moonbeam McSwine	Carmen Alvarez
Marryin' Sam	Stubby Kaye
Earthquake McGoon	Bern Hoffman
Daisy Mae	Edith Adams
Pappy Yokum	Joe E. Marks
Mammy Yokum	Charlotte Rae
Li'l Abner	Peter Palmer
Cronies	Marc Breaux, Ralph Linn, Jack Matthew, Robert McClure, George Reeder
Mayor Dawgmeat	Oran Osburn
Senator Jack S. Phogbound	Ted Thurston
Dr. Rasmussen T. Finsdale	Stanley Simmonds
Government Man	Richard Maitland
Available Jones	William Lanteau
Stupefyin' Jones	Julie Newmar
Colonel	George Reeder
Radio Commentators	James Hurst, Robert McClure, Jack Matthew
President	Lanier Davis
General Bullmoose	Howard St. John
Secretaries	Lanier Davis, Robert McClure, Jack Matthew, George Reeder
Appassionata Von Climax	Tina Louise
Evil Eye Fleagle	Al Nesor
Dr. Smithborn	George Reeder
Dr. Krogmeyer	Ralph Linn
Dr. Schleifitz	Marc Breaux
State Department Man	Lanier Davis
Wives	Carmen Alvarez, Pat Creighton, Lillian D'Honau, Bonnie Evans, Hope Holiday, Deedee Wood
Butler	James J. Jefferies
Colonel	Lanier Davis

Singers: Margaret Baxter, Joan Cherof, Pat Creighton, Joyce Gladmond, Hope Holiday, Jane House, Louise Pearl, Jeanette Scovotti; Don Braswell, Lanier Davis, James Hurst, Jack Matthew, Robert McClure, Oran Osborn, George Ritner, Anthony Saverino.

Dancers: Carmen Alvarez, Lillian D'Honau, Bonnie Evans, Maureen Hopkins, Barbara Klopfer, Christy Peterson, Sharon Shore, Rebecca Vorno, Deedee Wood; Chad Block, Marc Breaux, Grover Dale, Robert Karl, Ralph Linn, Richard Maitland, Anthony Mordente, Tom Panko, George Reeder.

And: Jan Gunnar, Lucky Kargo, Mario Lamm, Reed Morgan, Aldo Ventura, Robert Wiensko.

Act I.—Scene 1—Dogpatch, U.S.A. Scene 2—The Yokum cabin. Scene 3—The Fishing Hole. Scene 4—Cornpone Square. Scene 5—Dogpatch Road. Scene 6—Cornpone Square. Scene 7—Washington, D. C., sequence: A. Government laboratory; B. The President's office. Scene 8—General Bullmoose's office. Scene 9—

Dogpatch Road. Scene 10—Dogpatch. Scene 11—Dogpatch Road. Scene 12—Dogpatch. Act II.—Scene 1—Government testing laboratory, Washington. Scene 2—The Yokum cabin. Scene 3—General Bullmoose's office. Scene 4—Corridor in Bullmoose mansion. Scene 5—Ballroom in Bullmoose mansion. Scene 6—Corridor in Bullmoose mansion. Scene 7—The Government testing laboratory. Scene 8—Cornpone Square.

Staged by Michael Kidd; choreography by Mr. Kidd; scenery and lighting by William and Jean Eckart; costumes designed by Alvin Colt; musical direction, continuity and vocals by Lehman Engel; orchestrations by Philip J. Lang; ballet music arranged by Genevieve Pitot; production stage manager, Terence Little; stage manager, Lawrence N. Kasha; press representatives, Harvey B. Sabinson and Max Eisen.

Musical numbers—

ACT I

"A Typical Day" ....Dogpatchers
"If I Had My Druthers" ....Li'l Abner and Cronies
Reprise: "If I Had My Druthers" ....Daisy
"Jubilation T. Cornpone" ....Marryin' Sam and Dogpatchers
"Rag Offen the Bush" ....Dogpatchers
"Namely You" ....Daisy and Li'l Abner
"Unnecessary Town" ....Li'l Abner, Daisy and Dogpatchers
"What's Good for General Bullmoose" ....Secretaries
"The Country's in the Very Best of Hands" ....Li'l Abner and Marryin' Sam
"Sadie Hawkins Day" (Ballet) ....Dogpatchers

ACT II

"Oh Happy Day" ....Drs. Finsdale, Smithborn, Krogmeyer and Schleifitz
"I'm Past My Prime" ....Daisy and Marryin' Sam
"Love in a Home" ....Li'l Abner and Daisy
"Progress Is the Root of All Evil" ....General Bullmoose
Society Party ....Guests and Dogpatchers
Reprise:
  "Progress Is the Root of All Evil" ....General Bullmoose
"Put 'Em Back" ....Wives
Reprise: "Namely You" ....Daisy
"The Matrimonial Stomp" ....Marryin' Sam and Dogpatchers
Finale ....Entire Company

See "The Season on Broadway."

GIRLS OF SUMMER

(56 performances)

Play in three acts by N. Richard Nash. Produced by Cheryl Crawford at the Longacre Theatre, November 19, 1956.

Cast of characters—

Gene Mitchell ....Arthur Storch
Mickey Argent ....George Peppard
Hilda Brookman ....Shelley Winters
Binnie Brookman ....Lenka Peterson
Jules Taggart ....Pat Hingle
Tommy Brookman ....John Harkins
Phyllis Brookman ....Sandra Stevens
Mrs. Mitchell ....Nellie Burt

The action of the play takes place in Hilda Brookman's apartment, New York City, in early summer of the present day. Act I.—Morning. Act II.—Scene 1—The same night. Scene 2—The following night. Act III.—Scene 1—Immediately following. Scene 2—Early the next morning.

Staged by Jack Garfein; settings by Boris Aronson, assisted by Lisa Jalowetz; costumes by Kenn Barr; lighting by Lee Watson; production assistant, Sylvia Drulie; song "Girls of Summer" composed by Stephen Sondheim; trumpeter, Bob Manso; stage manager, Irving Buchman; press representatives, Ben Washer and Howard Newman.

See "The Season on Broadway."

(Closed January 5, 1957)

THE HAPPIEST MILLIONAIRE

(222 performances)
(Continued)

Comedy in two acts by Kyle Crichton, suggested by the book "My Philadelphia Father," by Cordelia Drexel Biddle and Mr. Crichton. Produced by Howard Erskine and Joseph Hayes at the Lyceum Theatre, November 20, 1956.

Cast of characters—

Emma	Kate Harrington
John Lawless	Martin Ashe
Livingston Biddle	Don Britton
Joe Mancuso	Rocco Bufano
Tony Biddle	Dana White
Cordelia Biddle	Diana van der Vlis
Charlie Taylor	Joe Bishop
Anthony J. Drexel Biddle	Walter Pidgeon
Mrs. Anthony J. Drexel Biddle	Ruth Matteson
Aunt Mary Drexel	Katharine Raht
Cousin Lucy Rittenhouse	Gaye Jordan
Angier Duke	George Grizzard
O'Malley	Lou Nova
Mrs. Benjamin Duke	Ruth White
Footman	Mark Allen

The action of the play takes place between September, 1916, and June, 1917, in the Biddle home, 2104 Walnut Street, Philadelphia. Act I.—Scene 1—Afternoon of a September day, 1916. Scene 2—March, 1917. Scene 3—The next night. Act II.—Scene 1—Early June, 1917. Scene 2—Early the next morning.

Staged by Howard Erskine and Joseph Hayes; setting and lighting by George Jenkins; costumes by Audre; production stage manager, William Weaver; stage manager, Joe Bishop; press representatives, Miriam Byram and Phyllis Perlman.

See "The Season on Broadway."

THE GLASS MENAGERIE

(15 performances)

Play in two acts by Tennessee Williams. Revived by the New York City Center Theatre Company (Jean Dalrymple, Director) at the New York City Center of Music and Drama, November 21, 1956.

Cast of characters—

The Mother	Helen Hayes
Her Son	James Daly
Her Daughter	Lois Smith
The Gentleman Caller	Lonny Chapman

Staged by Alan Schneider; adaptation of Jo Mielziner's original designs; lighting by Peggy Clark; original music composed by Paul Bowles; production stage manager, Willis Gould; stage manager, John Maxtone-Graham.

The Glass Menagerie was first produced by Eddie J. Dowling and Louis J. Singer at the Playhouse, March 31, 1945, for 561 performances.

(Closed December 2, 1956)

CRANKS

(40 performances)

Revue in two acts, written by John Cranko, with music by John Addison. Produced by Richard Charlton and John Krimsky at the Bijou Theatre, November 26, 1956.

Principals—

Hugh Bryant
Anthony Newley
Annie Ross
Gilbert Vernon
The "Cranks" Chamber Group:

Anthony Bowles and Philip Ingalls	Piano and harpsichord
Asunta Dell'Aquila	Harp
J. Morton	Clarinet
Bill Feinbloom	Bass
Alternates: Eugene Bianco	Harp
Irving Schlein	Piano

Staged by John Cranko; decor by John Piper; musical direction by Anthony Bowles; set supervision and lighting by Paul Morrison; stage manager, Jack Woods; press representatives, Richard Maney and Michel Mok.

Sketches and musical numbers—

ACT I

Who's Who
Adrift
Man's Burden
Where Has Tom Gone?
Boo to a Goose
Lullaby
Broadminded
Waiting Room
Bats
Passacaglia
Who Is It Always There?
Gloves
This is The Sign
Present for Gilbert
Sea Song
Valse Anglaise

ACT II

Tra La La
Don't Let Him Know You
Chiromancy
L'Après-Midi de Gilbert
I'm the Boy
Metamorphosis
Would You Let Me Know?
Arthur, Son of Martha
Blue
Elizabeth
Cove in Hove
Dirge
Telephone Tango
Goodnight

See "The Season on Broadway."

(Closed December 29, 1956)

BELLS ARE RINGING

(210 performances)
(Continued)

Musical comedy in two acts, with book and lyrics by Betty Comden and Adolph Green; music by Jule Styne. Produced by the Theatre Guild at the Sam S. Shubert Theatre, November 29, 1956.

Cast of characters—

Sue	Jean Stapleton
Gwynne	Pat Wilkes
Ella Peterson	Judy Holliday
Carl	Peter Gennaro
Inspector Barnes	Dort Clark
Francis	Jack Weston
Sandor	Eddie Lawrence
Jeff Moss	Sidney Chaplin
Larry Hastings	George S. Irving
Telephone Man	Eddie Heim
Ludwig Smiley	Frank Milton
Charles Bessemer	Frank Green
Dr. Kitchell	Bernie West
Blake Barton	Frank Aletter
Another Actor	Frank Green
Joey	Tom O'Steen
Olga	Norma Doggett
Man from Corvello Mob	John Perkins
Other Man	Kasimir Kokich
Carol	Ellen Ray
Paul Arnold	Steve Roland
Michelle	Michelle Reiner
Master of Ceremonies	Eddie Heim
Singer at Night Club	Frank Green
Waiter	Ed Thompson
Maitre d'Hotel	David McDaniel
Police Officer	Gordon Woodburn
Madame Grimaldi	Donna Sanders
Mrs. Mallet	Jeannine Masterson

Dancers: Norma Doggett, Phyllis Dorne, Patti Karr, Barbara Newman, Nancy Perkins, Marsha Rivers, Beryl Towbin, Anne Wallace; Doria Avila, Frank Derbas, Don Emmons, Eddie Heim,

Kasimir Kokich, Tom O'Steen, Willy Sumner, Ben Vargas, Billy Wilson.

Singers: Pam Abbott, Joanne Birks, Urylee Leonardos, Jeannine Masterson, Michelle Reiner, Donna Saunders; Frank Green, Marc Leon, David McDaniel, Paul Michael, Julian Patrick, Steve Roland, Ed Thompson, Gordon Woodburn.

Act I.—Scene 1—Office of Susanswerphone; late afternoon. Scene 2—Jeff Moss' living room. Scene 3—An alley at night. Scene 4—The office; early morning. Scene 5—A street in front of the office. Scene 6—Jeff Moss' living room. Scene 7—A street. Scene 8—A subway car. Scene 9—A street. Scene 10—Dr. Kitchell's office. Scene 11—A street. Scene 12—A drugstore. Scene 13—A street. Scene 14—The office; a week later. Scene 15—Jeff Moss' living room. Act II.—Scene 1—The office; the next night. Scene 2—The park. Scene 3—Larry Hastings' penthouse. Scene 4—The Crying Gypsy Cafe. Scene 5—The Pyramid Night Club. Scene 6—Bay Ridge subway platform. Scene 7—The office.

Staged by Jerome Robbins; dances and musical numbers staged by Mr. Robbins and Bob Fosse; sets and costumes designed by Raoul Pène duBois; lighting by Peggy Clark; orchestrations by Robert Russell Bennett; musical director, Milton Rosenstock; vocal arrangements and direction by Herbert Greene and Buster Davis; dance arrangements and incidental scoring by John Morris; general stage manager, Charles Atkin; stage manager, Ruth Mitchell; press representatives, John L. Toohey and Max Gendel.

Musical numbers—

ACT I

"It's a Perfect Relationship" ....Ella
"On My Own" ....Jeff and Ensemble
"You've Got to Do It" ....Jeff
"It's a Simple Little System" ....Sandor and Ensemble
"Is It a Crime?" ....Ella
"Hello, Hello There!" ....Ella, Jeff and Ensemble
"I Met a Girl" ....Jeff and Ensemble
"Long Before I Knew You" ....Ella and Jeff

ACT II

"Mu-Cha-Cha" ....Ella and Carl
Dance ....Carol, Carl and Dancing Ensemble
"Just in Time" ....Jeff, Ella and Ensemble
"Drop That Name" ....Ella and Ensemble
"The Party's Over" ....Ella
"Salzburg" ....Sue and Sandor
"The Midas Touch" ....Singer, Boys and Girls
"Long Before I Knew You" (Reprise) ....Jeff
"I'm Goin' Back" ....Ella
Finale ....The Company

See "The Season on Broadway."

CANDIDE

(73 performances)

Musical in two acts, based on Voltaire's satire, with book by Lillian Hellman; score by Leonard Bernstein; lyrics by Richard Wilbur, John Latouche and Dorothy Parker. Produced by Ethel Linder Reiner, in association with Lester Osterman, Jr., at the Martin Beck Theatre, December 1, 1956.

Cast of characters—

Dr. Pangloss .... Max Adrian
Cunegonde .... Barbara Cook
Candide .... Robert Rounseville
Baron .... Robert Mesrobian
Maximillian .... Louis Edmonds
King of Hesse .... Conrad Bain
Hesse's General .... Norman Roland
Man .... Boris Aplon
Woman .... Doris Okerson
Dutch Lady .... Margaret Roy
Dutch Man .... Tony Drake
Atheist .... Robert Rue
Arab Conjuror .... Robert Barry
Infant Casmira .... Maria Novotna
Lawyer .... William Chapman
Very, Very Old Inquisitor .... Conrad Bain
Very Old Inquisitor .... Charles Aschmann
Junkman .... Robert Cosden
Wine-Seller .... Stanley Grover
Bear .... Charles Morrell
Bear Man .... Robert Rue
Alchemist .... Charles Aschmann
Grocery Lady .... Margaret Roy
Beggars .... Margaret Roy, Robert
Cosden, Thomas Pyle
French Lady .... Maud Scheerer
Old Lady .... Irra Petina
Marquis Milton .... Boris Aplon
Sultan Milton .... Joseph Bernard
Pilgrim Father .... Robert Rue
Pilgrim Mother .... Dorothy Krebill
Captain .... Conrad Bain
Martin .... Max Adrian
Governor of Buenos Aires .... William Olvis
Officers .... George Blackwell, Tony
Drake, Thomas Pyle
Ferone .... William Chapman
Madame Sofronia .... Irra Petina
Duchess .... Maud Scheerer
Prefect of Police .... Norman Roland
Prince Ivan .... Robert Mesrobian
Scrub Lady .... Barbara Cook
Duke of Naples .... Charles Aschmann
Croupier .... Robert Barry
Lady Cutely .... Dori Davis
Lady Toothly .... George Blackwell
Lady Soothly .... Fred Jones
Lady Richmond .... Thomas Pyle

Singers: Peggyann Alderman, Charles Aschmann, Robert Barry, George Blackwell, Dori Davis, Jack DeLon, Tony Drake, Naomi Farr, Stanley Grover, Fred Jones, Mollie Knight, Dorothy Krebill, Vivian Laurence, Henry Lawrence, Robert Mesrobian, Lois Monroe, Doris Okerson, Thomas Pyle, Margaret Roy, Robert Rue, Mara Shorr, Dorothy White.

Dancers: Alvin Beam, Charles Czarny, Marvin Gordon, Carmen Gutierrez, Charles Morrell, Frances Noble, Liane Plane, Gloria Stevens.

Act I.—Scene 1—Westphalia. Scene 1A—Candide travels to Lisbon. Scene 2—Lisbon. Scene 2A—Candide travels to Paris. Scene 3—Paris. Scene 3A—They travel to Buenos Aires. Scene 4—Buenos Aires. Act II.—Scene 1—Buenos Aires. Scene 1A—Candide travels to Venice. Scene 2—Venice. Scene 3—Westphalia.

Staged by Tyrone Guthrie, assisted by Tom Brown; production associate, Thomas Hammond; production designed by Oliver Smith; costumes by Irene Sharaff; lighting by Paul Morrison; musical director, Samuel Krachmalnick; orchestrations by Leonard Bernstein and Hershy Kay; hair styles by Ronald de Mann; production stage manager, Peter Zeisler; stage manager, Jack Merigold; press representative, Howard Newman.

Musical numbers—

ACT I

Ensemble: "The Best of All Possible Worlds" . .Pangloss and Chorus
Duet: "Oh, Happy We" . . . . .Candide and Cunegonde
Song: "It Must Be So" . . . . .Candide
Lisbon Sequence . . . . .Infant Casmira, Conjuror, and Chorus
Song: "It Must Be Me" . . . . .Candide
Mazurka
Aria: "Glitter and Be Gay" . . . . .Cunegonde
Duet: "You Were Dead, You Know" . . . . . .Candide and Cunegonde
Pilgrims' Procession . . . . .Pilgrims
Serenade: "My Love" . . . . .The Governor, Cunegonde, Old Lady
Tango: "I Am Easily Assimilated" . . . . . .Old Lady, Cunegonde and
Chorus
Quartet Finale . . . . .Cunegonde, Candide, Old Lady and Governor

ACT II

Trio: "Quiet" . . . . .Cunegonde, Old Lady and Governor
Ballad: "Eldorado" . . . . .Candide
Schottische: "Bon Voyage" . . . . .Governor and Chorus
Waltz: "What's the Use?" . . . . .Old Lady, Bazzini, Ferone,
Ivan and Chorus
Gavotte . . . . .Pangloss, Old Lady, Cunegonde and Candide
Finale: "Make Our Garden Grow" . . . . .Entire Company

See page 148.

(Closed February 2, 1957)

NIGHT OF THE AUK

(8 performances)

Play in three acts by Arch Oboler. Produced by Kermit Bloom-
garden at the Playhouse, December 3, 1956.

Cast of characters—

Colonel Tom Russell . . . . .Wendell Corey
Lt. Mac Martman . . . . .Dick York
Lewis Rohnen . . . . .Christopher Plummer
Doctor Bruner . . . . .Claude Rains
Lt. Jan Kephart . . . . .Martin Brooks
    The action takes place in a rocket ship in interstellar space return-
ing from the first successful landing on the moon. Act I.—The day
after some tomorrow. Act II.—Scene 1—Two hours later. Scene
2—A short while later. Scene 3—Fifteen minutes later. Act III.—
Scene 1—Forty-five minutes later. Scene 2—One hour and forty-five
minutes later.
    Staged by Sidney Lumet; setting and lighting by Howard Bay;
production stage manager, Robert Carrington; stage manager, Ray
Boyle; press representatives, Arthur Cantor and Walrath J. Beach.

The scene is a rocket-ship returning to earth after man's first
landing on the moon. The atmosphere is not one of triumph or
jubilation but of egomaniac violences and dark murders; of the
discovery that atomic war has broken out on earth and that the
rocket ship is almost certainly doomed. Prophesying an atomic
age that may leave man as extinct as the auk, Mr. Oboler offered
ten frills for every *frisson,* ten Polonius-like truisms for each philo-

sophic truth, and constant forced use (and misuse) of language for every striking phrase.

(Closed December 8, 1956)

MISTER ROBERTS

(15 performances)

Comedy by Joshua Logan and Thomas Heggen, based on the latter's novel. Revived by the New York City Center Theatre Company (Jean Dalrymple, Director) at the New York City Center of Music and Drama, December 5, 1956.

Cast of characters—

Chief Johnson	Joe Hardy
Lieutenant (j.g.) Roberts	Charlton Heston
Doc	Fred Clark
Dowdy	Frank Campanella
The Captain	William Harrigan
Insigna	Joe Marcus
Mannion	Jack De Mave
Lindstrom	Rance Howard
Stefanowski	Stanley Beck
Wiley	Walter Massey
Schlemmer	Dick Button
Reber	Buddy Reynolds
Ensign Pulver	Orson Bean
Dolan	Walter Mathews
Gerhart	Steve Pluta
Payne	Clint Kimbrough
Lieutenant Ann Girard	Nancy Berg
Shore Patrolman	Jeff Harris
Military Policeman	David Davis
Shore Patrol Officer	Gerald H. Metcalfe
Seamen, Firemen and Others	Arthur Abelson, David Anthony, Rick Brymer, Barry Alan Grael, Ronald Louis House, Michael Jacobsen, Michael F. Kasdan, David Kurzon, Arthur LeRal and Bert Wechsler.

Staged by John Forsythe; settings and lighting based on designs by Jo Mielziner; production stage manager, Ray Parker; stage manager, John Maxtone-Graham.

Mister Roberts was first produced by Leland Hayward at the Alvin Theatre, February 18, 1948, for 1,157 performances.

(Closed December 16, 1956)

HAPPY HUNTING

(206 performances)
(Continued)

Musical comedy in two acts, with book by Howard Lindsay and Russel Crouse; lyrics by Matt Dubey; music by Harold Karr.

Produced by Jo Mielziner at the Majestic Theatre, December 6, 1956.

Cast of characters—

Sanford Stewart, Jr.	Gordon Polk
Mrs. Sanford Stewart, Sr.	Olive Templeton
Joseph	Mitchell M. Gregg
Beth Livingstone	Virginia Gibson
Jack Adams, a reporter	Seth Riggs
Harry Watson, a reporter	Gene Wesson
Charley, a photographer	Delbert Anderson
Liz Livingstone	Ethel Merman
Sam ⎫	Clifford Fearl
Joe ⎪	John Craig
Freddy ⎬ photographers	George Martin
Wes ⎭	Jim Hutchison
Mary Mills ⎫	Estelle Parsons
Dick Davis ⎬ reporters	Robert C. Held
Bob Grayson ⎭	Carl Nicholas
Maud Foley	Mary Finney
Police Sergeant	Marvin Zeller
Arturo	Leon Belasco
The Duke of Granada	Fernando Lamas
Count Carlos	Renato Cibelli
Waiter	Don Weissmuller
Ship's Officer	John Leslie
Barman	Warren J. Brown
Mrs. B.	Florence Dunlap
Mrs. D.	Madeleine Clive
Mrs. L.	Kelley Stephens
Terence, a groom	Jim Hutchison
Tom, a groom	Eugene Louis
Daisy	Moe
Mr. T., a member of the Hunt	John Leslie
Mr. M., a member of the Hunt	Jay Velie
Albert, a groom	George Martin
Margaret, a maid	Mara Landi

Singers: Peggy Acheson, Marilynn Bradley, Deedy Irwin, Jane Johnston, Jean Kraemer, Mara Landi, Betty McGuire, Estelle Parsons, Noella Peloquin, Ginny Perlowin, Mary Roche, Kelley Stephens, Helene Whitney; Delbert Anderson, Edward Becker, Warren J. Brown, David Collyer, John Craig, Jack Dabdoub, Clifford Fearl, Robert C. Held, Carl Nicholas, Seth Riggs, Charles Rule, Mark Zeller.

Dancers: Betty Carr, Alice Clift, Jane Fischer, Roberta Keith, Svetlana McLee, Patti Nestor, Wendy Nickerson, Fleur Raup, Sigyn; Bob Bakanic, John Harmon, Jim Hutchison, Dick Korthaze, Eugene Louis, George Martin, Jim Moore, Lowell Purvis, Don Weissmuller, Roy Wilson.

The action takes place in Monaco, on shipboard, and near Philadelphia. The time is the present. Act I.—Scene 1—Outside the Palace; Monaco. Scene 2—Liz Livingstone's suite, Hotel Riviera; Monaco. Scene 3—Terrace of the hotel. Scene 4—Veranda of the Duke's suite, Hotel Riviera. Scene 5—Quai. Scene 6—In the ship's bar. Scene 7—Afterdeck of the ship. Scene 8—In the ship's bar. Scene 9—Afterdeck of the ship. Act II.—Scene 1—Liz Livingstone's estate, near Philadelphia. Scene 2—The Livingstone stables. Scene 3—Summerhouse, Liz's estate. Scene 4—The Philadelphia Hunt Club. Scene 5—Another part of the forest. Scene 6—Liz's boudoir. Scene 7—The Hunt Ball.

Staged by Abe Burrows; settings and lighting by Jo Mielziner; costumes designed by Irene Sharaff; dances and musical numbers staged by Alex Romero and Bob Herget; musical direction by Jay Blackton; orchestrations by Ted Royal; dance music devised by Roger Adams; production stage manager, Robert Downing; stage managers, John Scott and Lo Hardin; press representatives, Leo Freedman and Abner D. Klipstein.

Musical numbers—

ACT I

Overture
Postage Stamp—Principality .... Tourists and Monegasques
Don't Tell Me .... Sandy and Beth
It's Good to Be Here .... Liz and the Reporters
Mutual Admiration Society .... Liz and Beth
For Love or Money .... The Girls
Bikini Dance .... Beth
It's Like a Beautiful Woman .... The Duke
Wedding-of-the-Year Blues .... Maud, Harry, Jack, the
                                          reporters and photographers
Mr. Livingstone .... Liz
If'n .... Beth, Sandy and the Passengers
This Is What I Call Love .... Liz

ACT II

Entr'acte
A New-Fangled Tango .... Liz, Beth, Arturo and the Guests
She's Just Another Girl .... Sandy
The Game of Love .... Liz
Happy Hunting .... Liz, the Duke and members of the Hunt
I'm a Funny Dame .... Liz
This Much I Know .... The Duke
Just Another Guy .... Liz
Everyone Who's "Who's Who" .... Jack, Harry and the Footmen
Mutual Admiration Society—Reprise .... Liz and the Duke

See "The Season on Broadway."

THE GOOD WOMAN OF SETZUAN

(24 performances)

Play in two acts by Bertolt Brecht, adapted from the German by
Eric Bentley. Produced by the Phoenix Theatre (T. Edward
Hambleton and Norris Houghton) at the Phoenix Theatre, December
18, 1956.

Cast of characters—

Wong, a water seller .... Gerald Hiken
First God .... Gene Saks
Second God .... Logan Ramsey
Third God .... George Ebeling
First Gentleman .... Bart Murphy
Shen Te .... Uta Hagen
Second Gentleman .... Richard Blackmarr
Mrs. Shin .... Irene Dailey
Wife .... Marion Paone
Husband .... Gerald McGonagill
Nephew .... Neil Vipond
Unemployed .... William Grannell
Carpenter .... Byrne Piven
Brother .... William Myers
Sister-in-Law .... Nancy Quint
Mrs. Mi Tzu .... Nancy Marchand
Grandfather .... Edward Morehouse
Boy .... Louis Negin
Niece .... Anne Meara
Policeman .... Jerry Stiller
Carpet Dealer's Wife .... Jenny Egan
Yang Sun .... Albert Salmi

Old Whore ....Rose Schulman
Shu Fu ....Zero Mostel
Carpet Dealer ....Mervin Williams
Mrs. Yang ....Jane Hoffman
Priest ....Bart Murphy
Waiter ....Richard Blackmarr
Little Child ....Shu-Ren Cheng
Young Boy ....Glen Cannon
Young Girl ....Kay Levy
    The action takes place in Setzuan and environs.
    Staged by Eric Bentley; scenery and costumes by Wolfgang Roth,
from the designs of Teo Otto; incidental music by Paul Dessau;
musical direction by Simon Sadoff; lighting by Klaus Holm; production stage manager, Robert Woods; stage manager, Stark Hesseltine;
publicity director, Ben Kornzweig.

(Closed January 6, 1957)

SPEAKING OF MURDER

(37 performances)

Play in three acts by Audrey and William Roos. Produced by
Courtney Burr and Burgess Meredith at the Royale Theatre, December 19, 1956.

Cast of characters—

Ricky Ashton ....Billy Quinn
Janie Ashton ....Virginia Gerry
Connie Barnes Ashton ....Neva Patterson
Charles Ashton ....Lorne Greene
Annabelle Logan ....Brenda de Banzie
Mrs. Walworth ....Estelle Winwood
Mildred ....Brook Byron
Mitchell ....Robert Mandan
    The entire action of the play takes place in the library of the
Ashton home, forty miles north of New York City. The time is the
present. Act I.—Scene 1—Late afternoon, early July. Scene 2—
Half an hour later. Act II.—Scene 1—The following Friday,
shortly before noon. Scene 2—Later that afternoon. Act III.—The
same afternoon, five o'clock.
    Staged by Delbert Mann; setting and lighting by Frederick Fox;
costumes by Alice Gibson; stage manager, Charles Durand; press
representatives, Phyllis Perlman and Marian Byram.

See "The Season on Broadway."

(Closed January 19, 1957)

UNCLE WILLIE

(141 performances)

Comedy in three acts by Julie Berns and Irving Elman. Produced
by Albert Lewis and Samuel Schulman, in association with I. B.
Joselow, at the John Golden Theatre, December 20, 1956.

Cast of characters—

```
Uncle Willie ................................Menasha Skulnik
Leo .......................................Norman Feld
Esther ....................................Arline Sax
Sheila ....................................Elaine Lynn
Kathy .....................................Eileen Merry
Peggy .....................................Kathy Dunn
Charlie ...................................John Connell
Francey ...................................Nita Talbot
Mrs. Simon ................................Dorothy Raymond
Ellen .....................................Edith Fellows
Sgt. McNamara .............................Martin Rudy
Mr. Smith .................................Gaylord Mason
The Victim ................................John Phelps
```

The play is set mainly in the Bronx, in the first decade of the 20th Century.

Staged by Robert Douglas; setting and lighting by Ralph Alswang; incidental music by Sol Kaplan; costumes by Guy Kent; production stage manager, Andy Anderson; stage manager, Kenneth Paine; press representatives, Nat Dorfman and Irvin Dorfman.

An outrageously sleazy vehicle for Menasha Skulnik, about a turn-of-the-century Jewish do-gooder whose greatest achievement is to convert a feuding two-family house (half Irish and half Jewish) into a bower of sweetness and light. Beyond a story that made *Abie's Irish Rose* seem downright avant-garde, *Uncle Willie* had a greasy benevolence.

(Closed April 20, 1957)

RUTH DRAPER

and

Her Company of Characters

(7 performances)

Monologues by Ruth Draper. Produced by Bowden, Barr and Bullock at the Playhouse, December 25, 1956. (The scheduled four-week engagement was cut short by Miss Draper's death on December 30, 1956.)

Selections from the following program—

"A Children's Party"
"In a Railway Station on the Western Plains"
"Three Women and Mr. Clifford"
```
    1. The Private Secretary ........................Miss Nichols
    2. In the Motor ................................Mrs. Clifford
    3. At Mrs. Mallory's
```
"A Scottish Immigrant at Ellis Island"
"Doctors and Diets"
    In a Restaurant
"In a Church in Italy"

Stage manager, Gerald O'Brien; press representative, Joseph G. Lustig.

(Closed December 29, 1956)

PROTECTIVE CUSTODY

(3 performances)

Play in three acts by Howard Richardson and William Berney. Produced by Anderson Lawler, in association with Will Lester Productions, at the Ambassador Theatre, December 28, 1956.

Cast of characters—

First Attendant	Howard Wierum
Marc Bradley	Fritz Weaver
Dr. Wilhelm Steidl	Thayer David
Helen Merrick	Olga Bielinska
Dolly Barns	Faye Emerson
A Nun	Barbara Lester
Second Attendant	Mitchell Erickson
Robert Fuller	Oliver Berg

The action of the play takes place in the former Convent of the Bleeding Heart twenty miles outside a large city behind the Iron Curtain.

Staged by Herbert Berghof; settings and costumes by Peter Larkin; lighting by Lee Watson; stage manager, George Quick; press representatives, Phillip Bloom and David Lipsky.

(Closed December 29, 1956)

SMALL WAR ON MURRAY HILL

(12 performances)

Comedy in two acts by Robert E. Sherwood. Produced by the Playwrights' Company at the Ethel Barrymore Theatre, January 3, 1957.

Cast of characters—

Lt. Lord Frederick Beckenham	Daniel Massey
Major Clove	Nicholas Joy
Orderly	Peter Foy
Sentry	Bill Becker
Sam Pieters	Harry Sheppard
General Sir William Howe	Leo Genn
Hawley, Batman to General Howe	William Strange
Hessian	Michael Lewis
General Graf von Donop	Stefan Schnabel
Robert Murray	Joseph Holland
Mary Murray	Jan Sterling
Captain DuPont	Nicholas Probst
Daisy	Jonelle Allen
Susan Lindley	Patricia Bosworth
Sergeant Galway	Elliott Sullivan
Corporal Mullet	Allan Stevenson
Amelie	Vinnette Carroll
Samuel Judah	Francis Compton
Mrs. Torpen	Sally Walker
Abigail Torpen	Susan Oliver
John	George Francis
Cora	Sharon Porter
Soldiers	Warner LeRoy, Leo Bloom
A Girl	Jan Jarrett

A Boy ....Marc Sullivan
    Act I.—Scene 1—Cook-house of a farm in the northern reaches of Brooklyn village in the middle of September, 1776. Subsequent scenes are all in the living room of Robert Murray's house, on Manhattan Island, during the next two days.
    Staged by Garson Kanin, assisted by Kip Good; production designed by Boris Aronson, assisted by Lisa Jalowetz and Robert Randolph; costumes designed by Irene Sharaff, assisted by Ann Roth; stage manager, Porter Van Zandt; press representatives, William Fields, Ted Goldsmith and Reginald Denenholz.

See "The Season on Broadway."

(Closed January 12, 1957)

A CLEARING IN THE WOODS

(36 performances)

Play in two acts by Arthur Laurents. Produced by Roger L. Stevens and Oliver Smith at the Belasco Theatre, January 10, 1957.

Cast of characters—

Virginia ....Kim Stanley
Nora ....Anne Pearson
Jigee ....Barbara Myers
Barney ....Onslow Stevens
Ginna ....Joan Lorring
George ....Pernell Roberts
Pete ....Robert Culp
Hazelmae ....Sybil White
The Boy ....Tom Hatcher
Andy ....Lin McCarthy
    Staged by Joseph Anthony; production designed by Oliver Smith; costumes designed by Lucinda Ballard; lighting by A. Feder; music by Laurence Rosenthal; production stage manager, Bill Ross; stage manager, Leonard Patrick; press representatives, William Fields, Walter Alford and Reginald Denenholz.

See page 170.

(Closed February 9, 1957)

THE WALTZ OF THE TOREADORS

(132 performances)

Comedy in three acts by Jean Anouilh; English version by Lucienne Hill. Produced by the Producers Theatre (Robert Whitehead) at the Coronet Theatre, January 17, 1957.

Cast of characters—

Mme. St. Pé ....Mildred Natwick
General St. Pé ....Ralph Richardson
Gaston, his secretary ....John Stewart
Sidonia, his daughter ....Mary Grace Canfield
Estelle, another daughter ....Sudie Bond

Doctor Bonfant ....John Abbott
First Maid ....Frieda Altman
Mlle. de Ste-Euverte ....Meriel Forbes
Mme. Dupont-Fredaine ....Louise Kirtland
Father Ambrose ....William Hansen
New Maid ....Helen Seamon
 The action of the play takes place in the home of General St. Pé in France, about 1910.
 Staged by Harold Clurman; designed by Ben Edwards; production stage manager, Frederic de Wilde; assistant stage managers, Jonathan Anderson and Chester Doherty; press representatives, Barry Hyams and Abner D. Klipstein.

See page 186.

(Closed May 11, 1957)

WAITING FOR GODOT

(6 performances)

Play in two acts by Samuel Beckett. Revived by Michael Myerberg, by arrangement with Independent Plays Limited, at the Ethel Barrymore Theatre, January 21, 1957.

Cast of characters—

Estragon (Gogo) ....Mantan Moreland
Vladimir (Didi) ....Earle Hyman
Lucky ....Geoffrey Holder
Pozzo ....Rex Ingram
A Boy ....Bert Chamberlain
 Act I.—A country road; a tree; evening. Act II.—Next day; same time; same place.
 Staged by Herbert Berghof; scenery by Louis Kennel; costumes by Stanley Simmons; production assistant, Frank Baldwin; assistant stage manager, Philip Dean; press representatives, Bill Doll, Robert Ullman and Robert Ganshaw.

Waiting for Godot was first produced by Michael Myerberg, by arrangement with Independent Plays Limited, at the John Golden Theatre, April 19, 1956, for 59 performances.

(Closed January 26, 1957)

MEASURE FOR MEASURE

(32 performances)

Comedy in three acts by William Shakespeare. Produced by the American Shakespeare Festival Theatre and Academy under the direction of John Houseman at the Phoenix Theatre, January 22, 1957.

Cast of characters—

The Duke of Vienna ....Arnold Moss
Escalus, a Lord ....Powys Thomas
Angelo, the deputy ....Richard Waring
Friar Peter ....Patrick Hines
Mistress Overdone, a bawd ....Gertrude Kinnell
Pompey, her tapster ....Hiram Sherman
Lucio ....Norman Lloyd
First Gentleman ....Mitchell Agruss
Second Gentleman ....Tucker Ashworth
Provost ....Morris Carnovsky
Claudio ....Richard Easton
Juliet, affianced to Claudio ....Jacqueline Brookes
Isabella, sister to Claudio ....Nina Foch
Francisca, a nun ....Pamela Saunders
Elbow, a constable ....Leon Janney
Froth ....Ellis Rabb
Servant to Angelo ....Tucker Ashworth
Mariana ....Nancy Wickwire
A Boy ....Brian Desmond
Abhorson, an executioner ....William Cottrell
Barnadine ....Jerry Stiller
    Ministers, Chamberlains and Citizens: James Cahill, Gary Glass,
John Ragin, Michael Miller, Robert Morris, Joseph Myers, Charles
Meier, Pat McAteer, Jill Livesey, Vivian Paszamont, Anita Michals,
Marion Caspary, Pamela Saunders, Edwin Sherin, Barbara Lord,
David Pierce, Anthony Holland, David Milton, James Ray.
    The Band: Ben Miller, Conductor; David Glickstein, Joseph
Castka, Robert Cecil, Bill Brown, Michael Gisondi.
    The play is laid in Vienna.
    Staged by John Houseman and Jack Landau; scenery and costumes
by Rouben Ter-Arutunian; production and lighting by Jean Rosenthal;
music by Virgil Thomson; production stage manager, Paul Leaf;
stage manager, Ronald Bates; press representative for the American
Shakespeare Festival Theatre and Academy, Frank Goodman; for the
Phoenix Theatre: publicity director, Ben Kornzweig, and press representative, Robert Ganshaw.

(Closed February 17, 1957)

THE HIDDEN RIVER

(61 performances)

Play in three acts by Ruth and Augustus Goetz, based on Storm
Jameson's novel. Produced by Martin Gabel and Henry Margolis
at the Playhouse, January 23, 1957.

Cast of characters—

Father Baussan ....Jack Bittner
Jean Monnerie ....Robert Preston
Francis Monnerie ....Peter Brandon
Marie Regnier ....Lili Darvas
Elizabeth Regnier ....Gaby Rodgers
Adam Hartley ....David King-Wood
Amalie ....Margot Lassner
Daniel Monnerie ....Dennis King
General Otto von Kettler ....Tonio Selwart
Doctor Montalti ....Roger DeKoven
    The action takes place in the Monnerie manor house on the banks
of the Loire River, in France. The time is late spring, 1950.
Act I.—Scene 1—Morning. Scene 2—Late afternoon. Act II.—

Scene 1—Early evening.   Scene 2—After dinner.   Act III.—
Midnight.
Staged by Robert Lewis; setting and lighting by Stewart Chaney;
costumes by Anna Hill Johnstone; stage manager, John Barry Ryan;
press representatives, Richard Maney and Michel Mok.

See "The Season on Broadway."

(Closed March 16, 1957)

THE POTTING SHED

(141 performances)
(Continued)

Play in three acts by Graham Greene.   Produced by Carmen
Capalbo and Stanley Chase at the Bijou Theatre, January 29,
1957.

Cast of characters—

Dr. Frederick Baston ....Lewis Casson
Anne Callifer ....Carol Lynley
Sara Callifer ....Leueen MacGrath
Mrs. Callifer ....Sybil Thorndike
John Callifer ....Stanley Lemin
James Callifer ....Robert Flemyng
Dr. Kreuzer ....Rudolf Weiss
Corner ....Richard Longman
Mrs. Potter ....Eda Heinemann
Miss Connolly ....Joan Croydon
Father William Callifer ....Frank Conroy
Act I.—Scene 1—The living room of the Callifers' house, Wild
Grove, in what was once the country; autumn afternoon.   Scene 2—
The same; evening, two days later.   Act II.—Scene 1—James
Callifer's lodging in Nottingham; four weeks later.   Scene 2—Father
William Callifer's Presbytery, somewhere in East Anglia; evening,
the next day.   Act III.—The living room at Wild Grove, the next
evening.
Staged by Carmen Capalbo; designed by William Pitkin; lighting
by Peggy Clark; costumes supervised by Patricia Zipprodt; production
stage manager, Gene Perlowin; stage manager, Rome Smith; press
representatives, Bill Doll and Robert Ullman.

See page 205.

MADELEINE RENAUD—JEAN-LOUIS BARRAULT
REPERTORY COMPANY

(30 performances)

Repertory of seven plays, in French, presented in six programs.
Produced by S. Hurok, under the auspices of the Government of the
French Republic, at the Winter Garden, January 30, 1957.

Repertoire—

> *Christophe Colomb,* a play in two acts by Paul Claudel, with music by Darius Milhaud
> *Volpone,* a play in five acts by Ben Jonson, adapted by Jules Romains and Stefan Zweig, with music by Georges Auric
> *Le Misanthrope,* a comedy in five acts by Molière
> *Les Nuits de la Colère* (Nights of Fury), a play in two acts by Armand Salacrou
> *Feu la Mère de Madame* (Dear Departed Mother-in-Law), a comedy by Georges Feydeau
> *Intermezzo,* a play in three acts by Jean Giraudoux, with music by Francis Poulenc
> *Le Chien du Jardinier* (The Gardener's Dog), a play in three acts by Georges Neveux, after Lope de Vega, with music on classic Spanish themes arranged by Pierre Boulez
> *Les Adieux* was a "farewell" to the audience, consisting of individual and collective skits, recitations, and songs.

Repertory Company—

Madeleine Renaud	Jean-Louis Barrault
Simone Valère	Jean Desailly
Marie-Hélène Dasté	Jean-Pierre Granval
Natalie Nerval	Georges Cusin
Françoise Golea	Beauchamp
Pierre Bertin	Régis Outin
Jean Juillard	Françoise Ledoux
Gabriel Cattand	André Batisse
Jacques Galland	Emile Noel
Dominique Rozan	Jean Lancelot
André Jobin	Gerard Dournel
René Lanier	Serge Merlin

Plays staged by Jean-Louis Barrault; musical director, Pierre Boulez; production stage manager, Marvin Krauss; stage manager, Jean Salerno; press representatives, Martin Feinstein and Michael Sweeley.

(Closed February 23, 1957)

EUGENIA

(12 performances)

Play in three acts by Randolph Carter, adapted from Henry James' "The Europeans." Produced by John C. Wilson, in association with Theatre Corporation of America, at the Ambassador Theatre, January 30, 1957.

Cast of characters—

Mr. Wentworth	Reynolds Evans
Gertrude Wentworth	Anne Meacham
Charlotte Wentworth	Irma Hurley
The Reverend Alfred Brand	Robert Duke
Felix Da Costa	Scott Merrill
Eugenia, Baroness Munster	Tallulah Bankhead
Robert Acton	Jay Barney
Elizabeth Acton	June Hunt
Clifford Wentworth	Tom Ellis
Marie	Therese Quadri

The action takes place in the guest house on the Wentworth estate near Boston. Act I.—Scene 1—A Sunday afternoon in June, 1878. Scene 2—Several weeks later. Act II.—Scene 1—An afternoon a week later. Scene 2—About eleven o'clock the night of July 4th. Act III.—Scene 1—Several days later. Scene 2—Morning, the following day. Scene 3—Later that day.

Staged by Herbert Machiz; production designed by Oliver Smith; lighting by Peggy Clark; costumes designed by Miles White; stage manager, Peter Pell; press representatives, Richard Maney and Martin Shwartz.

See "The Season on Broadway."

(Closed February 9, 1957)

VISIT TO A SMALL PLANET

(131 performances)
(Continued)

Comedy in three acts by Gore Vidal. Produced by George Axelrod and Clinton Wilder at the Booth Theatre, February 7, 1957.

Cast of characters—

General Tom Powers	Eddie Mayehoff
Roger Spelding	Philip Coolidge
Reba Spelding	Sibyl Bowan
Ellen Spelding	Sarah Marshall
Conrad Mayberry	Conrad Janis
Kreton	Cyril Ritchard
Aide	Bob Gothie
Rosemary	Grenadier Saadi
Cameraman	Earl Montgomery
Sound Man	John Hallow
A Friend	Francis Bethencourt

The action of the play takes place in the house of Roger Spelding outside Manassas, Virginia. The time is next summer. Act I.—Early evening of a summer's day. Act II.—Scene 1—The next morning. Scene 2—That evening. Act III.—An hour later.

Staged by Cyril Ritchard; setting by Oliver Smith, assisted by Robert O'Hearn; lighting by A. Feder; costumes supervised by Patricia Zipprodt; electronically-created vibrations by Louis and Bebe Barron; production stage manager, Pat Chandler; stage manager, Pat Fowler; press representatives, William Fields and Walter Alford.

See page 227.

THE TUNNEL OF LOVE

(124 performances)
(Continued)

Comedy in three acts by Joseph Fields and Peter DeVries, based on Mr. DeVries' novel. Produced by the Theatre Guild at the Royale Theatre, February 13, 1957.

Cast of characters—

Augie Poole ....Tom Ewell
Isolde Poole ....Nancy Olson
Dick Pepper ....Darren McGavin
Alice Pepper ....Elisabeth Fraser
Estelle Novick ....Sylvia Daneel
Miss McCracken ....Elizabeth Wilson
 The action of the play takes place in Westport, Conn., in Augie Poole's studio, a converted barn. Act I.—Prologue—June, 1957. Scene 1—An afternoon in late June, 1956. Scene 2—The following day. Act II.—Scene 1—Three months later (September). Scene 2—Six months later (March). Act III.—Three months later (late June).
 Staged by Joseph Fields; production associate, Philip Langner; production designed and lighted by Ralph Alswang; costumes by Virginia Volland; gowns for the Misses Olsen, Fraser, and Daneel from Larry Aldrich by Marie McCarthy; stage manager, Karl Nielsen; press representatives, Nat Dorfman and Irvin Dorfman.

See "The Season on Broadway."

HOLIDAY FOR LOVERS

(100 performances)

Comedy in two acts by Ronald Alexander. Produced by Shepard Traube at the Longacre Theatre, February 14, 1957.

Cast of characters—

Mary Dean ....Carmen Mathews
Robert Dean ....Don Ameche
Betsy Dean ....Sandra Church
Connie McDougal ....Audrey Christie
Joe McDougal ....George Mathews
Maid ....Denise Dorin
Margaret Dean ....Ann Flood
Paul Gattalin ....Thomas Carlin
Henri Berchat ....Rene Paul
 Act I.—Scene 1—A hotel in New York; the month of June. Scene 2—A hotel in Paris; seven days later. Scene 3—A hotel in Seville, Spain; ten days later. Act II.—Scene 1—A hotel in Rome, Italy; two weeks later. Scene 2—Paris; one week later.
 Staged by Shepard Traube; scenery and lighting by John Robert Lloyd; costumes designed by Helene Pons; production stage manager, Leonard Auerbach; stage manager, William Dodds; press representative, George Ross.

Travelogue of a well-heeled Minneapolis family's first trip abroad. Father is kindly but over-possessive; Mother Knows Better; one daughter emerges with a pianist, the other with a painter. *Holiday for Lovers* is not just a guided tour of a play: it is an always meticulously chaperoned one. There are amiable and even witty moments, and the suggestion of rancors and rages; but actions speak softer than words, no one—even in the easel-and-keyboard set—ever really misbehaves; and if often quite agreeable, *Holiday for Lovers* had no more guts as a satire than it had ribs as a play.

(Closed May 11, 1957)

THE TAMING OF THE SHREW

(23 performances)

Comedy in three acts by William Shakespeare. Produced by the American Shakespeare Festival Theatre and Academy under the direction of John Houseman at the Phoenix Theatre, February 20, 1957.

Cast of characters—

The Induction:
Christopher Sly, a tinker .... Mike Kellin
Hostess .... Pamela Saunders
A Lord .... Louis Edmonds
Bartholomew, a page .... Susan Lloyd
First Player .... Byron Russell
Huntsman and Servant to the Lord .... Tucker Ashworth
Huntsman and Servant to the Lord .... William Cottrell

The Players:
Lucentio, son to Vincentio .... Richard Easton
Tranio, servant to Lucentio .... Mitchell Agruss
Biondello, servant to Lucentio .... Jerry Stiller
Baptista, a rich gentleman of Padua .... Patrick Hines
Katherina, the shrew, daughter to Baptista .... Nina Foch
Bianca, also daughter to Baptista .... Barbara Lord
Gremio, suitor to Bianca .... Philip Bourneuf
Hortensio, suitor to Bianca .... Kendall Clark
Grumio, servant to Petruchio .... Morris Carnovsky
Petruchio .... Pernell Roberts
Curtis, servant to Petruchio .... Rod Colbin
Nathaniel, servant to Petruchio .... James Cahill
Peter, servant to Petruchio .... Michael Lindsay-Hogg
Joseph, servant to Petruchio .... Joseph Myers
Nicholas, servant to Petruchio .... David Milton
Sugarsop, servant to Petruchio .... Robert Morris
Tailor .... William Cottrell
Haberdasher .... Tucker Ashworth
Pedant, impersonating Vincentio .... Ellis Rabb
Vincentio .... Byron Russell
A Lusty Widow .... Pamela Saunders
Servants to Baptista .... Michael Miller, Charles Meier
  The scene is Padua and in Petruchio's house in the country.
  Staged by Norman Lloyd; festival stage by Rouben Ter-Arutunian; costumes by Dorothy Jeakins; lighting and additional decor by Jean Rosenthal; music by Irwin Bazelon; production stage manager, Paul Leaf; stage manager, Ronald Bates; press representative for the American Shakespeare Festival Theatre and Academy, Frank Goodman; for the Phoenix Theatre: publicity director, Ben Kornzweig, and press representative, Robert Ganshaw.

(Closed March 10, 1957)

A HOLE IN THE HEAD

(107 performances)
(Continued)

Play in two acts by Arnold Schulman. Produced by the Producers Theatre (Robert Whitehead) at the Plymouth Theatre; February 28, 1957.

Cast of characters—

Frank ....Milton J. Williams
Tina ....Louise Erickson
Mr. Goldblatt ....Jacob Mestel
Ally ....Tommy White
Mrs. Fessler ....Connie Sawyer
Herbert ....Larry Hart
Mr. Diamond ....Morris Strassberg
Lenny ....Tom Pedi
Shirl ....Joyce Van Patten
Sidney ....Paul Douglas
Max ....David Burns
Sophie ....Kay Medford
Mrs. Rogers ....Lee Grant

The action takes place at Miami Beach, Florida. The time is last August. Act I.—Scene 1—Afternoon. Scene 2—One o'clock in the morning. Scene 3—Two hours later. Act II.—Scene 1—The next afternoon. Scene 2—That evening. Scene 3—The next morning.

Staged by Garson Kanin, assisted by Kip Good; production designed by Boris Aronson, assisted by Lisa Jalowetz and Robert Randolph; lighting by Jean Rosenthal; costumes by Patton Campbell; production stage manager, Peter Zeisler; stage manager, Walter Neal; press representatives, Barry Hyams and Abner D. Klipstein.

See "The Season on Broadway."

ZIEGFELD FOLLIES

(106 performances)
(Continued)

Revue in two acts, with music and lyrics by Jack Lawrence, Richard Myers, Howard Dietz, Sammy Fain, David Rogers, Colin Romoff, Dean Fuller, Marshall Barer, Carolyn Leigh and Philip Springer; sketches by Arnie Rosen, Coleman Jacoby, David Rogers, Alan Jeffreys, Maxwell Grant. Produced by Mark Kroll and Charles Conaway at the Winter Garden, March 1, 1957.

Principals—

Beatrice Lillie   John Philip
Billy De Wolfe   Bob and Larry Leslie
Harold Lang   Carol Lawrence
Jane Morgan   Jay Marshall
Helen Wood   Tony Franco
Micki Marlo   Bruce Laffey

Ziegfeldians: Billie Bensing, Bette Graham, Faith Hilton, Frances Koll, Susan Shaute, Paula Wayne; Chuck Green, Robert Feyti, Ed Powell, James Stevenson, Gene Varrone.

Dancers: Vicki Barrett, Ruth Chamberlain, Dorothy D'Honau, Mary Jane Doerr, Wisa D'Orso, Nancy Hachenberg, Marcia Hewitt, Julie Marlowe, Sylvia Shay, Gini Turner, Shirley Vincent; Bob Bernard, James Brooks, Ron Cecill, Alan Conroy, Allan Craine, Hugh Lambert, Jack Leigh, Ted Monson, Lou Richards, Rod Strong, Merritt Thompson.

Ziegfeld Girls: Roberta Brown, Denise Collette, Ann Drake, Charlotte Foley, Pat Gaston, Nancy Westbrook, Barbara Hall, Gloria Kristy.

Staged by John Kennedy; sketch editor, Arnold Auerbach; dances staged by Frank Wagner; scenery and costumes designed by Raoul

Pène duBois; lighting by Paul Morrison; musical director, Max
Meth; orchestrations by Russell Bennett, Bill Stegmeyer, Joe Glover
and Bob Noelneter; dance composition by Rene Weigert; vocal
arrangements by Earl Rogers; production stage manager, Milton
Stern; stage manager, Bruce Laffey; press representatives, Karl
Bernstein and Anne Sloper.

Sketches and musical numbers—

ACT I

"Bring on the Girls" ....The Ziegfeldians and Ensemble
  (By Richard Myers and Jack Lawrence)
Double Indemnity (By Alan Jeffreys and Maxwell Grant)
  Secretary ....Charlotte Foley
  Mr. Wedgecliffe ....Billy De Wolfe
  Lola La Moundsville ....Jane Morgan
"If You Got Music" (By David Rogers and Colin Romoff)
  Danced and Sung by ....Harold Lang, Helen Wood and Ensemble
Milady Dines Alone (By Beatrice Lillie)
  The Lady ....Beatrice Lillie
  Waiter ....Bruce Laffey
"The Lover in Me" ....Micki Marlo
  (By Carolyn Leigh and Philip Springer)
High and Flighty (By Arnie Rosen and Coleman Jacoby)
  Hostess ....Beatrice Lillie
  Passengers ....John Philip, Bob Leslie, Larry
                     Leslie, Bette Graham, Robert Feyti
  Betty ....Mary Jane Doerr
"I Don't Wanna Rock" (By David Rogers and Colin Romoff)
  Juvenile Delinquent ....Billy De Wolfe
  Tenth Street Sheiks ....Vicki Barrett, James Brooks, Wisa
               D'Orso, Chuck Green, Nancy Hachenberg,
               Hugh Lambert, Julie Marlowe, Ed
               Powell, Lou Richards, Jim Stevenson,
               Rod Strong, Gene Varrone
Jay Marshall
"Music for Madame" (By Jack Lawrence and Richard Myers)
  The Boy ....Harold Lang
  The Girl ....Helen Wood
  Maitre D' ....John Philip
               Ziegfeldians and Dancers
"Intoxication" (By Dean Fuller and Marshall Barer)
  Sung by ....Beatrice Lillie
  Escort ....Allan Conroy
Dramatically Speaking ....Billy De Wolfe
Song of India
  The Rajah ....John Philip
  His Favorite ....Beatrice Lillie
  Assisted by ....Dancers and The Ziegfeldians

ACT II

"Two a Day on the Milky Way" (By Dean Fuller and Marshall Barer)
  Sung and danced by ....Harold Lang and Ensemble
  Agent ....Bob Leslie
Large Talk (By David Rogers)
  First Girl ....Charlotte Foley
  Second Girl ....Susan Shaute
  Lucille ....Beatrice Lillie
  Harriet ....Billy De Wolfe
"Salesmanship" (By Carolyn Leigh and Philip Springer)
  Sung by ....Jane Morgan, Micki Marlo, Carol
               Lawrence with The Ziegfeld Girls
Kabuki Lil (By Beatrice Lillie)
  Kabuki Lil ....Beatrice Lillie
"Honorable Mambo" (By Dean Fuller and Marshall Barer)
  Sung and danced by ....Carol Lawrence and Ensemble
"Miss Follies" (By David Rogers and Colin Romoff)
  Sung by ....Billy De Wolfe, Chuck Green, Ed
               Powell, Jim Stevenson, Gene Varrone
               and the Ziegfeld Girls

"Make Me" (By Tony Velone, Larry Spier and Uhpio Minucci)
Sung by ....Jane Morgan and The Ziegfeldians
"Miss (All You Don't Catch) Follies of 192—" (By Herman Hupfield)
Sung by ....Beatrice Lillie
Page Girl ....Nancy Hachenberg
Jay Marshall
"An Element of Doubt" (By Howard Dietz and Sammy Fain)
Sung by ....Harold Lang and Micki Marlo
"My Late, Late Lady" (By Dean Fuller and Marshall Barer)
Announcer ....Ed Powell
                                        { Beatrice Lillie
The Original Cast .... { Billy De Wolfe
                                        { John Philip
Finale ....Entire Company
    (By Jack Lawrence and Richard Myers)

See "The Season on Broadway."

GOOD AS GOLD

(4 performances)

Comedy in two acts by John Patrick, based on the novel by Alfred Toombs. Produced by Cheryl Crawford, with William Myers, by arrangement with Angus Equities, Ltd., at the Belasco Theatre, March 7, 1957.

Cast of characters—

Commentator ....Edward Fuller
Benjamin ....Roddy McDowall
Policeman ....Dana Elcar
Doc Penny ....Zero Mostel
Barbara ....Loretta Leversee
Congressman Fairweather ....Paul Ford
Congressman Jason ....Robert Emhardt
McDougal ....John Harkins
McFadden ....Dana Elcar
Jail Officer ....Tom Ahearne
Radio Announcer ....Edward Fuller
Radio Engineer ....Joseph Dooley
Reporter ....Clarence Stemler
Photographer ....Todd Patterson
Caucus Room Guard ....Clement Brace
Committeemen ....Lou Gilbert, Hugh Evans
U.S. Storage Vault Director ....Hugh Evans
Fredrica ....Juleen Compton
Pilsudski ....Lou Gilbert
    The action of the play takes place in Washington, D. C., at the present time. Act I.—Scene 1—The White House from Pennsylvania Avenue. Scene 2—Thomas Jefferson Jail, one hour later. Scene 3—Congressman Fairweather's office, the next day. Scene 4—Thomas Jefferson Jail, one hour later. Scene 5—Pennsylvania Avenue, a half-hour later. Scene 6—Thomas Jefferson Jail, later the same day. Scene 7—A caucus room, a few days later. Scene 8—The House of Representatives, the next day. Act II.—Scene 1—The Interior Weighing Room of the U.S. Storage Vault. Scene 2—Congressman Fairweather's office, the next day. Scene 3—Thomas Jefferson Jail, Christmas Eve. Scene 4—Lafayette Park, a week later.
    Staged by Albert Marre; settings designed by Peter Larkin; costumes by Noel Taylor; lighting by Al Alloy; production manager, Billy Matthews; production assistant, Sylvia Drulie; stage manager, Paul Davis; press representative, Ben Washer.

(Closed March 9, 1957)

THE SIN OF PAT MULDOON

(5 performances)

Play in three acts by John McLiam. Produced by Richard Adler and Roger L. Stevens at the Cort Theatre, March 13, 1957.

Cast of characters—

Theresa Muldoon ....Patricia Bosworth
Brigid Muldoon ....Katherine Squire
Cornelius de Lacey ....Edgar Stehli
Gertrude Muldoon ....Elaine Stritch
Pat Muldoon ....James Barton
Attendants ....James McGillicuddy, Ross Bennett
Dr. Glass ....John Heldabrand
Father Gallagher ....James Olson
Joe Vierra ....Gerald Sarracini

The action takes place in the kitchen and dining room of Pat Muldoon's house in Santa Clara, California. The time is the present. Act I.—Scene 1—A late morning in mid-July. Scene 2—After seven; the same evening. Act II.—Scene 1—A month later in the afternoon. Scene 2—Midnight the same day. Act III.—Five a.m. the following morning.

Staged by Jack Garfein; settings by Mordecai Gorelik; lighting by Paul Morrison; costumes by Anna Hill Johnstone; stage manager, Irving Buchman; press representative, Howard Newman.

Concerned with an elderly, unconjugal, money-wasting Irish-American scamp who for three acts lies dying of heart trouble in a big brass bed while his family try in vain to bring him back into the Church. A genre picture, or sort of slice-of-death, the play—with its lack of plot—needed an insight and freshness of detail it never had. At bottom sentimental, the merest Weak Hearts and Flowers, it was really as trite as it proved increasingly tedius.

(Closed March 16, 1957)

THE BEGGAR'S OPERA

(15 performances)

Musical in two acts by John Gay, adapted by Richard Baldridge. Produced by the New York City Center Light Opera Company (Jean Dalrymple, Director) at the New York City Center of Music and Drama, March 13, 1957.

Cast of characters—

Beggar Poet ....Peter Turgeon
Filch ....Charles Bolender
Macheath ....Jack Cassidy
Matt of the Mint ....Robert Burr
Jemmy the Twitcher ....Hal England
Crooked Finger Jack ....Maurice Edwards
Wat Dreary ....Macheath's Gang........Francis Barnard
Nimming Ned ....J. C. McCord
Slippery Sam ....Jack De Lon
Bob Booty ....David Nillo
Tom Tizzle ....William Inglis

Polly Peachum ....Shirley Jones
Mr. Peachum ....George S. Irving
Mrs. Peachum ....Zamah Cunningham
Mr. Lockit ....George Gaynes
Lucy Lockit ....Jeanne Beauvais
Mrs. Coaxer ....Paula Laurence

Jenny Diver ⎤   ⎡ Constance Brigham
Dolly   ⎥   ⎥ Maria Karnilova
Mrs. Vixen ⎥   ⎥ Anita Cooper
Betty Doxy ⎬ Ladies of the Town ....⎨ Jenny Lou Law
Mrs. Slammekin ⎥   ⎥ Adnia Rice
Suky Tawdry ⎥   ⎥ Shirley Chester
Molly Brazen ⎦   ⎣ Charlotte Ray

Prisoners, Guards and Other Ladies of the Town: William Ashley, Hal Barnet, George Broadhurst, Willie Cooper, Joan DuBrow, Jack Emrek, James Karr, Sara Meade, Louis Saporito, Lee Warren, Hurd Wiese.

Chorus of Prisoners: Louis Algarra, Jennie Andrea, Evelyn Aring, Robert Atherton, Nicola Barbusci, Don Becker, June Bucknor, Julia Gerace, Peter Held, Maurice Kostroff, Mary Lesawyer, Maria Martell, John Person, Thomas Powell, Robert Ruddy, Mary Thompson, Mara Yavne.

The action takes place at night in Newgate Prison, London.

Staged by Richard Baldridge; assistant to Miss Dalrymple, Alan Green; music adapted and arranged by Daniel Pinkham; musical staging by John Heawood; setting by Watson Barratt; costumes by Robert Fletcher; lighting by Jean Rosenthal; musical director and conductor, Miles Morgan; production supervisor, Burt Shevelove; production stage manager, Bernard Pollock; stage manager, John Maxtone-Graham; press assistant to Miss Dalrymple, Tom Trenkle.

Musical numbers—

ACT I

"Let Us Take the Road" ....Macheath and the Gang
"My Heart Was So Free" ....Macheath
Duet: "Were I Laid on Greenland Coast" ....Macheath and Polly
"Virgins Are Like the Fair Flower" ....Polly
Trio: "Our Polly Is a Sad Slut" ....Peachum, Mrs. Peachum, and Polly
"The Turtle Thus With Plaintive Crying" ....Polly
" 'Tis Woman That Seduces All Mankind" ....Lockit
Duet: "Through All the Employments of Life" ..Peachum and Lockit
"Hanging Is My Only Sport" ....Peachum
Reprise Duet: "Were I Laid on Greenland Coast" ....Polly and Macheath
"O, What a Pain It Is to Part" ....Polly and Macheath
"No Power on Earth Can E'er Divide" ....Polly
"Man May Escape From Rope and Gun" ....Prisoners
Trio: "Why How Now Madam Flirt" ....Lucy, Polly, and Macheath
Quartet: "Is Then His Fate Decreed, Sir?" ....Polly, Lucy, Peachum, and Lockit

ACT II

"Fill Every Glass" ....Matt, the Gang, and the Ladies of the Town
   Danced by ....Dolly Trull and Bob Booty
"The Ways of the World" ....Macheath and the Gang
Reprise: "Let Us Take the Road" ....The Gang and the Ladies of the Town
"If the Heart of a Man" ....Mrs. Coaxer
"Youth's a Season Made for Joys" ....The Ladies of the Town
"When Young at the Bar" ....Jenny Diver
Trio: "In the Days of My Youth" ....Mrs. Coaxer, Peachum, and Lockit
"At the Tree I Shall Suffer With Pleasure" ....Macheath
Reprise: "When Young at the Bar" ....Jenny Diver
"I'm Like a Skiff on the Ocean Toss'd ....Lucy
Duet: "Come Sweet Lass" ....Lucy and Polly
"The Charge Was Prepar'd" ....Macheath and Chorus

"Would I Might Be Hanged" ....Lucy, Polly, and
                                                         Macheath
"Since Laws Were Made for Every Degree" ....The Entire Company
Finale: "See the Conquering Hero" ....The Entire Company

(Closed March 24, 1957)

THE DUCHESS OF MALFI

(24 performances)

Play in two acts by John Webster. Produced by the Phoenix
Theatre (T. Edward Hambleton and Norris Houghton), in association with John Houseman, at the Phoenix Theatre, March 19, 1957.

Cast of characters—

Antonio, steward of the household of the Duchess.......Earle Hyman
Delio ....Richard Easton
Bosola ....Pernell Roberts
The Cardinal ....Hurd Hatfield
Ferdinand, Duke of Calabria, his brother ....Joseph Wiseman
Roderigo ⎫   ⎧ Louis Edmonds
Castruccio ⎪   ⎪ Justice Watson
Silvio   ⎬ Friends and Attendants at Malfi.....⎨ Charles Macaulay
Pescara   ⎪   ⎪ Patrick Hines
Grisolan ⎭   ⎩ William Cottrell
The Duchess of Malfi, sister of the
   Cardinal and Ferdinand ....Jacqueline Brookes
Cariola, her companion ....Priscilla Morrill
An Old Woman ....Dorothy Patten
Julia, Castruccio's wife ....Jan Farrand
A Doctor ....Ellis Rabb
A Footman ....Mitchell Agruss
                                            ⎧ Jack Cannon
Guests, Servants, Officers ....⎨ Anthony Holland
                                            ⎪ John Ragin
                                            ⎩ Barbara Lord

   Song and Litany are sung by Russell Oberlin.
   The scene: Malfi, Rome, Milan.
   Staged by Jack Landau; costumes by Saul Bolasni; music by Lee
Hoiby; festival stage by Rouben Ter-Arutunian; production and lighting by Jean Rosenthal; production stage manager, Robert Woods; stage
manager, Ronald Bates; publicity director, Ben Kornzweig; press
representative, Robert Ganshaw.

(Closed April 7, 1957)

ORPHEUS DESCENDING

(68 performances)

Play in three acts by Tennessee Williams. Produced by the
Producers Theatre (Robert Whitehead) at the Martin Beck Theatre,
March 21, 1957.

Cast of characters—

Dolly Hamma ....Elizabeth Eustis
Beulah Binnings ....Jane Rose

Pee Wee Binnings .... Warren Kemmerling
Dog Hamma .... David Clarke
Carol Cutrere .... Lois Smith
Eva Temple .... Nell Harrison
Sister Temple .... Mary Farrell
Uncle Pleasant .... John Marriott
Val Xavier .... Cliff Robertson
Vee Talbot .... Joanna Roos
Lady Torrance .... Maureen Stapleton
Jabe Torrance .... Crahan Denton
Sheriff Talbot .... R. G. Armstrong
Mr. Dubinsky .... Beau Tilden
Woman .... Janice Mars
David Cutrere .... Robert Webber
Nurse Porter .... Virgilia Chew
First Man .... Albert Henderson
Second Man .... Charles Tyner

The entire action of the play takes place in a general dry-goods store and part of a connecting "confectionery" in a small Southern town, during a rainy season, late winter, and early spring. Act I.—Scene 1 —Late dusk. Scene 2—A couple of hours later that night. Act II.— Scene 1—Afternoon, a few weeks later. Scene 2—Late that night. Act III.—Scene 1—Early morning, the Saturday before Easter. Scene 2—Sunset, the same day. Scene 3—Half an hour later.

Staged by Harold Clurman; production designed by Boris Aronson, assisted by Lisa Jalowetz; costumes by Lucinda Ballard, assisted by Florence Klotz; lighting by A. Feder; incidental music composed by Chuck Wayne, arranged by John Mehegan; music for "Heavenly Grass" by Paul Bowles, lyrics by Tennessee Williams; production stage manager, James Gelb; stage manager, Norman Kean; press representatives, Ben Kornzweig and Robert Ganshaw.

See page 248.

See page 248.

(Closed May 18, 1957)

BRIGADOON

(47 performances)

Musical in two acts, with book and lyrics by Alan Jay Lerner and music by Frederick Loewe. Revived by the New York City Center Light Opera Company (Jean Dalrymple, Director) at the New York City Center of Music and Drama, March 27, 1957.

Cast of characters—

Tommy Albright .... David Atkinson
Jeff Douglas .... Scott McKay
Archie Beaton .... Elliott Sullivan
Harry Beaton .... Matt Mattox
Angus MacGuffie .... Guy Gordon
Sandy Dean .... John Dorrin
Andrew MacLaren .... Russell Gaige
Fiona MacLaren .... Virginia Oswald
Jean MacLaren .... Virginia Bosler
Meg Brockie .... Helen Gallagher
Charlie Dalrymple .... Robert Rounseville
Maggie Anderson .... Lidija Franklin
Mr. Lundie .... John C. Becher
Sword Dancers .... { Glenn Olson
                                               { Keith Willis
Frank .... Jack Emrek
Jane Ashton .... Sloan Simpson
Bagpiper .... Duncan MacGaskill

Townsfolk of Brigadoon:
Singers: Misses Jennie Andrea, June Buckner, Marilyn Cooper, Dori
Davis, Julia Gerace, Patricia Hall, Jean Maggio, Maria Martell,
Sheila Mathews, Mary Thompson. Messrs. Robert Atherton, Don
Becker, Norris Brannstrom, Austin Colyer, Arthur Dilks, John Dorrin,
Peter Held, Vincent MacMahon, William Nahr, Stanley Page.
Dancers: Misses Jeanna Belkin, Pat Birsh, Anne Boley, Ann
Crowell, Geralyn Donald, Dorothy Etheridge, Rosemary Jourdan,
Evelyn Taylor, Mona Jo Tritsch. Messrs. Robert Barnett, Anthony
Blum, Jim Brusock, Walter Georgov, Charles McCraw, Glenn Olson,
Ray Pointer, Keith Willis, Emmanuel Winston.
Staged by George H. Englund; re-staged by James Jamieson; setting
by Oliver Smith; costumes by Paul duPont; lighting by Peggy Clark;
musical director, Julius Rudel; associate conductor, Samuel Matlovsky;
assistant to Miss Dalrymple, Alan Green; production stage manager,
Bernard Gersten; stage Manager, John Maxtone-Graham; press assistant to Miss Dalrymple, Tom Trenkle.

Brigadoon was first produced by Cheryl Crawford at the Ziegfeld
Theatre, March 13, 1947, for 581 performances.

(Closed May 5, 1957)

HIDE AND SEEK

(7 performances)

Play in three acts by Stanley Mann and Roger MacDougall.
Produced by Fred F. Finklehoffe, Mark Marvin and Gabriel Katzka
at the Ethel Barrymore Theatre, April 2, 1957.

Cast of characters—

Saul ....Peter Lazer
Michael ....Walter Brooke
Judy ....Marilyn Siegel
Ann Richards ....Geraldine Fitzgerald
Janice ....Dolores Dorn-Heft
Tom Richards ....Barry Morse
Sir Roger Johnson ....Basil Rathbone
Margo Johnson ....Isobel Elsom
Gregson ....Carl Harbord
The entire action takes place inside and outside a cottage in War-
wick, England. Act I.—A morning in spring. Act II.—That evening.
Act III.—Twenty minutes later.
Staged by Reginald Denham; setting and lighting by Ralph Alswang;
costumes by Virginia Volland; production stage manager, Herman
Shapiro; stage manager, Keith Herrington; press representative, David
Lipsky.

A play about a British nuclear scientist at work on a Government
project he loathes—for mutilating people before birth. If he quits,
however, he faces being made a security risk. The action involves
a lethal radioactive egg missing from the lab, which is very possibly the egg the scientist's young son is known to have been toting
around. This situation injects some scary moments into the final
act; but *Hide and Seek* puts all its egg in one basket, all its theatre

into one scene; the play in general is no less talky than unconvincing, and as full of digressions as of longueurs.

(Closed April 6, 1957)

THE MERRY WIDOW

(15 performances)

Operetta in three acts, with music by Franz Lehar; new book by Sidney Sheldon and Ben Roberts; lyrics by Adrian Ross. Revived by the New York City Center Light Opera Company (Jean Dalrymple, Director) at the New York City Center of Music and Drama, April 10, 1957.

Cast of characters—

The King	Jose Duval
Popoff	Melville Cooper
Cascada	Alex Alexander
Natalie	Helena Scott
Khadja	C. K. Alexander
Olga Bardini	Lucy Hillary
General Bardini	George Lipton
Novakovich	Lewis Brooks
Jolidon	Jim Hawthorne
Guests	Sonja Savig, Casper Roos
Nish	Norman Budd
Sonia	Marta Eggerth
St. Brioche	Warde Donovan
Danilo	Jan Kiepura
Clo-Clo	Monique Van Vooren
Gaston	Jose Duval
Premiere Danseuse	Mary Ellen Moylan
Premier Danseur	Michael Maule
Ballerina	Paula Lloyd

Singers: Misses Jeanne Anderson, Josephine Annunciata, Carol O'Day, June House, Claudine Manson, Sonja Savig, Jan Speers, Barbara Saxby, Yolanda Vasquez. Messrs. Charles O. Aschmann, Jr., Alan Cole, Wendell Grey, David London, Jack McMinn, Mitchell May, Casper Roos, David Smith, Marvin Solley.

Dancers: Misses Ann Barry, Marilyn d'Honau, Ruby Herndon, Joan Kruger, Eloise Milton, Charlotte Rae. Messrs. John Grigas, Scott Hunter, William Inglis, Bill Miller, Richard Monahan, Bobb St. Clair.

Lackeys: Bruce Blaine, James Feeney, Eben Snow.

Act I.—Prologue. Scene 2—The Marsovian Embassy in Paris; a summer evening in 1906. Act II.—Grounds of Sonia's house, near Paris; the following day, in the early evening. Act III.—Maxim's Restaurant, Paris; later that night.

Staged by Felix Brentano; original choreography by George Balanchine; dances by Edward Brinkman; musical director, Michael Kuttner; settings by George Jenkins; costumes by Paul duPont; lighting by Peggy Clark; assistant to Miss Dalrymple, Alan Green; production stage manager, Andy Anderson; stage manager, John Maxtone-Graham; press assistant to Miss Dalrymple, Tom Trenkle.

Musical numbers—

ACT I

"A Dutiful Wife"	Helena Scott and Jim Hawthorne
"In Marsovia"	Martha Eggerth with Alex Alexander, Warde Donovan and Male Chorus

"Maxim's" ....Jan Kiepura
"Polka" ....Paula Lloyd and Michael Maule
Finale ....Melville Cooper, Helena Scott, Jim Hawthorne,
Jan Kiepura, Marta Eggerth, George Lipton,
Alex Alexander, Warde Donovan and the Ensemble.

ACT II

Marsovian Dance ....Michael Maule, Mary Ellen Moylan
"Vilia" ....Marta Eggerth
"Never Give Your Heart Away" ....Monique Van Vooren and
Sonja Savig, Jan Speers,
June House, Jeanene
Anderson, Barbara Saxby
"The Pavilion" ....Jan Kiepura
"The Women"—
  (A) Melville Cooper, George Lipton, Jim Hawthorne, C. K.
     Alexander, Norman Budd, Lewis Brooks and Alex Alexander
  (B) The Above with Monique Van Vooren, Ann Barry, Ruby
     Herndon
  (C) Sonja Savig, June House, Jan Speers, Jeanene Anderson,
     Barbara Saxby
"I Love You So" ....Jan Kiepura and Marta Eggerth
  Danced by Mary Ellen Moylan, Michael Maule and Ballet
Finale ....Entire Company

ACT III

"Maxim's" ....Monique Van Vooren
  Danced by Paula Lloyd and Ballet Girls
"Kuiawiak" ....Sung in Polish by Jan Kiepura
"I Love You So" (Reprise) ....Jan Kiepura and Marta Eggerth
Finale ....The Entire Company

(Closed April 21, 1957)

HOTEL PARADISO

(60 performances)
(Continued)

Comedy in three acts by Georges Feydeau and Maurice Des-
vallières, adapted by Peter Glenville. Produced by Richard Myers
and Julius Fleischmann and Bowden, Barr & Bullock, by arrangement with Hardy W. Smith and H. M. Tennent Ltd., at Henry
Miller's Theatre, April 11, 1957.

Cast of characters—

Boniface (a builder) ....Bert Lahr
Angelique (his wife) ....Vera Pearce
Marcelle (the wife of Cot) ....Angela Lansbury
Cot (an architect) ....John Emery
Maxime (Cot's nephew) ....Carleton Carpenter
Victoire (the maid) ....Sondra Lee
Martin (a barrister) ....Douglas Byng
First Porter ....Neil Laurence
Second Porter ....Mark Lang
Third Porter ....Fred Baker
Fourth Porter ....Roy Johnson
Violette ....Joan-Ellen Caine
Marguerite ....Nancy Devlin
Paquerette ....Patricia Fay
Pervenche ....Helen Quarrier
Anniello (Manager of Hotel Paradiso) ....Ronald Radd

Georges (a page at the Hotel Paradiso) ....James Bernard
A Lady ....Lucille Benson
A Duke ....Horace Cooper
Tabu (a professor) ....James Coco
Police Inspector Boucard ....George Tyne
Policemen ....Roy Johnson, Fred Baker, Neil Laurence
    Act I.—The home of M. and Mme. Boniface in Passy, a suburb
of Paris; spring, 1910. Act II.—Hotel Paradiso; the same evening.
Act III.—The home of M. Mme. Boniface; the following morning.
    Staged by Peter Glenville; settings and costumes by Osbert Lan-
caster; New York production supervised by Charles Lisanby; as-
sociate producer, Will Lester Productions; music arranged by Lester
Lanin; production stage manager, Edmund Baylies; stage manager,
Fred Baker; press representatives, Marian Byram and Phyllis
Perlman.

See "The Season on Broadway."

SHINBONE ALLEY

(49 performances)

Musical in two acts, based on the "archy and mehitabel" stories
by Don Marquis, with book by Joe Darion and Mel Brooks, music
by George Kleinsinger and lyrics by Mr. Darion. Produced by
Peter Lawrence at the Broadway Theatre, April 13, 1957.

Cast of characters—

Voice of Newspaperman ....Julian Barry
archy ....Eddie Bracken
mehitabel ....Eartha Kitt
Phyllis ....Reri Grist
Mother ....Lillian Hayman
Ricky ....Dorothy Aull
Jail Cronies ....Buzz Halliday, Elmarie Wendel,
                            Cathryn Damon, Elizabeth Taylor,
                            Carmen Gutierrez, Nora Reho,
                            Gwen Harmon
"Copper" ....James Marley
Buzz ....Howard Roberts
Butch ....Moses LaMarr
Rusty ....Cathryn Damon
Big Bill ....George S. Irving
Broadway ....Ross Martin
Edie ....Gwen Harmon
Blackie ....Larry Montaigne
Gladys ....Carmen Gutierrez
Frankie ....Jacques D'Amboise
Fighting Dogs ....Don Farnworth, Gene Gavin,
                            Harold E. Gordon, Claude Thompson
Tyrone T. Tattersal ....Erik Rhodes
Shorty ....David Winters
Harry ....Jack Eddleman
Lady Bugs ....Dorothy Aull, Gwen Harmon, Buzz Halliday
Bartender ....Bruce MacKay
Penny ....Allegra Kent
Tall Cats ....Albert Popwell, James Tarbutton
    Dancers: Jacques D'Amboise, Cathryn Damon, Don Farnworth, Gene
Gavin, Carolyn George, Harold E. Gordon, Carmen Gutierrez, Allegra
Kent, Albert Popwell, Nora Reho, Dorothy Scott, James Tarbutton,
Elizabeth Taylor, Claude Thompson, Myrna White, David Winters.
    Singers: Dorothy Aull, Jack Eddleman, Reri Grist, Buzz Halliday,
Gwen Harmon, Lillian Hayman, Moses LaMarr, James Marley, Bruce
MacKay, Jack Rains, Howard Roberts, Elmarie Wendel.

The entire action takes place in Shinbone Alley and its environs. Act I.—Scene 1—A newspaper office. Scene 2—Shinbone Alley. Scene 3—The ASPCA Lock-Up. Scene 4—Shinbone Alley. Scene 5—A street. Scene 6—Shinbone Alley. Scene 7—A street. Scene 8— Tyrone's trunk apartment in Greenwich Village. Scene 9—Shinbone Alley. Act II.—Scene 1—A street. Scene 2—Shinbone Alley. Scene 3—A street corner. Scene 4—Shinbone Alley. Scene 5—Another street. Scene 6—mehitabel's new home. Scene 7—A bar beneath the street. Scene 8—A vacant lot. Scene 9—mehitabel's new home. Scene 10—A quiet street. Scene 11—Shinbone Alley.

Dances and musical numbers staged by Rod Alexander; production associate, Jerry Leider; music and choral direction by Maurice Levine; production designed by Eldon Elder; costumes by Motley; lighting by Tharon Musser; orchestrations by George Kleinsinger; additional orchestrations by Irwin Kostal; additional musical routines by John Morris; music materials under supervision of Arnold Arnstein; production stage manager, Morty Halpern; stage managers, Julian Barry and Gil Cates; press representatives, George Ross and Madi Blitzstein.

Musical numbers—

ACT I

"What Do We Care?" ....sung by mehitabel and the Singing
and Dancing Ensemble
"Toujours Gai" ....sung by mehitabel
"Queer Little Insect" ....sung by mehitabel, reprised by archy
"Big Bill' ....sung by Big Bill with Ladies
of the Dancing Ensemble
"True Romance" ....sung by mehitabel and Big Bill;
danced by mehitabel
"The Lightning Bug Song" ....sung by archy
"I gotta be" ....sung by Broadway and archy
Dog and Cat Ballet ....danced by Jacques d'Amboise
and the Ensemble
"Flotsam and Jetsam" ....sung by archy and mehitabel
"Come to Mee-ow" ....sung by Tyrone
"Suicide Song" ....sung by mehitabel
"Shinbone Alley" ....sung by Big Bill and Denizens
of Shinbone Alley

ACT II

"The Moth Song" ....sung by archy
"A Woman Wouldn't Be a Woman" ....sung and danced by
mehitabel and Ensemble
"The Lullaby" ....sung by mehitabel and the
Singing Girls
"What the Hell" ....sung by mehitabel
"Pretty Kitty" ....sung by Singing Girls,
danced by mehitabel
"Way Down Blues" ....sung by mehitabel
"The Lady Bug Song" ....sung by Dorothy Aull, Gwen
Harmon, Buzz Halliday
"Vacant Lot Ballet" ....danced by Jacques D'Amboise,
Allegra Kent, Cathryn Damon,
David Winters, and the Dancing Ensemble
"Be a Pussycat" ....sung by mehitabel
"Quiet Street" ....sung by archy
"Toujours Gai" ....sung by archy, mehitabel
and Ensemble

See "The Season on Broadway."

(closed May 25, 1957)

SOUTH PACIFIC

(23 performances)

Musical in two acts, adapted from "Tales of the South Pacific" by James M. Michener, with music by Richard Rodgers; lyrics by Oscar Hammerstein 2nd; book by Oscar Hammerstein 2nd and Joshua Logan. Revived by the New York City Center Light Opera Company (Jean Dalrymple, Director) at the New York City Center of Music and Drama, April 24, 1957.

Cast of characters—

Ngana	Lynn Kikuchi
Jerome	Alfredo DeArco
Henry	Mark Satow
Ensign Nellie Forbush	Mindy Carson
Emile de Becque	Robert Wright
Bloody Mary	Juanita Hall
Bloody Mary's Assistant	Julia Gerace
Abner	Jim McMillan
Stewpot	Lou Wills, Jr.
Luther Billis	Harvey Lembeck
Professor	Bill Mullikin
Lt. Joseph Cable, U.S.M.C.	Allen Case
Capt. George Brackett, U.S.N.	Martin Wolfson
Cmdr. William Harbison, U.S.N.	Alan Baxter
Yeoman Herbert Quale	Ray Weaver
Sgt. Kenneth Johnson	Van Stevens
Marine Cpl. Richard West	Dan Hannafin
Seabee Morton Wise	Evans Thornton
Sgt. Juan Cortez	Quinto Biagioni
Seaman Tom O'Brien	Jack McMinn
Radio Operator Bob McCaffery	Sam Kirkham
Marine Cpl. Hamilton Steeves	Lee Warren
Staff Sgt. Thomas Hassinger	Charles Aschman
Seaman James Hayes	Ralph Vucci
Lt. Genevieve Marshall	Miriam Gulager
Ensign Dinah Murphy	Christy Palmer
Ensign Janet MacGregor	Mildred Slavin
Ensign Cora MacRae	Pat Finch
Ensign Bessie Noonan	Barbara Saxby
Ensign Pamela Whitmore	Betty Graeber
Ensign Sue Yaeger	Peggy Hadley
Ensign Lisa Minelli	Betty McNamara
Liat	Imelda De Martin
Lt. Buzz Adams	Dick Button
Shore Patrol Officer	Peter Held
Islanders	Vie-Von Thom, Andrea Del Rosario, Claudia Satow

Staged by John Fearnley; musical director, Frederick Dvonch; settings by Jo Mielziner; adaptation and lighting by Peggy Clark; costumes by Motley; costume supervisor, Florence Klotz; assistant to Miss Dalrymple, Alan Green; make-up and hair styles supervised by Ernest Adler; production stage manager, Kermit Kegley; stage manager, John Maxtone-Graham; press assistant to Miss Dalrymple, Tom Trenkle.

South Pacific was first produced April 7, 1949, by Richard Rodgers, Oscar Hammerstein 2nd, Leland Hayward and Joshua Logan at the Majestic Theatre for 1,925 performances; and revived

May 4, 1955, by the New York City Center Light Opera Company at the New York City Center of Music and Drama for 15 performances.

(Closed May 12, 1957)

THE FIRST GENTLEMAN

(28 performances)

Play in three acts by Norman Ginsbury. Produced by Alexander H. Cohen and Ralph Alswang (in association with Arthur C. Twitchell, Jr.) at the Belasco Theatre, April 25, 1957.

Cast of characters—

Miss Cornelia Knight ....Dorothy Sands
Princess Charlotte, the Regent's Daughter............Inga Swenson
Mr. Henry Brougham ....Wesley Addy
Edward, Duke of Kent, the Regent's Brother.........Robert Goodier
The Bishop of Salisbury ....Clarence Derwent
Lady Conyngham ....Helen Burns
The Prince Regent of England......................Walter Slezak
William, Hereditary Prince of Orange ....John Milligan
Prince Leopold, of Saxe-Coburg ....Peter Donat
Charlotte, Queen of England, the Regent's mother ....Maud Scheerer
Princess Augusta   ⎫   ⎧ Meg Wyllie
Princess Elizabeth ⎬ the Regent's Sisters............⎨ Frances Greet
Princess Mary   ⎭   ⎩ Joyce Ballou
Servant to Caroline ....James Neylin
Caroline, Princess of Wales, the Regent's Wife .... Isobel Elsom
Servant in Claremont House ....Phena Darner
Mrs. Griffiths ....Ludi Claire
Sir Richard Croft ....Guy Spaull
Prince Regent's Dresser ....Le Roi Operti
    Guests: MacGregor Gibb, Edward Dunne, Earl Simmons, Jon Wiley, Rosanna San Marco, Sally Kemp.
    Footmen: Edmund Roney, Curt Lowens, Rex Partington, Dario Barri.
    Act I.—Scene 1—Carlton House, the Prince Regent's home in London; June, 1814. Scene 2—Princess Charlotte's rooms in Carlton House; some weeks later; afternoon. Act. II.—Scene 1—Connaught House, the home of Caroline, Princess of Wales; later that night. Scene 2—The Banqueting Hall, the Pavilion, Brighton; December, 1815. Act III.—Scene 1—Claremont House; Princess Charlotte's home in Surrey; October, 1817. Scene 2—The same; a month later. Scene 3—The Regent's dressing room, Carlton House; June, 1819.
    Staged by Tyrone Guthrie; scenery designed and lighted by Ralph Alswang; costumes by Motley; hair styles created by Ernest Adler; decor by French & Co.; clarinet, Emery Davis; harpsichord, Abba Bogin; violin, Isidor Lateiner; cello, Madeline Foley; stage manager, Rex Partington; press representatives, Harvey Sabinson and David Powers.

See "The Season on Broadway."

(Closed May 18, 1957)

LIVIN' THE LIFE

(25 performances)

Musical in two acts, based on Mark Twain's Mississippi River stories, with book by Dale Wasserman and Bruce Geller, lyrics by Mr. Geller, and music by Jack Urbont. Produced by the Phoenix Theatre (T. Edward Hambleton and Norris Houghton) at the Phoenix Theatre, April 27, 1957.

Cast of characters—

Marshall Rogers	Francis Barnard
Judge Thatcher	Jack DeLon
Mr. Dobbins	Earl Hammond
Captain Mumford	Dean Michener
Emmy Harper	Marijane Maricle
Muff Potter	Stephen Elliott
Jim	Lee Charles
Doc Robinson	Ronald Rogers
Aunt Polly	Alice Ghostley
Injun Joe	James Mitchell
Huckleberry Finn	Richard Ide
Tom Sawyer	Timmy Everett
Becky Thatcher	Patsy Bruder
Amy Lawrence	Lee Backer
Alfred Noble	Loren Hightower
Joe Harper	Tom Hasson
Ben Rogers	Kevin Carlisle
Jeff Hollis	George Liker
Bill Anders	Edward Villella
Susy Harper	Joan Bowman
Mary Austin	Julie Oser
Gracie Miller	Rettadel Tupper
Jennie Daniels	Paula Waring
George	Charles Queenan
Clem	Joe Nash
Frank	Irving Barnes
Zeke	James Hawthorne-Bey
Roxy	Ida Johnson
Hannah	Audrey Vanterpool
Annie Lou	Jacqueline Walcott
Sam Harper	Fred Jones
Emily Noble	Doris Okerson
Andy Douglas	Marvin Gordon
Lila Hollis	Annette Warren
Nancy Rogers	Joyce Carrol
Prosecutor	Tod Jackson
Henry Liggett	Dean Michener
Adele Sims	Sylvia Dick
Freda Walters	Doris Greb
Captain Leather	Ronald Rogers

The entire action takes place in and around Hannibal, Missouri, about 1850.

Staged by David Alexander; production associate, Sylvia Drulie; choreography and musical numbers by John Butler; scenery by William and Jean Eckart; costumes by Alvin Colt; lighting by Klaus Holm; dance music by Genevieve Pitot; orchestrations by Hershey Kay and Joe Glover; choral arrangements by Jack Urbont; additional musical arrangements by Ralph Burns, Jack Easton, James Mundy, and Sy Oliver; musical direction by Anton Coppola; production stage manager, Robert Woods; company stage manager, George Quick; publicity director, Ben Kornzweig; press representative, Robert Ganshaw.

Musical numbers—

ACT I

River Ballad ....Townspeople
"Someone" ....Jim and Polly
"Whiskey Bug" ....Muff Potter
"Livin' the Life" ....Tom and Huck
"Steamboat" .... Tom, Huck, Muff and Jim
"Take Kids"..................Polly, Emmy Harper, Emily Noble,
                                            Lila Hollis, Nancy Rogers
Mock Battle ....Tom, Amy, Alfred, Boys and Girls of the Town
"Probably in Love" ....Tom
Sunday Promenade ....Townspeople
"Don't Tell Me" ....Polly
"All of 'Em Say" ....Tom and Becky
"Late Love" ....Polly and Muff

ACT II

Jim's Lament ....Jim
"Ain't It a Shame" ....Townspeople
"Supersational Day" ....Minstrels and Townspeople
"Late Love" (Reprise) ....Polly
"Ain't It a Shame" (Reprise) ....Townspeople
Nightmare Ballet ....Tom, Injun Joe and Dancers
"MacDougal's Cave" ....Townspeople
River Ballad ....Townspeople
Finale ....Entire Company

(Closed May 19, 1957)

A MOON FOR THE MISBEGOTTEN

(34 performances)
(Continued)

Play in four acts by Eugene O'Neill. Produced by Carmen Capalbo and Stanley Chase at the Bijou Theatre, May 2, 1957.

Cast of characters—

Josie Hogan ....Wendy Hiller
Mike Hogan ....Glenn Cannon
Phil Hogan ....Cyril Cusack
James Tyrone, Jr. ....Franchot Tone
T. Stedman Harder ....William Woodson

The play takes place in Connecticut at the home of tenant farmer, Phil Hogan, between the hours of noon on a day in early September, 1923, and sunrise of the following day. Act I.—The farmhouse; around noon. Act II.—The same, but with the interior of sitting room revealed; eleven o'clock that night. Act III.—The same as Act I (no time elapses between Acts II and III). Act IV.—The same; dawn of the following morning.

Staged by Carmen Capalbo; designed by William Pitkin; lighting by Lee Watson; costumes by Ruth Morley; production stage manager, Gene Perlowin; stage manager, John Weaver; press representatives, Bill Doll and Seymour Krawitz.

See page 269.

THE GREATEST MAN ALIVE!

(5 performances)

Comedy in three acts by Tony Webster. Produced by Frederick Fox, in association with Elliott Nugent and John Gerstad, at the Ethel Barrymore Theatre, May 8, 1957.

Cast of characters—

```
Amos Benedict ...................................Dennis King
Tom Hopkins ..................................Russell Collins
Peggy Thomas ..............................Kathleen Maguire
Harry Dugan ..................................Richard Kelly
Steve Boyle .....................................Biff McGuire
Policeman .....................................Joseph Boland
Bishop Hansen .................................John Gibson
Ambulance Driver .............................Edgar Meyer
Hospital Aide ...............................William Windom
Photographer ..................................Stephen Gray
```

The action takes place in Amos Benedict's fifth-floor walk-up on East 11th Street, New York City. Act I.—5:30 P.M.; spring. Act II.—A half-hour later. Act III.—Six weeks later.

Staged by Elliott Nugent; production designed and lighted by Frederick Fox; Miss Maguire's gowns by Clare Potter; production stage manager, Sterling Mace; assistant stage manager, William Windom; press representative, George Ross.

(Closed May 11, 1957)

NEW GIRL IN TOWN

(21 performances)
(Continued)

Musical in two acts, based on Eugene O'Neill's play, "Anna Christie," with book by George Abbott, music and lyrics by Bob Merrill. Produced by Frederick Brisson, Robert E. Griffith and Harold S. Prince at the Forty-Sixth Street Theatre, May 14, 1957.

Cast of characters—

```
Lily .............................................Lulu Bates
Moll .............................................Pat Ferrier
Katie ............................................Mara Lynn
Alderman ...................................Michael Quinn
Chris .....................................Cameron Prud'homme
Johnson ........................................Jeff Killion
Seaman ........................................H. F. Green
Marthy .......................................Thelma Ritter
Oscar .........................................Del Anderson
Pete ..........................................Eddie Phillips
Mrs. Dowling .................................Ann Williams
Smith ........................................Stokley Gray
Mrs. Smith .................................Dorothy Stinnette
Bartender ....................................Mark Dawson
Ivy ..............................................Rita Noble
```

```
Rose ........................................Ginny  Perlowin
Anna ........................................Gwen  Verdon
Flo ..........................................Drusilla  Davis
Pearl ........................................Mara  Landi
Mat ..........................................George  Wallace
Mrs. Hammacher ..............................Jean  Handzlik
Reporter ......................................Herb  Fields
Masher ......................................John  Aristides
Svenson ......................................Ray  Mason
Violet ........................................Deedy  Irwin
Waiter ......................................Louis  Polacek
Dowling ......................................Ripple  Lewis
Politician ....................................H.  F.  Green
Krimp ........................................John  Ford
Henry ........................................Edgar  Daniels
```

Dancers: Claiborne Cary, Drusilla Davis, Dorothy Dushock, Pat Ferrier, Marie Kolin, Mara Lynn, Ethel Martin, Joan Petlak; John Aristides, Robert Bakanic, Harvey Hohnecker, Harvey Jung, Gale Moreda, John Nola, Eddie Phillips, Alton Ruff.

Singers: Jean Handzlik, Deedy Irwin, Mara Landi, Rita Noble, Ginny Perlowin, Dorothy Stinnette, Ann Williams; Del Anderson, Edgar Daniels, Herb Fields, John Ford, Stokley Gray, H. G. Green, Jeff Killion, Ripple Lewis, Ray Mason, Louis Polacek, Michael Quinn.

The action takes place near the waterfront, New York City, at the turn of the century.

Staged by George Abbott; dances and musical numbers staged by Bob Fosse; production designed by Rouben Ter-Arutunian; musical direction by Hal Hastings; orchestrations by Robert Russell Bennett and Philip J. Lang; dance music devised by Roger Adams; costumes executed by Helen Pons; hair styles by Ronald De Mann; production stage manager, Fred Hebert; stage manager, Dennis Murray; press representatives, Reuben Rabinovitch and Helen Richards.

Musical numbers—

ACT I

```
"Roll Yer Socks Up" ............H. F. Green, Dancers and Singers
"Anna Lilla" ............................Cameron Prud'homme
"Sunshine Girl" ....Del Anderson, Eddie Phillips and Mark Dawson
"On the Farm" ....................................Gwen Verdon
"Flings" ............Thelma Ritter, Lulu Bates and Mara Landi
"It's Good to Be Alive" ..........................Gwen Verdon
"Look at 'Er" ....................................George Wallace
"It's Good to Be Alive" (Reprise) ................George Wallace
"Yer My Friend, Aintcha?" ..........Thelma Ritter and Cameron
                                                    Prud'homme
"Did You Close Your Eyes?" .....Gwen Verdon and George Wallace
"At the Check Apron Ball" ..................Dancers and Singers
"There Ain't No Flies on Me" .........Gwen Verdon and Company
```

ACT II

```
"Ven I Valse" ......Gwen Verdon, Cameron Prud'homme, Dancers
                                                    and Singers
"Sunshine Girl" (Reprise) ..................Dancers and Singers
"If That Was Love" ............................Gwen Verdon
Ballet ................Gwen Verdon, John Aristedes and Dancers
"Chess and Checkers" .........Thelma Ritter, Dancers and Singers
"Look at 'Er" (Reprise) ........................George Wallace
```

THE PAJAMA GAME

(19 performances)
(Continued)

Musical in two acts, based on the novel, "7½ Cents" by Richard Bissell; book by George Abbott and Richard Bissell; music and lyrics by Richard Adler and Jerry Ross. Revived by the New York City Center Light Opera Company (Jean Dalrymple, Director) at the New York City Center of Music and Drama, May 15, 1957.

Cast of characters—

Hines	Paul Hartman
Prez	Stanley Prager
Joe	Sam Kirkham
Hasler	Ralph W. Chambers
Gladys	Pat Stanley
Sid Sorokin	Larry Douglas
Mabel	Marguerite Shaw
First Helper	Richard France
Second Helper	Cy Young
Charlie	Eugene Wood
Babe Williams	Jane Kean
Mae	Thelma Pelish
Brenda	Ann Buckles
Poopsie	Chele Graham
Salesman	Jack Waldron
Pop	William David

Dancers: Dorothy Etheridge, Chele Graham, Mickey Gunnerson, Rosemary Jourdan, Vivian Joyce, Barbara Siman, Bonnie West; Jim Brusock, Richard Colacino, Jack Konzal, Richard Monahan, Tom Snow, Keith Willis, Emanuel Winston.

Singers: Helen Baisley, Julia Gerace, Betty Graeber, Miriam Gulager, Peg Hadley, Sheila Mathews, Barbara Saxby, Mildred Slavin; Don Becker, Norris Branstrom, Arthur Dilks, Peter Held, Sam Kirkham, Vince McMahon, Stanley Page, Ralph Vucci.

Staged by Jean Barrere (original production staged by George Abbott and Jerome Robbins); scenery and costumes by Lemuel Avers; dances based on original choreography by Bob Fosse as executed by Erik Kristin; lighting by Peggy Clark; musical director, Frederick Dvonch; orchestrations by Don Walker; dance music arranged by Roger Adams; costume supervisor, Ruth Morley; assistant to Miss Dalrymple, Alan Green; production stage manager, Herman Shapiro; assistant stage manager, Bert Wood; press assistant to Miss Dalrymple, Tom Trenkle.

The Pajama Game was first produced May 13, 1954, by Frederick Brisson, Robert E. Griffith and Harold S. Prince at the St. James Theatre for 1,063 performances.

FACTS AND FIGURES

VARIETY'S TABULATION
OF FINANCIAL HITS AND FLOPS

HITS

Auntie Mame
Long Day's Journey into Night
Saint Joan

Separate Tables
Tunnel of Love

STATUS NOT YET DETERMINED

Apple Cart
Bells Are Ringing
Happiest Millionaire
Happy Hunting
Hole in the Head
Hotel Paradiso
Li'l Abner

Major Barbara
Moon for the Misbegotten
New Girl in Town
Potting Shed
Visit to a Small Planet
Waltz of the Toreadors
Ziegfeld Follies

FAILURES

Best House in Naples
Candide
Child of Fortune
Clearing in the Woods
Cranks
Double in Hearts
Eugenia
First Gentleman
Girls of Summer
Good as Gold
Greatest Man Alive
Harbor Lights
Hidden River
Hide and Seek
Holiday for Lovers
Loud Red Patrick
New Faces of '56

Night of the Auk
Orpheus Descending
Protective Custody
Reluctant Debutante
Shangri-La
Shinbone Alley
Sin of Pat Muldoon
Sixth Finger in a Five Finger
  Glove
Sleeping Prince
Small War on Murray Hill
Speaking of Murder
Too Late the Phalarope
Uncle Willie
Very Special Baby
Waiting for Godot (revival)

SPECIAL, MISCELLANEOUS (UNRATED)

Beggar's Opera
Brigadoon
Glass Menagerie
Merry Widow
Mister Roberts
Old Vic Repertory

Pajama Game
Renaud—Barrault Repertory
Ruth Draper
South Pacific
Teahouse of the August Moon

CLOSED DURING TRYOUT TOUR

Best of Steinbeck
Build with One Hand
Everybody Loves Me
Foolin' Ourselves

Joker
Liza
Maiden Voyage
Praise House

Holdovers from 1955-56 Season, Since Clarified

HITS

Lark
Middle of the Night
Most Happy Fella

My Fair Lady
Will Success Spoil Rock Hunter?

FAILURES

Fallen Angels
Mr. Wonderful
Pipe Dream

Ponder Heart
Waiting for Godot

STATISTICAL SUMMARY

(Last Season Plays Which Ended Runs After June 1, 1956)

Plays	Number Performances	Closing Date
Carmen Jones (revival)	24	June 17, 1956
Cat on a Hot Tin Roof	694	November 17, 1956
The Desk Set	296	July 7, 1956
Fallen Angels (revival)	239	August 11, 1956
Fanny	888	December 16, 1956
The Great Sebastians	174	June 2, 1956
A Hatful of Rain	398	October 13, 1956
Janus	251	June 30, 1956
The Lark	229	June 2, 1956
The Littlest Review	32	June 17, 1956
The Matchmaker	486	February 2, 1957
Middle of the Night	477	May 25, 1957
Mr. Wonderful	383	February 23, 1957
Pajama Game	1,063	November 24, 1956
Pipe Dream	246	June 30, 1956
The Ponder Heart	149	June 23, 1956
Waiting for Godot	59	June 9, 1956
Will Success Spoil Rock Hunter?	444	November 10, 1956
Witness for the Prosecution	645	June 30, 1956

LONG RUNS ON BROADWAY

To June 1, 1957

(Plays marked with asterisk were still playing June 1, 1957)

Plays	Number Performances
Life with Father	3,224
Tobacco Road	3,182
Abie's Irish Rose	2,327
Oklahoma!	2,248
South Pacific	1,925
Harvey	1,775
Born Yesterday	1,642
The Voice of the Turtle	1,557
Arsenic and Old Lace	1,444
Hellzapoppin	1,404
Angel Street	1,295
Lightnin'	1,291
The King and I	1,246
Guys and Dolls	1,200
Mister Roberts	1,157
Annie Get Your Gun	1,147
The Seven Year Itch	1,141
Pins and Needles	1,108
Kiss Me, Kate	1,070
Pajama Game	1,063
The Teahouse of the August Moon	1,027
Anna Lucasta	957
Kiss and Tell	957
The Moon Is Blue	924
Can-Can	892
Carousel	890
Hats Off to Ice	889
Fanny	888
Follow the Girls	882
The Bat	867

Plays	Number Performances
My Sister Eileen	865
* Damn Yankees	865
White Cargo	864
Song of Norway	860
A Streetcar Named Desire	855
Comedy in Music	849
You Can't Take It with You	837
Three Men on a Horse	835
Where's Charlie?	792
The Ladder	789
* Inherit the Wind	780
State of the Union	765
The First Year	760
Death of a Salesman	742
Sons o' Fun	742
The Man Who Came to Dinner	739
Call Me Mister	734
High Button Shoes	727
Finian's Rainbow	725
Claudia	722
The Gold Diggers	720
I Remember Mama	714
Tea and Sympathy	712
Junior Miss	710
Seventh Heaven	704
Cat on a Hot Tin Roof	694
Peg o' My Heart	692
The Children's Hour	691

Plays	Number Performances	Plays	Number Performances
* The Diary of Anne Frank	691	Show Boat	572
Dead End	687	The Show-Off	571
The Lion and the Mouse	686	Sally	570
Dear Ruth	683	One Touch of Venus	567
East Is West	680	Happy Birthday	564
* No Time for Sergeants	674	The Glass Menagerie	561
The Doughgirls	671	Wonderful Town	559
Irene	670	Rose Marie	557
Boy Meets Girl	669	Strictly Dishonorable	557
Blithe Spirit	657	Ziegfeld Follies	553
The Women	657	Floradora	553
A Trip to Chinatown	657	Dial "M" for Murder	552
Bloomer Girl	654	Good News	551
The Fifth Season	654	Let's Face It	547
Rain	648	Within the Law	541
Witness for the Prosecution	645	The Music Master	540
		Pal Joey	540
Call Me Madam	644	What a Life	538
Janie	642	The Red Mill	531
The Green Pastures	640	The Solid Gold Cadillac	526
The Fourposter	632	The Boomerang	522
Is Zat So?	618	Rosalinda	521
Anniversary Waltz	615	Chauve Souris	520
The Happy Time	614	Blackbirds	518
Separate Rooms	613	Sunny	517
Affairs of State	610	Victoria Regina	517
Star and Garter	609	The Vagabond King	511
The Student Prince	608	The New Moon	509
Broadway	603	* My Fair Lady	505
Adonis	603	Shuffle Along	504
Street Scene	601	Up in Central Park	504
Kiki	600	Carmen Jones	503
Wish You Were Here	598	The Member of the Wedding	501
A Society Circus	596		
Blossom Time	592	Personal Appearance	501
The Two Mrs. Carrolls	585	Panama Hattie	501
Kismet	583	Bird in Hand	500
Detective Story	581	Sailor, Beware!	500
Brigadoon	581	Room Service	500
Brother Rat	577	Tomorrow the World	500

NEW YORK DRAMA CRITICS CIRCLE AWARDS

At their annual meeting, the New York Drama Critics Circle chose Eugene O'Neill's *Long Day's Journey into Night* as the best new American play of the season. As the best foreign play, the Circle chose Jean Anouilh's *The Waltz of the Toreadors* (translated by Lucienne Hill) and as the best musical, Frank Loesser's *The Most Happy Fella*.

Circle awards have been—

1935-36—Winterset, by Maxwell Anderson
1936-37—High Tor, by Maxwell Anderson
1937-38—Of Mice and Men, by John Steinbeck
1938-39—No award.
1939-40—The Time of Your Life, by William Saroyan
1940-41—Watch on the Rhine, by Lillian Hellman
1941-42—No award.
1942-43—The Patriots, by Sidney Kingsley
1943-44—No award.
1944-45—The Glass Menagerie, by Tennessee Williams
1945-46—No award.
1946-47—All My Sons, by Arthur Miller
1947-48—A Streetcar Named Desire, by Tennessee Williams
1948-49—Death of a Salesman, by Arthur Miller
1949-50—The Member of the Wedding, by Carson McCullers
1950-51—Darkness at Noon, by Sidney Kingsley
1951-52—I Am a Camera, by John van Druten
1952-53—Picnic, by William Inge
1953-54—The Teahouse of the August Moon, by John Patrick
1954-55—Cat on a Hot Tin Roof, by Tennessee Williams
1955-56—The Diary of Anne Frank, by Frances Goodrich and
            Albert Hackett
1956-57—Long Day's Journey into Night, by Eugene O'Neill

PULITZER PRIZE WINNERS

For the fifth successive year the Pulitzer Prize went to the same play as the Critics Circle Award—in this case, *Long Day's Journey into Night.*

Pulitzer awards have been—

1917-18—Why Marry?, by Jesse Lynch Williams
1918-19—No award.
1919-20—Beyond the Horizon, by Eugene O'Neill
1920-21—Miss Lulu Bett, by Zona Gale
1921-22—Anna Christie, by Eugene O'Neill
1922-23—Icebound, by Owen Davis
1923-24—Hell-bent fer Heaven, by Hatcher Hughes
1924-25—They Knew What They Wanted, by Sidney Howard
1925-26—Craig's Wife, by George Kelly
1926-27—In Abraham's Bosom, by Paul Green
1927-28—Strange Interlude, by Eugene O'Neill
1928-29—Street Scene, by Elmer Rice
1929-30—The Green Pastures, by Marc Connelly
1930-31—Alison's House, by Susan Glaspell
1931-32—Of Thee I Sing, by George S. Kaufman, Morrie Rys-
        kind, Ira and George Gershwin
1932-33—Both Your Houses, by Maxwell Anderson
1933-34—Men in White, by Sidney Kingsley
1934-35—The Old Maid, by Zoë Akins
1935-36—Idiot's Delight, by Robert E. Sherwood
1936-37—You Can't Take It with You, by Moss Hart and George
        S. Kaufman
1937-38—Our Town, by Thornton Wilder
1938-39—Abe Lincoln in Illinois, by Robert E. Sherwood
1939-40—The Time of Your Life, by William Saroyan
1940-41—There Shall Be No Night, by Robert E. Sherwood
1941-42—No award.
1942-43—The Skin of Our Teeth, by Thornton Wilder
1943-44—No award.
1944-45—Harvey, by Mary Coyle Chase
1945-46—State of the Union, by Howard Lindsay and Russel
        Crouse

1946-47—No award.
1947-48—A Streetcar Named Desire, by Tennessee Williams
1948-49—Death of a Salesman, by Arthur Miller
1949-50—South Pacific, by Richard Rodgers, Oscar Hammerstein
       II and Joshua Logan
1950-51—No award.
1951-52—The Shrike, by Joseph Kramm
1952-53—Picnic, by William Inge
1953-54—The Teahouse of the August Moon, by John Patrick
1954-55—Cat on a Hot Tin Roof, by Tennessee Williams
1955-56—The Diary of Anne Frank, by Frances Goodrich and
       Albert Hackett
1956-57—Long Day's Journey into Night, by Eugene O'Neill

BOOKS ON THE THEATRE

1956-1957

Anouilh, Jean. *The Waltz of the Toreadors*. (Translated by Lucienne Hill.) Coward-McCann. $2.95.

Archer, William. *Masks or Faces?;* and Diderot, Denis. *The Paradox of Acting*. Hill and Wang. $1.25.

Barnes, Eric Wollencott. *The Man Who Lived Twice:* The Biography of Edward Sheldon. Scribner's. $5.00.

Barrymore, Diana, and Frank, Gerold. *Too Much, Too Soon*. Holt. $3.95.

Bentley, Eric (Editor). *From the American Repertory: Series Three*. University of Indiana Press. $7.50.

Bentley, Eric. *The Modern Theatre: Vol. 5*. (Five plays, by Büchner, Gogol, Ghelderode, Anouilh, O'Casey.) Anchor Books. $.95.

Bentley, Eric. *What Is Theatre?* Horizon Press. $3.50.

Blum, Daniel (Editor). *Theatre World 1955-56*. Greenberg. $5.00.

Capote, Truman. *The Muses Are Heard*. Random House. $3.00.

Chapman, John (Editor). *Theatre '56*. Random House. $5.00.

Chesterton, G. K. *George Bernard Shaw*. Hill and Wang. $.95.

Comden, Betty, and Green, Adolph. *Bells Are Ringing*. Random House. $2.95.

Craig, Edward Gordon. *On the Art of the Theatre*. Theatre Arts Books. $4.75.

Diderot, Denis. *The Paradox of Acting;* and Archer, William. *Masks or Faces?* Hill and Wang. $1.25.

Ervine, St. John. *Bernard Shaw*. Morrow. $7.50.

Farnsworth, Marjorie. *The Ziegfeld Follies:* A History in Text and Pictures. Putnam. $5.95.

Findlater, Richard. *Michael Redgrave, Actor.* Theatre Arts Books. $3.25.

Fitts, Dudley (Translator). *The Birds,* by Aristophanes. Harcourt, Brace. $4.00.

Fluchère, Henri. *Shakespeare and the Elizabethans.* Hill and Wang. $1.25.

Gassner, John W. (Editor). *Twenty Best European Plays on the American Stage.* Crown. $5.75.

Granville-Barker, Harley. *On Dramatic Method.* Hill and Wang. $.95.

Granville-Barker, Harley. *Preface to Hamlet.* Hill and Wang. $1.25.

Greene, Graham. *The Potting Shed.* Viking Press. $3.00.

Halliday, F. E. *Shakespeare: A Pictorial Biography.* Crowell. $5.95.

Hecht, Ben. *Charlie:* The Improbable Life and Times of Charles MacArthur. Harper. $3.95.

Hellman, Lillian. *Candide.* (Music by Leonard Bernstein, lyrics by Richard Wilbur, other lyrics by John Latouche and Dorothy Parker.) Random House. $2.95.

Henderson, Archibald. *George Bernard Shaw:* Man of the Century. Appleton. $12.00.

Knox, Bernard. *Oedipus at Thebes:* Sophocles' Tragic Hero and His Time. Yale University Press. $5.00.

Kronenberger, Louis (Editor). *Plays of R. B. Sheridan.* Hill and Wang. $1.45.

Kronenberger, Louis (Editor). *The Best Plays of 1955-1956.* Dodd, Mead. $5.00.

Krutch, Joseph Wood. *American Drama Since 1918.* Braziller. $5.00.

Laurents, Arthur. *A Clearing in the Woods.* Random House. $2.95.

Lee, Gypsy Rose. *Gypsy:* A Memoir. Harper. $3.95.

Lerner, Alan Jay. *My Fair Lady.* (Based on Shaw's *Pygmalion.*) Coward-McCann. $3.50.

Lindsay, Howard, and Crouse, Russel. *Happy Hunting.* Random House. $2.95.

Loesser, Frank. *The Most Happy Fella.* (Text, lyrics and score.) Frank Productions. $12.50.

Miller, Arthur. *Collected Plays.* Viking. $4.95.

Nicoll, Allardyce (Editor). *Shakespeare Survey 10.* Cambridge University Press. $4.00.

Niklaus, Thelma. *Harlequin.* Braziller. $7.50.

Pearson, Hesketh. *Beerbohm Tree:* His Life and Laughter. Harper. $3.75.

Pound, Ezra (Translator). *Women of Trachis*, by Sophocles. New Directions. $3.00.

Purdom, C. B. (Editor). *Bernard Shaw's Letters to Granville Barker.* Theatre Arts Books. $4.50.

Rattigan, Terence. *Separate Tables.* Random House. $2.95.

Rattigan, Terence. *The Sleeping Prince.* Random House. $2.95.

Richardson, Joanne. *Rachel.* Putnam. $4.50.

Roos, Audrey and William. *Speaking of Murder.* Random House. $2.95.

Scott, A. C. *The Classical Theatre of China.* Macmillan. $6.75.

Siegel, Paul N. *Shakesperean Tragedy and the Elizabethan Compromise.* New York University Press. $5.00.

Smith, Grove, Jr. *T. S. Eliot's Poetry and Plays.* University of Chicago Press. $6.00

Smith, Irwin. *Shakespeare's Globe Playhouse:* A Modern Reconstruction. Scribner's. $7.00

Sobel, Bernard. *A Pictorial History of Burlesque.* Putnam. $5.95.

Stanton, Stephen S. (Editor). *Camille and Other Plays.* Hill and Wang. $1.45.

Stevens, David H. (Editor). *Ten Talents in the American Theatre.* University of Oklahoma Press. $4.00.

Vidal, Gore. *Visit to a Small Planet and Other Television Plays.* Little, Brown. $4.00.

Wade, Allan (Editor). *The Scenic Art.* (Henry James' theatre essays.) Hill and Wang. $1.35.

Winsten, Stephen. *Jesting Apostle:* The Private Life of Bernard Shaw. Dutton. $5.00.

PREVIOUS VOLUMES OF BEST PLAYS

Plays chosen to represent the theatre seasons from 1899 to 1956 are as follows:

1899-1909

BARBARA FRIETCHIE, by Clyde Fitch. Life Publishing Co.
THE CLIMBERS, by Clyde Fitch. Macmillan.
IF I WERE KING, by Justin Huntly McCarthy. Samuel French.
THE DARLING OF THE GODS, by David Belasco. Little, Brown.
THE COUNTY CHAIRMAN, by George Ade. Samuel French.
LEAH KLESCHNA, by C. M. S. McLellan. Samuel French.
THE SQUAW MAN, by Edwin Milton Royle.
THE GREAT DIVIDE, by William Vaughn Moody. Samuel French.
THE WITCHING HOUR, by Augustus Thomas. Samuel French.
THE MAN FROM HOME, by Booth Tarkington and Harry Leon Wilson. Samuel French.

1909-1919

THE EASIEST WAY, by Eugene Walter. G. W. Dillingham and Houghton Mifflin.
MRS. BUMPSTEAD-LEIGH, by Harry James Smith. Samuel French.
DISRAELI, by Louis N. Parker. Dodd, Mead.
ROMANCE, by Edward Sheldon. Macmillan.
SEVEN KEYS TO BALDPATE, by George M. Cohan. Published by Bobbs-Merrill as a novel by Earl Derr Biggers; as a play by Samuel French.
ON TRIAL, by Elmer Reizenstein. Samuel French.
THE UNCHASTENED WOMAN, by Louis Kaufman Anspacher. Harcourt, Brace and Howe.
GOOD GRACIOUS ANNABELLE, by Clare Kummer. Samuel French.
WHY MARRY?, by Jesse Lynch Williams. Scribner.
JOHN FERGUSON, by St. John Ervine. Macmillan.

1919-1920

ABRAHAM LINCOLN, by John Drinkwater. Houghton Mifflin.
CLARENCE, by Booth Tarkington. Samuel French.
BEYOND THE HORIZON, by Eugene G. O'Neill. Boni & Liveright.

DÉCLASSÉE, by Zoë Akins. Liveright, Inc.
THE FAMOUS MRS. FAIR, by James Forbes. Samuel French.
THE JEST, by Sem Benelli. (American adaptation by Edward Sheldon.)
JANE CLEGG, by St. John Ervine. Henry Holt.
MAMMA'S AFFAIR, by Rachel Barton Butler. Samuel French.
WEDDING BELLS, by Salisbury Field. Samuel French.
ADAM AND EVA, by George Middleton and Guy Bolton. Samuel French.

1920-1921

DEBURAU, adapted from the French of Sacha Guitry by H. Granville Barker. Putnam.
THE FIRST YEAR, by Frank Craven. Samuel French.
ENTER MADAME, by Gilda Varesi and Dolly Byrne. Putnam.
THE GREEN GODDESS, by William Archer. Knopf.
LILIOM, by Ferenc Molnar. Boni & Liveright.
MARY ROSE, by James M. Barrie. Scribner.
NICE PEOPLE, by Rachel Crothers. Scribner.
THE BAD MAN, by Porter Emerson Browne. Putnam.
THE EMPEROR JONES, by Eugene G. O'Neill. Boni & Liveright.
THE SKIN GAME, by John Galsworthy. Scribner.

1921-1922

ANNA CHRISTIE, by Eugene G. O'Neill. Boni & Liveright.
A BILL OF DIVORCEMENT, by Clemence Dane. Macmillan.
DULCY, by George S. Kaufman and Marc Connelly. Putnam.
HE WHO GETS SLAPPED, adapted from the Russian of Leonid Andreyev by Gregory Zilboorg. Brentano's.
SIX CYLINDER LOVE, by William Anthony McGuire.
THE HERO, by Gilbert Emery.
THE DOVER ROAD, by Alan Alexander Milne. Samuel French.
AMBUSH, by Arthur Richman.
THE CIRCLE, by William Somerset Maugham.
THE NEST, by Paul Geraldy and Grace George.

1922-1923

RAIN, by John Colton and Clemence Randolph. Liveright, Inc.
LOYALTIES, by John Galsworthy. Scribner.
ICEBOUND, by Owen Davis. Little, Brown.
YOU AND I, by Philip Barry. Brentano's.
THE FOOL, by Channing Pollock. Brentano's.

MERTON OF THE MOVIES, by George Kaufman and Marc Connelly, based on the novel of the same name by Harry Leon Wilson.
WHY NOT? by Jesse Lynch Williams. Walter H. Baker Co.
THE OLD SOAK, by Don Marquis. Doubleday, Page.
R.U.R., by Karel Capek. Translated by Paul Selver. Doubleday, Page.
MARY THE 3D, by Rachel Crothers. Brentano's.

1923-1924

THE SWAN, translated from the Hungarian of Ferenc Molnar by Melville Baker. Boni & Liveright.
OUTWARD BOUND, by Sutton Vane. Boni & Liveright.
THE SHOW-OFF, by George Kelly. Little, Brown.
THE CHANGELINGS, by Lee Wilson Dodd. Dutton.
CHICKEN FEED, by Guy Bolton. Samuel French.
SUN-UP, by Lula Vollmer. Brentano's.
BEGGAR ON HORSEBACK, by George Kaufman and Marc Connelly. Boni & Liveright.
TARNISH, by Gilbert Emery. Brentano's.
THE GOOSE HANGS HIGH, by Lewis Beach. Little, Brown.
HELL-BENT FER HEAVEN, by Hatcher Hughes. Harper.

1924-1925

WHAT PRICE GLORY? by Laurence Stallings and Maxwell Anderson. Harcourt, Brace.
THEY KNEW WHAT THEY WANTED, by Sidney Howard. Doubleday, Page.
DESIRE UNDER THE ELMS, by Eugene G. O'Neill. Boni & Liveright.
THE FIREBRAND, by Edwin Justus Mayer. Boni & Liveright.
DANCING MOTHERS, by Edgar Selwyn and Edmund Goulding.
MRS. PARTRIDGE PRESENTS, by Mary Kennedy and Ruth Hawthorne. Samuel French.
THE FALL GUY, by James Gleason and George Abbott. Samuel French.
THE YOUNGEST, by Philip Barry. Samuel French.
MINICK, by Edna Ferber and George S. Kaufman. Doubleday, Page.
WILD BIRDS, by Dan Totheroh. Doubleday, Page.

1925-1926

CRAIG'S WIFE, by George Kelly. Little, Brown.

THE GREAT GOD BROWN, by Eugene G. O'Neill. Boni & Liveright.

THE GREEN HAT, by Michael Arlen.

THE DYBBUK, by S. Ansky, Henry G. Alsberg-Winifred Katzin translation. Boni & Liveright.

THE ENEMY, by Channing Pollock. Brentano's.

THE LAST OF MRS. CHEYNEY, by Frederick Lonsdale. Samuel French.

BRIDE OF THE LAMB, by William Hurlbut. Boni & Liveright.

THE WISDOM TOOTH, by Marc Connelly. George H. Doran.

THE BUTTER AND EGG MAN, by George Kaufman. Boni & Liveright.

YOUNG WOODLEY, by John van Druten. Simon & Schuster.

1926-1927

BROADWAY, by Philip Dunning and George Abbott. George H. Doran.

SATURDAY'S CHILDREN, by Maxwell Anderson. Longmans, Green.

CHICAGO, by Maurine Watkins. Knopf.

THE CONSTANT WIFE, by William Somerset Maugham. George H. Doran.

THE PLAY'S THE THING, by Ferenc Molnar and P. G. Wodehouse. Brentano's.

THE ROAD TO ROME, by Robert Emmet Sherwood. Scribner.

THE SILVER CORD, by Sidney Howard. Scribner.

THE CRADLE SONG, translated from the Spanish of G. Martinez Sierra by John Garrett Underhill. Dutton.

DAISY MAYME, by George Kelly. Little, Brown.

IN ABRAHAM'S BOSOM, by Paul Green. McBride.

1927-1928

STRANGE INTERLUDE, by Eugene G. O'Neill. Boni & Liveright.

THE ROYAL FAMILY, by Edna Ferber and George Kaufman. Doubleday, Doran.

BURLESQUE, by George Manker Watters and Arthur Hopkins. Doubleday, Doran.

COQUETTE, by George Abbott and Ann Bridgers. Longmans, Green.

BEHOLD THE BRIDEGROOM, by George Kelly. Little, Brown.

PORGY, by DuBose Heyward. Doubleday, Doran.

PARIS BOUND, by Philip Barry. Samuel French.

ESCAPE, by John Galsworthy. Scribner.

THE RACKET, by Bartlett Cormack. Samuel French.
THE PLOUGH AND THE STARS, by Sean O'Casey. Macmillan.

1928-1929

STREET SCENE, by Elmer Rice. Samuel French.
JOURNEY'S END, by R. C. Sherriff. Brentano's.
WINGS OVER EUROPE, by Robert Nichols and Maurice Browne. Covici-Friede.
HOLIDAY, by Philip Barry. Samuel French.
THE FRONT PAGE, by Ben Hecht and Charles MacArthur. Covici-Friede.
LET US BE GAY, by Rachel Crothers. Samuel French.
MACHINAL, by Sophie Treadwell.
LITTLE ACCIDENT, by Floyd Dell and Thomas Mitchell.
GYPSY, by Maxwell Anderson.
THE KINGDOM OF GOD, by G. Martinez Sierra; English version by Helen and Harley Granville-Barker. Dutton.

1929-1930

THE GREEN PASTURES, by Marc Connelly (adapted from "Ol' Man Adam and His Chillun," by Roark Bradford). Farrar & Rinehart.
THE CRIMINAL CODE, by Martin Flavin. Horace Liveright.
BERKELEY SQUARE, by John Balderston.
STRICTLY DISHONORABLE, by Preston Sturges. Horace Liveright.
THE FIRST MRS. FRASER, by St. John Ervine. Macmillan.
THE LAST MILE, by John Wexley. Samuel French.
JUNE MOON, by Ring W. Lardner and George S. Kaufman. Scribner.
MICHAEL AND MARY, by A. A. Milne. Chatto & Windus.
DEATH TAKES A HOLIDAY, by Walter Ferris (adapted from the Italian of Alberto Casella). Samuel French.
REBOUND, by Donald Ogden Stewart. Samuel French.

1930-1931

ELIZABETH THE QUEEN, by Maxwell Anderson. Longmans, Green.
TOMORROW AND TOMORROW, by Philip Barry. Samuel French.
ONCE IN A LIFETIME, by George S. Kaufman and Moss Hart. Farrar & Rinehart.
GREEN GROW THE LILACS, by Lynn Riggs. Samuel French.
AS HUSBANDS GO, by Rachel Crothers. Samuel French.

ALISON'S HOUSE, by Susan Glaspell. Samuel French.

FIVE-STAR FINAL, by Louis Weitzenkorn. Samuel French.

OVERTURE, by William Bolitho. Simon & Schuster.

THE BARRETTS OF WIMPOLE STREET, by Rudolf Besier. Little, Brown.

GRAND HOTEL, adapted from the German of Vicki Baum by W. A. Drake.

1931-1932

OF THEE I SING, by George S. Kaufman and Morrie Ryskind; music and lyrics by George and Ira Gershwin. Knopf.

MOURNING BECOMES ELECTRA, by Eugene G. O'Neill. Horace Liveright.

REUNION IN VIENNA, by Robert Emmet Sherwood. Scribner.

THE HOUSE OF CONNELLY, by Paul Green. Samuel French.

THE ANIMAL KINGDOM, by Philip Barry. Samuel French.

THE LEFT BANK, by Elmer Rice. Samuel French.

ANOTHER LANGUAGE, by Rose Franken. Samuel French.

BRIEF MOMENT, by S. N. Behrman. Farrar & Rinehart.

THE DEVIL PASSES, by Benn W. Levy. Martin Secker.

CYNARA, by H. M. Harwood and R. F. Gore-Browne. Samuel French.

1932-1933

BOTH YOUR HOUSES, by Maxwell Anderson. Samuel French.

DINNER AT EIGHT, by George S. Kaufman and Edna Ferber. Doubleday, Doran.

WHEN LADIES MEET, by Rachel Crothers. Samuel French.

DESIGN FOR LIVING, by Noel Coward. Doubleday, Doran.

BIOGRAPHY, by S. N. Behrman. Farrar & Rinehart.

ALIEN CORN, by Sidney Howard. Scribner.

THE LATE CHRISTOPHER BEAN, adapted from the French of René Fauchois by Sidney Howard. Samuel French.

WE, THE PEOPLE, by Elmer Rice. Coward-McCann.

PIGEONS AND PEOPLE, by George M. Cohan.

ONE SUNDAY AFTERNOON, by James Hagan. Samuel French.

1933-1934

MARY OF SCOTLAND, by Maxwell Anderson. Doubleday, Doran.

MEN IN WHITE, by Sidney Kingsley. Covici-Friede.

DODSWORTH, by Sinclair Lewis and Sidney Howard. Harcourt, Brace.

AH, WILDERNESS, by Eugene O'Neill. Random House.
THEY SHALL NOT DIE, by John Wexley. Knopf.
HER MASTER'S VOICE, by Clare Kummer. Samuel French.
NO MORE LADIES, by A. E. Thomas.
WEDNESDAY'S CHILD, by Leopold Atlas. Samuel French.
THE SHINING HOUR, by Keith Winter. Doubleday, Doran.
THE GREEN BAY TREE, by Mordaunt Shairp. Baker International
    Play Bureau.

1934-1935

THE CHILDREN'S HOUR, by Lillian Hellman. Knopf.
VALLEY FORGE, by Maxwell Anderson. Anderson House.
THE PETRIFIED FOREST, by Robert Sherwood. Scribner.
THE OLD MAID, by Zoë Akins. Appleton-Century.
ACCENT ON YOUTH, by Samson Raphaelson. Samuel French.
MERRILY WE ROLL ALONG, by George S. Kaufman and Moss Hart.
    Random House.
AWAKE AND SING, by Clifford Odets. Random House.
THE FARMER TAKES A WIFE, by Frank B. Elser and Marc Connelly.
LOST HORIZONS, by John Hayden.
THE DISTAFF SIDE, by John van Druten. Knopf.

1935-1936

WINTERSET, by Maxwell Anderson. Anderson House.
IDIOT'S DELIGHT, by Robert Emmet Sherwood. Scribner.
END OF SUMMER, by S. N. Behrman. Random House.
FIRST LADY, by Katharine Dayton and George S. Kaufman. Ran-
    dom House.
VICTORIA REGINA, by Laurence Housman. Samuel French.
BOY MEETS GIRL, by Bella and Samuel Spewack. Random House.
DEAD END, by Sidney Kingsley. Random House.
CALL IT A DAY, by Dodie Smith. Samuel French.
ETHAN FROME, by Owen Davis and Donald Davis. Scribner.
PRIDE AND PREJUDICE, by Helen Jerome. Doubleday, Doran.

1936-1937

HIGH TOR, by Maxwell Anderson. Anderson House.
YOU CAN'T TAKE IT WITH YOU, by Moss Hart and George S. Kauf-
    man. Farrar & Rinehart.
JOHNNY JOHNSON, by Paul Green. Samuel French.
DAUGHTERS OF ATREUS, by Robert Turney. Knopf.

STAGE DOOR, by Edna Ferber and George S. Kaufman. Doubleday, Doran.

THE WOMEN, by Clare Boothe. Random House.

ST. HELENA, by R. C. Sherriff and Jeanne de Casalis. Samuel French.

YES, MY DARLING DAUGHTER, by Mark Reed. Samuel French.

EXCURSION, by Victor Wolfson. Random House.

TOVARICH, by Jacques Deval and Robert E. Sherwood. Random House.

1937-1938

OF MICE AND MEN, by John Steinbeck. Covici-Friede.

OUR TOWN, by Thornton Wilder. Coward-McCann.

SHADOW AND SUBSTANCE, by Paul Vincent Carroll. Random House.

ON BORROWED TIME, by Paul Osborn. Knopf.

THE STAR-WAGON, by Maxwell Anderson. Anderson House.

SUSAN AND GOD, by Rachel Crothers. Random House.

PROLOGUE TO GLORY, by E. P. Conkle. Random House.

AMPHITRYON 38, by S. N. Behrman. Random House.

GOLDEN BOY, by Clifford Odets. Random House.

WHAT A LIFE, by Clifford Goldsmith. Dramatists' Play Service.

1938-1939

ABE LINCOLN IN ILLINOIS, by Robert E. Sherwood. Scribner.

THE LITTLE FOXES, by Lillian Hellman. Random House.

ROCKET TO THE MOON, by Clifford Odets. Random House.

THE AMERICAN WAY, by George S. Kaufman and Moss Hart. Random House.

NO TIME FOR COMEDY, by S. N. Behrman. Random House.

THE PHILADELPHIA STORY, by Philip Barry. Coward-McCann.

THE WHITE STEED, by Paul Vincent Carroll. Random House.

HERE COME THE CLOWNS, by Philip Barry. Coward-McCann.

FAMILY PORTRAIT, by Lenore Coffee and William Joyce Cowen. Random House.

KISS THE BOYS GOOD-BYE, by Clare Boothe. Random House.

1939-1940

THERE SHALL BE NO NIGHT, by Robert E. Sherwood. Scribner.

KEY LARGO, by Maxwell Anderson. Anderson House.

THE WORLD WE MAKE, by Sidney Kingsley.

LIFE WITH FATHER, by Howard Lindsay and Russel Crouse. Knopf.

THE MAN WHO CAME TO DINNER, by George S. Kaufman and Moss Hart. Random House.

THE MALE ANIMAL, by James Thurber and Elliott Nugent. Random House, New York, and MacMillan Co., Canada.

THE TIME OF YOUR LIFE, by William Saroyan. Harcourt, Brace.

SKYLARK, by Samson Raphaelson. Random House.

MARGIN FOR ERROR, by Clare Boothe. Random House.

MORNING'S AT SEVEN, by Paul Osborn. Samuel French.

1940-1941

NATIVE SON, by Paul Green and Richard Wright. Harper.

WATCH ON THE RHINE, by Lillian Hellman. Random House.

THE CORN IS GREEN, by Emlyn Williams. Random House.

LADY IN THE DARK, by Moss Hart. Random House.

ARSENIC AND OLD LACE, by Joseph Kesselring. Random House.

MY SISTER EILEEN, by Joseph Fields and Jerome Chodorov. Random House.

FLIGHT TO THE WEST, by Elmer Rice. Coward-McCann.

CLAUDIA, by Rose Franken Meloney. Farrar & Rinehart.

MR. AND MRS. NORTH, by Owen Davis. Samuel French.

GEORGE WASHINGTON SLEPT HERE, by George S. Kaufman and Moss Hart. Random House.

1941-1942

IN TIME TO COME, by Howard Koch. Dramatists' Play Service.

THE MOON IS DOWN, by John Steinbeck. Viking.

BLITHE SPIRIT, by Noel Coward. Doubleday, Doran.

JUNIOR MISS, by Jerome Chodorov and Joseph Fields. Random House.

CANDLE IN THE WIND, by Maxwell Anderson. Anderson House.

LETTERS TO LUCERNE, by Fritz Rotter and Allen Vincent. Samuel French.

JASON, by Samson Raphaelson. Random House.

ANGEL STREET, by Patrick Hamilton. Constable & Co., under the title "Gaslight."

UNCLE HARRY, by Thomas Job. Samuel French.

HOPE FOR A HARVEST, by Sophie Treadwell. Samuel French.

1942-1943

THE PATRIOTS, by Sidney Kingsley. Random House.

THE EVE OF ST. MARK, by Maxwell Anderson. Anderson House.

THE SKIN OF OUR TEETH, by Thornton Wilder. Harper.

WINTER SOLDIERS, by Dan James.

TOMORROW THE WORLD, by James Gow and Arnaud d'Usseau. Scribner.

HARRIET, by Florence Ryerson and Colin Clements. Scribner.

THE DOUGHGIRLS, by Joseph Fields. Random House.

THE DAMASK CHEEK, by John van Druten and Lloyd Morris. Random House.

KISS AND TELL, by F. Hugh Herbert. Coward-McCann.

OKLAHOMA!, by Oscar Hammerstein 2nd and Richard Rodgers. Random House.

1943-1944

WINGED VICTORY, by Moss Hart. Random House.

THE SEARCHING WIND, by Lillian Hellman. Viking.

THE VOICE OF THE TURTLE, by John van Druten. Random House.

DECISION, by Edward Chodorov.

OVER 21, by Ruth Gordon. Random House.

OUTRAGEOUS FORTUNE, by Rose Franken. Samuel French.

JACOBOWSKY AND THE COLONEL, by S. N. Behrman. Random House.

STORM OPERATION, by Maxwell Anderson. Anderson House.

PICK-UP GIRL, by Elsa Shelley.

THE INNOCENT VOYAGE, by Paul Osborn.

1944-1945

A BELL FOR ADANO, by Paul Osborn. Knopf.

I REMEMBER MAMA, by John van Druten. Harcourt, Brace.

THE HASTY HEART, by John Patrick. Random House.

THE GLASS MENAGERIE, by Tennessee Williams. Random House.

HARVEY, by Mary Chase.

THE LATE GEORGE APLEY, by John P. Marquand and George S. Kaufman.

SOLDIER'S WIFE, by Rose Franken. Samuel French.

ANNA LUCASTA, by Philip Yordan. Random House.

FOOLISH NOTION, by Philip Barry.

DEAR RUTH, by Norman Krasna. Random House.

1945-1946

STATE OF THE UNION, by Howard Lindsay and Russel Crouse. Random House.

HOME OF THE BRAVE, by Arthur Laurents. Random House.

DEEP ARE THE ROOTS, by Arnaud d'Usseau and James Gow. Scrib-
ner.
THE MAGNIFICENT YANKEE, by Emmet Lavery. Samuel French.
ANTIGONE, by Lewis Galantière (from the French of Jean Anouilh).
Random House.
O MISTRESS MINE, by Terence Rattigan. Published and revised by
the author.
BORN YESTERDAY, by Garson Kanin. Viking.
DREAM GIRL, by Elmer Rice. Coward-McCann.
THE RUGGED PATH, by Robert E. Sherwood. Scribner.
LUTE SONG, by Will Irwin and Sidney Howard. Published version
by Will Irwin and Leopoldine Howard.

1946-1947

ALL MY SONS, by Arthur Miller. Reynal & Hitchcock.
THE ICEMAN COMETH, by Eugene G. O'Neill. Random House.
JOAN OF LORRAINE, by Maxwell Anderson. Published by Maxwell
Anderson.
ANOTHER PART OF THE FOREST, by Lillian Hellman. Viking.
YEARS AGO, by Ruth Gordon. Viking.
JOHN LOVES MARY, by Norman Krasna. Copyright by Norman
Krasna.
THE FATAL WEAKNESS, by George Kelly. Samuel French.
THE STORY OF MARY SURRATT, by John Patrick. Dramatists' Play
Service.
CHRISTOPHER BLAKE, by Moss Hart. Random House.
BRIGADOON, by Alan Jay Lerner and Frederick Loewe. Coward-
McCann.

1947-1948

A STREETCAR NAMED DESIRE, by Tennessee Williams. New Direc-
tions.
MISTER ROBERTS, by Thomas Heggen and Joshua Logan. Houghton
Mifflin.
COMMAND DECISION, by William Wister Haines. Random House.
THE WINSLOW BOY, by Terence Rattigan.
THE HEIRESS, by Ruth and Augustus Goetz.
ALLEGRO, by Richard Rodgers and Oscar Hammerstein 2d. Knopf.
Music published by Williamson Music, Inc.
EASTWARD IN EDEN, by Dorothy Gardner. Longmans, Green.
SKIPPER NEXT TO GOD, by Jan de Hartog.

AN INSPECTOR CALLS, by J. B. Priestley.
ME AND MOLLY, by Gertrude Berg.

1948-1949

DEATH OF A SALESMAN, by Arthur Miller. Viking.
ANNE OF THE THOUSAND DAYS, by Maxwell Anderson. Sloane.
THE MADWOMAN OF CHAILLOT, by Maurice Valency, adapted from
the French of Jean Giraudoux. Random House.
DETECTIVE STORY, by Sidney Kingsley. Random House.
EDWARD, MY SON, by Robert Morley and Noel Langley. Random
House, New York, and Samuel French, London.
LIFE WITH MOTHER, by Howard Lindsay and Russel Crouse.
Knopf.
LIGHT UP THE SKY, by Moss Hart. Random House.
THE SILVER WHISTLE, by Robert Edward McEnroe. Dramatists'
Play Service.
TWO BLIND MICE, by Samuel Spewack. Dramatists' Play Service.
GOODBYE, MY FANCY, by Fay Kanin. Samuel French.

1949-1950

THE COCKTAIL PARTY, by T. S. Eliot. Harcourt, Brace.
THE MEMBER OF THE WEDDING, by Carson McCullers. Houghton
Mifflin.
THE INNOCENTS, by William Archibald. Coward-McCann.
LOST IN THE STARS, by Maxwell Anderson and Kurt Weill. Sloane.
COME BACK, LITTLE SHEBA, by William Inge. Random House.
THE HAPPY TIME, by Samuel Taylor. Random House.
THE WISTERIA TREES, by Joshua Logan. Random House.
I KNOW MY LOVE, by S. N. Behrman. Random House.
THE ENCHANTED, by Maurice Valency, adapted from a play by Jean
Giraudoux. Random House.
CLUTTERBUCK, by Benn W. Levy. Dramatists' Play Service.

1950-1951

GUYS AND DOLLS, by Jo Swerling, Abe Burrows and Frank Loesser.
DARKNESS AT NOON, by Sidney Kingsley and Arthur Koestler. Ran-
dom House.
BILLY BUDD, by Louis O. Coxe and Robert Chapman. Princeton
University Press.
THE AUTUMN GARDEN, by Lillian Hellman. Little, Brown & Co.

BELL, BOOK AND CANDLE, by John van Druten. Random House.
THE COUNTRY GIRL, by Clifford Odets. Viking Press.
THE ROSE TATTOO, by Tennessee Williams. New Directions.
SEASON IN THE SUN, by Wolcott Gibbs. Random House.
AFFAIRS OF STATE, by Louis Verneuil.
SECOND THRESHOLD, by Philip Barry. Harper & Bros.

1951-1952

MRS. MCTHING, by Mary Coyle Chase.
THE SHRIKE, by Joseph Kramm. Random House.
I AM A CAMERA, by John van Druten. Random House.
THE FOURPOSTER, by Jan de Hartog.
POINT OF NO RETURN, by Paul Osborn. Random House.
BAREFOOT IN ATHENS, by Maxwell Anderson. Sloane.
VENUS OBSERVED, by Christopher Fry. Oxford.
JANE, by S. N. Behrman and Somerset Maugham. Random House.
GIGI, by Anita Loos and Colette. Random House.
REMAINS TO BE SEEN, by Howard Lindsay and Russel Crouse.
    Random House.

1952-1953

THE TIME OF THE CUCKOO, by Arthur Laurents. Random House.
BERNARDINE, by Mary Coyle Chase.
DIAL "M" FOR MURDER, by Frederick Knott. Random House.
THE CLIMATE OF EDEN, by Moss Hart. Random House.
THE LOVE OF FOUR COLONELS, by Peter Ustinov.
THE CRUCIBLE, by Arthur Miller. Viking.
THE EMPEROR'S CLOTHES, by George Tabori. Samuel French.
PICNIC, by William Inge. Random House.
WONDERFUL TOWN, by Joseph Fields, Jerome Chodorov, Betty
    Comden and Adolph Green. Random House.
MY 3 ANGELS, by Sam and Bella Spewack.

1953-1954

THE CAINE MUTINY COURT-MARTIAL, by Herman Wouk. Double-
    day & Company, Inc.
IN THE SUMMER HOUSE, by Jane Bowles. Random House.
THE CONFIDENTIAL CLERK, by T. S. Eliot. Harcourt, Brace and
    Company, Inc.
TAKE A GIANT STEP, by Louis Peterson.
THE TEAHOUSE OF THE AUGUST MOON, by John Patrick. G. P.
    Putnam's Sons.

THE IMMORALIST, by Ruth and Augustus Goetz. Ruth and Augustus Goetz. Dramatists' Play Service.

TEA AND SYMPATHY, by Robert Anderson. Random House.

THE GIRL ON THE VIA FLAMINIA, by Alfred Hayes.

THE GOLDEN APPLE, by John Latouche and Jerome Moross. Random House.

THE MAGIC AND THE LOSS, by Julian Funt. Samuel French.

1954-1955

THE BOY FRIEND, by Sandy Wilson.

THE LIVING ROOM, by Graham Greene. Viking.

BAD SEED, by Maxwell Anderson. Dodd, Mead.

WITNESS FOR THE PROSECUTION, by Agatha Christie.

THE FLOWERING PEACH, by Clifford Odets.

THE DESPERATE HOURS, by Joseph Hayes. Random House.

THE DARK IS LIGHT ENOUGH, by Christopher Fry. Oxford.

BUS STOP, by William Inge. Random House.

CAT ON A HOT TIN ROOF, by Tennessee Williams. New Directions.

INHERIT THE WIND, by Jerome Lawrence and Robert E. Lee. Random House.

1955-1956

A VIEW FROM THE BRIDGE, by Arthur Miller. Viking.

TIGER AT THE GATES, by Jean Giraudoux, translated by Christopher Fry. Oxford.

THE DIARY OF ANNE FRANK, by Frances Goodrich and Albert Hackett. Random House.

NO TIME FOR SERGEANTS, by Ira Levin. Random House.

THE CHALK GARDEN, by Enid Bagnold. Random House.

THE LARK, by Jean Anouilh, adapted by Lillian Hellman. Random House.

THE MATCHMAKER, by Thornton Wilder. Harper.

THE PONDER HEART, by Joseph Fields and Jerome Chodorov. Random House.

MY FAIR LADY, by Alan Jay Lerner and Frederick Loewe. Coward-McCann.

WAITING FOR GODOT, by Samuel Beckett. Grove.

WHERE AND WHEN THEY WERE BORN

(Compiled from the most authentic records available)

Abbott, George .... Forestville, N. Y. 1889
Abel, Walter .... St. Paul, Minn. 1898
Addy, Wesley .... Omaha, Neb. 1912
Adler, Luther .... New York City 1903
Aherne, Brian .... King's Norton, England 1902
Aldrich, Richard .... Boston, Mass. 1902
Anderson, Judith .... Australia 1898
Anderson, Maxwell .... Atlantic City, Pa. 1888
Anderson, Robert .... New York City 1917
Andrews, Julie .... London, England 1935
Arthur, Jean .... New York City 1905
Ashcroft, Peggy .... Croydon, England 1907
Atkinson, Brooks .... Melrose, Mass. 1894

Bainter, Fay .... Los Angeles, Cal. 1892
Bankhead, Tallulah .... Huntsville, Ala. 1902
Barrymore, Ethel .... Philadelphia, Pa. 1879
Barton, James .... Gloucester, N. J. 1890
Begley, Ed .... Hartford, Conn. 1901
Behrman, S. N. .... Worcester, Mass. 1893
Bellamy, Ralph .... Chicago, Ill. 1904
Bergman, Ingrid .... Stockholm, Sweden 1917
Bergner, Elisabeth .... Vienna, Austria 1900
Berlin, Irving .... Russia 1888
Bernstein, Leonard .... Brookline, Mass. 1918
Best, Edna .... Hove, England 1900
Blackmer, Sidney .... Salisbury, N. C. 1898
Blaine, Vivian .... Newark, N. J. 1923
Bolger, Ray .... Dorchester, Mass. 1904
Bondi, Beulah .... Chicago, Ill. 1892
Booth, Shirley .... New York City 1909
Bourneuf, Philip .... Boston, Mass. 1912
Boyer, Charles .... Figeac, France 1899
Brando, Marlon .... Omaha, Neb. 1924

Brent, Romney .... Saltillo, Mex. 1902
Brown, Joe E. .... Holgate, Ohio 1892
Burke, Billie .... Washington, D. C. 1895
Byington, Spring .... Colorado Springs, Colo. 1898

Cagney, James .... New York City 1904
Cantor, Eddie .... New York City 1892
Carnovsky, Morris .... St. Louis, Mo. 1898
Carradine, John .... New York City 1906
Carroll, Leo G. .... Weedon, England 1892
Carroll, Madeleine .... West Bromwich, England 1906
Channing, Carol .... Seattle, Wash. 1921
Chase, Ilka .... New York City 1905
Chatterton, Ruth .... New York City 1893
Claire, Ina .... Washington, D. C. 1895
Clark, Bobby .... Springfield, Ohio 1888
Clift, Montgomery .... Omaha, Neb. 1921
Clurman, Harold .... New York City 1901
Cobb, Lee .... New York City 1911
Coburn, Charles .... Macon, Ga. 1877
Collinge, Patricia .... Dublin, Ireland 1894
Collins, Russell .... New Orleans, La. 1897
Conroy, Frank .... London, England 1885
Cook, Donald .... Portland, Ore. 1902
Cook, Joe .... Evansville, Ind. 1890
Cooper, Gladys .... Lewisham, England 1888
Cooper, Melville .... Birmingham, England 1896
Corbett, Leonora .... London, England 1908
Cornell, Katharine .... Berlin, Germany 1898
Coulouris, George .... Manchester, England 1906
Coward, Noel .... Teddington, England 1899
Crawford, Cheryl .... Akron, Ohio 1902
Cromwell, John .... Toledo, Ohio 1888
Cronyn, Hume .... London, Ontario 1912
Crothers, Rachel .... Bloomington, Ill. 1878
Crouse, Russel .... Findlay, Ohio 1893
Cummings, Constance .... Seattle, Wash. 1911

Dale, Margaret .... Philadelphia, Pa. 1880
Dana, Leora .... New York City 1923
Daniell, Henry .... London, England 1894
Derwent, Clarence .... London, England 1884
Douglas, Melvyn .... Macon, Ga. 1901

Dowling, Eddie .... Woonsocket, R. I. 1894
Drake, Alfred .... New York City 1914
Duncan, Todd .... Danville, Ky. 1900
Dunning, Philip .... Meriden, Conn. 1890
Durante, Jimmy .... New York City 1893

Eldridge, Florence .... Brooklyn, N. Y. 1901
Eliot, T. S. .... St. Louis, Mo. 1888
Elsom, Isobel .... Cambridge, England 1893
Evans, Edith .... London, England 1888
Evans, Maurice .... Dorchester, England 1901
Evans, Wilbur .... Philadelphia, Pa. 1908
Evelyn, Judith .... Seneca, S. Dak. 1913
Ewell, Tom .... Owensboro, Ky. 1912

Fabray, Nanette .... New Orleans, La. 1921
Fay, Frank .... San Francisco, Cal. 1897
Ferber, Edna .... Kalamazoo, Mich. 1887
Ferrer, José .... Puerto Rico 1912
Field, Betty .... Boston, Mass. 1918
Field, Virginia .... London, England 1917
Fields, Gracie .... Rochdale, England 1898
Fitzgerald, Barry .... Dublin, Ireland 1888
Fitzgerald, Geraldine .... Dublin, Ireland 1914
Flemyng, Robert .... Liverpool, England 1912
Fletcher, Bramwell .... Bradford, Yorkshire, Eng. 1904
Fonda, Henry .... Grand Island, Neb. 1905
Fontanne, Lynn .... London, England 1887
Forbes, Brenda .... London, England 1909
Foy, Eddie, Jr. .... New Rochelle, N. Y. 1907
Francis, Arlene .... Boston, Mass. 1908
Fry, Christopher .... England 1907

Gahagan, Helen .... Boonton, N. J. 1900
Gaxton, William .... San Francisco, Cal. 1893
Gazzara, Ben .... New York City 1930
Geddes, Barbara Bel .... New York City 1922
Geddes, Norman Bel ... . Adrian, Mich. 1893
George, Grace .... New York City 1879
Gershwin, Ira .... New York City 1896
Gielgud, Sir John .... London, England 1904
Gillmore, Margalo .... England 1901
Gilmore, Virginia .... El Monte, Cal. 1919

Gish, Dorothy .... Massillon, Ohio 1898
Gish, Lillian .... Springfield, Ohio 1896
Gordon, Ruth .... Wollaston, Mass. 1896
Green, Martyn .... London, England 1899
Greenwood, Joan .... London, England 1921
Guinness, Alec .... London, England 1914
Guthrie, Tyrone .... Tunbridge Wells, England 1900
Gwenn, Edmund .... Glamorgan, Wales 1875

Hagen, Uta .... Göttingen, Germany 1919
Hammerstein, Oscar, II ...... New York City 1895
Hardie, Russell .... Griffin Mills, N. Y. 1906
Hardwicke, Sir Cedric .... Lye, Stourbridge, England ... 1893
Harris, Julie .... Grosse Point, Mich. 1925
Harrison, Rex .... Huyton, Lancashire, England .. 1908
Hart, Moss .... New York City 1904
Havoc, June .... Seattle, Wash. 1916
Haydon, Julie .... Oak Park, Ill. 1910
Hayes, Helen .... Washington, D. C. 1900
Hayward, Leland .... Nebraska City, Neb. 1902
Heflin, Frances .... Oklahoma City, Okla. 1924
Hellman, Lillian .... New Orleans, La. 1905
Helmore, Tom .... London, England 1912
Helpmann, Robert .... South Australia 1911
Henie, Sonja .... Oslo, Norway 1913
Hepburn, Audrey .... Brussels, Belgium 1929
Hepburn, Katharine .... Hartford, Conn. 1909
Herlie, Eileen .... Glasgow, Scotland 1920
Hiller, Wendy .... Bramhall, England 1912
Holliday, Judy .... New York City 1924
Holloway, Stanley .... London, England 1890
Holm, Celeste .... New York City 1919
Homolka, Oscar .... Vienna, Austria 1898
Hull, Henry .... Louisville, Ky. 1890
Hunt, Martita .... Argentine Republic 1900
Hunter, Kim .... Detroit, Mich. 1922
Hussey, Ruth .... Providence, R. I. 1917

Ives, Burl .... Hunt Township, Ill. 1909

Johnson, Harold J. (Chic) ... Chicago, Ill. 1891
Joy, Nicholas .... Paris, France 1889

Kanin, Garson .... Rochester, N. Y. 1912
Karloff, Boris .... Dulwich, England 1887
Kaufman, George S. .... Pittsburgh, Pa. 1889
Kaye, Danny .... New York City 1914
Kazan, Elia .... Constantinople 1909
Keith, Robert .... Fowler, Ind. 1898
Kennedy, Arthur .... Worcester, Mass. 1914
Kerr, Deborah .... Helensburgh, Scotland 1921
Kerr, John .... New York City 1931
Killbride, Percy .... San Francisco, Cal. 1880
King, Dennis .... Coventry, England 1897
Kingsley, Sidney .... New York City 1906
Kirkland, Patricia .... New York City 1927
Knox, Alexander .... Ontario 1907
Kruger, Otto .... Toledo, Ohio 1885

Lahr, Bert .... New York City 1895
Landis, Jessie Royce .... Chicago, Ill. 1904
Laughton, Charles .... Scarborough, England 1899
Laurents, Arthur .... New York City 1920
LeGallienne, Eva .... London, England 1899
Leigh, Vivien .... Darjeeling, India 1913
Leighton, Margaret .... Barnt Green, England 1922
Lerner, Alan Jay .... New York City 1918
Lillie, Beatrice .... Toronto, Canada 1898
Lindsay, Howard .... Waterford, N. Y. 1899
Linn, Bambi .... Brooklyn, N. Y. 1926
Logan, Joshua .... Texarkana, Tex. 1908
Lukas, Paul .... Budapest, Hungary 1891
Lunt, Alfred .... Milwaukee, Wis. 1893

MacGrath, Leueen .... London, England 1914
MacMahon, Aline .... McKeesport, Pa. 1899
Mamoulian, Rouben .... Tiflis, Russia 1898
Mann, Iris .... Brooklyn, N. Y. 1939
Marceau, Marcel .... Near Strasbourg, France 1923
March, Fredric .... Racine, Wis. 1897
Martin, Mary .... Weatherford, Texas 1913
Mason, James .... Huddersfield, England 1909
Massey, Raymond .... Toronto, Canada 1896
Maugham, W. Somerset ..... England 1874
McClintic, Guthrie .... Seattle, Wash. 1893
McCormick, Myron .... Albany, Ind. 1907

McCracken, Joan .... Philadelphia, Pa. 1923
McDowall, Roddy .... London, England 1928
McGrath, Paul .... Chicago, Ill. 1900
McGuire, Dorothy .... Omaha, Neb. 1918
McKenna, Siobhan .... Belfast, Ireland 1923
Menotti, Gian-Carlo .... Italy 1912
Meredith, Burgess .... Cleveland, Ohio 1908
Merkel, Una .... Covington, Ky. 1903
Merman, Ethel .... Astoria, L. I. 1909
Middleton, Ray .... Chicago, Ill. 1907
Mielziner, Jo .... Paris, France 1901
Miller, Arthur .... New York City 1915
Miller, Gilbert .... New York City 1884
Mitchell, Thomas .... Elizabeth, N. J. 1892
Moore, Victor .... Hammonton, N. J. 1876
Moorehead, Agnes .... Clinton, Mass. 1906
Morgan, Claudia .... New York City 1912
Morley, Robert .... Semley, England 1908
Moss, Arnold .... Brooklyn, N. Y. 1910
Muni, Paul .... Lemberg, Austria 1895

Nagel, Conrad .... Keokuk, Iowa 1897
Natwick, Mildred .... Baltimore, Md. 1908
Neal, Patricia .... Packard, Ky. 1926
Nesbitt, Cathleen .... Cheshire, England 1889
Nugent, Elliott .... Dover, Ohio 1900

Odets, Clifford .... Philadelphia, Pa. 1906
Oenslager, Donald .... Harrisburg, Pa. 1902
Olivier, Sir Laurence .... Dorking, Surrey, England 1907
Olsen, John Siguard (Ole) ... Peru, Ind. 1892
O'Malley, Rex .... London, England 1906
O'Neal, Frederick .... Brookville, Miss. 1905
Osborn, Paul .... Evansville, Ind. 1901

Page, Geraldine .... Kirksville, Mo. 1925
Palmer, Lilli .... Posen, Austria 1914
Petina, Irra .... Leningrad, Russia 1900
Picon, Molly .... New York City 1898
Porter, Cole .... Peru, Ind. 1892
Portman, Eric .... Yorkshire, England 1903
Price, Vincent .... St. Louis, Mo. 1914

Quayle, Anthony .... Ainsdale, England 1913

Rains, Claude .... London, England 1889
Raitt, John .... Santa Ana, Cal. 1917
Rathbone, Basil .... Johannesburg, Africa 1892
Rattigan, Terence .... London, England 1911
Redgrave, Michael .... Bristol, England 1908
Redman, Joyce .... Newcastle, Ireland 1918
Reed, Florence .... Philadelphia, Pa. 1883
Rennie, James .... Toronto, Canada 1890
Rice, Elmer .... New York City 1892
Richardson, Sir Ralph .... Cheltenham, England 1902
Ritchard, Cyril .... Sydney, Australia 1898
Rodgers, Richard .... New York City 1902
Royle, Selena .... New York City 1905
Russell, Rosalind .... Waterbury, Conn. 1911

Sarnoff, Dorothy .... Brooklyn, N. Y. 1919
Saroyan, William .... Fresno, Cal. 1908
Schildkraut, Joseph .... Vienna, Austria 1895
Scott, Martha .... Jamesport, Mo. 1914
Segal, Vivienne .... Philadelphia, Pa. 1897
Sherman, Hiram .... Boston, Mass. 1908
Shumlin, Herman .... Atwood, Colo. 1898
Silvers, Phil .... Brooklyn, N. Y. 1911
Simms, Hilda .... Minneapolis, Minn. 1920
Skinner, Cornelia Otis .... Chicago, Ill. 1902
Slezak, Walter .... Vienna, Austria 1902
Smith, Kent .... Smithfield, Me. 1910
Stanley, Kim .... Tularosa, N. M. 1921
Stapleton, Maureen .... Troy, N. Y. 1926
Starr, Frances .... Oneonta, N. Y. 1886
Stickney, Dorothy .... Dickinson, N. D. 1903
Stone, Carol .... New York City 1917
Stone, Dorothy .... New York City 1905
Stone, Ezra .... New Bedford, Mass. 1918
Stone, Fred .... Denver, Colo. 1873
Straight, Beatrice .... Old Westbury, N. Y. 1918
Sullavan, Margaret .... Norfolk, Va. 1910

Tandy, Jessica .... London, England 1909
Tetzel, Joan .... New York City 1923
Thorndike, Sybil .... Gainsborough, England 1882

Tone, Franchot .... Niagara Falls, N. Y. 1906
Tozere, Frederick .... Brookline, Mass. 1901
Tracy, Lee .... Atlanta, Ga. 1898
Truex, Ernest .... Red Hill, Mo. 1890

van Druten, John .... London, England 1902
Van Patten, Dick .... New York City 1929
Varden, Evelyn .... Venita, Okla. 1893
Verdon, Gwen .... Culver City, Cal. 1926

Walker, June .... New York City 1904
Walker, Nancy .... Philadelphia, Pa. 1922
Wallach, Eli .... Brooklyn, N. Y. 1915
Wanamaker, Sam .... Chicago, Ill. 1919
Waring, Richard .... Buckinghamshire, England ... 1912
Waters, Ethel .... Chester, Pa. 1900
Watson, Douglas .... Jackson, Ga. 1921
Watson, Lucile .... Quebec, Canada 1879
Wayne, David .... Travers City, Mich. 1914
Webb, Alan .... York, England 1906
Webb, Clifton .... Indiana 1891
Webster, Margaret .... New York City 1905
Welles, Orson .... Kenosha, Wis. 1915
West, Mae .... Brooklyn, N. Y. 1892
Weston, Ruth .... Boston, Mass. 1911
Widmark, Richard .... Sunrise, Minn. 1914
Wilder, Thornton .... Madison, Wis. 1897
Williams, Emlyn .... Wales 1905
Williams, Rhys .... Wales 1903
Williams, Tennessee .... Columbus, Miss. 1914
Winwood, Estelle .... England 1883
Wood, Peggy .... Brooklyn, N. Y. 1894
Wyatt, Jane .... Campgaw, N. J. 1912
Wynn, Ed .... Philadelphia, Pa. 1886
Wynn, Keenan .... New York City 1917

Yurka, Blanche .... Bohemia 1893

NECROLOGY

June 1, 1956—May 31, 1957

Anderson, Phyllis Stohl, 49, producer. She received a B.A. from the University of Utah and a Master of Fine Arts in drama from Yale. She headed the drama department of the Erskine School in Boston and directed plays for Harvard, Radcliff and Wellesley Dramatic Clubs. For seven years she was head of the play department of the Theatre Guild and was associate producer with them of William Inge's play "Come Back, Little Sheba." She was the wife of playwright Robert Anderson ("Tea and Sympathy"). Born Brigham City, Utah; died New York, Nov. 28, 1956.

Arlen, Michael, 60, author. He wrote many novels and short stories, but the theatre knew him best for his dramatization of his novel "The Green Hat," which starred Katharine Cornell. He also wrote several motion pictures. Born Bulgaria; died New York, June 23, 1956.

Baker, Belle, 62, actress, singer. At 20 she was a star in vaudeville at the Palace, New York, sharing the program with Sarah Bernhardt. She began her career when Jacob Adler hired her for a part in his drama "The Homeless." In 1926 she starred in "Betsy" and was in several editions of "The Ziegfeld Follies." She introduced, in all, 163 songs and was a great success in England as well as America. Born New York; died Los Angeles, April 28, 1957.

Ballin, Hugo, 76, producer, director, painter. He studied painting in Rome and Florence. He went to Los Angeles 35 years ago and was in turn an art director, director and independent producer. He produced more than 100 motion pictures, among them "Pagan Love," "Baby Mine," "Jane Eyre" and his fine modernized "East Lynne." He was also famous as a mural painter, having done work in the Wisconsin State Capitol, the Carew Memorial Chapel in San Francisco and the B'nai B'rith Temple in Los Angeles. His wife, Mabel Ballin, was a well-known motion picture star and was in many of his films. Born New York; died Santa Monica, Calif., Nov. 27, 1956.

Bancroft, George, 74, actor. He spend his early life in the Navy. He became a Broadway actor in such plays as "The Trail of the Lonesome Pine" and "Paid in Full." His first Hollywood picture was "Code of the West," and he had many roles between 1929 and 1942 while under contract to Paramount. He usually portrayed such types as the gangster bully, the Western bad man, the Wall Street stock swindler or the political dictator. Born Philadelphia; died Los Angeles, Oct. 2, 1956.

Bedini, Jean, 85, producer. During the first 30 years of this century he was a leading producer of revues, vaudeville acts and burlesque shows. He is credited with having given Eddie Cantor, Clark & McCullough and many others their first professional chance. He produced "The Yankee Doodle Girl" and other shows in London and European cities. Birthplace not given; died New York, Nov. 8, 1956.

Belasco, Genevieve, 84, actress. A second cousin of David Belasco, she was said to have been the inspiration for Tosti's "Goodbye." For several years, as Genevieve Dolaro, she was with Weber and Fields. Other plays here include "Kismet," "Blood and Sand," "Zaza" and "Aphrodite." She made several motion pictures and performed on radio. Born London; died New York, Nov. 17, 1956.

Bogart, Humphrey, 57, actor. He attended Trinity School and Andover. His early stage roles in the twenties were in such plays as "Hell's Bells," "Cradle Snatchers," "Saturday's Children" and "It's a Wise Child." His most memorable Broadway role was that of Duke Mantee in "The Petrified Forest." He played the same role in pictures and this launched him on a tremendously successful screen career. He was in "Dead End," "The Maltese Falcon," "San Quentin," "Casablanca," "Key Largo," "The Big Sleep," "The Treasure of the Sierra Madre," "Sabrina" and a great many other films. He won an Oscar for his screen role in "The African Queen." Born New York; died Hollywood, Jan. 14, 1957.

Brecht, Bertolt, 58, playwright. One of Germany's most provocative playwrights, he wrote the libretto for the late Kurt Weill's "Threepenny Opera" recently revived Off Broadway with enormous success. After World War I he took over the Theatre am Schiffbauerdamm in Berlin, where he trained such actors as Peter Lorre and Oscar Homolka. His New York productions include "Mother" (1935), "Justice" (1938—Off Broadway), "The Private Life of the Master Race" (1945—Off Broadway) and "Galileo" (1947). A refugee from Hitler's Germany, he went to Switzerland in 1933. Later he lived in the Soviet Union and the United States. He spent some time in Hollywood and in 1947 was called before the House Committee on Un-American Activities which was investigating Communist influence in Hollywood. He testified that he was not and never had been a member of any Communist party; shortly thereafter he moved to East Berlin. Born Ausburg, Bavaria; died East Germany, Aug. 14, 1956.

Buck, Gene, 71, song writer and producer. Received his early schooling in Detroit and went to the Detroit Art School. He created over 5000 posterlike song covers. In 1911 he wrote "Daddy Has a Sweetheart and Mother is Her Name." He designed and directed an act for Lillian Lorraine, was then engaged by Florenz Ziegfeld and wrote most of the twenty editions of the "Follies" and sixteen editions of "Midnight Frolics." He discovered such stars as Ed Wynn, Eddie Cantor, Will Rogers and Joe Frisco as well as scenic artist Josef Urban. In 1926 he became an independent producer with "Yours Truly." He was president of ASCAP from 1924 to 1941, also president of The Catholic Actors' Guild. Among his songs were "Hello Frisco," "Garden of Dreams" and "Maybe." In 1940 he received the Henry Hadley Medal of the National Association of American Composers and Conductors in recognition of his effort to advance the cause of American music. Born Detroit; died Great Neck, L. I., Feb. 24, 1957.

Buckley, Floyd, 82, actor. He served as one of Theodore Roosevelt's Rough Riders and in 1899 joined Buffalo Bill's Wild West Show. He made his Broadway debut in 1903 in "The Fisher Maiden." On radio he was "Popeye the Sailor" and he also appeared in many films. At the time of his death he was appearing in "No Time for Sergeants" and was Broadway's oldest active performer. Born Chatham, N. Y.; died New York, Nov. 14, 1956.

Carroll, Albert, 61, actor. He began his career in Chicago at 16 and later came to New York, appearing in interludes between silent motion picture shows at the old Neighborhood Playhouse in Grand Street. He became a star of "The Grand Street Follies" and was in them when they moved uptown to Broadway. As an impersonator he won acclaim for his satires on famous persons. He was also seen in "The Dybbuk," "Lovers and Enemies," "Hamlet" (with Leslie Howard), "The Duke of Darkness" and others. He was in many musicals at the Paper Mill Playhouse in Millburn, N. J., and also at Highland Park. Born Chicago; died Chicago, Dec. 1, 1956.

Clapp, Charles Edwin, Jr., 57, writer, producer. A graduate of Hotchkiss and Yale, he was the author of three published books and many magazine and newspaper articles. In the twenties he was co-producer of two Broadway hits, "The Cat and the Canary" and "The Goose Hangs High." Born Pittsburgh; died Charlottesville, Va., Jan. 2, 1957.

Crawford, Anne, 35, actress. She was well known on the English stage, screen, radio and television. Her latest role in London was as the star of Agatha Christie's "Spider's Web." Her only appearance on Broadway was in the revival of "The Green Bay Tree" in 1951. Born Halfa; died London, Oct. 17, 1956.

Davis, Owen, 82, playright. He was America's most prolific and most produced playwright, being credited with more than 200 plays. He attended the University of Tennessee and Harvard. His first play, he said, was "Through the Breakers" produced in Bridgeport, Conn., in the nineties. For years he wrote popular-priced melodramas and when melodrama went out of fashion he gave his characters more sophistication and moved them into the drawing room. His plays include: "Her One False Step," "Nellie, the Beautiful Cloak Model," "Broadway After Dark," "Mile-a-Minute Kendall," "The Nervous Wreck," "The Detour" and the Pulitzer-Prize winner for 1923, "Icebound." Born Portland, Maine; died New York, Oct. 14, 1956.

Doro, Marie, 74, actress. She studied in private schools in New York and her first appearance on the stage was in St. Paul in 1901 in "Aristocracy." Until her retirement some twenty-odd years ago she appeared constantly in America and England and made pictures in Italy, France, England and America. William Gillette wrote "Clarice" for her and himself in 1905, and she was also with him in "The Admirable Crichton," "Diplomacy" and "Sherlock Holmes." In 1914 she played a command performance of "Diplomacy" before the King and Queen of England at Windsor Castle. She was famous in the title role of "Oliver Twist" and did the same role in pictures. She was a trained musician and wrote many popular songs. Her real name was Stewart. Born Duncannon, Pa.; died New York, Oct. 9, 1956.

Draper, Ruth, 72, monologuist. She was educated privately and as a girl attracted attention and the praise of distinguished people by her imitations in private homes. In 1915 she began doing her monologues professionally. She always wrote her own material. During her forty years on the stage she was painted by John Singer Sargent, gave a command performance at Windsor Castle, received honorary degrees from universities in this country and Britain and was made a Commander of the Order of the British Empire. Her only appearance in a play was in 1916 in "A Lady's Name" with Marie Tempest, in New York. Born New York; died New York, Dec. 30, 1956.

du Pont, Paul, 51, costume designer. He was trained as a singer and studied painting in Vienna. In 1923 he appeared with a ballet troupe in Chicago. His first designing was done for the Group Theatre and the Theatre Guild. In all, he did the costumes for 64 Broadway shows, among them "Porgy and Bess," "One Touch of Venus" and "Oh, Men! Oh, Women!" Born Bradford, Pa.; died New York, April 20, 1957.

Eaton, Walter Prichard, 78, drama teacher and author. He began his theatre career in 1902 as assistant drama critic on the New York Tribune, later becoming drama critic of The New York Sun. He was Professor of Playwriting at Yale University from 1933 to 1947. He wrote such books as "Plays and Players," "An Actor's Heritage" and "Ten Years of the Theatre Guild." He also wrote book reviews and articles for magazines. Born Malden, Mass.; died Chapel Hill, N. C., Feb. 26, 1957.

Eythe, William, 38, actor. A graduate of Carnegie Tech., in 1941 he began his career in stock. Later he came to New York and was in "The Moon Is Down." This was followed by such motion pictures as "The Eve of St. Mark" and "A Royal Scandal." He played the lead and was co-producer of the musical revue "Lend An Ear." Other Broadway productions in which he appeared were "The Liar" and "Out of This World." Born Mars, Pa.; died Hollywood, Jan. 26, 1957.

Garr, Eddie, 56, comedian. A night-club entertainer who for three years—one of them on Broadway—played Jeeter Lester in "Tobacco Road." He was also seen in "Thumbs Up," "Strike Me Pink" and "Hit the Deck." Born Philadelphia, Pa.; died Hollywood, Sept. 3, 1956.

Gildea, Mary, 70, actress. She made her stage debut in 1903 in the chorus of "The Governor's Lady," the first of a series of George M. Cohan productions in which she appeared. She turned to comedy in George Kelly's "The Torchbearers" and was afterwards in "Craig's Wife," "Philip Goes Forth," "Reunion in Vienna" and several others. Her most recent role was in "The Desk Set." Birth place not given; died upstate N. Y., Feb. 19, 1957.

Granlund, Nils T., 65, producer. He won early success as a motion-picture press agent and later became a great radio personality and night-club showman. During the twenties his initials

N. T. G. were famous in the entertainment field and his "girlie shows" were known from coast to coast. He was well known for poetry recitations on radio. He operated the Hollywood Restaurant and The Paradise on Broadway and the Florentine Gardens in Hollywood. He was an M.C. on early television shows. Born in Lapland; died Las Vegas, Nev., April 21, 1957.

Hale, George, 54, dance director. Starting as a tap dancer, he became a producer and director of musical numbers. He was the choreographer for many Broadway shows including "Heads Up," "Strike Up the Band," "Girl Crazy," "Of Thee I Sing" and "Red, Hot and Blue." He had also worked on musicals for Florenz Ziegfeld and George White. Born New York; died New York, Aug. 15, 1956.

Hersholt, Jean, 69, actor. He began performing screen roles in 1905 and continued for 50 years, playing more than 450 characters. He was in the first motion picture made in his native Denmark. He took his first Hollywood job in 1914. He was well known in films and on radio in the role of Dr. Christian. For four years he was President of the Academy of Motion Picture Arts and Sciences and received two special Oscars, 1939 and 1941, for his activities on behalf of his fellow actors. Born Copenhagen, Denmark; died Hollywood, June 2, 1956.

Hughes, Rupert, 84, author. His first published stories were serials for boys in St. Nicholas Magazine. He became a popular magazine and fiction writer and published a number of historical novels. He wrote plays and several motion pictures, among the latter being "The Wall Flower" starring Colleen Moore and Richard Dix, which he also directed. Born Lancaster, Mo.; died Los Angeles, Sept. 9, 1956.

Hull, Josephine, 71, actress. Under her maiden name of Josephine Sherwood she went on the stage in 1902, playing in Boston and around the country. Upon her marriage to Shelly Hull in 1910 she retired; after his death in 1919 she returned to the stage. She first attracted attention in 1924 in "Neighbors." This was followed by "Craig's Wife," "The Wild Man of Borneo," "Those We Love" and others. She was extraordinarily popular for her performances in "You Can't Take It with You," "Arsenic and Old Lace" and "Harvey." She officially became a star when in her sixties in "The Golden State" and was more recently starred in "The Solid Gold Cadillac." She made the the motion picture of "Arsenic and Old Lace" and won an Oscar for her performance in the movie version of "Harvey." Born Newtonville, Mass.; died Bronx, N. Y., March 12, 1957.

John, Alice, 75, actress. She came to this country as a child and her first stage appearances were in Chicago. She played with John Drew and was with Mrs. Fiske's traveling troupe in such plays as "Salvation Nell" and "Vanity Fair." She was with John and Lionel Barrymore in "Peter Ibbetson" and with Eva Le Gallienne in "The Swan." Her last role in New York was in "Crime and Punishment" in 1947. Born Llanelly, Wales; died Binghamton, N. Y., Aug. 9, 1956.

Johnson, William, 41, actor, singer. An engineering graduate of the University of Maryland, he started as a singer with his college band. Later he was a staff vocalist for NBC. In 1941 he was a juvenile in "Banjo Eyes" with Eddie Cantor, and later was with Ethel Merman in "Something for the Boys." He made one or two motion pictures in Hollywood and returned to Broadway in 1945 in "The Day Before Spring." Two years later he went to London to play Frank Butler in "Annie Get Your Gun" opposite Dolores Gray. Late in 1955 Broadway saw him in "Pipe Dream" with Helen Traubel and Judy Tyler. Born Baltimore, Md.; died Flemington, N. J., March 6, 1957.

Kane, Whitford, 75, actor. He toured in repertory in the British Isles before he came to the United States in 1912. He was in 56 Broadway shows, including a couple of dozen productions of "Hamlet," including those of John Barrymore, Walter Hampden and Maurice Evans. He was First Gravedigger for more than 40 Ophelias. Some of his other appearances were in "Hobson's Choice," "Tiger! Tiger!," "The Pigeon," "Children of the Moon," "Elizabeth the Queen," "The First Legion," "Excursion" and "Red Roses for Me." For David Belasco he wrote "Dark Rosaleen," produced in 1919. He also made several motion pictures. Born Larne, Ireland; died New York, Dec. 17, 1956.

Kelly, Paul, 57, actor. He made his stage debut at the age of eight in Belasco's production of "The Grand Army Man" and made his film debut that same year. "Seventeen" was his first big role, followed by "Penrod" and "Up the Ladder." In 1926 he went to Hollywood for several pictures. In 1930 he returned to Broadway appearing in "Bad Girl," "Just Remind You" and "Adam Had Two Sons." Perhaps his greatest success was in "Command Decision" in 1948. Born Brooklyn, N. Y.; died Hollywood, Nov. 6, 1956.

Kerby, Marion, 79, actress. She began her stage career at the turn of the century. Her best remembered performance was her portrayal of the mean sister in the original Broadway production of "Seventh Heaven" with Helen Menken. During the past few years she received wide recognition as a singer and collector of Negro spirituals and Kentucky mountain songs. Born in the South; died Hollywood, Dec. 18, 1956.

Latouche, John, 38, composer and lyricist. He attended the Richmond (Va.) Academy of Arts and Sciences, later coming to New York to go to Riverdale Preparatory School and Columbia. In his sophomore year at the latter he wrote the book and lyrics and some of the music for the Varsity Show. Some of his sketches and lyrics were in "Pins and Needles." He also did "Banjo Eyes," "Cabin in the Sky" and "The Golden Apple." His "Ballad for Americans" is especially well known. Born Richmond, Va.; died Calais, Vt., Aug. 7, 1956.

Lawton, Thais, 78, actress. She made her New York debut in "Lost River" in 1900 and later played Mercedes in James O'Neill's company of "The Count of Monte Cristo." She was under the direction of Winthrop Ames as a member of the New Theatre company and was prominently active in the American theatre since then. Her plays include "The Revellers," "The Blue Bird," "The Masqueraders," "A Royal Virgin" and "Love in My Fashion." Her last role was in "Romance of Mr. Dickens" in 1940. Born in Louisville, Ky.; died New York, Aug. 18, 1956.

Lockhart, Gene, 66, actor. He made his professional debut at the age of six, in Canada, and at 15 played in sketches with Beatrice Lillie. With Deems Taylor he composed "The World Is Waiting for the Sunrise." His first Broadway appearance was in "The Riviera Girl" in 1916. He was the star and co-author of "Bunk of 1926." He was lauded for his performance in "Ah! Wilderness" and in "Death of a Salesman," in which he replaced Lee J. Cobb. He made over 300 pictures, including "The House on 92nd Street," "Joan of Arc" and "Miracle on 34th Street." Born London, Ontario; died Santa Monica, Calif., March 31, 1957.

Lugosi, Bela, 71, actor. He studied at the Academy of Theatrical Art in Budapest and began his acting career in 1900. In 1911 he was leading man at the Magyar Szinhaz in Budapest and later became leading man at the Royal Hungarian National Theatre. His first appearance in New York was in "The Red Poppy" in 1922. There followed such plays as "Arabesque," "Open House," "Devil in the Cheese" and the very successful "Dracula." He also made such movies as "The

Wolf Man," "The Ghost of Frankenstein" and "Ninotchka." Born Lugis, Hungary; died Los Angeles, Aug. 16, 1956.

MacKaye, Percy, 81, dramatist. Son of the famous Steele MacKaye, he was born into the theatre and was well known on Broadway early in the century as a pioneering dramatist writing pageants and plays in verse. He graduated from Harvard and later studied at the University of Leipzig. The first fellowship in creative literature in the United States was founded for him at the University of Miami in 1900. He had many honorary degrees and awards. In all he wrote 25 plays produced on Broadway and more than a hundred books of poetry, essays and biography. In 1949 he completed his biggest work, a tetrology entitled "The Mystery of Hamlet, King of Denmark." It was produced at the Pasadena Playhouse in California. Born New York; died Cornish, N. H., Aug. 31, 1956.

Magrane, Thais, 79, actress. She began her career in 1902 in vaudeville. David Belasco then engaged her for "Naughty Anthony," and she appeared in many stock and repertory companies. She starred on Broadway in "Everywoman." Shortly after World War I she retired. Born St. Louis; died Suffern, N. Y., Jan. 28, 1957.

Mitchell, Grant, 82, actor. He was a graduate of Andover, Yale College and Harvard Law School. After a try at reporting he spent three years practicing law. He then became a student at the American Academy of Dramatic Arts. He made his debut in Chicago, in 1902, with Richard Mansfield in "Julius Caesar." Later the same year he appeared on Broadway in the same play. He supported such stars as Clara Bloodgood and Maxine Elliott. After "Get-Rich-Quick Wallingford" and "It Pays to Advertise" came one of his best and most successful plays—"A Tailor-Made Man." In 1921 he was in "The Hero." Beginning in 1929 he was in movies such as "Three on a Match," "Hell's Kitchen," "My Sister Eileen" and "Arsenic and Old Lace." Born Columbus, Ohio; died Los Angeles, May 1, 1957.

Morgan, Ralph, 72, actor. He was educated at Trinity School and Columbia University. He practiced real estate law before going into the theatre in 1908 in "Love's Comedy" in New York. He scored a hit in Clyde Fitch's "The Bachelor" followed by "Broadway Jones," "Turn to the Right," "Under Cover" and "Lightnin'." He also made numerous motion pictures. His last New York appearance was in "Three Wishes for Jamie" in

1952. He was the brother of actor Frank Morgan. Born New York; died New York, June 11, 1956.

Murray, Wynn, 35, singer. She entered show business at 13. She appeared on Broadway in "Babes in Arms" in which she won acclaim for her singing of "Johnny One Note." Other musicals include "Hellzapoppin" and "The Boys from Syracuse." She was a featured singer on radio. Born Carbondale, Pa.; died Ft. Meade, Md., Feb. 6, 1957.

Neilson-Terry, Julia, 88, actress. She first studied singing and later became a protégé of W. S. Gilbert. She made her theatrical debut in 1888 in "Pygmalion and Galatea" in her native England. She starred in a long succession of plays including "The Red Lamp," "The Merry Wives of Windsor" and "A Man's Shadow." In 1895 she made her first trip to America in "The Notorious Mrs. Ebbsmith." She was in many Shakespearean productions. Born London; died London, May 27, 1957.

Pinza, Ezio, 62, singer. As a performer he was successful in opera, musical comedy, motion pictures, television and radio. At the peak of his career in opera he left the Metropolitan, where he was a famous Figaro and Don Giovanni, to appear on Broadway and make a dazzling success in "South Pacific." He followed this with three motion pictures: "Mr. Imperium," "Strictly Dishonorable" and "Tonight We Sing." He toured New England in a non-singing role in "The Play's the Thing." More recently he was starred in "Fanny." Born Rome, Italy; died Stamford, Conn., May 9, 1957.

Sebastian, Dorothy, 51, actress. She was well known in motion pictures from 1925 to 1932, where she supported such stars as Alice Brady, Ben Lyon, Greta Garbo, Norma Shearer and others. She began her acting career in "George White's Scandals of 1924." Born Birmingham, Ala.; died Hollywood, April 8, 1957.

Sensenderfer, Robert E. P., 73, drama critic. He was the dean of Philadelphia's drama critics, attending more than 2,000 plays, most of which he reviewed for the newspapers. New York producers valued his reviews so highly they often solicited his suggestions when a new Broadway-bound play was in trouble. Born Philadelphia; died Ivyland, Pa., Jan. 2, 1957.

Short, Hassard, 79, director, actor. Hubert Hassard-Short, as he was originally known, got a walk-on part at 16 in London's "Cheer, Boys, Cheer" starring Fannie Ward. He later had small roles with Sir Beerbohm Tree and Lily Langtry. In 1905 Charles Frohman saw him and brought him to New York for

"The Second in Command" with John Drew. Thereafter he was very active, appearing in such plays as "Smith," "Peg O' My Heart," "The Man from Home," "East Is West" and others. In 1920 he directed "Honeydew" and later did the Music Box revues. He installed his own lighting system and did the sets and costumes as well. Thereafter he had many hits to his credit, directing, among others, such musicals as "Sunny," "The Great Waltz," "Oh, Please," "The Band Wagon" and "Carmen Jones." Born Eddington, England; died Nice, France, Oct. 9, 1956.

Sothern, Harry, 73, actor. A nephew of E. H. Sothern, he came to America in 1903 and three years later joined his uncle's company. He appeared in many roles in the Sothern and Marlowe company and was for nine years its production manager. He also supported such stars as Robert Mantell, Otis Skinner, Laurette Taylor, Jane Cowl and Walter Hampden. Some of his more important roles were in "Lean Harvest," "Bird in Hand," "Berkeley Square" and "Shadow and Substance." Born England; died New York, Feb. 22, 1957.

Sparks, Ned, 73, comedian. He made his theatrical debut at 17 as a ballad singer in the gold camps of the Klondike. Then followed five years of acting in every conceivable sort of show in the West and Northwest. He first appeared in New York with Madge Kennedy in "Little Miss Brown," where he scored as a comedian. Other successes included "The Show Shop," "Nothing But the Truth" and "My Golden Girl." He was in many motion pictures, including "Alias the Deacon," "The Boomerang," "The Big Noise," "Love Comes Along" and five Constance Talmadge features. He was also on radio and wrote three plays and many sketches. He was a founder of Actors' Equity. Died Victorville, Calif., April 3, 1957.

Sullivan, Francis, 53, actor. He studied at Stonyhurst College and Neuchatel, Switzerland. He then began to study engineering but in 1920 tried his luck on the stage, touring with a Shakespearean company. His London debut was in 1924 in "Peter Pan." He created a number of George Bernard Shaw characters. He made his New York debut in "Many Waters" in 1929. His picture career started in 1931 and he made many films, notably "Great Expectations." He was also seen in New York in "The Winslow Boy" and most recently in "Witness for the Prosecution." Born London; died New York, Nov. 19, 1956.

Trimble, Jessie, 83, playwright. Graduating from Western College in Oxford, Ohio, she began her career as a newspaper woman for the Chicago Herald. In 1909 her play "Wedding Day" was done on Broadway. She then became a play reader for Daniel Frohman and later joined the staff of the American Play Company. In 1924 her play "The Leap" was done at the Cherry Lane. Born Toledo, Ohio; died New York, April 14, 1957.

Von Tilzer, Albert, 78, composer. He was one of five brothers who made popular-music history in New York at the turn of the century. Among his most famous songs were "Take Me Out to the Ball Game," "O By Jingo" and "Oh How She Could Yacki Hacki Wicki Wacki Woo." His musical comedies included "The Gingham Girl," "Honey Girl," "Bye, Bye, Bonnie" and "Somewhere." Born Indianapolis; died Los Angeles, Oct. 1, 1956.

Wycherly, Margaret, 74, actress. She attended the Boston Latin School and the American Academy of Dramatic Arts and started her stage career at 17 in "What Dreams May Come." She was the first wife of playwright Bayard Veiller, who wrote "The Thirteenth Chair" for her in 1920. Some of her other plays were "Jane Clegg," "Mixed Marriage," "Six Characters in Search of an Author" and "Tobacco Road." She went to Hollywood for several pictures, including "Sergeant York" in 1941. Born London; died New York, June 6, 1956.

THE DECADES' TOLL

(Prominent Theatrical Figures Who Have Died
in Recent Years)

	Born	Died
Adams, Maude	1872	1953
Anderson, John Murray	1886	1954
Arliss, George	1869	1946
Bennett, Richard	1873	1944
Bernstein, Henri	1876	1953
Calhern, Louis	1895	1956
Carroll, Earl	1893	1948
Carte, Rupert D'Oyly	1876	1948
Christians, Mady	1900	1951
Cochran, Charles B.	1872	1951
Collier, Willie	1866	1943
Cowl, Jane	1884	1950
Craven, Frank	1890	1945
Crosman, Henrietta	1865	1944
Davis, Owen	1874	1956
Digges, Dudley	1879	1947
Duncan, Augustin	1872	1954
Errol, Leon	1881	1951
Fields, W. C.	1879	1946
Gaige, Crosby	1883	1949
Garfield, John	1913	1952
Golden, John	1874	1955
Hampden, Walter	1879	1955
Hart, Lorenz	1895	1943
Hart, William S.	1870	1946
Hooker, Brian	1881	1947
Howard, Willie	1883	1949
Jolson, Al	1886	1950
Jouvet, Louis	1887	1951
Kane, Whitford	1882	1956
Kern, Jerome D.	1885	1945
Lawrence, Gertrude	1898	1952

	Born	Died
Lehar, Franz	1870	1948
Loftus, Cecilia	1876	1943
Lord, Pauline	1890	1950
Mantle, Burns	1873	1948
Marlowe, Julia	1866	1950
Merivale, Philip	1886	1946
Molnar, Ferenc	1878	1952
Moore, Grace	1901	1947
Nazimova, Alla	1879	1945
Nethersole, Olga	1870	1951
O'Neill, Eugene	1888	1953
Patterson, Joseph Medill	1879	1946
Perry, Antoinette	1888	1946
Pinza, Ezio	1895	1957
Powers, James T.	1862	1943
Reinhardt, Max	1873	1943
Romberg, Sigmund	1887	1951
Scheff, Fritzi	1879	1954
Selwyn, Edgar	1875	1944
Shaw, G. B.	1856	1950
Sheldon, Edward	1886	1946
Sherwood, Robert E.	1896	1955
Shubert, Lee	1875	1953
Tarkington, Booth	1869	1946
Tauber, Richard	1890	1948
Tyler, George C.	1867	1946
Ward, Fannie	1872	1952
Warfield, David	1866	1951
Webster, Ben	1864	1947
Whitty, Dame May	1865	1948
Woods, Al H.	1870	1951
Woollcott, Alexander	1887	1943
Youmans, Vincent	1899	1946

INDEX OF AUTHORS AND PLAYWRIGHTS

INDEX OF PLAYS AND CASTS

Bold face page numbers refer to pages on which
Cast of Characters may be found.

432

INDEX OF PRODUCERS, DIRECTORS, DESIGNERS, STAGE MANAGERS, COMPOSERS, AND CHOREOGRAPHERS